Social Problems

THE COAUTHORS

H. C. BREARLEY, *George Peabody College*

JOHN N. BURRUS, *Mississippi Southern College*

THOMAS R. FORD, *Air University, Maxwell Air Force Base*

S. EARL GRIGSBY, *University of Florida*

HOMER L. HITT, *Louisiana State University*

MARION T. LOFTIN, *Mississippi State College*

C. A. McMAHAN, *Air University, Maxwell Air Force Base*

LOUIS J. MALOOF, *University of Florida*

LOWRY NELSON, *University of Minnesota*

PAUL H. PRICE, *Louisiana State University*

JOSEPH S. ROUCEK, *University of Bridgeport*

EDGAR A. SCHULER, *Wayne University*

GUS TURBEVILLE, *Northland College*

JOSEPH S. VANDIVER, *Oklahoma A. and M. College*

CLYDE B. VEDDER, *University of Florida*

IRVING L. WEBBER, *University of Florida*

•

New York — 1955

Social Problems

T. LYNN SMITH
University of Florida

and

Associates

THOMAS Y. CROWELL COMPANY

MANUFACTURED IN THE UNITED STATES OF AMERICA
BY THE VAIL-BALLOU PRESS, INC., BINGHAMTON, N. Y.

Preface

This book has been written as an introduction to the study of contemporary social problems in the United States. Into its planning and production have gone the best efforts of men who have had intimate and extensive experience with the course in social problems as it is given in all parts of the nation.

The range and complexity of social problems, and of the verified knowledge about each of them, are now so great that no one scholar can become and remain fully informed about more than a few of them. Those who can well be expected to write, for example, in the field of marriage and the family, of population, of personality and culture, of rural or urban sociology, of race and minority problems, of criminology and penology, of social psychology, or of social theory cannot be expected to have equally complete knowledge about most of the other subdivisions of their extensive subject. At the same time, teachers of courses in social problems, who have in most instances become highly proficient in one or two areas covered by such a course, must rely heavily upon a textbook for an adequate coverage of the numerous topics that lie outside their own realms of major interest.

The need, therefore, is for a text that is both comprehensive and authoritative, in which each of the chapters—although written for students at the freshman and sophomore level—will meet the standards of those best informed about the subject matter of that chapter. Thus it was that the preparation of this book was predicated upon division of labor and specialization. Difficult as is this type of collaboration, it is believed that such is the only way in which a book that will fully meet the needs of instructors and students can be produced.

Once the decision had been made that only by applying the principle of specialization and division of labor could we hope to produce the kind of text that is needed, our second aim was to eliminate from this book as many as possible of the usual defects of a symposium. To begin with, most of those invited to participate had been closely associated with one another or with the editor over a period of years. This past association did much to facilitate mutual understanding and appreciation among the contributors, especially with respect to the basic objectives, scope, and frame of reference of the book. A majority of these coauthors took part in a conference in which the editor's preliminary plans were exposed to critical analysis and revision and the division of labor and general procedures agreed upon. All engaged in the interchange of ideas with the editor in connection with the planning and outlining of the specific chapters; and, in those cases in which there was a likelihood of undesirable duplication, groups of the coauthors were in later communication with one another. With very few exceptions at least one member, and in most cases two or more members, of the team besides the editor gave the author of each chapter the benefit of their criticisms and suggestions. Finally, in close consultation with the authors, the entire manuscript was carefully edited for the purpose of reducing duplication, eliminating apparent ambiguities, and resolving seeming contradictions. The work remains the joint product of numerous authors, but it is hoped that integration, short only of what would have done violence to the thoughts and individualities of the respective authors, has been achieved.

We have aimed to keep the problems considered in this volume closely in line with those presented in the outlines of the various courses offered in American colleges and universities. However, in the light of certain new and emerging developments in the United States, we have also tried to present comprehensive introductions to several social problems not previously given extensive treatment in the texts used in such courses. In this connection we wish to call attention specifically to Chapters 3, "Manpower and Labor Force Problems," 4, "Problems of Aging and the Aged," and 16, "Problems Arising from Cultural Contacts."

T. Lynn Smith

February, 1955

Contents

The Nature and
Variety of
Social Problems

Social problems are of concern to all. They are part of the legacy everyone receives along with his membership in the human race. For a society, as for a person, life may easily appear as just one problem after another. Yearly, monthly, or perhaps almost daily, perplexing new questions and situations arise. Matters difficult to solve, to handle, or even to be allowed to remain as they are confront man and society on every hand. Misconduct and maladjustment appear in the most surprising places. Frequently it is found that tensions and strains have arisen in a social institution, the social agency, the family, the neighborhood, the community, the state, and in groups of all other kinds, formal and informal; or it is discovered that the individual or the group must move along new and uncharted lines of action. Even the group that seeks to avoid problems by holding strictly to the tried and tested soon finds its life hopelessly complicated because of changes that have taken place in other parts of society. In a word, social life is an endless series of questions to be faced and solved, of problems that must be dealt with in one way or another. It is not by accident that many a successful play or novel presents concretely and seriously a problem of human conduct or relationships. It is just because they do deal with social or sociological problems, with the perplexing situations not too unlike those with which the audience is acquainted, with matters of real life and not with mere phantasy, that many of these plays enjoy a tremendous popularity.

A DEFINITION OF SOCIAL PROBLEMS

It is essential in the beginning of this volume to attempt a clarification and definition of the basic topic under consideration, namely, the concept of *social problems*. Of the two words involved, there need be relatively little concern about the first. *Social* denotes the collective aspects of life as distinct from the personal or individual. An interplay of stimulus and response and a patterning of behavior is, of course, present among animals other than those classified as human; but in this book the only problems considered are those of mankind. Hence for our purposes, social is here restricted to the group activities of the species *homo sapiens*.

The second word in the term is more difficult. Any *problem*, social or personal, involves a perplexing situation or a perplexing question. It is a matter requiring action of some kind which it is difficult to solve, to settle, or to handle in any other way. How can war, which might destroy civilization itself, be prevented? What can and should be done about the rapidly increasing number of aged people in the United States? Is mankind faced with starvation because the population is tending to increase more rapidly than the food supply? Are we plundering our planet? Must we abandon our great metropolitan centers and adopt a more dispersed manner of living? These are only a few of the questions disturbing the people of the United States as we move well along into the second half of the twentieth century.

Many social problems involve the idea of misconduct or maladjustment, which frequently are considered detrimental to the welfare, or at least to the self-respect, of other members of the group. Prostitution, juvenile delinquency, and crime—to mention only three—involve behavior generally considered as contrary to the well-being of the group; and ways and means of protecting and caring for abandoned children, the mentally deficient, and the mentally ill frequently have developed largely because a sense of shame has been produced when the people in one country or community have come in contact with those from more "advanced" parts of the world.

Technically speaking, if only one family in a community or neighborhood has a "problem" child, a social problem might be said to exist. In an exaggerated form such a situation may constitute a genuine problem for the larger group. However, the case is much more definite if numerous families have "problem" children, and if the phenomenon is not confined to a few localities. Indeed, wayward children in large metropolitan centers, when organized into gangs, sometimes become a concern of people generally throughout the nation. For a social problem to be serious, it must arouse awareness and stimulate concern in a considerable proportion of the members of the society, be it neighborhood, community, state, region, or nation.

A social situation that is considered as a problem by one society is not necessarily so regarded by another. Probably the thousands of homeless waifs who thronged the growing cities of the United States during the second half of the nineteenth century were not considered as a serious social problem by the majority of the people of that era. However, before many decades had elapsed remedial measures on a considerable scale were devised and applied. Even today, however, one cannot visit the world's major cities without finding many in which thousands of very young children appear to be confronting life strictly on their own. They manage to get enough to keep body and soul together by begging a few pennies, shining shoes, carrying packages, or engaging in petty theft. They sleep in doorways, and they live by their wits. Their chances in life appear slim to the ordinary citizen of Berlin, or London, or New York. As yet, however, these children seem to arouse little concern on the part of the well-to-do and middle-class citizens of the cities in which they abound. The situation apparently is taken for granted; too few of those in a position to do something about it have been challenged, either by its relation to their own welfare or by self-respect, to take the lead in proposing remedial measures. As yet the situation poses no problem for the societies directly concerned. It has not been defined by them as a social problem, and, as is repeatedly emphasized throughout this book, no phenomenon is a social problem until it is so defined by the members of a society.

Once a social situation or condition, a social matter of any kind, is widely recognized and appraised as undesirable, corrective action is

demanded as a matter of course.   Then a problem arises because no
tried and tested line of action is evident.   There may be several alternatives, none of which guarantees satisfactory results; or there may be
an absolute impasse with no apparent course to pursue.   Eventually,
satisfactory solutions are found for some of the questions and they
cease to be problems; others seem to linger on generation after generation, or to keep cropping up in one form or another every few years.
At any given time, however, a society is always confronted with a multitude of perplexing matters, calling for action, and for which no tried-
and-tested solutions are available.

The discussion in the preceding paragraphs leads to the definition
of social problems used in this book, namely: A social problem is a
situation or condition (1) of which a considerable share of a society's
members are aware, (2) which they judge to be sufficiently out of line
with their standards or such a threat to their well-being or self-respect
that corrective action must be taken, but (3) about which the best
course to pursue is highly perplexing and debatable.

THE ORIGIN OF SOCIAL PROBLEMS

From what has been said above it should be evident that social
problems may originate in a multiplicity of ways.   In a rapidly changing civilization such as that of the United States, however, a large
share of the most serious social problems are those that are associated
with social change or that grow out of the introduction of new elements or factors into our social situation.   Even a gradual process of
social change helps produce the perplexing situations a society comes
to define as its problems.   This is well illustrated by the case of a
society, such as ours, which once was almost exclusively rural and
agricultural and now is overwhelmingly urban and industrial.   In a
highly rural society the family serves as a general-purpose welfare
agency in addition to performing a host of other social and economic
functions.   Largely self-sufficient economically, with living quarters
that are roomy and easily expanded at little cost, such a family has the
responsibility for a multiplicity of enterprises and tasks at which those

of all ages and both sexes are actively and beneficially employed. It is burdened to a minimum by the presence in the household of the aged parents of husband or wife, spinster cousins, widowed sisters or aunts, orphaned children, or others in need of food, clothing, shelter, and human association. In a strictly rural stage of existence rare indeed is the community in which all the cases of dependency of any kind are not handled directly by the family groupings.

In sharp contrast, the typical urban family simply is not in a position to serve, to any extent, as a welfare agency. Houses or apartments are small and very expensive to expand, if, indeed, they can be enlarged at any cost. All the food for every mouth must be purchased, almost exclusively at retail prices. There is little in the way of household tasks or domestic industries to furnish employment for those outside the immediate family circle. In brief, the process of change from the rural to the urban mode of existence has made it almost impossible for the family to function extensively as a welfare agency for relatives and others who are in need.

Throughout the United States and Canada, however, as the village grew into the town and the town became a city, the specialized agencies needed to assume the welfare functions once performed by the family were slow in making their appearance. As indicated above, thousands of homeless waifs cluttered the streets of an emerging metropolis for years before the existing situation was recognized as a problem of sufficient magnitude to bring about the development of orphanages, placement homes, and the like. Widowed mothers struggled almost alone with their own overwhelming problems for many decades—aided perchance by religious or private charity—before society made more adequate provisions to give them and their children a somewhat fairer chance in life. As for the aged—who are increasing rapidly, both relatively and absolutely, in number and whose financial problems are almost hopelessly worsened by rampant inflation—no provision has yet been made for their welfare at all comparable to that enjoyed by aged people in the rural family of a hundred years ago.

New factors introduced into social situations which are in a fair degree of adjustment or balance are another aspect of social change that give rise to many of the most serious social problems with which a given society is concerned.   Indeed, much of the price a group must pay for what is called progress is the train of problems, many of them wholly unforeseen, that arise as a result of inventions and discoveries that had been eagerly sought for the benefit of mankind.   Consider, for example, some of the problems the invention and perfection of the automobile have brought to twentieth-century societies.   The introduction of this rapid, adaptable, personally operated, and dangerous mode of transportation has affected, often disadvantageously, all of our social and economic structures and institutions.

Obvious to all is the fact that the automobile greatly extended the range of activities of persons of all ages, those engaged in every type of activity, socially approved and socially disapproved, legal and illegal. The family car quickly became a prime necessity for almost every domestic unit in the United States and in so doing completely revolutionized the time budgets of all members of the household, father, mother, junior, sister, and any other children that came along.   By and large it contributed immensely to the satisfactions implicit in the phrases "American standard of living" and "American way of life." But it also greatly extended the possibilities and opportunities for actions which lack society's approval, including those of the racketeer, the criminal, and the criminal gang.   Note merely a few of the charges that frequently are leveled against the automobile.   Many say that it disrupts the family, weakens parental authority over the children, and contributes greatly to juvenile delinquency.   Others contend that it demoralizes the study habits of students in those high schools, colleges, and universities that permit cars to be used by those in attendance. Frequently it is said that the car absorbs money that more properly should be expended on necessities such as food, clothing, and housing. Some, attuned to the problems of religion in the modern world, insist that the use of the car for pleasure on Sundays keeps people from the churches.   All are agreed that every kind of crime, from bootlegging to bank robbery, is facilitated by the automobile; and that the rapid flight it makes possible greatly handicaps officers of the law in their efforts to apprehend criminals.

Other most serious problems created by the automobile afflict every urban center of any size in the United States.   Life is greatly complicated for all by the lack of enough parking places, the traffic congestion, and the danger to life and limb that threaten constantly the inhabitants of all of our towns and cities. Even such cities as Los Angeles and Miami, places built largely after the automobile was perfected, are confronted with almost insuperable traffic problems; while older cities are even less well planned to make possible the circulation of the great numbers of automobiles possessed by their inhabitants. The fact is, of course, that the pattern of urban life inherited from past generations became hopelessly antiquated when cities were invaded by hosts of gasoline-powered vehicles. The planning problems with which American municipalities are confronted on an ever enlarging scale grow in a large measure directly out of the invention and perfection of the automobile.

The germ theory of disease and the measures based upon it for the control of illness and the postponement of death are another illustration of the fact that a train of social problems arises from the introduction of a new factor into a situation that previously was in a fair degree of adjustment or balance. Man's endless quest for ways and means of lessening the grief and sorrow caused by sickness and by the loss of loved ones still in their childhood or in the prime of life was facilitated immeasurably by the development of the germ theory of disease. In a few decades killers that had been the scourges of mankind, such as smallpox, diphtheria, yellow fever, malaria, and typhoid fever, were reduced to minor positions among the causes of death in the United States, Canada, the countries of northwestern Europe, Australia, New Zealand, and South Africa. In addition they were brought under control to a considerable degree in the remainder of the world, including the countries in the tropical zones. Judged by the standard that is almost universally accepted, that health is better than illness and that life is better than death, the health and sanitary measures that have done so much to reduce sickness and death from transmissible diseases in the years since the close of World War I must be viewed as among man's greatest accomplishments. But even this humanitarian achievement has brought problems in its wake.

The reduction of the death rates from the germ diseases brought quick and substantial reductions in mortality rates generally. But there was no accompanying decline in the birth rates, high ones that in the past had served merely to offset the ravages of the commu-

nicable diseases. As a result, the rate of natural increase was substantially raised and the population in many parts of the world began
to mount at a dizzy pace. Around the middle of the twentieth century, the population upsurges were particularly great in precisely those
countries that already were experiencing the most difficulty in feeding, clothing, and housing their people at anything like a human level
of existence. In those countries—bound by routinary methods of
production, great disregard for the worth of human labor, and the
lack of many of the things considered as resources—the saving of lives
from the ravages of the germ diseases might mean merely that there
were more people to suffer chronically from the lingering curses of
malnutrition and starvation. As a result, the specter of famine again
caused thoughtful people to become concerned with the problem of
feeding the rapidly increasing millions who inhabit the earth. Books
outlining the issues came to rank among the best sellers, and articles
debating the dilemma filled the professional journals and found eager
acceptance in the popular magazines.[1] Society became aware of another situation from which there was no readily apparent and readily
acceptable way out; a population problem had arisen for which there
was no tried and true answer. Thus once more success in moving
toward one of man's most universally accepted goals brought in its
train serious problems to confront the societies that had achieved it.

It is still too early to identify all of the social problems that will
arise from the discoveries in physics having to do with nuclear energy
and their application either to weapons or to peaceful uses. Suffice
it to say, however, that in all aspects of our social life, from those connected with community planning to those involving relations between
nations, these discoveries are having the most profound effects. Measures designed by our leaders are out of date almost before they can be
blueprinted. Probably these developments are the most momentous
that have ever confronted mankind. The problems are recognized;
but their solution seems almost to defy human imagination.

[1] See, for example, William Vogt, *Road to Survival* (Sloane, 1949); Guy I. Burch
and Elmer Pendell, *Human Breeding and Survival: Population Roads to Peace and
War* (Penguin Books, 1947); and Fairfield Osborn, *Our Plundered Planet* (Little,
Brown, 1948).

THE RANGE OF SOCIAL PROBLEMS

An examination of the table of contents of this volume, or that of one of other texts in the field, serves to bring out the tremendous range and variety of current social problems. In the realms of economics and education, in urban areas and rural districts, in domestic politics and international relations, in relation to population as a whole or to that of several of its segments, in the relationships between races and the contacts of cultures, in industry and in the family, with relation to the handicapped or in respect to health in general, in unsanctioned and unlawful activities and in those that are not prescribed—in all of these areas society in the United States is confronted with problems of great magnitude. An analysis of texts used in similar courses a decade ago or of those studied a quarter of a century ago would still further expand the list of topics that might be listed under the heading of social problems.

A glance at the history of our own country also helps illustrate the extremely great range of phenomena that are or have been considered as social problems. Even the most abbreviated list would have to include such topics as the following: relationships with the Indians, and with the French, the Spaniards, and the Dutch; the control of the western lands; the distance at which one might reside from a church; taxation without representation; independence versus continuance in colonial status; the nature of the federal union; freedom and the rights of the individual; the relations between church and state; the conditions under which corn may be made into alcohol; the manner of securing title to a part of the national domain; slavery; tariffs; the restriction of immigration; the regulation of the railroads; the coinage of money; monopolies; involvement in European troubles; and international organization.

If one turns to another country, the list can easily be made equally long, although most of the specific items included might be different. During World War II the writer was amazed to discover, on the occasion of some of his first visits to Colombia, that the paramount social problem in that republic was the so-called "invasions" of private estates by squatters seeking places on which to grow subsistence crops for their families.   A headline *Problema Social* in the newspapers was always followed by an account of the peasants of this or that district entering upon lands claimed by the proprietor of one of the large haciendas and proceeding to make use of them to produce food for themselves and the members of their families.   Later the same problem in an aggravated form was encountered in several of the Central American republics.

In 1934 a noted Brazilian writer prepared a list of the 27 "unfavorable realities" with which his country was confronted.   Since this list more adequately than any other that has come to the attention of the writer serves to bring out the range of social problems prevailing throughout much of the world today, it is presented in full:

1. The excessive dispersion of the population, which determines that a large part of the people live in complete social isolation, which is often accompanied by extreme physical and moral degradation.
2. The insufficiency, in some places, of religious participation, facilitating the moral regression provoked by other factors.
3. The lack, sufficiently general, of urban hygiene, and even of domestic and personal hygiene among some social strata.
4. Extreme misery among a part of the agricultural proletariat, subjecting this stratum of the population to the most precarious conditions of diet, dress, and shelter.
5. Frequent appearance of outbreaks of banditry.
6. The widespread abuse of alcohol.
7. The worst sanitary conditions in some zones, resulting from frequent recurrence of one or more of the greater maladies prevailing in the Brazilian interior (syphilis, lung troubles, digestive and intestinal ailments, leprosy, goiter, constipation, malaria and other fevers, grippe, etc.).
8. The exercise with impunity, in all parts, of the pernicious quackery of fetish doctors and charlatans.
9. The lack of medical and pharmaceutic assistance for the great mass of the rural population, and even in numerous centers of relative importance.
10. The injurious development of gambling.
11. Routine in the processes of work.
12. The blind, wasteful, and often unproductive and unnecessary devastation of the forests.
13. Deficient means of communication and transportation.

14. An insufficient number of cities, deserving of the title, as co-ordinating elements in the social and economic life.

15. Lack of technical and administrative organization in the great majority of agricultural undertakings.

16. Illiteracy among the mass of the rural population and even among a large part of the urban population.

17. Lack of the most rudimentary knowledge of practical life among most social classes.

18. Regression to illiteracy of the ex-students of the primary schools because the backwardness of social life does not provide them an opportunity to utilize the knowledge acquired.

19. Insufficient administrative assistance to the producing classes.

20. The corruptive action of motion pictures without the necessary censorship.

21. Extremely numerous cases in which landed estates are not divided among the heirs, are unmarked, and lack a legal title.

22. Great confusion in weights and measures.

23. The most rudimentary system of institutions of credit.

24. Irrationality in the administrative division of the territory.

25. Imperfect and deficient conduct in the administration of the municipios [counties], resulting from the lack of knowledge of the boundaries, from extravagant cases of extraterritoriality of local governmental powers, and from the lack of co-ordination and combination of forces between the various municipios.

26. Lack of harmony and convergence in the undertakings of the various branches of public administration.

27. Deficient selection, discipline, stimulus and remuneration for the general body of public servants.[2]

Fortunately many of the social problems still afflicting Brazilian society have been pretty well solved in the United States. Banditry in this country is far less important now than in the days of Jesse James, although modern city gangs and gangsters, with their internecine strife, killings, rackets, and intimidation of businessmen, may hardly be considered an improvement. Our weights and measures are now highly standardized, and our credit institutions surely are much more satisfactory than they were in 1929. Quack doctors, healers, and charlatans of various types continue to ply their trades, but not to the same degree as is the case in Brazil. Illiteracy no longer

[2] Translated from M. A. Teixeira de Freitas, *Educação Rural*, Nos. 18–19 (Rio de Janeiro, March–April, 1934), pp. 56–57. Also quoted in T. Lynn Smith, *Brazil: People and Institutions* (Louisiana State University Press, 1946), pp. 10–11.

is a serious problem in the United States, although the level of education still might be raised substantially and with beneficial results.
Health and sanitation still have their problem aspects, but they are less
acute problems here than in Brazil. Lack of facilities for communication and transportation hardly constitutes a social problem any longer
in the United States, but the situation in this respect has changed
greatly from that prevailing in 1900 or even in 1925.

Some of the problems listed are, of course, peculiar to the Brazilian
situation; but others are much the same as some of those treated in
this volume. Gambling, alcoholism, the defective nature of local
government, and the lack of harmony and cooperation among various
governmental agencies trouble us fully as much as they do the Brazil-
ians. But irrespective of whether the problems are the same as ours,
are specific to Brazilian society, or are those that were serious in this
country only at an earlier period, the list as given helps us greatly in
appreciating the tremendous range of phenomena that may come to
be considered as social problems.

THE CHANGING PANORAMA OF SOCIAL PROBLEMS

Society's social problems are in a constant state of flux. Some of
them, it is true, in one form or another, seem to be with us always.
Others, however, are solved definitively and cease to be of serious
concern to succeeding generations. But for every social problem
solved, a new one, often of even greater proportions, makes its appearance, and the sum total of the problems with which those living
at a given time have to deal does not seem to decrease. As a matter
of fact, many of those who have considered the matter most thought-
fully are inclined to believe that society's problems become more
numerous and more difficult of solution as time passes and social differentiation proceeds. Slavery (but not all of its aftermath), the
lack of standardized weights and measures, the menace of hostile
Indians, the ravages of such diseases as smallpox and yellow fever, all
of which once constituted problems of the first magnitude in the
United States, are among those that seem definitely to have been

eliminated. But criminal activities, alcoholism, prostitution, the proper handling and care of the mentally deficient and the mentally ill, the dilemmas associated with the gyrations of the business cycle, domestic political enigmas, and many other social problems, have not been overcome. They are of fully as much concern to those living in the second half of the twentieth century as they were to those alive at its opening or those making up the population of the nation one hundred years ago. In addition, since the outbreak of World War II a host of new social problems has arisen to fill the front pages of newspapers, cram news magazines, and demand the attention of the citizen during his waking hours and haunt his dreams at night. Greatest of these are, of course, war, both "hot" and "cold," the control of atomic energy, and the problem of international organization.

The changing panorama of social problems is well illustrated by a comparison of the sociology textbooks used in the early years of the twentieth century with those that have come from the press since 1950. In 1900 the new discipline of sociology was merely beginning to get a foothold in the colleges and universities of the United States. Courses in social problems, however, were among the first to be given, and the consideration of the pathological occupied a prominent place in the more general ones. Before the first decade of the new century had passed, much of the materials used in the courses had appeared in printed form, and those books are most enlightening for comparative purposes. Consider, for example, the handling of social problems in the early works of Charles Richmond Henderson, of the University of Chicago, James Q. Dealey, who taught at Brown University, Frank W. Blackmar, of the University of Kansas, and Charles A. Ellwood, who for many years influenced large groups of students at the University of Missouri.[3]

Henderson was one of the first to offer university courses on social problems, and he was the first of the four mentioned to get his materials available in book form. Although he did not make use of the words "social problems" in the title, his entire volume was devoted to the subject. The same was true of another book, *Social Duties, from*

[3] Charles Richmond Henderson, *The Social Spirit in America* (Scott, Foresman, 1908); Frank W. Blackmar, *The Elements of Sociology* (Macmillan, 1908); James Q. Dealey, *Sociology* (Silver Burdett, 1909); and Charles A. Ellwood, *Sociology and Modern Social Problems* (American Book, 1910).

the Christian Point of View, he had published in 1909 by the University of Chicago Press. First consideration was given to domestic problems, including a brief discussion of divorce. The ill effects and necessity of correcting the situation with respect to child labor came next, followed by treatments of charities and corrections. Under the latter heading came a treatment of relief, crime, and juvenile delinquency. Problem aspects of housing, public health, and the lack of good roads and communications were next in order; and then came a lengthy analysis of industrial reform, with attention focused upon the problems of toiling mothers, child labor, unemployment, population, and profit sharing. Political reform and educational problems complete the list of topics to which Henderson gave primary attention.

Blackmar, the next of the four to see his volume in print, was concerned with four major problems—charities, poverty, crime and punishment, and what he called social degeneration. The last of these was subdivided into the problems of intemperance and immorality. As was so generally true during the period in which the compilations of materials about the Jukes and the Kallikaks were rather generally accepted as reliable scientific evidence, the hereditary or zoological factors were relied upon heavily in the explanation of the problems outlined.

Dealey, whose book appeared shortly after that by Blackmar, divided his work into two almost exactly equal parts and gave the title "Applications of Sociological Teachings to Some Social Problems" to the second part. His attention was concentrated first upon racial problems, which, interestingly enough, he did not view as a "Negro" problem. Rather his principal concern was with immigration, particularly that of the "lower races" from southern Europe and western Asia. "Race suicide" on the part of the "higher native racial stock" also he thought a special cause for alarm. The regulation of economic interests was considered of primary importance by Dealey, and he dwelt at some length on the problems of a large unskilled proletariat, child labor, preying corporations and trusts, and the exploitation of the masses in general. Educational problems he analyzed and discussed largely in terms of class versus mass education. In a lengthy section devoted to the elimination of the social evils, attention was once again centered on the problems of immigration and the control of economic organizations. Poverty and pauperism also were given considerable attention, and Dealey lamented that charity was no remedy for them and that those in the "submerged tenth" of the population were enabled to maintain and perpetuate themselves by means of assistance from the philanthropic agencies. Crime, sexual immorality, and intemperance are three other principal problems which figure in his treatment.

Ellwood, the only one of the four to use the term "social problems" in the title of his book, went over much the same ground as Dealey. He included, however, family problems in the list and, under that heading, an extensive discussion of divorce. He also employed the term "population problems," one that was designed to enjoy great popularity in future years. For Ellwood, however, the population problem of the day was the declining birth rate of the native white stock. He also treated as problems immigration, the Negro, poverty and pauperism, and crime. Ellwood made explicit an idea implicit in much of the sociological and other writing of his time by singling out and discussing the "problem of the city." In this section he sought to prove that the city has a higher incidence of insanity, suicide, poverty, pauperism, crime, and illegitimacy than does the country.

The selected bibliographies included in these early works also serve to illustrate the matters considered as social problems by pioneer sociologists at the opening of the twentieth century. As gleaned from a perusal of the titles in the bibliography supplied by Dealey—certainly one of the more adequate—the recognized social problems may be listed as follows: charities and corrections, including preventive philanthropy or welfare; crime and juvenile delinquency; unemployment; the drink problem, the temperance problem, or the liquor problem; the "Negro" problem; race adjustment, or a pure versus a mongrel population; social disease; poverty; and degeneracy.

The manner in which the problems of basic concern to society at the opening of the twentieth century differ from those confronting us today may easily be determined by comparing the lists presented in the preceding paragraphs with the table of contents of this volume or that of one of other recent texts in the field. It is hoped, however, that the brief comments made in the discussion above, along with an examination of current texts, will indicate that such titles as "race problems," "domestic problems," "educational problems," and so forth, do not have exactly the same meaning now as they had fifty years ago. In race matters, for example, segregation and not amalgamation seems to be the current problem in the United States; in education, it is not the problem of class versus mass education, but the problems of more equal opportunities for all, of the quality of the instruction, and of the nature of the educational process that arouse bitter and prolonged struggles in our contemporary communities; and the consideration of modern family and domestic problems must include far more than a discussion of the "divorce evil." Since we are no longer a rural nation greatly disturbed by the social maladjustments accompanying the rise of towns and cities, our society's view of the city and its problems today is vastly different from that of our fathers and grandfathers. The consequences of two world wars, the development of the airplane and atomic and hydrogen bombs, and the seemingly insuperable problem of international organization and peace have now made problematical the continued existence of urban agglomerations in anything resembling their present form.

In brief, the panorama of social problems is continuously changing. Those confronting a given generation may include many of the same ones with which earlier generations had to deal, some of them in essentially the same form. Others, however, although the area and the name may be the same, have a much different specific content. A few problems are solved or dropped from the list for other reasons. But new ones emerge, it would seem, in ever greater numbers. The net effect of all is to make for continuous change in the perplexing situations or matters with which society is confronted.

CURRENT SOCIAL PROBLEMS

The chapters which follow are intended to be comprehensive, concise, and reliable introductions to the study of the major social problems in the United States. Before one begins the examination of any particular set of them, however, it is well to have in mind the broad outlines of the entire lot. The titles of the chapters of this volume were planned to secure the desired organization and sequence; and by drawing on them and the various subdivisions the authors have used in their respective contributions, one may secure the necessary bird's-eye view of the field.

Our consideration of current social problems begins with those in which the people themselves give rise to the enigmatical social situations. Population problems, among the first of these, are placed first because they are the most general. Many persons now think that these are among the most serious with which mankind is faced. Some hold that the "population explosion" occasioned by a substantial reduction in death rates throughout the world, without a corresponding drop in the birth rates, is a more serious threat to human welfare than atomic or hydrogen bombs. Since the close of World War II, the fear of "population outrunning the food supply" has been revived to play keenly upon the fears of informed people of the United States and other parts of the Western world. A particularly important set of population problems is that having to do with the proper inventory, allocation, and utilization of our manpower resources. To change an industrial nation from an all-out war basis to one in which peaceful pursuits are paramount, or vice versa, calls for the most careful planning, and even then the dislocations may almost paralyze the economy. A nation runs the risk of facing serious shortages even before the policies it has designed and established to cure serious unemployment problems have had time to take effect. Currently the problem of a rapidly aging population is one of the most serious of the relatively new dilemmas with which our society has to deal. With those in the advanced ages increasing steadily in relative as well as absolute importance at the very time when our traditional rural civilization is giving way to relatively untried urban ways of life, the problem has become especially complicated. For the most part we still must determine the future roles of the aged in our social and economic patterns, and meanwhile our numerous aged persons are confronted with acute problems involving finances, living arrangements, health, personal adjustment, and social participation.

Many of the social problems in which persons themselves are directly concerned are very old, with the list including the proper care and handling of the mentally deficient, the mentally ill, the blind, the deaf, and those incapacitated, handicapped, or afflicted in other ways. Perplexities in all of these areas promise to remain with us for many decades to come. The problems of crime and juvenile delinquency also come in this category, and although chronic in our society they seem to be particularly acute since the close of World War II. The increasing incidence and cost of crime, the difficulties of detecting and apprehending the criminal, the extent to which the guilty escape and innocent persons are convicted, and the best ways of handling offenders are matters of intense concern to those in all walks of life and every part of the country. No less perplexing are the problems involving children who get athwart the law. We lack even an adequate definition of juvenile delinquency. We definitely are not agreed upon the way in which juvenile offenders should be handled, and we are frequently shocked by what we learn of the ways in which they are treated. Seriously we raise a question as to the extent to which the community, and not the child, is responsible for the deviant behavior involved.

All of the problems cited so far, those in which the people themselves are directly involved, occur more or less generally throughout society. Next to be mentioned, however, are certain ones that are more specific to one or the other of the two great segments, rural and urban, of which our society is composed.

In a rural society the institutional relationships of man to the land, and particularly the nature of the property rights of those who till the soil in the land upon which they work, are of paramount importance, socially, economically, and politically. Most of the world is still overwhelmingly rural and agricultural; and probably more than one half of all the world's agriculturists are farming by more rudimentary, inefficient, and labor-devouring methods than the Egyptians were using at the dawn of history. As a result, levels of living in many parts of the world are so low as to provide for little more than a mere creature level of existence, whereas modern means of communication and transportation have made people in many lands aware of better situations elsewhere, and have helped raise the standards to which they aspire. Therefore, it is no accident that, amid the ferment and instability that overspread the world, some of the most burning questions confronting mankind are those relating to land tenure and the size of the holdings. People generally desire the security and the chance for improvement that come from the ownership, individual possession, and control of a tract of land. The bulk of mankind no longer is content with a precarious existence as workers on soil that is owned by others, even though the proprietor may be the state. Land reform, that is, land for the peasants, is an effective rallying cry in almost all parts of the world.

Fortunately for the internal situation in the United States, its middle-class society and resulting middle-class mentality have insured that problems of the concentration of land ownership would never become acute in most parts of its rural territory. In external relationships, however, this highly satisfactory situation at home may prove to be disadvantageous. It means that most of our own cultivators and almost all of our urban people have a profound lack of appreciation for the acute sufferings which afflict their fellows in many other parts of the earth; and this renders people throughout the United States generally unable to understand the lengths to which the common people of other lands are willing to go in order to bring about a change in the status quo. It makes it difficult for us to understand and evaluate the strength of a militant, cynical, imperialistic communism, a force which has no scruples about promising land to the masses as one of the means toward its own selfish ends. These international complications are among our most acute contemporary problems, although, as will be shown in Chapter 7, the current domestic rural social problems are by no means insignificant. Concentration of land ownership and the poor functioning of the agricultural ladder does adversely affect some segments of our rural society; the changes in the rural neighborhood and the rural community are creating untold perplexities for those in the farming districts; and the rural church and the rural school are having to meet one crisis after another.

Just as the inhabitants of rural communities are faced by perplexing situations arising directly from their way of life, those who reside in towns and cities are confronted on every hand with the problems which develop because thousands of people are crowded together in a small space. In many ways the dilemmas of city life are even more difficult to solve than those of the country, since men have had much less experience in urban communities than in rural ones. On the other hand, the weight of traditionalism, the reluctance to attempt the new and the untried, is less a handicap to the heterogeneous urban population than to the more homogeneous groups who live in the country districts. Currently, city people, particularly those living in the great centers of industry, transportation, and commerce, the most important targets in any "all out" war, are the ones threatened most gravely, most immediately, and most personally, by international tensions and the awesome weapons of the hydrogen age. Currently, the possibility of the almost complete destruction of its major cities must be considered as among the nation's greatest social problems.

Another set of serious social problems is found in the maladjustments which hamper the effective functioning of our principal social institutions, domestic, economic, educational, governmental, and health. Since the family is the basic cell in the social body, problems which affect any considerable proportion of the domestic units are of national concern. Today, as was also the case fifty years ago, the instability of the family, as reflected in high divorce rates, along with many desertions and separations, must be ranked high in the list of social problems. The difficulties of adjusting the family unit to the changed and changing circumstances of city living, including the trend toward the suburbs, constitute other basic perplexities in our rapidly urbanizing society.

For many the economic problems are thought to be of paramount importance among all the social difficulties confronting the modern generation. The long-continued inflation, which has effectively destroyed the purchasing power of the savings of millions, acutely affects large numbers of the aged and the aging. The possibilities of another serious depression, with resulting widespread unemployment and dependency, must be considered by all until it has been established more certainly that our society has learned how to control the "boom and bust" gyrations of the business cycle. Demoralizing poverty is still the lot of large numbers of people, even in the richest country in the world; and world economic relationships, including our economic policies with respect to other countries, friends and allies, foes, and neutrals, are by no means fully determined or unanimously agreed upon.

As the world's greatest industrial nation, one that has forged to the front comparatively recently, the United States is beset with a wide variety of serious industrial and labor problems. The dispersal of industrial plants, especially those vital to national defense and to our ability to retaliate against attack, seems a prime necessity, but it involves a long series of complications. We currently are struggling with the problem of what controls, if any, government should exercise over capital, management, and labor. We have not yet learned how to improve the relationships between management and labor to the extent that paralyzing strikes may be averted.

The first of the great nations to plan and put into operation a program of universal education, requiring many years of each child's life, the United States constantly is faced with tremendous social problems in its educational system. Great inequalities in educational opportunities and gross differences in the burdens of supporting the schools prevail. Rural districts, for example, probably rear and educate about two children for every one who ultimately makes a home of the farm. On the other hand, the city, with comparatively small proportions of children to educate, merely by relying upon the schools within its own limits, cannot be certain of having a well-educated citizenry in the next generation. But we cannot agree upon ways and means for equalizing educational opportunities on a national scale. The power struggle for control of the schools, the issue of private versus public education, and the roles of teachers also have given rise to problems that are far from solution in most parts of the United States.

In the realm of political institutions and government, modern American society also is confronted with a host of serious questions. Many of these stem merely from the attempt to be democratic. Others arise from the nature of the two-party system and the seemingly inevitable conflict between party welfare and social welfare. The activities of pressure groups, the conflicts between state and national interest, the long-continued tendency toward centralization of governmental functions and control, and bureaucracy are almost certain to be listed among the problems under discussion, whether the forum be one that attracts television cameras or merely a lounge car on a train. The demand for constitutional reform, the problems of local government, and the proper roles, functions, and organization of the Congress and its committees all give rise constantly to new and vital issues on which public opinion divides sharply.

Although the United States has made phenomenal progress since 1900 in the control of sickness and death, health problems continue to be among those of greatest concern to the individual and to society. Sickness and disability, much of which might be prevented, still constitute heavy burdens on our social and economic life. For many families they are tragic; and no person can be sure that they may not strike within the circle of his own family. An inadequate distribution, if not an inadequate supply of physicians, other medical personnel, and health facilities in general, handicaps the nation. The manner in which medical services should be paid for is a highly debatable question; and the proper role of the state, the issue of socialized medicine, has by no means been settled to the satisfaction of any of the sides engaged in the chronic dispute.

Some of the most burning social questions with which our modern American society must deal have arisen in the field of social relationships. This area includes, in the first place, the problems involved in the relationships between races and problems of the minority groups. These problems are very old. Slavery gave rise to our most persistent problems, and contributed greatly to the blindness and dogmatism of those in our various regions with respect to the situation and problems of people who live in the others. The mere mention of race prejudice, discrimination, segregation, disenfranchisement, mob violence, race riots, lynching, and the Fair Employment Practices Act are sufficient to call to mind the fundamental, unsettled problems in the area of race and minorities. In the second place, perplexing situations that arise from the contact of cultures make up some of the fundamental problems in the area of social relationships with which we are forced to deal. These include the unsolved matters of relationships between the various nationality and cultural groups which are found in the United States, problems of adjustment, acculturation, assimilation, and intermarriage or amalgamation; and, as rapid communication and transportation increasingly bring our citizens into contact with the inhabitants of all other parts of the world, the contacts of highly different cultural systems multiply the problem situations on every hand.

Finally, the field of international relations is one in which some of the most vital social problems have arisen; indeed, the problem of war is undoubtedly the most serious one in the modern world, and *it* is closely rivaled by that of international organization. Can mankind survive unless it develops a workable system of international controls by which war and other threats to existence and welfare can be eliminated?

THE STUDY OF SOCIAL PROBLEMS

The study of social problems leaves much to be desired. In our scientific age, it is a truism to say that careful, unbiased, objective, scientific study of the facts should be made and these facts carefully considered before any corrective policies whatsoever are decided upon and put into effect. In connection with problems and policies that affect every member of the community and every citizen of the nation, the need for thorough and comprehensive analyses should seem self evident to nearly all. But the truth is that relatively little effort and pitifully inadequate funds are being devoted to scientific studies designed to contribute to the understanding and solution of social problems. One finds in most communities, it is true, small groups of dedicated men and women who are making every effort to understand local problem situations and to devise ways and means for ameliorating them. Were it not for their efforts, many of the problems would be even more acute than they are. But the interest is by no means commensurate with the task. Few indeed are those seriously concerned about social problems who also are trained and experienced in the use of the scientific method in the study of social phenomena.

Most of the work that is done is carried on by the nation's sociologists and other social scientists. They, however, are few in number and widely scattered. For the most part, too, their research activities are merely volunteer undertakings. Because of their own intense interest in one problem or another, they devote large amounts of their "leisure" to such studies, over and above the work, such as teaching in the colleges and universities, which society has seen fit to institutionalize and for which they are paid their salaries. Society has not yet provided to any extent for research activities in the field of social problems. Few indeed are the men and women who can dedicate their lives to prolonged, intensive, specialized, concentrated efforts in the theoretical and applied aspects of any social problem, comparable, for example, to the intense study by the specialist in the diseases of a certain plant, or by one who concentrates on the control of this or that insect. It is not that enthusiastic young people with the capacity and the inclination to carry on are lacking; each year the colleges graduate them in considerable numbers, just as they do those who find successful research careers in other fields. The basic deficiency is the lack of established agencies with adequate quarters and money for salaries, equipment, supplies, and other necessary costs, comparable to those of the research institutes that flourish in so many other areas. Finding ways and means for securing an intensive application of the scientific method to the study of social problems may be said to be one of American society's most pressing needs.

Study Questions

1. Give, in your own words, a definition of a social problem.

2. Outline briefly the range of social problems.

3. Compare and contrast the list of social problems treated in this book with that given in another recent text in the field.

4. Select a current social problem that was important at the opening of the twentieth century and indicate the ways, if any, in which it has changed in the last fifty years.

5. In what ways may social problems originate? Explain rather fully.

6. How do the principal social problems of the United States compare with those of another country of your own choosing?

7. From the specific social problems mentioned in this chapter, select the five you consider most serious and list them in the order of their importance.

8. What are the ways and means by which our society could provide for more adequate scientific study of its social problems?

9. Indicate three currently important social problems which you think will decrease in importance during the next twenty-five years; three which

you think will increase in importance; and three which you believe will not change substantially.

10. Discuss the ways in which social and cultural changes produce situations which come to be defined as social problems.

Selected References

Bernard, Jesse, *American Community Behavior* (Dryden, 1949), ch. I. A brief analysis of the nature of community problems.

Brown, Lawrence Guy, *Social Pathology* (Crofts, 1945), ch. I. An introduction to a socio-psychological approach to the problems of personal and social disorganization.

Dealey, James Q., *Sociology* (Silver Burdett, 1909), pp. 187–339. One of the first comprehensive attempts to outline and treat the field of social problems. The bibliography is very useful.

Gillette, John M., and James M. Reinhardt, *Current Social Problems* (American Book, 1933), chs. I and II. A representative discussion of the nature of social problems as they were recognized in the early 1930's.

Gillen, John Lewis, *Social Pathology* (3rd ed., Appleton-Century, 1946), ch. I. A general introduction to social maladjustments and the study of social pathology.

Herman, Abbott P., *An Approach to Social Problems* (Ginn, 1949), ch. II. An excellent treatment of the role of social and cultural change in generating social problems.

Nordskog, John Eric, Edward C. McDonagh, and Melvin J. Vincent, *Analyzing Social Problems* (Dryden, 1950), ch. I. A compilation of extracts from the writings of many authorities who have discussed the nature of social problems.

Odum, Howard W., *American Social Problems* (Holt, 1939), ch. I. The social problems of the United States as they appeared to one of the nation's leading sociologists on the eve of World War II.

Reinhardt, James M., Paul Meadows, and John M. Gillette, *Social Problems and Social Policy* (American Book, 1952), ch. I. An excellent discussion of the nature and field of social problems.

Queen, Stuart A., and Jennette Rowe Gruener, *Social Pathology* (rev. ed., Crowell, 1940), Part I. Summary treatments of the relation of social participation to social problems, teaching and studying social problems, and approaches to social problems.

2

Population Problems

The student, on being exposed to population materials, might ask, "Facts for what?" or "Why population data, anyhow?" Though on the face of them these figures may look dull and lifeless, few things are so important to all of us—whether we are rich or poor, young or old, male or female—as are these demographic data. They pertain to our most precious resource—the people. They are indispensable to governmental agencies, business enterprises, professional persons, and private citizens. Almost all activities in which we participate are influenced by population facts and trends. Few, if any, social problems are entirely free from some aspect or implication of population.

THE NATURE OF POPULATION PROBLEMS

The Basic Importance of Social Values

Population problems, like all social problems, reflect a discrepancy or gap between what is desired by a society and what actually exists. Since the values and aspirations of societies differ, their definitions or conceptions of what constitutes a population problem also differ. Identical demographic phenomena, such as high birth rates or low migration rates, may be evaluated in quite contradictory ways by similarly situated societies. Moreover, the variation in value orientation within a society makes for varying assessments of demographic phenomena. A rapidly expanding national population may at the same time be deplored by economists and welcomed by militarists. Thus, within a society there may be a wide range of opinion as to whether or not specific aspects of the population picture constitute problems, or as to the degree of severity of a demographic phenomena deemed pathological. There are no absolute standards for identifying and evaluating population problems. They must be approached within a given value system which itself is not subscribed to by all members of a society. Some measure of agreement does prevail in our society and the present discussion reflects the writer's own interpretation of this consensus. In any event, it should be remembered that population phenomena *per se* are not social problems. They become problems only if they are so regarded by members of society.

Population, Social Change, and Social Problems

Population processes both result from and produce social change, and social change frequently, if not always, underlies problem situations in society. A great many of the significant social developments of our time have been rooted in basic demographic phenomena. All about us is evidence of this vital and all-pervasive interrelationship between population and social change. As cases in point, one might cite the close linkage of urbanization and population redistribution with the fringe-area problems of cities, the need for revising the corporate limits of urban centers, and the acute housing shortage which confronted the returning veterans from World War II; the linkage of increased fertility during and after the war with crowded and inadequate school facilities since the late 1940's; or the relationship between the rapid increase of persons in the older age groups and the growing significance of old-age benefits and the wide range of problems involving the aged. Indeed, it behooves those who aspire to understand the evolving world in which we live to take heed of the underlying demographic factors.

The Interdependence of the Population and Other Factors

While bearing upon a great many social pathologies, perhaps most of them, the population factor taken alone rarely explains the genesis of a social problem or offers a simple solution for its amelioration. Social problems, for the most part, result from a complex of factors, only one of which is frequently of a demographic character. No drastic change in the population factor preceded the Great Depression of the 1930's though at the time many extremists explained its origin in demographic terms. Heavy national population growth coupled with meager living standards has been singled out by some as the prime cause of war. Yet, as the relatively peaceful histories of India and China reveal, population pressure alone does not cause war; it must be accompanied by cultural factors that make war seem to be a feasible course of action. Even heavy rates of migration out of an area cannot be accounted for by population pressure alone, as international and our own domestic experience has demonstrated. The population factor must be evaluated in terms of the other elements comprising the problem matrix, especially the value system of the society. In developments having problem connotations the usual interrelationship of the population factor with other phenomena often makes the labeling of these social maladjustments as population problems somewhat misleading. This name imputes undue influence to the demographic variable both as a cause and as a possible remedy. Perhaps a more logical phrasing would refer to them as social problems related to the population factor.

Types of Problems Related to Population

A variety of classifications has been employed for the description and analysis of the major social problems related to population phenomena. Usually these problems are identified in terms of the particular aspects of population contributing to their origin and existence. For the purposes of this exposition it is deemed sufficient to delineate two broad classes of problems for special attention. One of these classes includes those *problems related to the number and spatial distribution of the population.* The other category embraces those *problems arising from the composition or make-up of the population.* The inclusive nature of these categories enables the classification of virtually all problem situations associated with population.

PROBLEMS RELATED TO POPULATION
NUMBER AND DISTRIBUTION

The last decade has witnessed an extraordinary resurgence of interest in world population growth and redistribution. Several circumstances have contributed to this development of widespread concern for what is happening and is likely to happen to the number and distribution of the earth's inhabitants. Of first-rate importance in this regard is general awareness not only that the world's people have been increasing rapidly for three centuries, but also that their current rate of growth is greater than any previously recorded. This demographic fact, viewed against the backdrop of knowledge that millions already exist at subsistence levels and hundreds of thousands actually die annually from starvation and malnutrition, has caused considerable anxiety among many thinking people. Widely publicized warnings from some authorities emphasizing the progressive exhaustion of the world's resources have in no sense diminished this apprehension. Nor, for that matter, has the anxiety been lessened by the realization that political power and influence, and consequently the struggle between the communists and the Free World, are affected by the growth and redistribution of population. Another element in the situation has been the emergence of the "one-world" humanitarian conception of social problems that places some responsibility on the more fortunate peoples for the difficulties of the less fortunate.

The Problem of a Teeming World

The world's population, according to the most reliable estimates, was slightly in excess of 2.4 billion in 1950. The pattern of growth leading to this figure has given rise to widespread fear that the future will bring a crowded, teeming world of perhaps 10 to 20 billion people who at best will be able to eke out a bare livelihood. Let us examine briefly the character of past global population growth insofar as it can be pieced together from the fragmentary evidence available.

World population growth, in the long view, appears to have been slow, halting, and erratic until it burst forth in a veritable explosion during the past three centuries.[1] Throughout the vastly greater part of man's existence on the earth, his number, it seems, increased with microscopic slowness. For temporary periods in some areas growth was probably rapid, whereas in other localities human groups dwindled and disappeared. Greater density of population became possible with the domestication of animals, improvement in agriculture, and development of skills for producing pottery and textile goods. The ever-continuing and expanding stream of cultural evolution paved the way for larger numbers of persons. Growth of population, however, was so exceedingly slow until the middle of the seventeenth century that it would be considered almost stationary by modern standards.

TABLE 2.1: ESTIMATED POPULATION OF WORLD, 1650–1950

Year	Estimated World Population (millions)	Annual Per Cent Growth during Preceding Period
1650	545	—
1750	728	0.29
1800	906	0.44
1850	1,171	0.51
1900	1,608	0.63
1950	2,411	0.84

Source: Figures for 1650 through 1900 are taken from A. M. Carr-Saunders, *World Population* (Oxford: Clarendon Press, 1936), p. 42. Figures for 1950 are taken from United Nations, *Demographic Yearbook, 1952, Fourth Issue* (Statistical Office of the United Nations, Department of Economic Affairs, 1952), Table 1A, p. 102.

The Industrial Revolution with its sweeping social, economic, political, and technological changes provided the impetus for unparalleled population growth. Originating in Europe, these forces were rapidly diffused throughout the world where their impact on population trends was momentous. Their immediate result was to reduce the death rate and, in so doing, establish a new and less wasteful balance between births and deaths. The effect on population

[1] A. M. Carr-Saunders, *World Population: Past Growth and Present Trends* (Oxford: Clarendon Press, 1936), p. 43. See also Kingsley Davis, *Human Society* (Macmillan, 1949), p. 595.

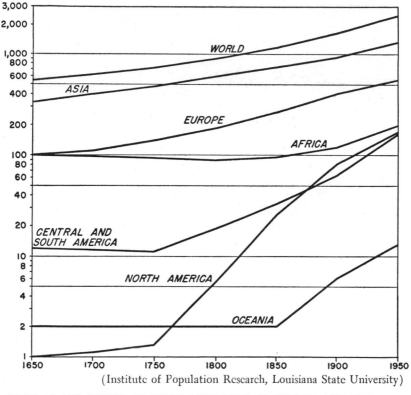

(Institute of Population Research, Louisiana State University)

FIGURE 2.1: THE GROWTH OF WORLD POPULATION, IN MILLIONS, 1650–1950

growth was phenomenal. According to the best available estimates, which are presented in Table 2.1 and Figures 2.1 and 2.2, the world's population increased more than fourfold in the three centuries between 1650 and 1950. Moreover, the rate of growth reflected in these estimates has been accelerating within this 300-year period. Amounting to .29 per cent per year between 1650 and 1750, it climbed steadily during each successive half century until it reached the amazing level of .84 per cent per year between 1900 and 1950. The impact of this increasing rate of growth on population size is shown by the fact that the world's inhabitants more than doubled in number in the last century (between 1850 and 1950) and increased by 50 per cent during the last half century (between 1900 and 1950).

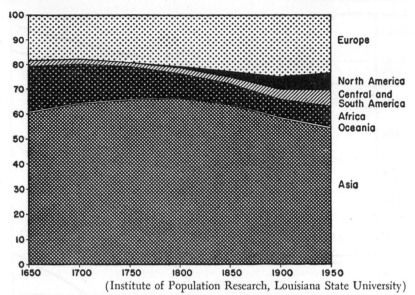

(Institute of Population Research, Louisiana State University)

FIGURE 2.2: PERCENTAGE DISTRIBUTION OF WORLD POPULATION, BY CONTINENTS, 1650–1950

One compelling basis for the widespread alarm as to future crowding on the earth is the known consequences of the continuation of the present rapid rate of population increase. For example, if the world were to continue the same rate of population growth that prevailed between 1900 and 1950, the earth's inhabitants would number over 31 billion by the year 2250. It is difficult for us to imagine such a vast number deriving at one time any kind of living from the earth.

Several writers have concerned themselves with the ultimate number of people the world can support. In discussing this subject, Kuczynski comes to the conclusion that 11 billion persons represent the maximum.[2] Such estimates, for the most part, are based upon calculated assumptions of the world's potential food production. One obvious weakness in this procedure is the fact that in arriving at a figure for food production technological advancements of the next few centuries cannot be anticipated and taken into account. These estimates also

[2] Robert P. Kuczynski, *Population*, Harris Foundation Lectures, 1929 (University of Chicago Press, 1930), pp. 283–286.

assume the food supply will be the limiting factor upon population growth. This may not be the case. Davis has suggested that "Rather it may well be that comfort and convenience will determine the limit." [3]

Widely differing opinions exist among scholars as to the probable long-time future trend of world population and its likely influence upon the level of living. Amid all the claims and counterclaims centered on the dynamic world-wide relationship of population to resources, two distinct and opposing views as to future prospects have emerged. One in an optimistic vein holds that human society through the abundance of natural resources and the ingenuity of science can cope successfully with the population increase of the future. A leading exposition of this interpretation is Mather's book bearing the hopeful title *Enough and to Spare*.[4] Supporting in a general way this encouraging thesis that science and resources will not be found wanting is the recent work by Castro entitled *The Geography of Hunger*.[5] The other and opposing view pessimistically points to a dire and distressing time ahead which will result from the combined effects of diminishing resources and a fast growing population. This idea is keynoted in two widely acclaimed volumes, Vogt's *Road to Survival* [6] and Osborn's *Our Plundered Planet*.[7] The debate still continues and its resolution is not now possible because of the imponderables in the equation. No one can know what science holds for the years ahead nor can the pattern of future population growth be foretold with certainty. There is no doubt, however, that social welfare and, hence, social problems are inextricably bound up with world population developments.

Apprehension remains widespread that "standing room only" with an attendant subsistence pattern of life may become a world-wide phenomenon. Kingsley Davis has developed in some detail the thesis that this view is based on illusion, not on probability.[8] The

---

[3] Davis, *op. cit.*, p. 598.
[4] Kirtley Mather, *Enough and to Spare* (Harper, 1944).
[5] Josue de Castro, *The Geography of Hunger* (Little, Brown, 1952).
[6] William Vogt, *Road to Survival* (Sloane, 1948).
[7] Fairfield Osborn, *Our Plundered Planet* (Little, Brown, 1948).
[8] Davis, *op. cit.*, pp. 610–613.

main points of Davis' thesis are as follows: There is an inherent contradiction between an advancing living standard and a proportionate growth of population, a fact which those who fear a mere subsistence pattern of life ignore. Basic to the fear is the assumption that highly developed societies may channel all of their resources into the support of an increasing population. This they cannot do. Inventions, for the most part, are directed at other areas of living than the increase of the food supply. Yet it often happens that such developments, conceived with no thought of their possible aid to food production, eventually contribute to this also. As a result, those societies that entirely reject the subsistence approach are thereby in a position to support more people than would otherwise be the case. Their expanded food supply provides a better living for more people, rather than the same living for more people. The increased food supply is the consequence of technological advancement and the technological advancement, in turn, results from the high level of consumption. If the high level of consumption were lowered by a return to subsistence standards, the increased food supply could not be maintained. It is contingent, as has been emphasized, on a variety of capacities which could not exist under subsistence conditions.

According to this view, the fear of a teeming world population of many submerged billions doomed to a scanty existence does not seem well founded. An industrial civilization cannot divert all of its resources and energies to feeding the maximum number of people at a subsistence level. Its technology requires a high level and wide range of consumption. The danger, thus, is not that a "beehive" world will come to pass. Rather, it is that a complete transition from subsistence agriculture to industrial civilization with its less wasteful demographic balance may not be achieved in certain backward areas.

The Problem of Unequal Levels of Living

Fantastic differences exist between the level of living characterizing our society and that of many peoples of the world. Although no simple cause and effect relationship between population and level of living is posited, the number of people is an important element in the over-all picture. Other primary factors influencing the level of living include natural resources, technology, and social organization. Attention in this context will be centered on population size as one of the fundamental variables bearing on economic welfare.

In general, relatively high levels of living prevail in those industrialized countries that have achieved a demographic balance of low birth and death rates. Among these countries are Canada, the United States, Australia, and the nations of western and northern Europe. They have been termed populations of *incipient decline*. The lowest levels of living, on the other hand, are present in those subsistence-agricultural countries with the balance of high birth rates and high death rates. Among these, which are referred to by demographers as areas of *high growth potential*, are China, India, southeast Asia, most of Africa, and most of South America. A third category of population, characterized by a demographic balance of high birth rates and low death rates, is said to be in a stage of *transitional growth*. These populations, for the most part, are entering a period of industrial development and enjoy levels of living somewhat above those prevailing in populations of high growth potential.

Developments in recent years have increasingly focused our attention and our efforts on the raising of living standards in the so-called "underdeveloped" areas. Our solicitude has been partly humanitarian, predicated on the sincere desire to lend a helping hand. Some of our concern has undoubtedly been based on self-interest. Economic development and higher levels of living and consumption in these areas make for a healthier world economy and for increased international trade. Such improvements may also forestall the defection of these peoples to the communistic sphere of influence. In any event, the existence of these low levels of living has been defined by our leaders and thinkers as a bona fide social problem meriting the expenditure of billions of dollars of public funds and the efforts of thousands of highly trained technicians.

The population factor looms large in most of these underdeveloped areas. In some, however, as in most of Latin America, ample room remains for substantial population growth. In other underdeveloped countries, such as India, China, Egypt, Java, Formosa, and Korea, the populations have already increased to the point that millions are struggling on the land for the barest livelihood. The fastest population growth occurring anywhere is taking place in these crowded areas, contributing further to the pressure of people on resources and to the disadvantageous position of these areas as compared with that of industrialized nations.   These areas, primarily agricultural, are already veritably swarming with people, and the prospect is for an even greater human glut in the future.   With high birth rates and relatively high death rates, these peoples press constantly on the means of subsistence. Starvation to some extent and malnutrition help account for their high mortality.   What is the solution for their predicament?

A program of alleviation is, as our government has discovered, a highly complex and expensive undertaking.   It can be stated with confidence that food relief by itself is not a solution.   The provision of food will temporarily reduce the mortality rate.   Fewer will die and population will increase.   The growth in number will in time take up the slack in the larger food supply.   Then the mortality rate will again rise, with more people present to starve now than there were before. The new situation is as critical as the original one—and withdrawal of the additional supply of food will make it infinitely worse.   Food alone will not solve the population problem in such underdeveloped areas as India and Egypt.   Whatever else is done, fertility has to be reduced.   If it remains high, then mortality, too, will in the long run be high.   The reduction of mortality without also bringing fertility under control "is at best a temporary and hazardous experiment." [9] This means, in effect, that the program for underdeveloped countries must be aimed at bringing fundamental changes in the economic and social organization.   These changes, if the program succeeds, must induce a reduction of fertility.

The Problem of Shifting National Power

The population factor bears an important relationship to national power and military strength.   In general, manpower available for the armed forces as well as for the labor force varies with total population size.   The populations of nations and world areas have grown at varying rates during the past three centuries.   These differentials, for the

[9] Davis, *op. cit.*, p. 611.

most part, have favored the Western world (primarily Europeans and their descendants) in general, and the United States in particular. The relative numerical importance of the peoples of these areas in the world's population has increased significantly. This population expansion has not been unrelated to the protracted primacy of European countries in international relations nor to the emergence of the United States as the world's Number One Power.

Population has grown at a phenomenal rate in the United States. It is estimated that in 1650 only 52,000 white persons lived in the area now comprising the United States. By 1700 this number had increased more than fivefold, reaching 275,000. The lapse of the next half century brought almost another fivefold increase, to a total of 1,207,000 in 1750. Rapid population growth continued after the thirteen colonies merged to form the United States. When the first federal census was taken in 1790, the inhabitants of the young Republic numbered slightly less than 4,000,000. For the ensuing 70 years, the increase exceeded 30 per cent each decade. In 1860, just prior to our civil war, the nation boasted a population of 31,502,000. Although its rate of growth slowed considerably during the last four decades of the nineteenth century, the nation's population kept on expanding, reaching almost 76 million by 1900. In the last 50 years, while the rate of increase generally continued to decline, the total population doubled, rising to the 151 million level in 1950. By March, 1954, according to an official estimate, the figure had exceeded 161.5 million. In the 160 years between the first (1790) and the last (1950) federal censuses, the nation's population increased thirty-eight fold, a truly spectacular expansion.

The role of the population factor is also effectively illustrated by the rise of Russia and Japan to the status of world powers. Consider first the case of Russia. Only two centuries ago the population of Russia was smaller than that of France. In 1950, with an estimated population of 195 million, she had well over four times as many inhabitants as France and more than twice as many as had the territory which comprised prewar Germany. Moreover, as a country in the stage of transitional growth, Russia promises to outdistance the nations of western Europe in population growth even more decisively in the next few decades. Among the nations of the world, only China, India, and the United States will be in the same general class in terms of population size.

Japan, whose present eclipse as a world power is probably temporary, came to the fore rapidly on a wave of phenomenal population expansion. This nation in 1870 was an isolated island kingdom devoted primarily to agriculture, with only 35 million inhabitants. During the next 70 years, the population more than doubled, reaching the figure of 73 million in 1940. In the meantime, Japan had acquired an empire by successful aggressive military ventures which boosted her total human reservoir to 105 million prior to Pearl Harbor. This remarkable population expansion took place during a period of rapid urbanization and industrialization in which the decline in fertility lagged well behind that in mortality. It is anticipated that should Japan reassume her role as a leading industrial power, her population will become stationary sometime after the year 2000. The intervening decades, while she completes the stage of transitional growth, will be marked by further rapid population gains. It has been estimated that by 1970 the inhabitants of her home islands will exceed 85 million.[10]

The changing relative population sizes of nations and world areas depend largely upon the nature of their respective balances of fertility and mortality; and as has been pointed out, the demographic balance, in turn, is influenced primarily by the socio-economic development of the areas concerned. The thoroughly industrialized and modernized countries, in the stage of incipient decline characterized by low birth and death rates, can for the most part look to a future of relatively slow growth, or population stability, or decline. The nations in transitional growth, with their birth rates still high and their death rates already lower are experiencing and will continue to experience rapid population increases for some years before fertility comes into balance with mortality. Finally, the countries of a high growth potential with a balance of high fertility and mortality will enter a long period of fast population growth if their death rates can be brought under control by modernization and industrialization. It is anticipated that this expansion would ultimately be slowed by the new

[10] Davis, *op. cit.*, p. 606.

balance of fertility and mortality, but the intervening decades would witness spectacular population growth.

Table 2.2 presents a backward look at the changing relative importance of the populations of selected world powers during the past three decades and a forecast based on population estimates as to what the picture will be in 1970. In preparing this table, the populations of the U.S.S.R., the U.S.A., Japan, Germany, Great Britain, and France were totaled and used as a base in computing the percentage distributions in specified years. The lack of corresponding reliable data for such countries of high growth potential as China and India precluded them from this comparison. It will be noted that Germany, Great Britain, and France, among the first countries to enter the stage of incipient decline, have been steadily slipping in relative importance, population-wise, since 1920, and it appears that their demographic situation as reflected by relative population size will deteriorate further in the next two decades. The United States has held her own generally during the past 30 years, reaching her greatest

TABLE 2.2: PERCENTAGE DISTRIBUTION OF POPULATION AMONG SELECTED WORLD POWERS: 1920–1970

	1920	1930	1940	1950	1970
U.S.S.R.	34.2	34.1	35.1	32.8	38.3
U.S.A.	23.0	23.9	23.7	25.5	24.4
Japan	11.9	12.4	12.8	14.0	14.5
Germany *	13.1	12.7	12.5	12.1	10.6
Great Britain	9.4	8.9	8.7	8.5	6.6
France	8.4	8.0	7.2	7.1	5.6
Total	100.0	100.0	100.0	100.0	100.0

Source: Data for 1920 through 1950 are from United Nations, *Demographic Yearbook, 1952, Fourth Issue* (Statistical Office of the United Nations, Department of Economic Affairs, 1952), Tables 1A, 3, and 4, with the exception of the 1950 information for Germany. Those data and the 1970 data for the U.S.S.R., Great Britain, and France are from projections given by Frank W. Notestein *et al.*, *The Future Population of Europe and the Soviet Union: Population Projections: 1940–1970* (Geneva: League of Nations, 1944). The data for Japan are taken from Frank W. Notestein, "Population—the Long View," *Food for the World*, Theodore W. Schultz (ed.) (University of Chicago Press, 1945), p. 48. The forecast for the population of the United States in 1970 is from P. K. Whelpton, *Forecasts of the Population of the United States, 1945–1975* (Government Printing Office, 1947), Table II.
* The percentage allocated to Germany is based on its prewar territory.

relative importance numerically in 1950. By 1970, according to the estimates employed, the relative demographic position of the United States will have receded slightly from the 1950 level. The 1970 estimate for the United States is probably too low in view of the continuing high rate of natural increase occasioned by the high level of births since World War II. Japan has improved her relative position somewhat and will continue to do so in the years immediately ahead. Apparently Russia, now in a period of transitional growth, will improve her relative position in the next two decades more than any other of the powers being compared. The weakening of her position between 1940 and 1950 resulted, for the most part, from heavy war and war-related casualties. In evaluating these and similar materials, it is important to remember that national strength and power, while influenced by population, are not determined by it.

PROBLEMS RELATED TO POPULATION COMPOSITION

A great many problem situations in society are related to the composition or make-up of the population. The composition of a population refers to the nature of its component parts (or sub-populations) as identified by certain characteristics. The more common characteristics employed in analyzing population make-up are race and nativity, residence, age, sex, marital status, occupational status, and religious affiliation. It often happens that the absolute and relative sizes of these component groups in given social and cultural situations are such as to contribute to the emergence of problem developments. In a given area, for example, the economy, in order to operate most efficiently, may require fewer farmers and unskilled laborers, but more industrial workers and technicians. The age distribution may be characterized by what is adjudged to be an excessive number of aged persons and children in proportion to the productive workers available. A nation's females at the termination of a disastrous war may greatly outnumber her males. The number of divorced persons may assume alarming proportions.   All of these societal maladjustments are related to the composition of population.

Under this general heading may also be subsumed those societal maladjustments usually referred to as *problems of quality*.   These problems are concerned with those physical, mental, and social characteristics that are regarded as undesirable.   Value judgments, an element in the emergence of all social problems, loom particularly large in this field of qualitative problems.   Considerable disagreement prevails as to the identity of undesirable characteristics and even more as to means of eliminating or reducing them.   These problems lend themselves less to empirical methods of analysis than other phases of population study, and consequently have become central issues in heated controversies.

Problems of Age Composition

Many stresses in contemporary society are linked to the manner in which population is distributed among the various age groups.   Most of the problems related to age structure are rooted in the relative importance of the three broad age groups: children, productive adults, and the aged.   To a very considerable extent, the persons in the productive years, roughly between the ages of 15 and 65 years, have the responsibility of supporting both the children and the oldsters. Changes in the relative importance of these broad age categories disturb an established equilibrium and, in so doing, give rise to a rash of social and economic maladjustments.   As cases in point, both the recent rapid increase of children and the longtime aging of the population have confronted the nation with a wide assortment of perplexing difficulties.

The relative excess of children in "underdeveloped" areas.   Populations with a high birth rate and a high death rate, which have been referred to as having high growth potential, are generally characterized by an extremely squat age structure.[11]   These populations, in other

[11] T. Lynn Smith, "The Population Problems of the Tropics," *The Proceedings of the Fourth International Congresses on Tropical Medicine and Malaria* (Government Printing Office, 1948), pp. 1530–1540.

words, contain a relatively high percentage of children but a low proportion in the productive years and an extremely small number of elderly persons. The heavy concentration of children places an excessive economic burden upon the relatively small number of producers. Consequently, the level of living for the entire population is usually low, with want and deprivation widespread. The women in these populations are devoting a relatively high proportion of their energy to the bearing of large numbers of infants, many of whom are destined to suffer from malnutrition and in time to be decimated by the high death rate.

This general type of age profile characterized by a disproportionate concentration of children prevails in the underdeveloped areas which have been either untouched or largely unaffected by forces of industrialization and modernization. Their inhabitants comprise approximately 60 per cent of the world's people. The high fertility and high mortality in such areas as India, China, southeast Asia, most of South America, and most of Africa produce this typically squat age structure. Consider the high proportion of persons under 15 years of age in selected countries. This percentage was 40 in India in 1931, 38.7 in Burma in 1938, 38.0 in Egypt in 1947, 41.5 in Brazil in 1940, 41.9 in Colombia in 1938, 40.9 in Venezuela in 1941, 40.2 in El Salvador in 1930, and 43.2 in Puerto Rico in 1950. In sharp contrast is the proportion of persons under 15 years of age in western Europe and the United States. For example, in 1950 the percentage was 22.0 in England and Wales and 26.9 in the United States.

The ratio of dependents to producers is a revealing index of the burden falling on productive adults in populations with a relative excess of children. Such an index may be computed by relating the number of persons under 15 and over 65 years (the dependents) to the number of persons between the ages of 15 and 65 years (the producers). The number of dependents for each 100 producers was 73.0 in India (1931), 70.3 in Burma (1938), 70.0 in Egypt (1947), and 85.5 in the Philippines (1918). The same ratio was also high in various countries of the Western Hemisphere, amounting to 75.4 in Brazil (1940), 77.9 in Colombia (1938), 88.5 in Puerto Rico (1950), 75.7 in El Salvador (1930), and 76.8 in Venezuela (1941). In comparison, England and Wales had only 49.0 dependents for each 100 producers in 1950, and in the United States the index was 53.9 in the same year. This 1950 figure for the United States reflects the upsurge of the birth rate since World War II. The corresponding index was only 46.8 in 1940.

The relative excess of the aged in "advanced" areas. One of the most widely publicized demographic facts of our time is that the nation's population is aging. The application of the term "aging" to our population means simply that increasingly large proportions of the people are in the advanced age brackets. This aging process is not unique to the United States. It is taking place in all of the so-called advanced countries sharing Western civilization. That proportionately more people in these countries are reaching old age is the result of the balance of low death rates and low birth rates that typify populations of "incipient decline." This balance is the product of the social, economic, and technological changes referred to as the Industrial Revolution. The relatively large number of the aged is a modern development and the host of social and economic problems occasioned by these oldsters are new problems, among the more pressing ones of our time.

European countries moving into the industrial cycle ahead of the United States exhibited earlier the characteristics of aging and have advanced further in the process. Among these countries are France, England, and Sweden. On the other hand, in the populations of preindustrial areas, or in areas in which industrialization is only beginning, the proportion of the aged is relatively small. Indeed, underdeveloped areas may be differentiated from advanced areas in terms of the proportion of oldsters in their respective populations.

An increase in the proportion of aged persons has been discernible in the United States since the first census in 1790. The increasing absolute number of the aged assumes especially great importance when related to the size of the general population, because the aged to a considerable extent represent nonproducing but consuming members of society. The burden of supporting them, insofar as it is a burden, varies with the number among whom it can be shared. This makes the proportion of aged persons in the total population a highly meaningful measurement. In the United States this proportion has been increasing for several decades. In 1900 only 4.1 per cent of the

nation's population were aged 65 years and over. By 1920 the figure
had risen to 4.7 per cent. In 1940 it had reached 6.8 per cent, and by
1950 had grown to 8.1 per cent. See Figure 2.3. The aged in the
nation, then, are proportionately twice as numerous now as at the turn
of the century.

Problem implications of the recent upsurge in births. The prolonged decline in fertility in the United States, perceptible for more
than a century, was interrupted in the late 1930's by an increase in the
birth rate. This recent upward trend of births, cresting in 1947 at
the rate of 25.8 live births per 1,000 persons, continues above the
previous level, which in 1933 had dipped to 16.6. The immediate
impact upon age composition has been the rapid increase of the absolute and proportionate number of children in the nation's population.
This unexpected wave of children, for which society at large had not
prepared, confronted communities throughout the land with a host
of·problems. To cite only a few, health and medical services were
frequently found wanting, housing units were too few and too small,
recreational facilities were insufficient for the demand, and school
plants and teaching staffs proved to be entirely inadequate.

The imbalance between children and schools has perhaps been the
area of most critical maladjustment. All over the nation, large and
small communities alike were caught shockingly unprepared in the fall
of 1949 for the large influx of pupils (especially first and second grad-
ers) who showed up in record numbers to take advantage of one of the
most cherished of all American privileges, attending free public
schools. The youngsters all too often had to begin their education
with inadequate transportation facilities, inadequate schoolroom facilities, and inadequate cafeteria facilities. Proper attention to population developments could have greatly cushioned the shock by alert-
ing communities well in advance to expected enrollments. In any
event, this relatively large wave of children is moving up the age
structure and is successively requiring school adjustments at advancing levels; by the late 1950's, their impact will be felt on college
campuses and the workday world.

Coincidentally with the rapid increase in children in the United
States, unprecedented numbers of adults have been reaching the advanced age groups. The resultant age structure, with relatively large

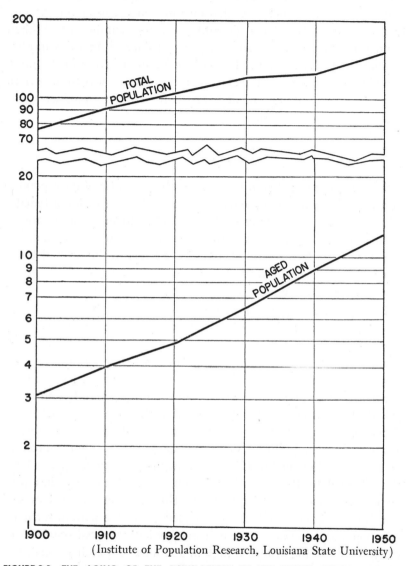

(Institute of Population Research, Louisiana State University)

FIGURE 2.3: THE AGING OF THE POPULATION OF THE UNITED STATES—GROWTH OF TOTAL AND AGED POPULATIONS, IN MILLIONS, 1900–1950

45

numbers of persons in both the very young and the old age classes, places a particularly heavy burden on those in the economically productive years. Between 1940 and 1950 the number of children (under 15 years of age) per 100 producers (aged 15–65 years) increased from 36.7 to 41.4. The corresponding increase in the number of aged (65 years and over) per 100 producers was from 10.1 to 12.5. The total number of dependents for each 100 producers rose from 46.8 to 53.9 persons.

Problems of Sex-Composition

Some imbalance between the sexes is characteristic of most populations. In many of them the relative excess of either males or females assumes such magnitude as to be conducive to problem situations. Such a disproportion results from the influence of one or more of the following three factors: (1) an imbalance between the sexes at birth, (2) a sex selectivity of death, and (3) a sex selectivity of migration. These factors, by and large, operate in a roughly predictable manner.

Problem implications for marriage. In our monogamous society a heavy preponderance of either males or females probably exerts on marriage its most telling pathological influence. When one sex greatly outnumbers the other, the sex in short supply is at an advantage in mate selection and most of its members so inclined can get married. The more numerous sex, on the other hand, has an insufficient supply of potential mates available. It is inevitable that some, depending upon the extent of the imbalance, should not be able to locate a marriage partner. Generally speaking, the sex composition of the population in the United States until recent years has been characterized by the numerical dominance of males and has thus favored the marriage of women. In this situation, the values and standards of women undoubtedly tended to set the pattern for mate selection and many men were unavoidably left mateless. Since 1910 when there was the historical high of 106 males for each 100 females, the sex ratio has been declining, reaching 100.7 in 1940 and 98.6 in 1950. Now, for the first time in the history of the nation, females outnumber males.

In the United States the classic examples of marriage problems stemming from differing sex distributions are found in the rural and urban populations. Rural people are characterized by a high sex ratio, i.e., a predominance of males, whereas urbanites typically include a relative excess of females. In 1950, the number of males for each 100 females was 110.1 on farms, 103.6 in rural-nonfarm territory, and only 94.6 in urban areas. These disproportions result primarily from the fact that more females than males migrate from rural to urban areas. These residential imbalances take on added significance for the unmarried adults when it is remembered that the sexes are approximately equally represented among the married and among children. The possibility of the unmarried farmer's finding a mate is thus even more limited than the sex composition of the entire farm population indicates. In a similar manner, the chances of the single urban female's finding a mate are greatly reduced. This situation in urban areas has undoubtedly been conducive, especially in the past, to the frequency with which women have crossed cultural lines and married foreign-born males. The inequitable distribution of males and females in urban and rural areas lowers marriage and birth rates and probably conditions the whole pattern of sex behavior and family relationships in both populations.

In other segments of the nation's population extreme disparities between the sexes give rise to marriage problems. The male selectivity of long-distance migration has resulted historically in a predominance of males among foreign-born whites. In 1910 this group was characterized by a sex ratio of 129.2, but since then it has been steadily declining. By 1930 it had fallen to 115.8 and by 1950 had dropped to 103.8. This last figure represents the nearest approach of foreign-born whites to an equitable distribution of the sexes. The sex ratio among Negroes has consistently been lower than among whites, in 1950 standing at 94.3 as compared with 98.6. The participation of many more male than female Negroes over the years in the long trek to northern industrial centers has brought about high sex ratios among members of this race in the North. The most extreme disproportions, however, prevail among "other races." In 1950 there were 117.7 males per 100 females among the Japanese and 189.6 among the Chinese. The corresponding rates in 1900 were 2,369.6 and 1,887.2, respectively. The impact upon marriage, fertility, and family

patterns of such disparities, significant as it is at the present, obviously
assumed tremendous proportions several decades ago.

Problems of the male-dominated population. Many types of populations contain an extremely heavy preponderance of males. Among
these are the inhabitants of frontier communities, mining and lumber
camps, and colonial areas. The rough and rugged nature of life, the
emphasis upon "get-rich-quick" exploitative enterprises, and the almost exclusive demand for strenuous labor combine to attract a disproportionately large number of males to these areas. In turn, the
relative absence of females exerts a profound influence on the general
pattern of behavior and social relationships. Many facets of life
assume pathological manifestations. An air of transiency pervades
the scene. Churches and schools are few and far between and their
stabilizing influences are sorely missed. The bulk of the population
cannot and does not live and interact within the family pattern.
Homes and homemaking in the traditional sense are lacking. Prostitutes openly ply their trade; and brothels, gambling houses, and
saloons flourish as social centers. Life takes on the stamp of reckless
abandon with violence and debauchery widespread. That such pathological conditions as these have characterized to some degree male-
dominated communities is abundantly documented in historical and
sociological literature. Our own frontier was no exception.

Problems of the female-dominated population. Females rarely assume the extreme degree of numerical dominance in populations that
males do, and the problem manifestations arising from their relatively
greater number are less conspicuous. There is, nevertheless, some evidence that the pattern of life in populations containing disproportionately large numbers of females is thereby significantly, if subtly, conditioned. It has already been pointed out that the urban centers
of the nation typically have low sex ratios. In many communities
with a concentration of economic enterprises depending upon female
labor, the excess of women among the residents becomes pronounced.
In such populations, it has been observed that the inability of many
females to marry has fostered a deviant pattern of sex behavior which
may be reflected in more aggressive courting activity by females,
higher divorce rates, and more extra-familial entanglements. Some
have suggested that the necessity for many females to accommodate

themselves to a life without men may promote among them patterns of feminism and crusades for women's rights. While the precise problem implications of a female-dominated population lack documentation, their existence to some degree is rather generally conceded among social scientists.

Problem Implications of Racial Composition

Many social problems of modern society have their basis in the crowding together or intermingling of peoples of diverse races. This recognition of the problem implications of racial composition does not presuppose any biological interpretation of history or the existence of hereditary racial differences in mental capacity. Frequently, however, the existence of such innate differences are assumed by large proportions of society, and social behavior is accordingly patterned. Moreover, cultural differences are usually associated to some extent with racial differences; and, while the two are not causally related, they are thought so to be by many people. As a result, race is imputed an importance which, though not supported by biological evidence, is nevertheless expressed in social consequences. The relatively ineffaceable character of the physical traits of race contributes to the persistence of fictions regarding the innate importance of race. The fact that technological advances in transportation and communication are increasingly making spatial neighbors of heretofore relatively isolated racial groups assures the emergence of new social stresses in this field of interracial contacts.

Danger of Asiatic world domination. The pressure of population upon resources in vast areas of Asia is already alarming, with teeming millions existing at sub-standard levels. Considerably more than half of the world's more than 2.4 billion people live on that continent. While this proportion, according to the best estimates, has declined from the high of 66.4 per cent in 1800 to 55.0 per cent in 1950, the present demographic situation in Asia is such that a phenomenal population increase may take place there in the next several decades. The more than a billion people inhabiting India, China, and southeast Asia are characterized by high birth rates and high death rates and consequently are populations of high growth potential. Already experiencing a rapid rate of natural increase, these populations will expand at a spectacular pace if their high death rates can be brought under control by social and economic advancement.

Against this background, it is not surprising that many harbor deep-seated fears that Asiatic peoples will in time overwhelm the rest of the world as a result of sheer numerical superiority and then impose their Oriental way of life upon all people. Such a phrase as "the yellow peril" reflects this anxiety in some quarters. This view, as Kingsley Davis has pointed out, neglects the independence of race and culture.[12] The only way Asiatics could become dominant, or even powerful, in the world is through Westernization and modernization, and by this process their culture or mode of living (which is feared) would necessarily change, becoming more like that of Europe and the Western world in general. While remaining Asiatics in a racial sense, they would lose their present Oriental pattern of living— which is not transmitted in their genes. Eventually, their birth rates would decline as has been the case in all countries that have been subjected to the forces of modernization and industrialization. The experience of Japan is a case in point. This country borrowed a great deal from the West, and, as a result, rose to the status of a world power. However, in time, her birth rate began the downward trend, as had previously occurred in Western nations.

Sociological analysis has shown that it is not possible for Asiatics to select and adopt only such few cultural traits from the West as would contribute to their drive for dominance.[13] The functional interrelatedness of Western culture precludes this. Consider, for example, the vital problem of controlling the death rate. The measures for effective control include science, medicine, and technology, and these in turn rest on a whole series of Western institutions and values. It is true that some piecemeal transference of cultural traits from the West can be accomplished through the authority and leadership of colonial administrators, but such fragmentary borrowing encouraged by the lenders does not contribute to the dominance of the receiving people. Either Western civilization must be embraced in

[12] *Op. cit.*, p. 608.
[13] *Ibid.*, p. 609.

its broader aspects, or the Asiatics cannot hope to achieve a dominant position in the world. There is no reason, therefore, to fear their imposing the present-day Oriental mode of existence upon the entire world. It is true, of course, that they could become formidable political and military enemies if they did modernize and industrialize, but they would be formidable precisely because they had adopted in large measure our civilization. This is not to contend that their culture would assume any narrowly limited form; the framework of Western civilization allows for a wide range of cultural expressions. It appears, indeed, that Western civilization, broadly conceived, is in the process of being diffused throughout the world.

Demographic bases of Negro-white relations. Many social maladjustments in the United States have arisen from the heterogeneous racial make-up of the population. The greater portion of these sources of social friction has involved relations between Negroes—who constitute the major nonwhite group in the nation—and the dominant whites. In 1950, whites comprised 89.6 per cent of the nation's population, Negroes accounted for 9.9 per cent, and the remaining .5 of a per cent were classified as "other races" (primarily American Indian and Asiatic groups). While no attempt will be made in this context to elaborate upon the pathological aspects of Negro-white relations, it is significant to review briefly some of the demographic bases of this general problem.

Negroes in the United States have increased in number from approximately 750,000 in 1790 to slightly more than 15,000,000 in 1950. Natural increase, or the excess of births over deaths, has been largely responsible for this twenty-fold increase. Despite their rapid absolute increase during the last 160 years, the significant thing is that Negroes have been steadily losing, not gaining, in relative importance throughout our national history. In 1790, almost one-fifth (19.3 per cent) of the population was comprised of Negroes. By 1860, their proportion of the population had dwindled to approximately one-seventh (or 14.1 per cent); and by 1930 they constituted less than one tenth (9.7 per cent) of the total population. The last two decades witnessed a very slight increase in their proportionate importance, but even in 1950 Negroes still accounted for slightly less than 10 per cent of the population. The dissemination of information concerning their long-time decline in relative importance would do much to allay the fear in many of a "rising tide of color."

Future stresses in the field of race relations will be influenced by the geographical distribution of Negroes in the United States. They remain concentrated for the most part in the southeastern states. In 1950, almost one half (45.5 per cent) of Mississippi's population was made up of Negroes. Over thirty per cent of the population in four other states—South Carolina (38.9 per cent), Louisiana (33.1), Alabama (32.1), and Georgia (30.9)—was comprised of Negroes. Notwithstanding their continued persistence in the South, Negroes have been and are still migrating in substantial numbers to other regions. World War I generated a heavy migration of Negroes to northern industrial centers. The years of World War II witnessed the comparable movement of hundreds of thousands of Negroes to the West Coast to work in aircraft and other defense industries. Moreover, in recent years there has been a westward movement of Negroes into the cotton areas of the Southwest. The time definitely seems to be near when the Negro will be of great interest and concern to the entire nation—not only to one region.

Problems of Nativity Composition and Immigration Controls

Nativity composition as a source of social problems. The native-born and the foreign-born whites differ widely in cultural background and economic status. Moreover, groups of the foreign born classified according to country of birth differ from one another in culture and in economic level. These differences are reflected in many social and demographic variables, such as birth rates, death rates, educational status, incidence of migration, occupational composition, and religious affiliation. The cultural diversity stemming from nativity coupled with *assumed* biological differences has given rise to a plethora of social maladjustments and social frictions in our society. At the outset, the point should be made crystal clear that biological and sociological investigations have yielded no conclusive evidence of the innate general physical or mental superiority of one nationality (or racial) group over another. The tendency among scholars is increasingly to attribute differences in the achievements of these groups to socio-cultural rather than to biological factors.

Throughout our history, but especially during this century, discussion and controversy have raged over the implications of immigration for the quality of our population. The foreign born have been variously criticized on the basis of their moral behavior, their mental capacity, and their physical endowments. The more sustained and concerted attacks have been directed against the immigrants from southern and eastern Europe who exhibit the greatest cultural and physical differences from the numerically dominant western European stock of the nation. Questions have been raised as to the possible dilution of the nation's mentality and the general biological degeneration through the amalgamation of the foreign born and the natives (whose ancestors migrated earlier). Skepticism has been expressed as to whether the immigrants could be assimilated into the "American way of life," whether they could understand and participate effectively in our political system, and whether they would represent a permanent threat to organized labor.

Nativity composition of the population. The more than 135 million whites in the nation in 1950 were comprised of approximately 125 million natives and 10 million foreign-born persons. The foreign born were drawn largely from European countries and from other countries in the Western Hemisphere. More came from Italy (1,427,145) than from any other country. Germany, the country of birth of 984,331, ranked second, followed by Russia (894,844) and Poland (861,104). Despite this impressive contingent of foreign-born whites, for more than two decades our people have rapidly been becoming more homogeneous from the standpoint of nativity and culture. The foreign-born white population is decreasing both absolutely and relatively. In 1930 it had reached the historical high of 13,983,405. By 1940, it had dropped to 11,419,138, and in the next ten years it dwindled still further, sinking to 10,161,168 in 1950. The percentages of the total population comprised of foreign-born whites in 1930, 1940, and 1950 were 11.4, 8.7, and 6.7, respectively. This trend suggests that the stresses and strains occasioned by the heterogeneous nativity composition of the population are on the wane in the United States.

Immigration and United States population growth. Immigration
has been a tremendous force in population growth in the United States.
Since the nation's beginning, a substantial but changing segment of
the population has been made up of the foreign born. Official immigration records, which go back to 1820, reveal that almost 40 million
persons have been admitted to the United States from all countries.
It has been estimated that more than 32 million of these have remained. The volume of immigration generally increased until the
outbreak of World War I in 1914. In the main, prosperous years
brought larger increases in the influx from Europe, and periods of
depression resulted in its temporary shrinkage. Arrivals increased
from about 350,000 annually at the middle of the nineteenth century
to the high level during the first decade and a half of this century of
approximately a million per year. World War I brought the virtual
cessation of immigration into the United States. Before the inward
movement could regain its momentum after the termination of hostilities, quota restrictions rigidly limiting numbers and countries of origin
were imposed by Congress.

The composition of the immigrant stream to the United States
changed radically at the beginning of the twentieth century. During
the nineteenth century, the foreign born had been drawn primarily
from northern and western Europe; the heaviest absolute influx from
these areas occurring between 1881 and 1890, when approximately 4
million entered. The largest proportion of immigrants contributed
by northern and western Europe, however, was in the 1851–1860 decade, when they amounted to more than nine of every ten entering.
After 1900 the movement from southern and eastern Europe increased
sharply to a position of dominance. Immigration from these areas
reached a peak during the first decade of the twentieth century, when
more than 6 million poured into the United States. In this period,
newcomers from southern and eastern Europe accounted for over
seven of every ten immigrants.

This shift in the character of American immigration aroused greater
apprehension concerning the deleterious influences of the foreign born
upon the quality of population. The new immigrants differed more
sharply than did their predecessors from the prevailing pattern in physi-

cal appearance as well as in culture. These differences were assumed by many to reflect biological inferiority. It was further observed that the adjustment and assimilation of the recent immigrants were slower and more difficult. The widespread concern, reaching a new pitch in the early part of the twentieth century, set the stage for restrictive immigration policies establishing larger quotas for countries of northern and western Europe than for those of southern and eastern Europe.

Immigration restrictions as a means of controlling population quality. The kind or quality of immigrants entering the United States has long been a matter of general concern. Early emphasis was placed on the *selection*, rather than on the *restriction* of the number, of immigrants. During the periods of colonial, state, and early federal control, the primary aim was to screen out persons considered undesirable through the application of various tests of admissibility. The first federal immigration act, that of 1875, denied admission to alien convicts and prostitutes. The act of 1882 added two bases for exclusion—mental defectiveness and the likelihood that the immigrant become a public charge. Succeeding acts rapidly expanded the grounds for exclusion. Several measures sought specifically to prohibit the entry of contract laborers who had been persuaded to migrate by persuasive assurances of employment. The Immigration Act of 1917 brought the selective approach to immigration control to its most advanced and complete development. It spelled out in greater detail the definitions of those classes denied admission because of physical, mental, and moral defectiveness, and added two new causes for exclusion. One of these was illiteracy in persons over 16 years of age, and the other was the restriction called the Asiatic Barred Zone provision which forbade the entry of natives from specified areas of southern and eastern Asia. At present our immigration laws set forth more than 35 grounds for the exclusion of aliens. Among these are included illiteracy, certain specific diseases, a variety of physical and mental defects, immorality, likelihood of becoming a public charge, and subversive beliefs.

In the years immediately after World War I, when it became evident that the criteria of selection were not appreciably limiting the number of immigrants, a direct means of controlling the numbers as well as the countries of origin was developed in the form of quota restrictions. The first legislation specifically directed at the numerical limitation of immigrants was incorporated into the quota act of 1921. This act, leaving intact the selective controls already in force, set annual quotas for immigration from all European countries. The quotas were assigned on the basis of nationality, each country being allotted a quota of three per cent of the number of immigrants already in the United States in 1910 who were born in that country. The total of the various national quotas for a year approximated 357,000. This means of determining quotas gave some advantage to northern and western European nations over those of southern and eastern Europe, the former receiving a combined quota about one-fourth greater than the latter. Modifications introduced three years later in a new act enormously increased the preferential position of northern and western Europe. Specifically, the 1924 act shifted the quota base year back two decades to 1890 (which was before the heavy influx of immigrants from southern and eastern Europe) and stipulated that quotas would be two per cent of the foreign-born of the various countries then residing in the United States. The result was a combined quota for northern and western Europe six times as large as that for southern and eastern Europe and a reduction in the total number of immigrants to be admitted in a year to around 165,000. Still a different formula, the so-called national origins plan, went into effect in 1929. While basing quotas on the estimated national origins of the nation's white population in 1920, it preserved the same relative distribution of quotas among the broad sections of Europe, but further reduced the total immigrants per year to about 153,000. The double intent of these quota laws was to restrict the number of immigrants to be admitted each year and to favor the entry of persons from northern and western Europe.

A new comprehensive immigration statute, the McCarran-Walter Immigration Act, became the law of the land in 1952. This new act retained essentially unchanged the basic restrictive and quota provisions which had been in effect since 1929. Annual national quotas were specified as six tenths of one per cent of the population in 1920 which was attributable to the various national origins. The 1952 law further expanded and elaborated the selective criteria for exclusion, setting forth additional grounds of inadmissibility. It also stipulated that the process of screening prospective immigrants should be more rigorous and careful. Reflecting an interest in positive selection, the McCarran-Walter Act provided that preference in filling quotas should be given to those possessing characteristics considered desirable, such as high educational status, technical training, or exceptional ability. Some critics have attacked this law as repudiating American traditions. Others have called attention to the extensive grounds of inadmissibility, claiming, in particular, that many are phrased so vaguely that they could be used as the basis for disqualifying almost any applicant.

For more than a quarter of a century, American immigration laws have remained basically the same. They have provided for the selection of immigrants possessing desirable characteristics, primarily by excluding those with specified undesirable traits; they have provided for the restriction of the total number to be admitted in a given year; and they have favored immigrants from northern and western Europe as opposed to those from southern and eastern Europe. No quota restrictions have been placed on Western Hemisphere nations, though, of course, tests of admissibility do apply to them. Also, nominal or token quotas have been extended to certain Asiatic countries from which immigration had previously been prohibited altogether.

The entire matter of immigration policy is and has been highly controversial. Continuing bitter and sharp disagreement has particularly been in evidence with respect to the preferential position given to northern and western European countries, and many have felt that the limitations on the number of immigrants are too restrictive. Public opinion, however, has been such that the basic controls have been maintained essentially unchanged since the early 1920's. That these controls have had considerable influence upon the number and types of immigrants entering the United States is certain. Their precise impact upon the quality of the nation's population is not subject to empirical investigation and must remain for the most part in the realm of controversy.

Problems of Differential Fertility

Differential fertility refers to differences in the rate of reproduction among the groups comprising a population. It may be approached broadly from the standpoint of differences in fertility levels among the populations of world areas, continents, and nations; or it may be more narrowly viewed in terms of residence, regional, racial, and socio-cultural variations in reproduction within a more restricted population, as that of a nation. Whatever the scope of consideration may be, it is rather generally agreed by demographers that fertility differentials are primarily due to variations in culture and value orientation rather than to differences in fecundity (biological capacity to reproduce). In this context, attention will be directed specifically to the differing rates of increase characterizing certain socio-cultural groups in our population and the implications of these differentials for population quality.

Numerous investigations over the years have shown that fertility in the United States (and in urban Western society generally) is inversely related to wealth and income, occupation, and educational status. The more advanced groups with respect to these criteria are characterized by the lower productive rates, whereas the more depressed groups exhibit the higher levels of population increase. By and large, in moving from the top to the bottom of the income, occupational, and educational scales, the researcher has discovered increasing fertility rates. Several studies have determined the relative extent to which such groups (stratified according to these criteria) reproduce themselves. The results have rather generally demonstrated that the higher classes in society, as identified by income, occupation, and education, have been failing by a considerable margin to reproduce themselves, whereas the lower ranking groups have been maintaining their own numbers and producing in addition a substantial surplus. Some evidence coming to light since World War II suggests that changes are taking place in this pattern of differentials. More specifically, it seems that the groups traditionally characterized by the lowest fertility levels may have increased their birth rates most rapidly in this recent upsurge. The data, however, remain as yet inconclusive.

One consequence for society of the pattern of differential fertility which has prevailed for several decades is clear: the future generation is being disproportionately drawn from the lower classes. The implications for the quality of the nation's population are less definite. Indeed, the nature and extent of possible harmful results are much debated among both scholars and laymen. Contradictory claims have been profuse; and controversy abundant and heated. Most of the claims and counter claims and the discordant points of view can be summarized under the two headings of (1) biological implications and (2) social implications.

The most severe disagreement centers on the question of biological implications. One leading viewpoint endorsed by many scholars holds that the biological stock of the population is deteriorating as a result of the continuous disproportionate recruitment of the next generation from the lower strata of society. Basic to this view is the assumption that native ability is roughly correlated with social stratification, that is, that by and large the individuals with superior capacity occupy the higher ranks in the social structure and that those possessing more limited inherent ability tend to concentrate at the base of the social pyramid. Cited in support of this assumption are studies that have found an inverse relationship between I.Q. (test intelligence) and fertility. From this assumption it follows that a dysgenic selection is taking place. The inherently more able persons are not replacing themselves, whereas the less able are producing a surplus of offspring which must fill the gaps in the higher strata. The long-run effect accordingly will be the decline of the hereditary capacity of the population.

Opponents of this view are outspoken. They reject the thesis that the correlation between native ability and the social structure is such as to bring about a dysgenic selection from differential fertility. These partisans challenge the assumption that farmers, poorly-paid wage workers, and immigrants (all of whom are more than replacing themselves) are biologically inferior. Rather, they are impressed with the physical vigor of these groups and with the capacity for intellectual development which they exhibit under favorable circumstances. The I.Q. test performances, in their view, result primarily from the environmental conditioning of the members of the upper classes.

All in all, they see no reason for concern as to the possible deleterious influences of differential fertility on the biological constitution of the population.

That differential fertility may have detrimental social implications is rather generally conceded. These harmful effects stem from the fact that those groups in society most poorly equipped from an economic and educational standpoint to provide their children with favorable opportunities for social and cultural development have the responsibility of bearing and training a disproportionately large share of the next generation. A great many of these socially disadvantaged children will be called upon to fill highly responsible positions in society. Insofar as their backgrounds have been inadequate, society stands to suffer. Thus, while proof of the biological selectivity of differential fertility is inconclusive, the evidence seems strong that the social selectivity is significant.

Study Questions

1. What has been the general pattern of world population growth during the past three centuries? Explain.

2. Do you think a teeming world with a general low level of living is a definite future prospect? Why?

3. What population changes would you recommend for underdeveloped world areas as means of improving their levels of living? Explain.

4. In what sense are Russia and Japan in a relatively advantageous demographic position? Explain.

5. What recent changes in the age composition of the United States have placed an increased burden on those in the productive ages?

6. Compare the problems of a male-dominated population with those of a female-dominated population.

7. Is there any basis for the fear that whites in the United States will be submerged in a "sea of color"? Why?

8. What types of immigration regulations have been used as means of controlling the quality of the nation's population?

9. Are the social problems associated with the heterogeneous racial and nativity composition of a population caused primarily by biological or by cultural differences? Explain.

10. Discuss the biological and social implications of differential fertility.

Selected References

Davis, Kingsley, *Human Society* (Macmillan, 1949), ch. 21. An excellent, brief treatment of "World Population in Transition" which lucidly interrelates demographic fact and theory. Its emphasis of oft-neglected points serves to diminish the alarm permeating many analyses of emerging population problems.

Ford, Thomas R., and C. A. McMahan, "Population Problems," in Morris G. Caldwell and Laurence Foster (eds.), *Analysis of Social Problems* (Harrisburg, Pa.: The Stackpole Co., 1954), pp. 52–92. An up-to-date, systematic survey of the major population problems of the day within a social-problems frame of reference.

Hatt, Paul K. (ed.), *World Population and Future Resources* (American Book, 1952). A timely collection of twenty authoritative papers on population, food resources, material resources of industry, and energy resources. While the first five papers bearing specifically upon the population factor are most relevant, these demographic materials assume added significance when related to the ensuing papers on resources and technology.

Hitt, Homer L., "America's Aged at Mid-Century: Number, Distribution, and Pattern of Change," in T. Lynn Smith (ed.), *Living in the Later Years* (University of Florida Press, 1952), pp. 9–29. An analysis, based on census data, of the number, geographical distribution, and recent changes in the nation's aged population. This inquiry suggests that migration is becoming an increasingly important vehicle of population distribution among the aged.

Landis, Paul H., and Paul K. Hatt, *Population Problems: A Cultural Interpretation* (American Book, 1954). A highly readable, comprehensive volume on population organized around problems, and stressing the socio-cultural approach.

National Resources Committee, *The Problems of a Changing Population* (Government Printing Office, 1938). A general, thorough-going analysis of the nation's population in the late 1930's which relates demographic trends and differentials to the economy, to health and physical development, and to social development and education. While outmoded to a considerable extent by unanticipated population developments of the past 15 years, this volume remains a landmark in its coverage of the problem implications of our changing population.

Pendell, Elmer, *Population on the Loose* (New York: Wilfred Funk, Inc., 1951). A breezy, unconventional volume that stresses the existing and imminent maladjustments stemming from unrestrained repro-

duction.   An example of one extreme point of view on problem implications of population growth.

Smith, T. Lynn, *Population Analysis* (McGraw-Hill, 1948).   A systematic treatment that effectively summarizes the fundamental body
of population knowledge and describes the methods and techniques
whereby it was attained.   Avoiding pathological emphasis, this volume provides an excellent basic framework for the study of the
problem implications of population.

————, "The Population Problems of the Tropics," *The Proceedings of the Fourth International Congresses on Tropical Medicine and
Malaria* (Government Printing Office, 1948), pp. 1530–1540.   A
brief, lucid exposition of the major population problems of the
tropics.   Singled out for special attention are maladjustments associated with race, age, sex composition, marital status, and natural
increase.

Thompson, Warren S., *Population Problems* (4th ed., McGraw-Hill,
1953).   A recently revised edition of the first textbook to appear in
the field.   It is widely recognized as an excellent, well-balanced volume which integrates population fact and theory with pathological
implications.

3

Manpower and Labor Force Problems[*]

The middle of the twentieth century finds the world with problems which have their roots in the prevailing conditions of world tension and military preparedness. Under such circumstances a nation's future depends not only upon its physical resources, but also upon the wise utilization of its most vital resource, its manpower. The alignment of political power in the world of today places about one fourth of the world's population in communist-dominated countries. This block of manpower puts the communist in a position which appears to threaten the security of the free world, if the expendability of human beings can be truly regarded as an asset. For most of the Western nations where the numbers added to the populations in recent decades have been smaller than in many other parts of the world, the problem is how to survive in the face of a relative shortage of manpower—a shortage of either quantity or quality or both. The manpower problem is particularly acute for the United States in view of its relatively small population, its tremendous productive capacity, its high level of living, and its assumed role in the world.

World leadership demands power. In the atomic age military power does not come from having a large supply of fighting men only.

[*] The author is indebted to the officials of the Human Resources Research Institute for their support of manpower research. However, the subject matter of this chapter should and must not be interpreted as representing the opinions of any agency or institution, governmental or otherwise. The author is personally responsible for the materials presented herein, although he is indebted to many persons for stimulating discussions and criticisms; he is particularly indebted to Mr. Stephen W. Fotis for contributing to the subject matter and for editorial assistance.

Increasingly a nation's power has come to depend upon its productive capacity as well. This capacity depends not alone on the utilization of manpower but on the utilization of manpower in a balanced combination with other factors of production. Some writers have referred to these fundamental factors of production as the five M's: *material, machines, money, management,* and *manpower.* However, in order to make an over-all estimate of a nation's power to influence the world, one must probably take into account such additional factors as location, size and shape of the country, type of terrain, climate, social organization, political stability, and armaments on hand. The present chapter is limited to the treatment of only one of these factors —manpower; but it is necessarily related to the others.[1]

THE NATURE OF MANPOWER AND LABOR FORCE PROBLEMS

When a society or group becomes conscious of a dislocation or gap between desired conditions and existing conditions, a social problem might be said to exist. Manpower and labor force problems are no exception to this proposition. These desired conditions might be regarded as a function of the values and standards held by a particular society at a particular time. When the question of labor conscription arose during World War II, many people agreed that all able-bodied citizens of the United States should work or fight; at the same time the system of values held by most people in this country was such as to cause the rejection of the idea. Thus, although in times of national crisis the value of national survival is by and large placed ahead of the values and interests of individual and special group, there is

[1] "How to Measure a Nation's Strength," *Armed Forces Talk* 359 (Government Printing Office, 1951), p. 2. Of necessity the treatment of manpower problems in this chapter is suggestive in nature only. The serious student should make an intensive analysis of the problems listed herein and should consider in addition such manpower problems as the following: marginal manpower; community problems associated with concentration of manpower; health and education problems related to manpower; problems arising from the growth of white collar workers; manpower problems of selected industries, particularly the machine tool industry; problems of selection, rejection, and classification of military manpower; psychiatric problems of military manpower; problems of industrial training programs; and the way in which these problems are attacked in foreign countries.

always the problem of reconciling conflicts among values. Not only do value references differ between society and its sub-groups, but they differ also from group to group. For example, a shortage of skilled workers in the machine tool industry may represent an undesirable condition for the manufacturers, but from the standpoint of the labor union concerned this is a condition quite favorable to its bargaining power.

Since the values of North American culture form the basis of this discussion, it should be recognized that American tradition holds that human resources should not be wasted and that a man should be able to secure and hold a job which will provide him and his family with an "adequate" level of living.

Manpower Terminology

In discussions of manpower problems, one frequently hears the terms manpower resources, manpower requirements, manpower allocation, and manpower utilization. In a sense these concepts are analogous to the concepts of supply, demand, distribution, and consumption as they are used in economic analysis, but the analogy should not be pushed too far. They are actually convenient terms to apply to major problems in the area of manpower. The principal problem within our present frame of reference is *allocation*.

Ordinarily the placement of individuals in jobs is merely part of the broader process of social placement by which people are trained and channeled into the essential functions which society needs performed. The placement process takes a variety of forms. Family training, the class structure, the educational system, the economic processes of the market place, and religious institutions all play a part in motivating competition for, or restricting access to, positions in society. Placement in economic functions might be thought of as being subject to the law of supply and demand, but it is much broader than that. In times of crisis, such as those involving national survival, extreme manpower needs arise. Large numbers of persons are required for the armed forces themselves, and the parts of the economy devoted to production of war materiel must be greatly expanded. As a result, special requirements are presented and special problems of allocation to meet these requirements arise. Of course, effective decisions regarding allocation of personnel demand knowledge of the requirements to be met and of the resources available. The requirements, in turn, depend not only upon the ultimate demands for production, but also, in part, on how effectively personnel are utilized (effectiveness being measured from the standpoint of both using qualified personnel, and of using them most economically).

The utilization of manpower in the interests of national security introduces a grave dilemma—the problem of preserving the traditional freedom of America while implementing the necessary regimentation with which to protect this freedom. This is the old problem of reconciling the values of freedom and security. For the first time in United States history it appears that we must maintain peacetime conscription for a long period of time, but we cannot afford to do so at the sacrifice of our scientific and intellectual resources. If the technical capacities of the nation were permitted to become stagnant, ultimately both the capacity for self-protection and freedom of self-determination would be jeopardized. Even if freedom were not the question, the allocation of human resources to optimum use would still pose a precarious problem; a failure of judgment could prove fatal.

MANPOWER RESOURCES

The supply of manpower is composed of all people who are capable of performing work. By definition, then, "total manpower" resources would exclude small children, mothers of very small children, extremely aged and disabled persons, and inmates of mental institutions. On the other hand, manpower resources include many persons who are not a part of the labor force, since the labor force excludes such able-bodied persons as students, housewives, and retired persons, and those who are neither working nor seeking work. Thus, although the three terms are related, there is a distinction between population and manpower and the labor force—a distinction that the student should be aware of from the outset.   Further discussion of this relationship will follow presently.   Meanwhile it should be emphasized that manpower problems of our modern society also bear a definite relationship to world manpower problems.   This relationship should not be overlooked if manpower is to be considered in a realistic sense rather than as an abstraction; the discussion in this chapter, however, concerns itself, in the main, with the manpower problems of the United States. In order to present the manpower position of the United States in relation to the international manpower pools, Figure 3.1 was prepared.[2]

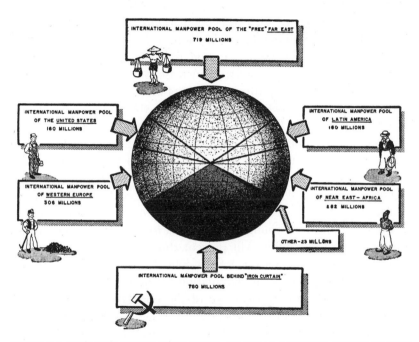

FIGURE 3.1: ESTIMATED WORLD POPULATION, BY BROAD DIVISIONS—"FREE," "SLAVE" (BEHIND THE IRON CURTAIN), AND "OTHER"—OF POPULATION AND MANPOWER, 1953

[2] The data for this figure were taken from Department of State Publication No. 4301, *Why Foreign Aid* (Government Printing Office, 1951).   No attempt has been made to define the size of the various manpower pools; only the estimated population from which manpower is drawn has been shown.

Population of the United States

It has been pointed out that the manpower pool comprises that part of the population which is capable of work; that is, the greatest number of possible workers, or the potential working force. Since population changes affecting numerical strength and composition are gradual, the manpower of a nation increases or decreases slowly. These changes in the size and composition of the population of the United States have keenly affected the availability of manpower for defense. Some of the most significant changes may be listed as follows:

1. Between 1900 and 1950 the population approximately doubled, increasing from 76 million to 151 million.

2. In the decade between 1940 and 1950 the population increased 20 million with the greatest relative increase taking place among those under 10 years of age and those 65 years of age and older. But in the age group 10–19 from which new entrants to the military and civilian working groups were to be drawn, there was a decrease of over two million. It will probably be 1958 before the number of boys reaching 18 will exceed the number of boys reaching 18 in 1940 (Figure 3.2).[3]

3. The birth rate increased during the decade 1940–1950. These higher birth rates will augment the military and civilian working force in the 1960's; in the meantime, however, the stringency will continue as millions of growing youngsters are cared for, educated, and trained. Furthermore, these duties will prevent thousands of young mothers from leaving their homes for defense jobs.

4. The average age of the population of the United States has increased. In 1900 the median age of the population of the United States was 22.9 years; in 1950 it was 30.2 years. While the population approximately doubled between 1900 and 1950, the population aged 65 and above quadrupled.

5. The death rate declined from over 17 in 1900 to less than 10 in 1953. Life expectancy at birth increased from less than 50 years in 1900 to nearly 70 years in 1950.

Relation between manpower and the labor force. According to

[3] Bureau of Labor Statistics, *Fact Book on Manpower* (Government Printing Office, 1951), pp. A1–A4.

the Bureau of the Census the nation's total labor force is that part of the manpower pool which is made up of workers who are actually working or who are actually seeking work; it includes, therefore, the employed, and self-employed, as well as unemployed persons. Members of the armed forces are also included in the labor force. The

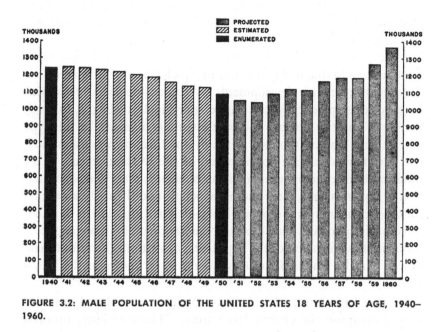

FIGURE 3.2: MALE POPULATION OF THE UNITED STATES 18 YEARS OF AGE, 1940–1960.

size of the labor force is normally smaller than the total manpower pool, although the flexibility in size of the labor force is far greater than that of manpower, since manpower supply is dependent upon population changes while the variability of the labor force is subject to human "decision."

In a free society the decision of whether to participate in the labor force is left up to the individual, who in many instances is influenced by seasonal and cyclical factors. For instance, during the harvest season there is a tendency for an increased number of people to participate in the working force, and during summertime the labor force tends to be augmented by the participation of students. In periods of economic depression the labor force is affected, for obvious reasons,

by the participation of people who normally would not be required
to work.   In periods of prosperity the size of the labor force tends
to respond positively to the demand for labor.   In wartime the civilian labor force is inflated by the entry of housewives, students, children, partially disabled people, retired persons, and persons of delayed
retirements.   For purposes of total mobilization the increase of the
labor force to about the size of the total manpower pool is an important goal.

Aside from seasonal and cyclical variations, the size of the labor
force relative to the total manpower of a society is also affected by the
state of its economic development.   Within agricultural or subsistence societies practically every able individual is obliged to work
merely in order to produce the bare essentials of life.[4]   In this type
of economy workers produce primarily for their own consumption,
and very few people are not members of the working force.   In an
industrialized economy where division of labor is great and concentration of capital is large, more and more people find themselves working
for others; and in a "free economy" in which participation in the labor
force is left up to individual decision, the working force has come to be
thought of as a segment of the population apart from the rest of manpower.   In the United States it has come to be known as the "labor
force."

Civilian labor force.   All civilians classified as employed or unemployed comprise the civilian labor force.   Those civilians fourteen
years of age and over who are not classified as employed or unemployed are "not in the labor force."   Those not in the labor force are
further classified as "engaged in own house-work," "in school,"
"permanently unable to work," and "other."   (The "other" includes
retired persons, the aged, and the like.)   Selected data on age, sex,
employment status, and color of the civilian labor force are presented
in Tables 3.1, 3.2, and 3.3.

Wartime labor force above normal.   For this discussion the prewar (World War II) trends in age-sex labor force participation rates
are assumed to be normal.   In April of 1945, as World War II drew
to a close, the labor force included about 8 million more workers than

---

[4] For an elaborate discussion, see A. J. Jaffe and Charles D. Stewart, *Manpower
Resources and Utilization* (Wiley, 1951), pp. 1–33.

TABLE 3.1: AVERAGE CIVILIAN LABOR FORCE, BY AGE AND SEX, FOR THE UNITED STATES, 1952 *

Age in Years	NUMBER OF PERSONS			PER CENT			Sex Ratio
	Both Sexes	Male	Female	Both Sexes	Male	Female	
Total 14–over	62,966,000	43,454,000	19,513,000	100.0	100.0	100.0	222.7
14–15	829,000	585,000	244,000	1.3	1.3	1.3	239.8
16–17	1,807,000	1,101,000	706,000	2.9	2.5	3.6	155.9
18–19	2,256,000	1,210,000	1,046,000	3.6	2.8	5.4	115.7
20–24	5,840,000	3,338,000	2,502,000	9.3	7.7	12.8	133.4
25–34	14,905,000	10,585,000	4,320,000	23.7	24.4	22.1	245.0
35–44	14,383,000	9,945,000	4,438,000	22.8	22.9	22.7	224.1
45–54	11,961,000	8,326,000	3,636,000	19.0	19.2	18.6	229.0
55–64	7,981,000	5,950,000	2,032,000	12.7	13.7	10.4	292.8
65–over	3,005,000	2,415,000	590,000	4.8	5.6	3.0	409.3

Source: Bureau of the Census, "Annual Report on the Labor Force, 1952," Current Population Reports—Labor Force, Series P-50, No. 45, July 1953, p. 15.
* Due to rounding, totals may be slightly inaccurate.

TABLE 3.2: ESTIMATED CIVILIAN NONINSTITUTIONAL POPULATION, BY EMPLOYMENT STATUS AND SEX, FOR THE UNITED STATES, 1952 *

	Number of Persons 14-over in Civilian Noninstitutional Population	CIVILIAN LABOR FORCE			NOT IN LABOR FORCE			
		Total	Employed	Unemployed	Total Not in Labor Force	Keeping House	Going to School	Other
Annual Average								
Both sexes	109,676,000	62,966,000	61,293,000	1,673,000	46,710,000	33,334,000	6,040,000	7,335,000
Male	51,955,000	43,454,000	42,391,000	1,062,000	8,502,000	69,000	3,002,000	5,431,000
Female	57,720,000	19,513,000	18,902,000	611,000	38,208,000	33,266,000	3,038,000	1,904,000
Per Cent								
Both sexes	100.0	57.4	55.9	1.5	42.6	30.4	5.5	6.7
Male	100.0	83.6	81.6	2.0	16.4	0.1	5.8	10.5
Female	100.0	33.8	32.7	1.1	66.2	57.6	5.3	3.3
Sex Ratio	90.0	222.7	224.3	173.8	22.3	0.2	98.8	285.2

Source: Bureau of the Census, "Annual Report on the Labor Force, 1952," Current Population Reports—Labor Force, Series P-50, No. 45; July 1953, p. 13.
* Totals may be slightly inaccurate due to rounding of numbers.

TABLE 3.3: EMPLOYMENT STATUS OF THE CIVILIAN NONINSTITUTIONAL
POPULATION, BY COLOR AND SEX, FOR THE UNITED STATES:
WEEK OF AUGUST 2–8, 1953

	WHITE			NONWHITE		
Employment Status	Both Sexes	Male	Female	Both Sexes	Male	Female
	(Percentages)					
Total population, 14 years and over	100.0	100.0	100.0	100.0	100.0	100.0
In labor force	57.5	84.9	32.4	61.9	85.0	42.8
Not in labor force	42.5	15.1	67.6	38.1	15.0	57.2
Total in labor force	100.0	100.0	100.0	100.0	100.0	100.0
Employed	98.2	98.3	97.9	97.1	96.9	97.4
In agriculture	10.5	12.8	4.8	18.2	19.1	16.5
In nonagricultural industries	87.7	85.5	93.1	78.9	77.8	80.9
Unemployed	1.8	1.7	2.1	2.9	3.1	2.6

Source: Bureau of the Census, "The Monthly Report on the Labor Force: August 1953," *Current Population Reports—Labor Force*, Series P-57, No. 134,
September 11, 1953, p. 11.

would have normally been expected.[5]   These extra workers included
about 4 million women, 2 million boys under twenty, and slightly less
than two million men who would normally have been considered too
old or unable to work.   Only six years later, had this country been
faced with a need for widespread mobilization, it has been estimated
that the population of 1951 would have yielded only about five million
extra workers under conditions prevailing at the end of World War II.
Further expansion of needs would have presented a critical problem
and probably would have necessitated drawing upon high-school students and mothers of very young children.

Armed forces.   During periods of war and mobilization or military
readiness the personnel strength of the armed forces represents a significant proportion of the supply of able-bodied manpower.   Figure
3.3 was constructed in order to show the relationship of the population of the United States, the civilian labor force, and the armed
forces.[6]

[5] *Fact Book on Manpower*, pp. B1–B5.
[6] This figure is based upon an estimated population of 155,767,000 as of July 1,
1952.   The age distribution used was that of Bureau of Census, *Current Popula-*

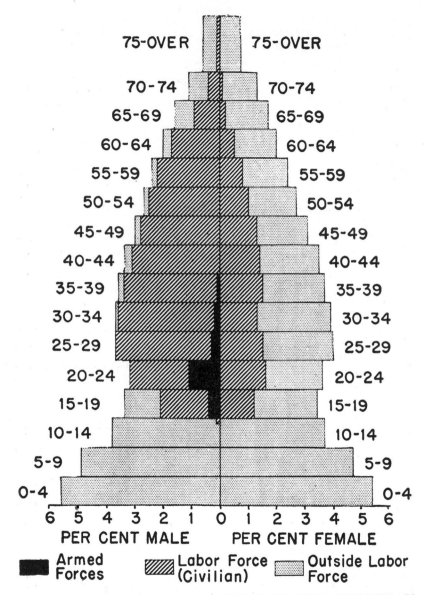

FIGURE 3.3: ESTIMATED AGE-SEX DISTRIBUTION OF THE TOTAL POPULATION, OF THE LABOR FORCE, AND OF THE ARMED FORCES OF THE UNITED STATES, 1952.

Specialized and technical personnel. It is a well-known fact that a nation's strength is not in manpower alone; it lies considerably in the scientific, the technical, and the industrial capabilities of that manpower. Today many of the most significant aspects of the manpower problem are connected with these qualitative aspects of the subject which will be discussed more fully at the end of this chapter.

MANPOWER REQUIREMENTS

Basically, the demand for manpower rests upon the elemental human needs for food, clothing, shelter, and protection. As a society develops its economic capacity to sustain its elemental needs, it experiences a growing demand for manpower with which to provide for less elemental needs such as education, mobility, health care, recreation, and the like. With increasing development of social organization, advancing technology, and growth of large-scale production, tasks become more specialized, and skilled and semi-skilled workers play an increasingly important role in the productive process. This type of development introduces a new dimension into problems of manpower, for the problem then goes beyond mere numbers of people and enters into the realm of *quality* of manpower. Meanwhile, as population grows and the economy expands, demand for manpower continues to increase. The responsibilities of the United States in its role of world leadership have also affected the complexion of its manpower requirements. These requirements charged to the civilian

---

tion Reports—*Population Estimates*, "Estimates of Population of the U.S. by Age, Color and Sex, July 1, 1950, 1951, 1952," Series P-25, No. 73, June 16, 1953, p. 4. The civilian labor force was based upon Bureau of Census, "Annual Report of the Labor Force 1952," *Current Population Reports—Labor Force*, Series P-50, No. 45, July 1953, p. 15. The size of the labor force of 1952 averaged 62,966,000. The 5-year age distribution used in this figure was computed from the above by using the same age-sex distribution as that of the labor force of 1950. It was assumed that the armed forces included 3.5 million persons. The age distribution of the armed forces was based upon the 1950 Census under the following assumptions: (1) that 60 per cent of the addition to the armed forces since the outbreak of the Korean war was in the age group 20–24; (2) that 14 per cent of the increase fell in the age group 15–19 and an additional 14 per cent fell in the group 25–29; and (3) that 8 per cent of the increase fell in the age group 30–34 and 4 per cent fell in the age group 35–39. The above percentages were estimated.

manpower pool of the United States in 1953 derive their character
from at least five basic functions, as is shown in Figure 3.4.[7]

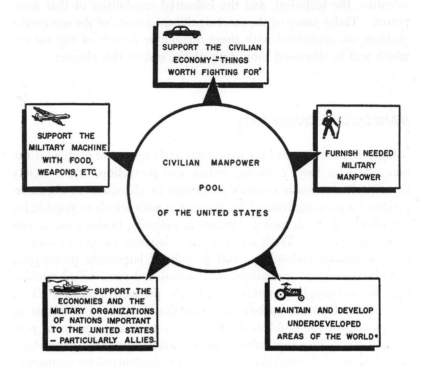

SUPPORT THE CIVILIAN
ECONOMY—"THINGS
WORTH FIGHTING FOR"

SUPPORT THE
MILITARY MACHINE
WITH FOOD,
WEAPONS, ETC.

CIVILIAN   MANPOWER

POOL

OF THE UNITED STATES

FURNISH NEEDED
MILITARY
MANPOWER

SUPPORT THE
ECONOMIES AND THE
MILITARY ORGANIZATIONS
OF NATIONS IMPORTANT
TO THE UNITED STATES
— PARTICULARLY ALLIES.

MAINTAIN AND DEVELOP
UNDERDEVELOPED
AREAS OF THE WORLD*

*ABOUT ONE HALF OF THE TOTAL UNITED STATES FOREIGN TRADE IS WITH "UNDERDEVELOPED AREAS".
SEVENTY PER CENT OF CRITICAL MATERIALS FOR STOCKPILING COMES FROM SUCH AREAS.

FIGURE 3.4: FIVE DIMENSIONS OF MANPOWER—SUGGESTED REQUIREMENTS UPON
THE CIVILIAN MANPOWER POOL OF THE UNITED STATES, 1953.

As a whole, manpower requirements represent the sum total of
jobs in existence, whether filled or unfilled. However, it is the *unfilled* requirements which pose the problems that arise in this connection. These problems loom largest in periods of high economic
activity and full employment and become critical at times of mobiliza-

[7] The illustration was based upon comments by Philip Hauser in Leonard
Carmichael and Leonard C. Mead (eds.), *The Selection of Military Manpower—
A Symposium* (Washington: National Academy of Sciences—National Research
Council, 1951), pp. 61–65.

tion. Because of the interdependence that pervades the economic system, shortages in one sector tend to generate shortages in another. The hoarding of labor and the pirating of workers tend to become prevalent problems in industry when the pressure of requirements becomes heavy.

The determination of overall civilian manpower requirements is not an official activity of the government, since the autocratic allocation of manpower is not practiced in this country. But for purposes of manpower analysis, requirements can be estimated by such means as observing the size of the labor force and the study of economic and population trends. The armed forces are obliged to make requirements analyses as best they can by using tables of authorized and assigned strength. Job analysis is a conventional technique used by industrial establishments for the specification of manpower requirements. Organization charts also furnish a useful aid in this respect. However, a major problem of military manpower requirements is the lack of a thorough-going survey of job requirements to match with manpower resources. That is, a comprehensive demand schedule and a supply schedule, both of which are needed in the allocation of manpower, seem to be lacking. Thus one of the major problems of manpower analysts is to develop a methodology whereby requirements (physical, psychological, and otherwise) can be related to job profiles.

MANPOWER ALLOCATION

The process by which manpower resources and requirements are equated may be thought of as the allocation of manpower.[8] During periods of mobilization, the problem of allocation tends to become a matter of national concern. In such emergencies the allocation between military and civilian use of resources which may be in stringent

[8] In a free economy, according to classical economic theory, the process is relatively automatic and operates through the interaction of supply and demand for manpower. These forces help determine the price of labor—or the wage rate—and this, in turn, operates as one factor in channeling the flow of labor as well as in regulating the rate of flow. The process, however, fails in being completely autonomous because of such factors as governmental control, collective bargaining, and monopolistic situations.

supply can hardly be left to natural forces. Through enabling legislation and the administration of conscription manpower is channeled
into the military forces. Other means also are employed to bring
about the desired allocation; such means include programs of recall of
military reserves to active duty and intensive promotional campaigns
based on appeals to sentiments of patriotism and self-interest ("learn-
a-trade") as an inducement to voluntary enlistment. Although the
federal government did not exercise complete control over the allocation of industrial manpower resources during World War II, most of
the needed allocation came about indirectly as a by-product of other
regulatory policies. The expansion of defense industries, induced by
government purchases and allocation of materials and equipment,
diverted large numbers of workers from consumer-goods industries;
and wage ceilings helped to keep labor migration and mobility within
reasonable bounds. The results of the "placement" processes in
terms of the occupational structure in 1940 and 1950 are shown in
Figure 3.5.[9]

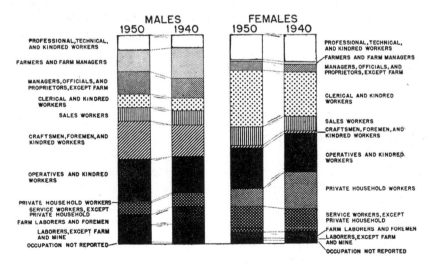

**FIGURE 3.5: PROPORTIONS OF EMPLOYED PERSONS IN THE MAJOR OCCUPATION
GROUPS, BY SEX, FOR THE UNITED STATES, 1940 AND 1950.**

[9] Based upon Bureau of the Census, *U.S. Census of Population*, 1950, II,
Characteristics of the Population, Part 1, U.S. Summary, ch. C (Government
Printing Office, 1953), 1–267—1–269.

Selective Service

One of society's basic problems is to to determine who will do the fighting; that is, of allocating personnel to the military establishments. Age is a dominant factor in the solution of this problem and action (both legislative and administrative) is necessarily strongly affected by it.[10]   Largely on the basis of broad age groups the male population of a nation may be divided into (1) those best qualified for military service, (2) those questionably qualified for military service because of dependency, (3) and those best qualified by reason of experience or education, or both, for production and community service.   If these groups were mutually exclusive, selection for the armed forces would be simplified.   But the dividing line is not always clear cut.[11]

Registration of males between the ages of 18 and 64 in the event of total war has been recommended.   Based upon the lessons of the past, the Selective Service System has proposed a schedule for the control of registrants of the different age groups 18–25, 26–29, 30–33, 34–37, 38–44, and 45–64.   This schedule establishes criteria for occupational deferment according to varying degrees of indispensability ranging from no deferment for the 18–25 group, and extremely rigid requirements for the 26–29 group, to virtually no requirements applicable to the 45 to 64 group.   No provisions for control of the groups under 18 and over 64 were outlined except for a restriction on voluntary enlistment among the former.

Allocation by Compulsory National Service

Whereas compulsory military service is accepted as a necessity in modern war, the question of whether citizens should be drafted into civilian jobs is still highly debatable.[12]   "Work-or-fight" legislation

[10] For more complete treatment, see Selective Service System, *Age in the Selective Service Process* (Government Printing Office, 1946), Special Monograph No. IX.

[11] By the end of World War II, men over 30 years of age composed the bulk of the industrial force.   In fact, the nucleus of the labor force during World War II was composed of men over 37 and of women.   Besides military rejects, this group was largely made up of occupationally deferred registrants and, up until late 1943, of men who were fathers previous to December 7, 1941.

[12] See "Manpower and National Security," *Armed Forces Talk* 195 (Government Printing Office, 1947), pp. 5–6.

was not enacted during World War II, although the issue was debated in Congress. Such legislation was supported by the Secretary of War and the Secretary of the Navy, but opponents held that compulsory civilian service would be undemocratic—would be "slave labor." Management and organized labor joined forces in arguing that voluntary methods based on cooperation were far more effective than extensive government controls. Finally the government agreed that to administer civilian service would be most difficult, and by common agreement other policies were adopted for dealing with the problem. Among the ways used for channeling workers into essential jobs were (1) moving workers between locations and between industries, and (2) locating new factories near available supplies of manpower in order to minimize problems of housing, transportation, and schooling.

MANPOWER UTILIZATION

In general, the utilization of manpower is reflected in levels of employment. The number of persons employed and the number of man-hours worked provide crude measures of utilization. For example, during the week of October 4–10, 1953, the 60,647,000 persons 14 years of age and over who were at work averaged 42.4 hours worked (50.4 hours in agriculture and 41.4 hours in nonagricultural industries).[13] Output per worker (or per man-hour) also furnishes an index to the productivity of labor, that is, the efficiency of manpower utilization. Utilization of manpower is determined not only by the extent of employment and the number of hours worked, but also by practices and techniques of internal management that "team up" manpower and machines in the most productive working arrangement possible. The ability to utilize manpower in the productive process depends upon the availability of the other factors of production (the other M's), so that the ability to utilize manpower is limited by the degree in which these factors are lacking.

[13] Bureau of the Census, *Current Population Reports—Labor Force,* "The Monthly Report on the Labor Force: October 1953," Series P-57, No. 136, November 6, 1953, p. 10.

In one sense, problems of manpower utilization constitute what is perhaps the cardinal social issue of modern mankind outside the problem of international hostility. The mere mention of the unemployment situation of the world during the great depression of the thirties (in the United States alone nearly 13 million persons or one fourth of the total labor force could not find jobs) should suffice as a reminder of the profound social implications of that experience. In those years the outlook for full economic recovery was bleak indeed, and people began to wonder if this seemingly chronic scarcity of jobs had not become a permanent fixture of the economy as an evolutionary consequence of its maturation.

Aside from the problem of unemployment, the utilization of manpower has ramifications that involve the level of living and, indeed, the very way of life of a society. For upon the utilization of manpower depends productivity and therefore the quantity and kinds of goods which men can have. Furthermore, the effects of utilization rebound upon manpower itself, since any furtherance of the utilization process will tend to have the commensurate effect of maximizing manpower resources and minimizing requirements. To illustrate, during World War II, labor, management, and government attempted to use manpower more efficiently by such means as lengthening the scheduled work week in industry to 48 hours, cutting down manpower waste by placing ceilings on the number of workmen to be hired, and by discouraging labor hoarding, absenteeism, racial and religious discrimination.

SELECTED PROBLEMS OF SPECIALIZED
AND TECHNICAL PERSONNEL

Discussion of the problems related to manpower resources, requirements, allocation, and utilization will here be limited to a single category—that of specialized and technical personnel. Even with this limitation the coverage must be incomplete.

Expanding research and development for production and for defense have directed attention to scientific and technical manpower.

Educational institutions, the government (including the armed forces), and industry are all encountering serious problems in this field. To help illustrate the nature of these problems the following sample questions are raised: *Resources*—What are the human resources? How can an inventory of trained personnel be made? What form of registration is needed? How can resources be expanded? *Requirements*—How are requirements determined? In the event of war, how much specialized personnel will be needed? How many physicians, engineers, physicists will be required? How much new specialized personnel is needed yearly? When requirements subside, how is the surplus to be used? *Allocation*—What requirements are to be given priority? What measures are to be used for allocating personnel? A draft? Increased pay? Appeals to patriotism? How can the best qualified young persons be attracted into specialized fields to build up trained resources? *Utilization*—How much of a physician's time should be taken up by administration?

Resources of Specialized Personnel

As the first step in any analysis of specialized manpower resources there should be a descriptive inventory of the supply on hand. This involves the problems of identifying, locating, and registering scientific and technical personnel. As late as 1953 it was difficult to obtain sound estimates of the nation's resources of specialized personnel. Crude approximations based on fragmentary sources had to be used since no one source or method was satisfactory. Nevertheless, considerable progress had been made in the period 1948–1953. It was hoped that the situation would be improved by the decennial census, but many imperfections showed up in the data of 1950. Most of the estimates that have been made were based upon the membership of professional societies.

In January, 1953, the National Science Foundation assumed responsibility for the *National Scientific Register*. The general aim was to provide a relatively complete manpower information program, and the specific aims were: (1) to develop methods of locating persons with scientific and technical skills, (2) to make studies of requirements and supplies of scientists and engineers, and (3) to act as a clearing house for data on scientists and engineers.[14] Even in 1953 an adequate knowledge of the ages of scientists did not exist. Yet a knowledge of age is fundamental to any estimate of the replacements needed for those who retire or die or are called into military service. For example, with respect to physicists, there was a differential in age between physicists specializing in the "old" as compared to the "new" fields of physics.[15] In the "old" fields of optics, acoustics, and classical theory about 35 per cent were under 35 years of age; while in the "new" fields of quantum and nuclear physics 60 per cent were under 35; and in the "new" fields of atomic, molecular physics, and electronics, 46 per cent were under 35. Since about one fifth of these physicists under 35 years of age were reservists, a call-up of reservists would materially affect defense production and research.

In 1951 about one in each 350 chemical engineers was a woman, about one in each 33 physicists was a woman, and about one in each 13 chemists was a woman. The problem implied in such facts is obvious: these professions which have failed to attract large numbers of women to their ranks are exposed to serious depletion in case of mobilization. The fact that women who are now engaged in these professions appear to be underpaid relative to men of comparable age and qualifications probably helps account for this situation. If a greater number and proportion of women are to be attracted into these professions, opportunities for them to advance in the profession must be expanded.

Engineers. Engineering is the largest of the technical professions. In 1950 the number of engineers was estimated at between 450,000 and 530,000 or about double the number in 1940; in 1890 there were only about 30,000 engineers. The problem or threat of a surplus of personnel has been hanging over this field from time to time since World War II.[16] A serious surplus of engineers was predicted for

---

[14] Bowen Dees, "The Fellowship Program of the National Science Foundation" in Panel on Manpower, Committee on Human Resources, Research and Development Board, *Symposium on Scientific and Specialized Manpower*, June 15–16, 1953, pp. 34–35.

[15] Helen Wood, "Characteristics of Our Present Resources of Scientific and Specialized Personnel," in *Symposium on Scientific and Specialized Manpower*, pp. 85–86.

[16] Henry H. Armsby, "Current Trends in U.S. Colleges and Universities: Production of Engineers," in *Symposium on Scientific and Specialized Manpower*, p. 13.

1950, this prediction being based on the observation of (1) heavier-than-usual enrollments in engineering schools in the fall of 1946, and (2) reportedly light demand for engineers in industry in 1950. However, due in part to the Korean War, this surplus did not materialize to the extent anticipated.

Scientists. While the population of the United States doubled between 1900 and 1950, the supply of scientists with doctor's degrees increased nearly 40 times.[17] This phenomenal production of scientists took place despite the interruptions of two world wars and at least one severe depression; these three upheavals resulted in a loss of scientists estimated at about 11,500. The fact that this loss amounts to one fourth of the number (46,000) of living scientists (Ph.D.'s under 70 years of age), in the United States in 1953 is one indication of the acuteness of this problem. The academic world is not the only area affected by such losses; for only about one half of scientists with doctor's degrees are employed in educational institutions; industry and government employ practically all the other half. Furthermore, industry and government depend frequently upon the consultative services of academic scientists.

Physicians. The number of physicians is a crude measure of resources, but mere numbers do not always give the complete picture since ideally the quality of available medical service should also be taken into consideration. In quantitative terms there were approximately 214,000 physicians in the United States late in 1952, or a ratio of 1 : 728 for the total population.[18] An uneven distribution of physicians over the nation presents a problem of equitable share in the medical resources of the nation. The ratio of physician to population in the Middle Atlantic States was 1 : 625 and in the South it was 1 : 1300. In 1949 nearly two thirds of the active physicians in private practice were located in the East, the Midwest, and on the Pacific Coast.

[17] Douglas E. Scates, "Recent Production and Distribution of Highly Educated Scientists in the United States," in *Symposium on Scientific and Specialized Manpower*, pp. 65–68. The first earned doctor's degree was granted by Yale University in 1861.

[18] National Manpower Council, A *Policy for Scientific and Professional Manpower* (Columbia University Press, 1953), p. 220.

Requirements for Specialized Personnel

After the outbreak of the Korean conflict, empirical proof existed that requirements for American manpower in selected fields were not being met since more jobs were available in certain critical engineering and scientific occupations than there were qualified job candidates. A few of the problems that arise in connection with determining requirements have been selected for discussion.

Problems of estimation. One of the difficulties in estimating future demand for employment in scientific occupations is that there is a lack of basic historical data on employment in these occupations; and thus it is hazardous to estimate future manpower requirements by occupational field. Yet, the importance of being able to project personnel requirements in the technical and scientific occupations is very real despite the comparatively small number of persons involved. Scientists and engineers are instrumental not only in the production of material goods but also in the development of techniques and knowledge that may be used to create more and different kinds of manpower requirements—even requirements for a greater number of scientists and engineers.[19] Furthermore, estimates of demand and supply of workers can be useful in formulating employment policies, in planning programs of education and training, in planning facilities, and in furnishing information on opportunities for employment to be used in vocational guidance.

One approach to the problem of estimating demand has been to canvass firms and government agencies as to the anticipated number which they planned to hire in the following year, but only a partial response from firms has been forthcoming in the past. A refinement of this approach involves the study of the functions performed by the existing workers in the occupation: that is, what they were hired to

[19] John F. Hilliard, "U.S. Requirements for Scientific and Specialized Personnel," in *Symposium on Scientific and Specialized Manpower,* p. 9. Current techniques for analyzing the labor market, developed to study the craft and production type occupations, are especially inadequate for the study of scientists and engineers. The requirements among the latter pertain largely to mental and creative talents rather than to physical skills. The fact that professionals often function in a specific occupation for which they have not been directly trained tends to obscure the demand picture.

do; the factors affecting the decision to hire them; the factors creating a market for their services; and the relationship of these factors to other economic or social occurrences that are capable of being projected into the future; and the influences that may modify these past relationships. Another approach to the study of the future demand for scientific personnel makes use of budgetary projections. The first step is to study the functions performed by scientists—teaching, work directly related to production, and research and development activities. The next step is to examine the prospective dollar outlays for future programs involving these functions. Finally, by applying to this amount the prevailing dollar ratio of cost per worker it may be possible to arrive at a crude estimate of the manpower that is needed to carry out a program of a given cost.

Problem of need versus demand for physicians. As physicians become able to "do more" for people, the demand for medical services seems to increase. Medical care, which was formerly thought of as a luxury, has now become a necessity. Thus from a manpower point of view as well as from the standpoint of social values, the problem is to estimate need as contrasted to demand. Gregg estimated that there would be a "need" for 210,600 active physicians for 1954.[20]

Trends in medicine and national life have worked in opposite directions in regard to the demand for physicians. Better hospitals, earlier and better diagnosis, more effective drugs, preventive medicine, higher levels of living, more auxiliary personnel, good roads and automobiles —all have in some respects lessened the demands upon physicians. On the other hand the growth in population has increased the need for physicians. Estimated on the basis of one doctor per 850 civilians, the increase in population between 1940 and 1950 would have produced a need for 23,000 more physicians in 1950 than in 1940. If an armed force of 3.5 million is to be maintained with a doctor ratio of 35 physicians per 10,000 men (this is about three times the number of physicians needed for a civilian population of comparable size), there will be an additional demand for physicians.

Precisely what constitutes a shortage of physicians and whether a shortage of physicians actually exists are highly debatable. Probably

[20] Unless stated otherwise, this discussion of physicians is based upon Alan Gregg, "Doctors," *Scientific American* (September 1951), pp. 79–85.

the function of professional groups must be defined before the question of relative shortages can be determined. Some writers have been accused of assuming shortages rather than proving shortages.[21]

Allocation of Specialized Personnel

Let us consider now the problem of getting personnel possessing selected characteristics into specialized fields and categories of work.

In terms of long-range manpower, the problem of specialized personnel is (1) to identify the most intelligent members of the younger generation; (2) to motivate them to remain in school; (3) to provide them with a challenging education; and (4) to furnish opportunity for training that will enable them to contribute most effectively to the national welfare.[22] The immediate problem, until about 1964, has no easy solution. It must be borne in mind that one cannot change the number of boys in the age group since these boys are already in college, high school, or junior high school. However, consideration may be given to the following ways for increasing the number of scientists and engineers: (1) increasing the proportion of high-school graduates who go to college; (2) increasing the proportion of college students who study engineering (without disturbing other professions); and (3) increasing the proportion of engineering students who graduate. Closely related is the problem of increasing the output of the present corps of engineers.[23] All of these actions may be workable in varying degrees.

The problem of quantity and quality of potential specialized personnel. One of the characteristics of a complex technological system is that a large proportion of the population must be trained for jobs requiring considerable knowledge and skill. The educational system serves this function to a great extent and thus operates as a selective force in the earlier stages of the allocation process affecting potential professional manpower. Educational institutions must constantly adapt to foreseeable manpower requirements, and often their pro-

[21] Frank G. Dickinson, *Supply of Physician Service* (Chicago: Bureau of Medical Economic Research, American Medical Association, 1951).

[22] Dael Wolfle, "The Quality and Quantity of Potential Students," in *Symposium on Scientific and Specialized Manpower*, pp. 57–62.

[23] Armsby, *op. cit.*, pp. 19–20.

cedures have been criticized on the grounds that by focusing on mass production the quality of the product is lowered. Hence it might be advisable at this point to examine the developments that have been taking place in schools and colleges, the breeding grounds of future specialists.

Following World War II college enrollments experienced a sharp increase over previous years (Figure 3.6).[24] After the first wave of veterans passed through college, a decline in the aggregate size of graduating classes set in. The decline is expected to continue in progress through the year 1955. By 1960, however, the size of the graduating classes should have resumed its upward trend, and by 1970 the number of graduates is expected to total 590,000.

The anticipated growth of the college population will not necessarily bring about a lowering of the general intellectual level of the students. This conclusion is based on a strong belief that large numbers of young men and women qualified for higher education have not been going to college. If it were supposed that only the brightest youth went to college, then an increase in the proportion of college entrants to non-entrants would certainly lower the average quality. But there is no good evidence that all college students, past or present, have come from levels of those with the highest ability. The following facts need to be considered here: (1) the large loss between high school and college seems to be spread over the entire range of intelligence; (2) college entrants have been averaging only slightly better on intelligence tests than all high school graduates; (3) college students who drop out before graduation appear to be spread over the entire range of intelligence, although there probably is a greater tendency for the less intelligent to drop out than for the more intelligent; (4) in terms of intelligence and grades, high-school graduates of top quality have been finishing college at seemingly limited rates (see Figure 3.6); and (5) even though college graduates have an average intelligence superior to that of the total population, thousands of average high-school graduates who do not finish college could make at least average members of scientific and professional groups. In view of the above, it seems that factors other than intelligence have an important influence upon the determination of which high-school

[24] This figure was based upon information by Wolfle, *op. cit.*

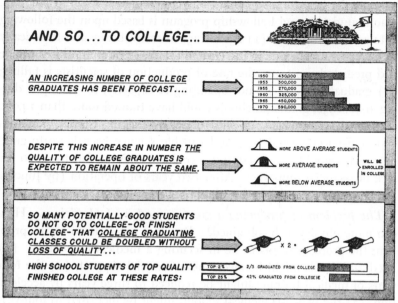

AND SO...TO COLLEGE...

AN INCREASING NUMBER OF COLLEGE
GRADUATES HAS BEEN FORECAST....

1950	430,000
1953	300,000
1955	270,000
1960	325,000
1965	450,000
1970	590,000

DESPITE THIS INCREASE IN NUMBER THE
QUALITY OF COLLEGE GRADUATES IS
EXPECTED TO REMAIN ABOUT THE SAME.

MORE ABOVE AVERAGE STUDENTS
MORE AVERAGE STUDENTS
MORE BELOW AVERAGE STUDENTS
WILL BE ENROLLED IN COLLEGE

SO MANY POTENTIALLY GOOD STUDENTS
DO NOT GO TO COLLEGE-OR FINISH
COLLEGE-THAT COLLEGE GRADUATING
CLASSES COULD BE DOUBLED WITHOUT
LOSS OF QUALITY...

X 2

HIGH SCHOOL STUDENTS OF TOP QUALITY
FINISHED COLLEGE AT THESE RATES:

TOP 2%   2/3 GRADUATED FROM COLLEGE
TOP 25%   42% GRADUATED FROM COLLEGE

(Bureau of Agricultural Economics)

FIGURE 3.6: ESTIMATED NUMBER AND QUALITY OF COLLEGE GRADUATES, UNITED STATES, 1950–1970.

graduates enter college, and which ones who enter go on to graduate.

It appears, therefore, that the educational system should be made more efficient as a selective force. Its present critical weakness is due, perhaps, to the chasm that exists between secondary school and college. How is the chasm to be bridged so as to permit free passage for *all* able students irrespective of handicaps other than those related to ability? It should be noted that the problem is not altogether one of economic capacity to finance a program of higher education; other factors such as motivation to pursue higher learning must be dealt with.

In order to improve the general welfare of the nation, and to strengthen its scientific potential, Congress passed legislation establishing the National Science Foundation. The function of this Foundation is to award scholarships and fellowships to American citizens; the recipents are to be chosen "solely on the basis of ability."

To date the board has supported only a graduate fellowship program. The Foundation and Fellowship program is based upon the following data and assumptions: (1) A shortage of scientifically and technically trained personnel exists in the United States; (2) despite this shortage and predicted shortages, the rate of production of scientists is falling; (3) graduate schools are not operating to capacity; for example, during 1951–1952, graduate schools could have trained more than 14,000 additional science students with presently existing training facilities and staffs; (4) several thousand capable science baccalaureate graduates who would like to continue graduate training fail to do so for lack of financial support.[25] After two years of operation (by June of 1953), nearly 1,200 fellowships had been awarded.

The problem of producing a greater number of physicians. How can more physicians be obtained? Pay does not seem to be the problem; the problem seems to be in securing a medical education. (1) Medical schools might be given more financial support, (2) the four years of medical training might be reduced to three years by acceleration, (3) the two-year medical schools might be increased to four-year schools, (4) states such as Montana and New Mexico which have no medical schools could establish schools. However, this line of thought assumes shortages which may or may not be real.

Is "migration and mobility" of scientists a problem? As compared to most occupational groups, scientists are highly mobile in their movements from state to state and from region to region. Since about 80 per cent of the scientists, according to one study, had worked in two or more states, it would appear that location is not a limiting factor in the placement of scientific personnel.[26] Moreover, a majority of the group had been employed by at least two of the major types of employers, private industry, government, and educational institutions. Their work histories also indicated that they could be expected to transfer from one speciality to another within a major branch of science such as physics, chemistry, and biology, but not from one major scientific field to another, for instance, from physics to biology.

[25] Dees, *op. cit.*, pp. 31–32.
[26] *Occupational Mobility of Scientists: A Study of Chemists, Biologists, and Physicists with Ph.D. Degrees* (Government Printing Office, 1953), pp. 2, 4, and 48.

During 1951, engineers and scientists left their jobs at a rate of 16 per 100 employed at the end of the year.[27] Previously only during World War II was the rate this high. The reasons for this turnover are not entirely clear since less than one fifth of all separations of scientists and research engineers from industry could be attributed to calls to military service. This would appear to suggest a worth-while area of investigation, for turnover can be wasteful, disruptive, time-consuming, and especially aggravating to any manpower shortage in these professions. In fact, whether these current rates are excessive or not it is difficult to say.

Utilization of Specialized and Scientific Personnel

Of all workers, scientific and specialized personnel as a group probably have the highest potential of usefulness to society. Any waste of their capacities means irrevocable loss to this and future generations. Even worse would be the consequences of a wide-spread feeling of discontent among them.

Problems of specialized personnel in industrial research. The outlay for scientific research and development in 1952 was more than four times the yearly expenditure at the outbreak of World War II.[28] Of the more than $3,500,000,000 spent in 1952 two thirds of this sum went for work done in laboratories that were either privately owned or operated; the federal government spent about one fourth for research and development carried on in government laboratories, and the remainder went to colleges and universities for work done by them. According to a survey that covered 85 per cent of industrial research and development in 1951, the surveyed companies reported 94,000 scientists and research engineers employed. Almost 90 per cent of these were employed in the manufacturing industries, primarily the aircraft, chemical, and electrical-machinery industries which accounted for more than half of the total. Research staffs (combined

[27] This discussion of turnover and problems of specialized personnel in industrial research is based upon Bureau of Labor Statistics, *Industrial Research and Development* (Government Printing Office, 1953).

[28] The largest section of the research and development resources of the nation exists within the activities of private industries. Yet, as compared to knowledge of the research operations of government and educational institutions, few data have been compiled relating to industrial research in toto in the United States.

professional and supporting personnel) totaled some 234,000, so that there were about 1.5 supporting workers for each scientist and research engineer. The foregoing discussion of scale of utilization could be pursued in terms of both dollar outlay and number of workers employed. However, in order to measure more accurately the extent of dollar support devoted to the activities of research personnel one could employ a ratio of dollar cost to manpower employed. The average cost per scientist in industrial research and development in 1951 was $22,100.

The problems of productivity in the professions. The question of how far society is prepared to go with its subsidy of scientific activity is wrapped up with the question of how productive these activities prove to be. This problem of productivity is not, however, one which the individual can solve for himself, since he is limited by the system in which he is forced to work. The professional occupations cover a rather wide range of activities, each with its own set of requirements in terms of mental capacities, technical skills, and even personality traits. For instance, a researcher with a desire for pure research can be rendered ineffectual if saddled with onerous administrative responsibilities. In his case the problem of productivity is related to questions of optimum organization for research as well as to questions of adequate provision of the facilities needed for the job. Although this is essentially a management problem, it is rather difficult to deal with it by means of conventional management techniques. The type of productivity that stems from mental and creative effort cannot readily be measured in quantitative terms in the same way as physical production can be measured in units of output.

Other problems of utilization. Among the other imponderable factors that enter into problems of utilization are conflicting values, such as the individual versus the organization, age versus youth, male versus female, and leadership versus followship. Also tied up with utilization are problems of career development: in-service training, vocational guidance, promotion policies, opportunities for participation in outside professional activities, and the like. The utilization of human resources in general is at best a difficult problem to deal with, but in the case of professional and scientific personnel the difficulties are perhaps the most challenging. To elaborate, engineers become executives, medical officers become general officers, a man fails to work a maximum number of hours per week, many qualified men fail to get promotions. Are all of these people malutilized? [29]

THE PROBLEM OF POLICY

One of the major barriers in dealing with manpower problems, according to the opinions of many informed persons, is the lack of a basic manpower policy. Administrative skill, though a fundamental ingredient of effective action, is clearly not enough. There can be no implementation of a policy which does not exist; nor can policy be formulated out of thin air. Today sound policy seems to be an outcome of mature analysis based largely on research; and it is generally agreed that more research and development are needed in the manpower area of social problems.

Study Questions

1. List at least five critical manpower problems and show why they are important.

2. Discuss the relationship, as well as the associated problems, of underemployment, unemployment, full employment, and new technology.

3. Compare attitudes toward certain occupations of your choice and relate them to the problems of obtaining workers.

4. What items and problems should be considered in the formulation of a manpower policy for the United States?

5. Compare the percentages of persons engaged in each major group of occupations from 1870 to 1930. What are some of the problems of the occupational statisticians?

6. From the latest *Monthly Report on the Labor Force* and other current publications, determine United States manpower as follows: (1) the number employed (industries, farms, etc.), (2) the strength of the armed forces, (3) the number able to work but unemployed, (4) the number of high-school and college students (not employed during learning period), and (5) the number able to work but not forced to work (includes the retired and dependent). In addition, determine the number of people in the United States who are excluded from a count of man-

[29] Eli Ginsberg in Irving C. Whittemore, "The Manpower Symposium at the 1952 Annual APA Meeting," *American Psychologist* (March 1953), p. 121.

power; those, that is, who are not able to work because of their youth, their age, or severe disability.

7. Trace the growth in importance of semi-skilled workers and white-collar workers in the United States since 1900. What problems related to training, the apprentice system, and education have accompanied this growth?

8. Analyze the importance of personnel in the machine tool industry. What are some of the problems in this area during peacetime and during periods of mobilization?

Selected References

Bureau of the Census, *Sixteenth Census of the United States: 1940,* "Population, Comparative Occupation Statistics for the United States, 1870 to 1940" (Government Printing Office, 1943). A somewhat comparable series of occupation statistics from 1870 to 1930 are presented along with selected comparisons for the 1930 and 1940 censuses.

Bureau of Labor Statistics, *Manpower Requirements of the Machine Tool Industry in the Current Mobilization Program* (Government Printing Office, 1951). An example of requirements for critical manpower during periods of mobilization.

————, *Scientific Research and Development in American Industry* (Government Printing Office, 1953). The report of a nationwide survey of industrial research and development in the United States in 1952 emphasizing research engineers and scientists, supporting personnel, turnover, and research costs.

Dewhurst, J. Frederick, and Associates, *America's Needs and Resources* (New York: Twentieth Century Fund, 1947). A comprehensive study of the American economy in which many aspects of manpower and labor force problems are treated.

Durand, John D., *The Labor Force in the United States, 1890–1960* (New York: Social Science Research Council, 1948). The influence of population factors upon the working force is the primary theme of this book.

Jaffe, A. J., and Charles D. Stewart, *Manpower Resources and Utilization* (Wiley, 1951). This book analyzes past and present factors that are and have been operating upon the working force of the United States.

Knapp, R. H., and H. B. Goodrich, *Origins of American Scientists* (University of Chicago Press, 1952). A comprehensive study of the factors associated with the interest of undergraduate college students in science as a vocation.

Monthly Labor Review, "Labor during National Emergencies" (October 1951), pp. 383–419. These articles are oriented primarily toward *labor* problems during periods of emergency rather than to *labor force* problems; however, the student should find them appropriate and the bibliography especially useful.

National Manpower Council, *Student Deferment and National Manpower Policy* (Columbia University Press, 1952). The issues involved in student deferment, deferment policy, and selection for deferment are examined in this publication.

Strausz-Hupe, Robert, and Stefan T. Possony, *International Relations* (McGraw-Hill, 1950), chs. IV and V. These chapters present a summary of the relationship of manpower to political power.

Williams, Benjamine H. (ed.), "The Search for National Security," *The Annals of the American Academy of Political and Social Science,* vol. 278 (1951). Many aspects of manpower and labor force problems that are associated with national survival are treated in this particular volume.

Problems of Aging and the Aged

Modern industrial society faces a perplexing dilemma with regard to its older people. The Biblical injunction, "Honor your father and your mother," has become increasingly difficult to comply with, both as a personal and as a social commandment. On the one hand, the elderly now comprise, in absolute numbers and in proportion to the total, a much more significant segment of our population than they did a century, a half century, or even a decade ago. On the other hand, our rapidly changing society places its highest value on the young, the active, and the dynamic. Hence the aged tend to be pushed aside, to be left to grapple alone with the problems of physiological and psychological decline, economic maintenance, living arrangements, and personal adjustment. In a sense old people are members of a minority group that has not worked out a satisfactory accommodation to the majority group in American society.

Primitive societies differ markedly from contemporary literate societies in that few people in the former ever reach old age. In some tribes people considered old can boast of relatively few years, according to modern ideas; a person is "aged" if he has attained thirty-five or forty years, far short of the Biblical three score and ten.

The respect accorded old people in primitive groups and the treatment of those who because of physical and mental deterioration can no longer take part in tribal activities vary surprisingly. Among the now extinct Tasmanians, for example, old men and women enjoyed a certain prestige, but the nomadic life of the group made it difficult if not impossible to care for the feeble. Hence they were left to die while the remaining members of the tribe moved on. On the nearby continent of Australia the Aranda, by contrast, never abandoned or killed the aged when they became incapacitated. Instead old people received kind treatment, including the exclusive right to eat certain highly esteemed foods. Still another pattern of behavior prevailed among the Hottentots of South Africa. The members of this tribe held the aged in the highest respect and cared for them lovingly; despite their high status, however, the infirm were sometimes left in a shelter with a little food to await death.

Wide variations in the treatment of the elderly are not limited to preliterate peoples. Indeed, the modern world provides striking examples of both high and low status for the aged—the former illustrated by the example of China, the latter by practice in the United States.

In China the aged traditionally have higher status, wield greater authority, and enjoy more prestige than the members of any other age group. Among the Chinese obedience to parents is looked upon as the greatest of virtues. Chinese society, at least until in relatively recent years it felt the impact of Western ideas, experienced an extremely low rate of social change; the patriarchal type of family, usually headed by the oldest man, reigned supreme as it had for centuries. In contrast, our own society, like those of western Europe generally, has been marked by a high rate of social change. As an end result of numerous social trends, our old people have no well-defined roles to play, and their status, compared with that of children, adolescents, and those in the economically productive years, is doubtful and uncertain. Instead of according respect, authority, and prestige to our elders, we are more likely to characterize them as "behind the times," questioning or denying their right to impose their ideas upon us. The statement, "They've lived their lives; they should let us live our own lives," sums up fairly well a widespread reaction toward the aged in the United States today.

In what ways does old age constitute a problem? The answer to this question must touch on at least the social, economic, psychological, and medical spheres. Social welfare agencies must look after the needs of the indigent, the blind, the handicapped, whatever the factors that have led to their condition. Families face, with perplexity and often with feelings of guilt, the problem of caring for aged parents and grandparents. In the economic realm, problems cluster around the changing abilities of the older worker, unemployment, the compulsory retirement age, and pensions. Failure of the aged to find satisfaction for basic psychological needs—the desire to feel wanted, to be useful, to be appreciated—leads to severe maladjustments and, indirectly, to mental and physical disease. Finally, physiological aging complicated by disease creates increased medical expenses at a time in life when the vast majority of older people are least able financially to cope with them.

How can we explain the fact that the aged in our society are a problem group? No factor has been more important than the amazing increase in the number of people reaching the older years and the almost equally surprising increase in the share of the total population that they comprise. In this country the population aged 65 and over was 10.7 times larger in 1950 than it was in 1870, whereas the total population was only 3.9 times greater. During the same 80-year period, the proportion of the nation's population in these advanced ages increased from 3.0 per cent to 8.2 per cent. By 1950 there were in the continental United States nearly 12,300,000 men and women who had passed their 65th birthdays. Thus maladjustments affecting old people involve more persons and these persons make up a larger proportion of our population than ever before.[1]

Several other interrelated factors, the origin of which may be traced to the Industrial Revolution, have also played an important part in bringing about the situation in which the aged often are a problem. Industrialization is primary among these factors. The application of mechanical power to the process of producing goods led—most importantly from this point of view—to the end of a rural way of life. It helped bring about an economic system in which money is all-important, and in which most people are dependent for financial

[1] There is little or no agreement as to when "old age" begins. All of us recognize that in our own experience people do not age at the same rate; at 60 one person seems young while another shows all the outward evidences of advanced age, such as grey hair or baldness, slow and uncertain gait, poor eyesight, partial deafness, stooped posture, poor memory for recent events. For statistical purposes, however, age 65 is usually employed as the lower limit of the aged category.

security on the satisfactory operation of a highly complex system of production largely beyond the control of the individual. Along with industrialization has come urbanization, the trend toward residence in the city. Among other things, urban life means houses no larger than required for the immediate family; it means smaller families; and it necessitates tighter work and play schedules. Accompanying the spread of industrial life and the rise of the city came highly significant changes in the structure and functions of the family. The patriarchal family of medieval times consisted of husband, wife, children, grandparents and unmarried relatives; and it had diverse functions. The modern democratic family, which had its origin in the Industrial Revolution, consists of husband, wife, and children. Its emphasis is increasingly placed on such psychological values as affection, companionship, and emotional security; and it is of slight importance as an economic producing unit. It makes little or no provision for the care of older relatives.

Such long-range trends have developed a society in which the aged are more often viewed as a troublesome care than as a highly respected elite.

AGING AS A BIOLOGICAL AND SOCIOLOGICAL PHENOMENON

Those human beings who survive the assaults of accident and disease pass through the several stages of the life cycle. In modern American society, unlike in many primitive societies, there are no ceremonies to mark clearly, for all to see, the beginning and end of these stages. Of the several possible classifications of the life cycle, the following seems to be most useful for our purpose: infancy, childhood, adolescence, adulthood, old age. Each of these stages involves certain rights, privileges, and responsibilities. And since they are age grades, the roles and statuses of the individuals in each of them are all related to the progress of the aging process. Important for present purposes are the physiological, psychological, and sociological changes that accompany the transition from adulthood to old age.

Aging actually begins at conception and therefore the human organism is aging throughout the entire life cycle. But the rate of change in the organism is not at all uniform from conception to old age. During infancy and childhood the process of growth predominates, whereas in adulthood the process of atrophy or degeneration comes to play a more significant part. In old age the atrophic process is of paramount importance.

Physiologists believe that certain basic changes are a part of the aging process as such and are not attributable to diseases.[2] In general terms we may say that the body tissues gradually dry out, cell division slows and the capacity for cell growth and tissue repair is retarded, and the metabolic (speed of living) rate declines. Cell atrophy and gradual decrease in tissue elasticity result in decreased speed, strength, and endurance; in degeneration of the nervous system; and in the slow impairment of the mechanisms for keeping a satisfactory internal environment for the cells and tissues.

These changes with age are interrelated and it is not yet known which, if any, is the most significant. The process is further complicated by the fact that it is difficult to separate the phenomena of aging *per se* from those of disease. Death usually results, ultimately, not from "old age" but from the degenerative diseases, such as arthritis, rheumatism, cardiovascular ailments, and arteriosclerosis. It is important to bear in mind two significant generalizations by Shock: (1) individuals differ widely in the rate of aging; and (2) within the same individual different organ systems age at different rates.[3]

Psychological changes are, of course, closely related to the physiological changes just discussed. In general, mental abilities gradually decline with age. General intelligence begins to wane in the early twenties and this trend continues at an increasing rate, at least up to the age of sixty. Memory for recent events falls off rapidly following a peak reached in the late teens and early twenties, but the ability to retain old learning declines much less with age than the capacity for learning new material. These findings must be interpreted cautiously,

[2] See Anton J. Carlson and Edward J. Stieglitz, "Physiological Changes in Aging," *The Annals of the American Academy of Political and Social Sciences*, CCLXXIX (1952), 22.
[3] Nathan W. Shock, "Biology of Aging," in T. Lynn Smith (ed.), *Problems of America's Aging Population* (University of Florida Press, 1951), pp. 37–46.

however, because of the serious difficulties involved in constructing tests and administering them to the aged.

Psychologists corroborate the commonplace observation that both hearing and vision become increasingly impaired with age after reaching a peak in the late teens. The speed of many motor responses begins a gradual decline about the age of 40 to 50 years. Donahue has pointed out that a man of 65 who sees an approaching automobile requires 0.06 seconds more for applying the brakes than he needed when he was 23. Thus if his car is traveling at the rate of 50 miles per hour, he must have five additional feet to stop the vehicle.[4]

Judgment and reasoning ability develop slowly and reach their peak later than the other abilities. The better judgment of older people tends to compensate for the decline of sensory and motor functions; hence they are less likely to be involved in serious automobile accidents, for example, than younger people. Finally, creative imagination suffers relatively little if at all from the inroads of aging.

Despite the basic nature of the biological changes, it is the social and cultural systems in which physical and mental changes occur that ultimately determine how older people fare. This has been suggested by the sharply varying situations of the aged in different cultures mentioned above. The sociological factor in the aging process is understood most readily in terms of the roles people play and the status they enjoy. A *role* may be thought of as a set of activities organized around some function which the group believes is useful. Thus the schoolteacher plays a role, as do the doctor, the policeman, the fireman, the parent, and the child. Each of us plays many roles. For example, at a given time one man may have the roles of parent, child, grandparent, merchant, PTA member, Kiwanian, church warden —and dozens of others.

The community places values on the various roles. It determines the *status* of an individual, his relative position or standing in the community or other social group, largely on the basis of the roles played by him. Moreover, society assigns markedly different values to roles. That of doctor, for example, rates much higher than that of clerk, and the role of parent higher than that of unmarried adult.

[4] Wilma T. Donahue, "Psychological Aspects of Aging," in Smith (ed.), *op. cit.*, p. 54.

In American society childhood is primarily the period of preparation for the active years of adulthood. From the earliest years the individual yearns for the attainment of adulthood, the period in which he will be free from the limitations imposed upon young people and able to exercise a greater personal choice in his behavior. The hardships occasioned by discipline, education, and training therefore tend to be rationalized away as justified by the nature of the goal of adulthood. For the American male the period of highest status is middle and later adulthood, or the ages of from about 30 to 60. The female enjoys the highest status during the child-bearing period, or from approximately 20 to 50 years of age.

The coming of old age means giving up the social roles that carry the highest status. The adjustment to the roles of old age is a difficult process, and this is especially so in our society because we place so much emphasis on work—which to an individual may mean many things in addition to a way of getting a living. Of course along with these changes in role and status there usually is a marked reduction in income, a development which makes the adjustment doubly hard to accomplish satisfactorily. Loss or reduction of income plays an extremely important part in creating the problem aspects of advanced age.

We may conclude, therefore, that a person is "old," from a sociological point of view, when he has relinquished the social roles and relationships typical of adulthood (mainly full-time employment for men and household management for women) and has accepted the social roles and relationships typical of the later years (such as becoming dependent on others, financially or otherwise, and subordinate in decision-making to one's adult children or to social workers).[5]

ECONOMIC DEPENDENCY AND EMPLOYMENT OF THE AGED

Economic Position of the Aged

The unsatisfactory position of the aged in the United States is due largely to the fact that as a group they are at a severe economic dis-

[5] See Ruth S. Cavan et al., Personal Adustment in Old Age (Chicago: Science Research Associates, 1949), pp. 6–7.

advantage. Their handicap in this respect shows up clearly in the data regarding their incomes. In 1949 the median income for all families in the nation was $3,107; but it was $3,466 for families whose heads were from 45 to 54 years old, and only $1,883 for those headed by persons aged 65 and over. About one fourth of the families whose heads were in the aged category had money incomes of between $1,000 and $2,000; 13.4 per cent received less than $500 during the year; and it was estimated that in the preceding year (1948) about 3 million persons aged 65 and over had no money income whatever.[6] In 1949, only the persons aged 14 to 19 years had a lower median income than those of 65 and over, the figure for the youths being $410.

In addition to the handicap of low incomes, many older people must face an uncertain future with very small estates to rely upon. A national study of beneficiaries of old-age and survivors insurance conducted in 1951 indicated that 4.5 per cent of the men receiving such payments had liabilities greater than their assets, and 22.8 per cent of them had no assets or liabilities whatever. The median net worth for all beneficiaries amounted to only $2,983; and for those who had some positive net worth the median was $6,334. This meager backlog against misfortune included the values of their homes.

Additional light is shed on the precarious economic position of the aged through an examination of the sources from which they derive their incomes. Although the aged tend to be at work in larger proportions during periods of prosperity and full employment, through the years the proportion of elderly persons in remunerative jobs has been declining. It has been estimated that in June, 1952, 31 per cent of all persons 65 and over were employed or were the wives of earners. In general, this group, less than a third of the total, may be regarded as living a more or less normal life. From an economic point of view, it presents relatively few problems.

On the same date about one third of the aged group were receiving income from social insurance and related programs, including old-age and survivors insurance, railroad retirement, federal civil-service retirement, state and local government retirement, and the veterans program. About one fifth were dependent to a greater or less extent

[6] See Jacob Fisher, "Income of Aged Persons, 1948," *Social Security Bulletin,* XIV (1951), 10–13.

upon public assistance (old-age assistance). Much smaller proportions received their income from private insurance (5.3 per cent) and
private pensions (3.0 per cent). Finally, about 30 per cent were dependent upon still other sources, including about one million persons
who were receiving income from investments and rent, and two millions who were either primarily dependent upon relatives or were
without visible means of support. (Since many older persons receive
income from more than one of these sources, the several percentages
do not total 100.)

The economic significance of the sources from which the aged receive their income lies in the recognition that to a large degree they
are dependents. In this respect their position resembles that of children. Since the unemployed old people no longer contribute to the
national product, they constitute consumers rather than producers.
Hence, whether their incomes come from public assistance, social
insurance programs, or assistance from friends and relatives, to a considerable extent they are a burden on society.

Of primary importance in the support of the aged are two programs
operated under the Social Security Act—Old-Age and Survivors Insurance, and Old-Age Assistance. The Social Security Act, which
also provides for unemployment insurance, employment services, and
maternal, child-health, and child-welfare services, was passed by Congress in 1935. The legislation had a background of widespread unemployment and distress due to the Great Depression. Since its passage, the act has been amended several times.

Old-age and survivors insurance is a federally administered program
affecting those who have worked for specified periods of time in employment covered by the act. Now that the coverage has been greatly
broadened, the most important groups of workers not participating
are certain self-employed persons such as lawyers, physicians, and
dentists, as well as many casual agricultural workers. The benefits
paid under the act are secured through assessments on wages paid by
employees and their employers. The situation in 1955 may be used
for illustrative purposes; employees and employers each paid two per
cent on earnings up to $4,200 per year. Monthly benefits were paid
to the retired worker who had reached age 65; to his wife, if she was
65 or over; to his unmarried children under 18; to his wife, regardless

of her age, if their child, under 18 and entitled to benefits, was in her care; and to a retired woman worker's dependent husband, if he was 65 or over. The payments were made without reference to the need of the recipient, except that no further benefits were paid in a given calendar year after the beneficiary had earned $1,200—unless the recipient was 72 years old or over.

The scope of this great federal program may be grasped from the fact that 5.6 million persons were receiving monthly benefits at the end of July, 1953, the payments for that month totaling $236.4 million. The Social Security Administration estimated that 66.5 million persons were insured under old-age and survivors insurance at the beginning of 1953.

The role of old-age and survivors insurance benefits in cases where there is no other important source of income and where illness occurs may be illustrated by the following case: [7]

When Mr. A in 1945 left his job as a skilled worker in a steel mill at the age of 65 to care for his ailing wife, the couple had some assets in addition to the home they owned. He immediately became entitled to old-age insurance benefits. Mrs. A, who was 2 years younger than Mr. A and nearly blind, did not become entitled until 1947. Their benefits— $61.08 a month in 1949—were among the highest paid, for his average monthly wage was $223.59, but in the survey year they constituted the couple's only money income. Mrs. A had a serious operation in 1948 which took the last of the couple's savings and all they had left in 1949 was their home, an 8-room house valued at $7,000, in which they were living by themselves. The house, however, was mortgaged for over half its value. Both Mr. and Mrs. A had life insurance policies for $1,000 each. In 1948 they were unable to make any payments on the house and in 1949 made only two payments of $50 each. Their debts increased $275 during the survey year. Although he felt able to engage in certain kinds of employment, Mr. A had not attempted to add to the couple's income by working after his retirement because his wife needed him at home. A married son was not in a position to help his parents. They were not familiar with the old-age assistance program.

Old-Age Assistance is the other social-security program that plays an important role in providing, more or less adequately, for the mate-

[7] Margaret L. Stecker, *Resources of Old-Age and Survivors Insurance Beneficiaries in Philadelphia and Baltimore, 1949* (Bureau of Old-Age and Survivors Insurance, 1950), pp. 12-13.

rial needs of those 65 and over.   It differs from old-age and survivors insurance in a number of ways.   Old-age assistance is a federal-state program administered by state governments (or by county governments under state supervision).   The national government participates by contributing somewhat more than half of the cost of the assistance and administration.   Moreover, benefits are payable only on the basis of need; and since the payments are made under state laws, the amounts paid vary from state to state.

During 1952 a total of $1,468,060,000 was paid to 2,635,000 old-age assistance recipients in the United States.   Although in July, 1953, the average monthly payment for the nation was $50.99, the average payments in the various states ranged from $79.19 in Connecticut to $27.01 in Virginia.   These figures should be measured against the cost of living.   The official estimates of a modest budget for an elderly couple, at October, 1950, prices, ranged from $1,602 in New Orleans to $1,908 in Milwaukee.

As we have seen, earnings from employment, social insurance, and old-age assistance account for most of the income of the aged in the United States.   Private pensions and individual accumulations, such as savings, security holdings, and insurance annuities, are other sources that must be mentioned.   Private pension systems, under which an employer pays a stipulated sum, usually monthly, to the retired employee, have become increasingly significant since World War II.   A number of unions have been successful in their demands for the establishment of such pension plans.   In many instances the employer has agreed to supplement Old Age and Survivors Insurance benefits in order to provide a combined retirement income of a given amount. In 1950 it was estimated that about 11,500,000 workers were covered by industrial pension systems but that only about 250,000 retired persons were actually receiving such payments.   At that time, however, many of the pension plans in large industries had been in existence but a short time.   Undoubtedly this source of income will become more and more important as additional plans are placed in effect and progressively more covered workers reach retirement ages.

Under modern conditions, adequate self-provision for the older years has become increasingly difficult.   The rapid inflation which occurred during and after World War II is an important factor in the situation.   The marked increases in price levels make practical planning for retirement income doubly hard.   But more important is the fact that for a large proportion of the population adequate savings simply cannot come out of current earnings.   If the average person were to provide for a life income of $100 per month beginning at age 65, he would have to possess an accumulation of $17,000 at that age.[8] It is unrealistic to expect such amounts of savings in a society in which, as late as 1949, one-half of all *families* received less than $3,107 annually.

Employment of the Aged

Employment would probably play a much more important part in the support of the aged were it not for widely prevalent discrimination against the hiring of older people and even against retaining them on the payroll.   Although the proportion of the population in the 65-and-over category has been increasing steadily, the percentage they constitute of the total labor force has remained relatively stable, as these figures show: [9]

Year	Percentage of Population Aged 65 and Over	Percentage of Total Labor Force Aged 65 and Over
1890	3.8	4.3
1930	5.5	4.3
1952	7.8	4.4

The reluctance of employers to hire or rehire older workers begins long before age 65 is reached.   For women it begins to be evident as early as 30 or 35; for men it is apparent after 40 or 45 years of age. Some studies have shown that as many as one third of the companies surveyed have explicit policies against employment of workers over

[8] Edwin E. Witte, "Social Provisions for the Aged," in Milton Derber (ed.), *The Aged and Society* (Champaign, Ill.: Industrial Relations Research Association, 1950), p. 116.
[9] Figures from Bureau of the Census.   See U.S. Senate, *Retirement Policies and the Railroad Retirement System, Report of the Joint Committee on Railroad Retirement Legislation, Part 2, Economic Problems of an Aging Population* (Government Printing Office, 1953), p. 43.

stated ages, and in a much higher proportion of firms the same policy prevails even though it is not specifically formulated.

Discrimination against older workers is based on a variety of beliefs, including the following: that older people are less productive than younger people; that they are harder to get along with; that they have higher rates of absenteeism; that their accident rates are higher and consequently they endanger other workers; that they are sick too often; that there is more labor turnover in the aged group; and, in retail establishments, that customers prefer to deal with younger people, especially younger as opposed to older women. Most of these beliefs are based on nothing more substantial than impressions. Undoubtedly they stem in large part from our society's pronounced tendency to evaluate youth more highly than age. In many instances the empirical studies necessary to prove or disprove the validity of the specific reasons assigned for discriminating against the employment of older people have not yet been made, but there is a growing body of findings that strongly suggest the fallaciousness of many of the claimed justifications for discrimination. For example, the rates of absenteeism for older workers are not higher than those of their younger fellows. There is also increasing evidence that any loss in speed and in muscular strength among workers over 40 years of age is compensated for by increased skills and better judgment.

The difficulties of unemployed older persons in obtaining work have led in recent years to the development by a number of governmental and private employment agencies of special counseling and placement programs for clients of this type. In general, the results of such efforts have been gratifying, although the total effect has been small in the light of the total need. The following extracts from the report of a Canadian experimental program illustrate the possibilities of the special counseling approach. Of a total of 1,138 unemployed persons over 45 years of age who were counseled during the one-year study period, 630 obtained work; and 426 of these clients secured their own jobs after their confidence had been restored through interviews with trained counselors.[10]

[10] W. G. Scott, *Report of the Counseling Service for Applicants for Employment Over 45 Years of Age* (Toronto: National Employment Service, 1948 [?]), pp. 9–10.

A.B.—69. Strong and virile man. 38 years with a large national firm —had risen from office boy to office manager. Reported to simplify and improve almost every business system with which he was associated. Unemployed eleven months.

After counseling, together with other recommendations, it was suggested, that he be a "resurrector of failing businesses."

With his morale restored, he immediately sold his services to a contracting firm engaged in the rapid building of houses. Because of his business ability and experience, he vitalized this business. One month after his appointment he became a Director of the firm; four months later he was made Vice-President!

E.F.—63. A pleasant, cooperative woman, much discouraged because of her inability to obtain factory employment. Arthritis caused some discomfort in walking. Unemployed ten months.

As a hobby she was greatly interested in and did considerable knitting, crocheting, and sewing. Counsellor suggested that she take samples of her work to some of the neighborhood stores dealing with this type of merchandise. Three days later she reported that she had followed the suggestion and had obtained sufficient orders to keep her gainfully employed for two months and probably six months.

The task of evaluating fairly the older worker depends first of all upon getting the true facts concerning his performance on the job. A second step involves changing the attitudes of both the employer and the older worker toward the latter's potentialities. Meanwhile the present widespread discrimination represents a serious social waste and a substantial barrier to the successful adjustment of many older people. As Havighurst has pointed out, work provides a basis for self-respect and a sense of worth; it is a source of prestige or recognition by others; it provides a place for social participation; it is a means of expressing one's self creatively; and it is a way of being of service to others. It has value to the worker even if it is no more than a way of making time pass.[11]

[11] Robert J. Havighurst, "What It Means to Retire from Work," *The University of Chicago Round Table*, No. 690 (June 17, 1951), pp. 14–17.

LIVING ARRANGEMENTS OF THE AGED

The twin keys to an understanding of the problems of housing and living arrangements for the aged are the evolution of the individual family and the reduction in income that often accompanies the transition to old age. The typical family begins with the marriage of two people, grows in size as children are born, decreases in size as the grown children leave home to establish their own living arrangements, and finally again consists of the original married pair. But whereas the typical older man is married, the typical older woman is a widow. Thus throughout the family cycle housing needs of the average family gradually change. The advent of old age, with its altered living requirements due to the changed composition of the household as well as to illness and physical disabilities, also unfortunately is, as indicated above, usually accompanied by a serious loss of income.

Although well over two thirds of those aged 65 and over in 1950 were living in their own households, only 44 per cent of these households consisted of married couples. About one tenth of the older people were living with relatives other than husbands or wives, and 14 per cent were either living alone or with persons to whom they were not related. One fourth of the older people of the nation were living in the households of others, that is, they were living in homes headed by someone else. Finally, six per cent of the older group resided in quasi-households, that is, institutions, hotels, or large rooming houses. From another point of view, 76 per cent of the aged were living in families (with one or more relatives present), and 24 per cent were living alone or in groups that could not be classified as families.

The housing arrangements of older people in non-farm areas (villages, towns, suburbs, and cities) run heavily to one and two-person households, and there is a noticeable lack of congestion in the homes. The fact that the families of older persons have larger quarters than those of the younger ones is due to the reduction in size of their households by the departure of children and the death of the husband or the wife. This is not, however, an unmixed blessing. The heads of

households who are 65 and over own their homes in larger proportions (68 per cent) than those of any other age group; but it is often
true that home ownership constitutes a heavy physical and financial
burden for them. Actually a somewhat larger share of our elderly
people live in substandard houses than is the case with those who are
younger. In 1950 the Census Bureau found, moreover, that nearly
12 per cent of the dwellings rented by older people were in a dilapidated condition, and that 40 per cent of the elderly renters paid less
than $30 a month.

We should not conclude that all old people have a severe housing
problem. However, the figures just presented, interpreted in connection with the relatively poor economic status of the aged, should
make it clear that the later years of life bring to many persons overwhelming problems. Large numbers of the aged must endure living
conditions seriously below what is generally considered to be an acceptable standard.

Only about 6 per cent of the aged live in institutions, hotels, and
large rooming houses, but this group merits special attention. It
consists largely of those who, because of physical impairments, inadequate financial means, and the lack of close relatives, cannot maintain households of their own. In 1950 some 3 per cent of all persons over 65 resided in institutions. More than half of these were
in homes for the aged, over a third were in mental hospitals, and the
remainder were cared for in chronic-disease hospitals, tuberculosis
hospitals, correctional institutions, homes and schools for the mentally
handicapped, and other establishments.

Traditionally the almshouse or poor farm was the last resort of the
indigent aged. This institution, in which the destitute of all ages
were thrown together under often wretched conditions, is gradually
disappearing in this country.[12] Today about 12 per cent of the aged
institutional population resides in local public homes, while more
than 40 per cent is cared for in private homes, either voluntary (non-
profit) or proprietary. This category includes nursing homes. Fra-
ternal organizations, churches, and labor unions operate many of them.
There is an unmistakable trend toward more progressive social, recrea-

[12] Nathan W. Shock, *Trends in Gerontology* (Stanford University Press, 1951),
p. 51.

tional, and rehabilitative programs by such institutions. However, most homes for the aged provide little more than the basic necessities of food and shelter; and the inmates often simply vegetate, giving little comfort to themselves or to others.

In recent years an increasing recognition of the inadequacies of living arrangements for older people has resulted in the launching of several experimental programs. For example, some social agencies place their clients in foster homes, just as has been done with children. A few small communities exclusively for older people, such as the cottage colony at Millville, New Jersey, have been established. Apartment buildings for the elderly have been constructed in large cities, notably in New York City. A novel proposal for the building of "mother-in-law annexes"—small apartments connected with an ordinary single dwelling which can be closed off from the remainder of the house—has received enthusiastic approval. Such units can provide for elderly relatives a desirable degree of privacy and also facilitate social contacts and assistance. Moreover, architects and gerontologists are studying the need for incorporating in housing for the aged such features as ramps instead of stairs, special night-lighting and non-slip floors, all of which are desirable because of the progressive physical deterioration of old people.

Students of the problem seem to agree that the main question is one of providing suitable low-cost housing, not only in communities where substantial numbers of the aged now live but also in those climatically favored areas to which they are migrating in large numbers. Such an undertaking is fraught with difficulties because of the limited financial resources and short life expectancy of those in the group concerned.

THE PROBLEM OF HEALTH IN OLD AGE

Everyday observation demonstrates that the incidence of chronic disease and disability increases rapidly with advancing age. It is not so generally recognized, however, that in recent decades progressively more of the deaths occurring are those of persons at the older ages. In

1900, deaths of those aged 65 and over accounted for 24.3 per cent of all deaths in the United States. By 1950, deaths occurring at those ages made up 52.7 per cent of the total. On the other hand, mortality of persons under 15 years of age accounted for 34.6 per cent of all deaths in 1900 and only 9.4 per cent in 1950.

To some extent the increasing concentration of deaths in the older ages may be attributed to the increasing proportion of the aged in our population. But more significant is the greater progress made in reducing the death rate at the younger ages. Advances in medical knowledge and treatment and in sanitation have controlled in a large degree the infectious diseases of childhood and early adulthood.[13] Hence more persons survive the earlier years only to fall prey to other diseases and accidents in the later years.

More than four fifths of all deaths among white persons in the age-range 65–84 now result from the principle cardiovascular-renal diseases (those affecting the heart, circulatory system, and kidneys), cancer, pneumonia and influenza, and accidents. It is especially significant that many of these ailments are attended by long-continued disability before death comes. Persons so afflicted may become a partial or complete burden on their relatives or on the community. Care of the chronically ill and disabled thus burdens society and necessitates suitable nursing and hospital facilities.

Unfortunately, the illnesses of old age strike at a stage in the life cycle when the individual often is not able to pay for medical attention and hospital or nursing care. The fact that group-insurance plans providing hospitalization and surgical care usually terminate with the end of employment aggravates the matter.

The health problems of the older segment of the population are now receiving greater attention as it is more generally recognized that they are a basic concern of the community. Most physicians agree that early diagnosis of the degenerative diseases offers the best hope for reducing mortality and keeping older people active, productive, and happy. To accomplish this, a number of programs have been undertaken. One of the most promising is multiple or multiphasic screening, or testing for several pathological conditions at the same

---

[13] "Shift in Mortality to Older Ages," *Metropolitan Life Insurance Company Statistical Bulletin*, XXXIV (1953), 3–5.

time. Such multiple screening, combined with health education and
medical research, ultimately will go far toward insuring early detection of the illnesses that take a high toll among the aged. Only a
beginning has been made, however, in utilizing this technique.

Another trend is the development of the medical specialty of geriatrics, treatment of the ailments of old age. About two hundred
physicians now are members of the American Geriatrics Society, but
there is disagreement among practitioners as to the wisdom of establishing geriatrics as a special field of medicine. Many doctors feel
that it is unwise to segregate the aged for treatment since the diseases
from which they suffer could be dealt with within the existing framework of specialization. It is notable, however, that similar objections
were voiced when pediatrics was being set off as a medical specialty.[14]

Geriatric clinics established by a few hospitals have made important
contributions to the care of older patients and, through research, have
added to our knowledge of the medical aspects of aging. Out-patient
care of older people is also being developed in connection with some
hospitals. There is evidence that programs of medical and hospital
care for elderly patients can achieve a surprising degree of rehabilitation. Such programs are much further advanced in Great Britain
and the Scandinavian countries than in our own country.[15]

We may look to biological research for important discoveries that
will aid in working out positive programs to achieve and prolong
health. Already workers in the field of nutrition have published
findings of utmost significance. It has long been known, for instance,
that keeping a thin body is of the greatest moment in achieving long
life. Recent studies have given us more exact knowledge as to what
diets will help in attaining this goal. It seems quite clear, nevertheless, that only pioneering efforts have yet been made in the direction
of maintaining health and treating disease in the older years. The
combined efforts of scientists, educators, national, state, and local
health departments, the medical profession, institutions for the aged,
and hospital administrators will be required for a broad and comprehensive attack on the problems of health in old age.

[14] Shock, *op. cit.*, pp. 39–40.
[15] *Ibid.*

PROBLEMS OF PERSONAL ADJUSTMENT TO OLD AGE

The adjustment of any group of persons has two aspects, personal and social. Personal adjustment refers to the changes a person makes in his attitudes and behavior in response to the requirements of a new situation. One's adjustment may be successful or unsuccessful. In other words, the individual faced with a new set of life conditions may adjust himself satisfactorily and hence be more or less happy; or he may fail to make the necessary changes in attitudes and behavior and remain unhappy. Social adjustment, on the other hand, relates to alterations in society itself in response to different conditions resulting from social change.[16] Thus the passage of the Social Security Act was a social adjustment brought about by new conditions facing certain segments of American society.

It should already be clear that the process of aging confronts the individual with numerous zoological, psychological, and social changes which disturb personal adjustment. As the aging person loses his roles, such as that of provider, which are highly prized in our society, he must accept other less desirable ones such as that of dependent. Thereafter he no longer enjoys the relatively higher status associated with the roles he formerly played. In any given instance, these changes in roles and statuses create a condition of strain, and the individual typically goes through a difficult period of unadjustment. Eventually, a large proportion of older persons adjust satisfactorily to their new situations. But for many of the older group, as the case records of social service agencies demonstrate, the period of unadjustment is succeeded by a more or less permanent state of maladjustment. Probably the failure to adjust satisfactorily is due to the inability to satisfy basic human needs. Pollak lists these as follows: (1) physical health and comfort, (2) affection and love, (3) recognition, (4) expression of interests, and (5) emotional security.[17]

[16] Ernest W. Burgess, "Personal and Social Adjustment in Old Age," in Milton Derber (ed.), *The Aged and Society* (Champaign, Ill.: Industrial Relations Research Association, 1950), p. 138.

[17] Otto Pollak, *Social Adjustment in Old Age* (New York: Social Science Research Council, 1948), pp. 45–46.

A basic difficulty involved in making the transition to old age is, for a majority of elderly people, the refusal to accept realistically the undeniable fact that they are growing old. One study shows, for example, that most men and women think of themselves as "middle-aged" until they reach seventy. In the seventies a majority consider themselves "elderly." Even in the nineties far less than one half of the older persons included in the investigation designated themselves as "aged." [18] It follows, of course, that orderly preparation for the acceptance of new roles and statuses can hardly proceed smoothly among persons who resolutely resist the idea that a transition is necessary.

Although the specific problems of personal adjustment are numerous and differ markedly from individual to individual, certain changes in role and status recur rather generally. Potentially each of them may result in acute maladjustment. Particularly widespread is one which has already been mentioned, the loss of the role of provider. As economic mainstay and functional head of a family unit, a man or woman plays one of the most highly regarded roles in our society, one which carries with it many desirable privileges and a high status in any particular group. Giving up that role means losing independence and authority and accepting a relatively inferior status. At about the same time the older person loses his role of leader in organizations—business, governmental, civic, and so forth—and this loss helps develop the feeling that he is no longer important to others.

Death of the husband or wife, resulting in the acceptance of the role of widow or widower, likewise is a widespread experience. Widowhood prevails among older women to a marked extent; nearly half of all adult women aged 65–74 and over two thirds of those aged 75 and over are widows. Widowhood may make severe inroads on physical health and comfort, affection and love, recognition, and emotional security. Remarriage, which is far more frequent for widowers than widows, is accompanied by serious dangers of failure to achieve marital happiness.

Another problem of personal adjustment in old age involves changes in living arrangements necessitated by reduced income, family alterations, and illness. For a person who has headed a household to

[18] Burgess, *op. cit.*, pp. 148–149.

become a member of another household in which the paramount position is held by someone else may impose a severe emotional strain. Accepting the role of inmate in an institution likewise taxes the readjustment capacities of an older person. Another frustrating experience confronts those who are forced by illness or physical disabilities to adapt themselves to decidedly limited social contacts, a monotonous routine, or perhaps to economic dependency.

For the attainment of a situation in which the elderly more generally achieve satisfactory personal adjustment, progress must be made on a broad front. Of fundamental importance is the matter-of-fact recognition by our society generally and by middle-aged and older people in particular that physical, psychological, and social changes do occur with aging and that these changes are natural and inevitable. As a more immediate goal, numerous groups should develop adequate programs to prepare adults for aging and retirement. A few universities, public-school systems, and business firms have made a start in this direction. Hand in hand with instruction, which may be carried on in classroom situations, group discussions, and even through correspondence courses, should go comprehensive counseling and guidance programs. Skilled professional people may greatly assist the aged in solving personal adjustment problems as they arise. Finally, social adjustments to insure better societal provisions for the economic needs, housing, health, and leisure-time activities of our older people are basic.

THE AGED AND RECREATION, EDUCATION, RELIGION, AND POLITICS

The tardiness with which our society has become aware of the growing importance of our aged population has also created problem situations in other major institutional fields. A brief consideration of some unmet needs in recreation, education, religion, and politics demonstrates the serious lag in our society's adjustment to its older members.

Recreation

The American "cult of youth," the glorification of vigorous activity, speed, and efficiency, has brought about a situation in which recreational institutions specialize in the activities of young people. Our numerous youth centers, boys' clubs, the Boy Scout and Girl Scout movements, and athletic and hobby programs provide evidence of this. Most older people have ample leisure and need to develop new interests and activities to substitute for those they were preoccupied with as adults. Nevertheless, city recreational departments, civic organizations, clubs, and religious groups have been concerned largely with establishing and operating programs intended primarily for younger people.

Although little provision has been made for avocational activities of most older people, there are a number of promising developments. At present recreational personnel are demonstrating a growing awareness of unmet needs in their field. In several cities activity centers for older people are now in operation. At one of the earliest of these, the Hodson Community Center in New York, older people may, in the atmosphere of a social club, talk with their contemporaries, play cards, read newspapers, listen to the radio, have tea, coffee, and cake. In addition, members play in a musical ensemble, publish a mimeographed monthly magazine, take part in poetry-reading sessions, and build household furniture in a carpentry class. A program of another type has worked well in Philadelphia and other cities, where Golden Age Clubs have been organized to serve leisure-time needs. Pioneering ventures have also included hobby and craft shops. In many Florida cities older people themselves operate their recreational programs through clubs, with supervision and assistance from local recreation departments. These are among the many indications that communities are belatedly beginning to discharge their obligations to older citizens.

Education

Traditionally, in America, we have educated only our young people, assuming that the legitimate objective of education is to prepare children for adult roles. Although the adult education movement has gained great momentum, it has addressed itself largely to active adults, not to old people. Consequently, until very recent years, education ignored completely this segment of the population. A new concept of education is now taking form. It is being recognized that training cannot safely be stopped without impairing the ability of citizens to make adjustments required throughout the life cycle. Also it is being realized that, on logical as well as practical grounds, it is as important to prepare to meet the problems posed by the transition from adulthood to old age as to be ready to handle those involved in the change from youth to adulthood. In view of these developments our traditional limitation of education to man's earliest years seems much too narrow and short-sighted. Furthermore, much of the maladjustment now associated with old age might be eliminated through effective use of educational techniques for persons in adulthood and later maturity.

The evidences of this trend are numerous and encouraging. Several colleges and universities offer experimentally courses intended to help older people use their own and other resources to solve their problems. A few public-school systems, notably in California, Michigan, and New York, are placing new emphasis on education for the older adult. In recent years have appeared magazines, newspaper articles and columns, and popular books devoted to the task of helping older readers to stay abreast of the times and to tackle their own difficulties effectively.

Religion

The advent of the last stage of the life cycle brings for many persons a renewed interest in the spiritual element. In old age, special spiritual needs probably appear—for relief from heightened emotions, from the pangs of loneliness, and for reassurance in general. Organized religion has important resources with which to meet spiritual crises. However, the problems of adjustment are exceedingly varied and diverse and it is doubtful that most churches employ their resources to best advantage. In order to serve the peculiar needs of older people, to help enable them fully to realize their potentialities, churches will probably find it necessary to provide additional services and facilities.

Numerous indications suggest that spiritual leaders are awakening more fully to their responsibilities to the elderly. Representatives of religious organizations participated enthusiastically in the First National Conference on Aging, held in Washington in 1950. *Older People and the Church*, a book dealing with the aging process, pastoral care, group work, and social resources of the church, appeared in 1949.[19] Some churches have established special counseling arrangements. A few have made such physical modifications in church structures as ramps in place of stairs, and have provided hearing aids and other accommodations for the infirmities of old age. In 1953 the National Council of Churches of Christ in the U.S.A. held, at Lake Geneva, Wisconsin, its First International Conference on the Church and Older Persons. It seems certain that henceforth organized religion will play a more significant role in facilitating the adjustment of the elderly.

Politics

The belief or fear that the aged constitute a problem in the political sphere rests essentially on two assumptions. The first is that voting behavior is related more or less directly to age. Specifically, older people are thought to be more conservative than younger people. The second assumption is that older voters tend to form a bloc when confronted with issues that directly affect them. Unfortunately, evidence to prove or disprove these two assumptions has not been assembled, although a few studies have been suggestive. It is true, however, that as the years pass, the aged make up a larger and larger proportion of our potential voters. In 1950, 12.6 per cent of those aged 21 and over had passed their sixty-fifth birthdays. It has been forecast that in the year 2000, 25 per cent of those eligible to vote will be 65 or over.[20]

[19] Paul B. Maves and J. Lennart Cedarleaf, *Older People and the Church* (New York: Abingdon-Cokesbury Press, 1949).

[20] Walter C. McKain, Jr., *The Social Participation of Old People in a California Retirement Community* (unpublished Ph.D. thesis, Harvard University, 1947), p. 12.

The widespread support given by older people to such movements as the Townsend Plan for universal pension payments indicates that under certain conditions they may operate as a major political force. When issues directly affecting their welfare are at stake, they, aided by friends and relatives, may also exert considerable additional pressure. Consequently there is an important need for additional facts that will enable us to assess realistically the political interests, roles, and power of the aged.

TOWARD THE INTEGRATION OF THE AGED IN AMERICAN SOCIETY

In the second half of the twentieth century, the situation of the aged in America is thus unsatisfactory in many respects. In numerous areas of social life older citizens pose problems which must be solved if our society is to function smoothly and if the elderly are to live as full-fledged citizens. Behind these social problems and coupled with increases in the numbers and proportions of older people are the derivative effects of highly significant trends set in motion by the Industrial Revolution—industrialization, urbanization, changes in family structure and function, and other institutional changes.

How can the aged be more fully integrated into American society? The task will not be easy, but from a sociological point of view it seems to center on the concepts of role and status. Modern social trends have gradually closed to most older people many of the roles that our society values highly. The old man or the old woman no longer functions as patriarch or matriarch. They are more likely to be relegated to the role of dependent, to be receiving assistance either from the state or from their children. The roles they have lost have not been replaced by other equally desirable ones in the developing institutional structure. Since a person's status is based on the community's evaluation of the roles he plays, the average of the statuses assigned to older people is relatively low.

To remedy this situation, which puts high hurdles in the way of personal and social adjustment, the effort should be made to develop more desirable roles for older people. The most fruitful way to accomplish this is to re-evaluate the importance of the aged. From the economic viewpoint, it is easy to demonstrate that while older people remain in the labor force, they contribute to the total national product; they do not constitute dependents. Moreover, the aged possess experience and maturity of judgment that should not be lost merely because the societal structure does not provide means for channeling these resources into useful outlets. To avail ourselves of these assets we must insure that the aged remain a part of the on going life of the community. The realities of physiological and psychological aging cannot of course be denied and no good purpose would be served by underemphasizing their effect upon adjustment. Nevertheless, adequate preparation for old age, which to be effective must begin early in life, should enable a person to visualize later maturity as an inviting and challenging period of life, one which—like all other life periods—brings problems, but which also offers rich opportunities. With proper preparation, the years of retirement can be the ones in which a person thoroughly enjoys the things in which he is most interested.

Study Questions

1. Why have the elderly recently assumed widespread importance as a problem group in the United States?

2. Discuss the significance of role and status in the aging process.

3. Give several examples of societal adjustments to the aged during this century.

4. Discuss the relationship of the economic factor to the over-all adjustment of the aged.

5. How do employers justify employment policies which discriminate against the aged?

6. Why does illness constitute a special problem in old age? What diseases take the greatest toll? Why?

7. What do you consider the most feasible ways of preventing personal maladjustments of older people? Discuss.

8. What is the significance of the concept of cultural lag in connection with the problems of the aged?

9. Discuss the aged as a potential political pressure group.

10. What can our society do to remove the disadvantages presently handicapping the aged?

Selected References

The Annals of the American Academy of Political and Social Sciences, vol. 269 (1952). The entire issue is devoted to articles by leading students of aging and retirement.

Cavan, Ruth Shonle, Ernest W. Burgess, Robert J. Havighurst, and Herbert Goldhamer, *Personal Adjustment in Old Age* (Chicago: Science Research Associates, 1949). An excellent short exploration of personal adjustment in old age.

Derber, Milton (ed.), *The Aged and Society* (Champaign, Ill.: Industrial Relations Research Association, 1950). A valuable symposium on the social and economic aspects of aging.

Donahue, Wilma, and Clark Tibbitts, *Planning the Older Years* (University of Michigan Press, 1950), and *Growing in the Older Years* (University of Michigan Press, 1951). Worthwhile papers on the social, economic, educational, and medical problems of the aged.

Gilbert, Jeanne G., *Understanding Old Age* (Ronald, 1952). A textbook of psychological gerontology, important as a pioneering effort.

Journal of Gerontology. This quarterly constitutes an important source of information about current research on the biological, psychological, and social aspects of aging.

Lansing, Albert I. (ed.), *Cowdry's Problems of Aging* (3rd ed., Williams & Wilkins, 1952). The standard reference work on the biological and medical aspects of aging.

Lieb, Clarence William, M.D., *Outwitting Your Years* (Prentice-Hall, 1949). Advice for the lay reader on how to grow old gracefully.

Maclachlan, John M. (ed.), *Health in the Later Years* (University of Florida Press, 1953). The proceedings of the Third Annual Southern Conference on Gerontology, devoted to medical problems of the aging.

Shock, Nathan W., *A Classified Bibliography of Gerontology and Geriatrics* (Stanford University Press, 1951). A comprehensive bibliography covering the biology of aging, organ systems, geriatrics, psychological processes, and social and economic aspects.

Smith, T. Lynn (ed.), *Problems of America's Aging Population* (University of Florida Press, 1951); and *Living in the Later Years* (University of Florida Press, 1952). The proceedings of the First and Second Annual Southern Conferences. These two volumes contain a number of significant papers concerned mainly with population, economics, living arrangements, and health.

5

The Handicapped,
The Incapacitated, and
The Afflicted

This chapter is concerned with the social problems that arise because of the handicapped and the incapacitated. It is not a technical discussion of various inadequacies, but a survey of the social consequences of the disorders. Statistical data are held to a minimum.

According to the French sociologist Emile Durkheim there are two types of society—the *mechanistic* and the *organic*.[1] The former variety is one in which there is little division of labor, and in which the relationships are what Cooley called *primary*. In such a society the social group tends to be small, isolated, homogeneous, and stable. The latter is one in which there is a considerable amount of division of labor and in which group contacts are *secondary*. In such a situation the social groups tend to be large, heterogeneous, and dynamic. Experience has shown that social problems are less prevalent in a *mechanistic* type society than in an *organic* one. The chief trend in social groups today is toward the *organic* type of society, with the result that social problems of all kinds are increasing. In this chapter we shall limit the discussion to the problems besetting the mentally and physically handicapped or incapacitated in an organic society such as our own.

[1] George Simpson, *Emile Durkheim on the Division of Labor in Society* (Macmillan, 1933), pp. 86–131 and *passim*.

MENTAL DISEASES AS SOCIAL PROBLEMS

For purposes of simplicity psychologists frequently use a two-fold classification for mental diseases. One type is known as psychoneurosis, or, more simply, neurosis. The other type is known as psychosis. The difference between the two is a matter of degree. Neuroses are less severe than psychoses and usually do not require hospitalization. There are many borderline cases between the two which are difficult to classify as either neuroses or psychoses.

Neuroses

There are several forms of neuroses, the most common of which will be discussed in turn. In *anxiety states* the individual is characterized by extreme and unreasonable feelings of fear. Some psychologists state that all cases of neuroses have an anxiety basis.[2] Since anxiety rests on fear, it seems that neurotics are fearful.

A second form of neurosis is *conversion hysteria*. In this type there is a physical manifestation of a mental disorder. An individual may lose his sight without there being any organic basis for his blindness. The army reported many cases of conversion hysteria in which soldiers on the battlefield became paralyzed, deaf, blind, mute, or afflicted with some other physical ailment without there being a demonstrable organic cause. These individuals who sincerely believed that they were without the use of the mechanisms affected, were finding some reason why they should not continue in the battle. To turn back would be cowardice, but if because of paralysis, blindness, or deafness, they could not proceed, then obviously they should not be censured. Usually rest, accompanied by psychiatric treatment, restored these individuals to their normal condition. In the opinion of many psychiatrists the dramatic cases of faith-healing are instances of the curing of a form of conversion hysteria. It is doubtful whether any organic lesion can be cured by faith alone.

A third form of neurosis is *neurasthenia*. In this disorder the indi-

[2] See Sigmund Freud, A General Introduction to Psychoanalysis (Garden City Publishing Co., 1943), pp. 341–356.

vidual is characterized by chronic fatigue. He is always so tired that he can hardly go through the motions of living. Women are especially prone to this affliction.

A fourth type of neurosis is the *obsessive-compulsive* reaction. In the obsessive-type reaction there is a recurring idea or thought of which the subject cannot rid himself. He may get the idea that his best friend is very ill, and this thought will keep running through his mind even though he sees that his friend is in the prime of health. In the compulsive-type reaction the individual thinks that he must perform some task. For example, he may feel the necessity of avoiding the cracks in a sidewalk, or he may have to check the mailbox several times a day even though he knows he has already picked up the mail.

So much for these neuroses as such. If people do not look upon these aberrations of behavior as problems, then for them they are not problems. Among certain preliterate people, such as the Dobuans of New Guinea, certain of the anxiety states are said to be normal.[3] Social isolation apparently is a very strong factor in producing neuroses. In a *mechanistic* type of society, there is comparatively little social isolation for most people, and hence the neuroses are less frequent. But in an *organic* type of society, because of the over all complexity of the social disorganization, social isolation may be wide spread and individuals suffering from a neurosis of some kind may therefore be numerous.

Psychoses

In general, psychoses may be divided into two chief types, organic and functional. As their names imply, the former has a physical basis, whereas the latter apparently has a mental etiology.

Organic. The chief varieties of organic psychoses are as follows. *Paresis* is syphilis of the central nervous system. Usually many years pass after the first infection before the symptoms begin to appear; then a businessman who previously was very stable and conservative suddenly may begin writing checks for exorbitant amounts; or he may claim that he is fluent in seven languages. He may be obsessed with

[3] Ruth Benedict, *Patterns of Culture* (Houghton Mifflin, 1934), pp. 130–172.

the idea that he is a famous statesman, or that he is an eminent musician. At one time it was believed that there was no cure for paresis, but now fever treatments are very promising. Of course, once damage is done to the brain cells they cannot be repaired, but further damage can be prevented.

Meningitis is inflammation of the meninges which are the three membranes that envelop the brain and spinal cord. To the extent that this inflammation causes brain damage, the person's mental capacities are impaired. Another disease caused by brain inflammation is *encephalitis lethargica*, or sleeping sickness. There are various forms of this disease, some apparently caused by the tsetse fly. An outbreak in California in 1952–1953 apparently was caused by an insect associated with cattle and other livestock. The person afflicted with this disease may become irritable, drowsy, have a fixed expression on his face, and be very amenable to any command.

Brain trauma or injury is another organic psychosis. Severe blows on the head or birth injuries frequently account for this disorder.

An affliction which is far more common among old people than young is *cerebral arteriosclerosis,* or hardening of the arteries. Although this is an organic condition it may be exaggerated by emotional excitement that stimulates the sympathetic nervous system, and the result may be a stroke.

Epileptic seizures have been described for centuries. The two chief types are the *grand mal* and the *petit mal.* The former is more serious than the latter, and the sufferer loses consciousness after the attack. The latter type may merely entail a momentary lapse of memory. Repeated attacks may cause brain injury, and hence bring about a psychosis. A number of famous persons have been afflicted with epilepsy, including such individuals as Julius Caesar and the Russian novelist, Dostoevski.

The final type of organic psychosis to be described at this time results from *brain tumors.* The characteristics of the psychotic suffering from a brain tumor are similar to those of any individual suffering from any other type of brain damage in a comparable area. With more advanced techniques of treating malignant growths, it is thought that this kind of psychosis will diminish.

Although all of the above types of psychoses have physical origins they are coupled with social implications, but they become social problems only when defined by the people as such. Epileptic seizures in fact, are looked upon by some societies with approbation in the belief that the person having the attack is having direct communication with the spiritual world.

There is no reason to believe that our increasingly *organic* type of society is a cause of these organic psychoses. One possible exception would be cerebral arteriosclerosis; there may be an increase of this type psychosis because more people are reaching advanced years, and also possibly because of the greater use of alcohol, tobacco, coffee, and tea, which have an influence on hardening the arteries. This latter assumption is still a subject of debate within the medical profession.

Functional. The most prevalent form of functional psychosis is *schizophrenia*, formerly called *dementia praecox*. Classically it has been stated that schizophrenia has no organic basis, but there is increasing evidence that the brain structure of schizoids is different from that of normal people.

One of the four kinds of schizophrenia is the *simple* type. In this variety the individual is withdrawn, shy, taciturn, and is characterized by a great amount of social isolation. He interacts with very few people, and then only at low rates of interaction; his part is usually that of responding and not originating. Schizophrenia usually manifests itself in the relative early years, chiefly in the teens and twenties. A second variety of schizophrenia is the *hebephrenic* type with a pattern of behavior in which there is much foolish laughing and giggling. The third type of schizophrenia is the *catatonic*. The most striking characteristic of this variety is the assumption by the subject of odd and apparently uncomfortable postures for long periods of time. The individual may also have a fixed stare and answer all questions with merely a grunt or brief acknowledgment. The final type of schizophrenia is the *paranoid*. This is the most dangerous form because the individual so afflicted has delusions of persecution. He may believe that certain individuals are trying to poison him, or to do him damage in other ways. As a result of this he may decide that it is safer to kill them first.

None of these four types of schizophrenia is clear cut and distinct.

Some schizoids manifest characteristics of all four states, whereas it is difficult to classify others under any of these headings.

Schizophrenia is a distinct social problem. A person who loses contact with reality, as does the schizoid, cannot adjust to the folkways and mores. In school the embryonic schizoid may be the very quiet and timid student who never causes any disturbance in class. He has few friends and plays little with the other children. Because he does not cut up in class the teacher frequently fails to realize that he is a serious problem. However, his personality problem is far more severe than that of the student who causes the teacher frequently the most trouble, namely, the show-off and the cut-up. The latter type merely wants attention, but the former type needs immediate psychiatric attention.

The *manic-depressive* is the second chief type of functional psychosis. As classically described, one so afflicted goes through alternating periods of great elation, or mania, and of extreme depression. In fact, however, few patients follow such a rhythmical cycle. Most of them tend to be depressed, and they remain so for long periods of time. They are dangerous to themselves because when in the depressed stage they have a propensity toward suicide. Before ending their own lives they may also decide to kill close friends or relatives. The newspapers are replete with stories of such cases.

Whereas schizophrenia tends to be more prevalent among young people, manic-depression is more common among people in middle age or past. The latter develops in people who have lost much of the idealism and optimism of youth, and are wondering what life holds for them. Frequently among women the onset of this psychosis is associated with the menopause, and the affliction is known technically as *involutional melancholia*. But involutional melancholia, although far more frequent among women than men, is not confined to females. Persons suffering in this way mistakenly feel that their sex life is over, and they worry about it. Some of them engage in a series of affairs, an attempt at a last fling. But the sex angle is not the only one. They may feel that their employment is less secure, and that if they lose their jobs, they will have difficulty securing new ones.

The final type of psychosis is known as *paranoia*. Some psychiatrists consider this to be a form of schizophrenia, but others say that it has a distinct pattern of its own. The chief characteristic seems to be that the individual has completely systematized delusions. He may think he is Jesus Christ, Napoleon, or some other famous individual. His delusion is so complete that it is virtually impossible to catch him in an inconsistency. He never steps out of his role. Cases of pure paranoia are extremely rare.

The description just given is the standard one when discussing the psychoses. Dr. Karl Menninger of the famed Menninger Clinic in Topeka, Kansas, has stated that he feels students of mental deviations would do well to drop the standard terminology now employed in the description of functional psychoses. In its stead he would substitute a four-fold classification: he would arrange the four forms in order and designate number one as being the least serious and number four as the most serious. It is his belief, based on many years of experience, that all the functional psychoses have such similar characteristics that their chief differences are in degree.

Psychopathy

There is an old saying among students of mental aberrations that when you can't find any other classification for a mental disorder, designate it as psychopathic personality. This has been a more or less catch-all category, but apparently it does have some utility.

Individuals who have the so-called psychopathic characteristics are those who are well oriented in time and place, but who apparently have no social conscience at all. Intellectually they can distinguish between right and wrong, but they show virtually no emotional response. Frequently chronic liars, they find it almost impossible to set goals for themselves, their work habits are spotty, and they do not respond warmly to persons who are close to them. A psychopath may commit the most sadistic murder, re-enact it for the benefit of the police and court records, and yet show no emotional reaction whatsoever.

The social factors that contribute to the formation of psychopathic personality are obscure, but it would certainly appear that a lack of a primary-group orientation is one of consequence. It is largely within a primary group that a social conscience emerges, and if one lacks such groups, then the social conscience will have barren soil on which to grow.

Psychopaths are responsible for many of the heinous crimes which inflame public indignation. A harsh punishment is demanded by society to set an example for others who may be so disposed. Such reasoning, however, is faulty because fear of punishment is no deterrent to the true psychopath. In fact, there is some evidence that the psychopath may be unconsciously seeking punishment when he commits his acts.

MENTAL HYGIENE MOVEMENT

Society is largely indebted to the late Clifford W. Beers (1876–1943) for a mental hygiene movement. Beers, a graduate of Yale University, was at one time confined to a mental institution. After his recovery he wrote the vastly influential book, A Mind That Found Itself.[4] Remembering the experiences he had had in various mental institutions, Beers was so angered by the ineffectual and even brutal treatment he had received that he determined to do something about it. With others he founded, in 1909, the Mental Hygiene Movement, which not only has attempted to clean up conditions in institutions for the psychotic, but has also emphasized preventive measures in the realm of mental disorders.

Most of the large cities in America today have mental-hygiene clinics, but few of our smaller communities are able to afford them. In order to be most effective, these clinics need one or more psychiatrists plus psychiatric social workers and nurses. These are not easily secured, and there has always been opposition to any form of publicly supported medicine or mental treatment.

Another very serious difficulty is that the mental hygiene clinic seldom gets a patient until the latter has a severe emotional disorder. If schools could develop more effective techniques of diagnosing embryonic mental illnesses, and then have these cases handled and

[4] A Mind That Found Itself: An Autobiography (Longmans, Green, 1908).

supervised by trained personnel, much of the problem would be solved. Apparently, however, modern society has not yet defined mental aberrations as a social problem serious enough to arouse mass indignation. Whenever society does so define them far more positive, preventive, and curative steps will be taken.

MENTAL DEFECTIVES AS SOCIAL PROBLEMS

In this section various forms of mental defects are discussed. For present purposes the social and emotional significance of the mental defects is more important than their technical aspects. The descriptions below are in no sense complete ones; rather they point out some of the chief types of defectives and their social consequences.

Amentia or Feeble-mindedness

The usual procedure is to classify cases of feeble-mindedness into two types, hereditary and nonhereditary. For many years it was believed that almost all feeble-mindedness was hereditary. Some time ago a number of studies were published that purported to demonstrate such as a fact. Two of the best known of these concerned the Jukes and the Kallikaks.[5] These studies were purported to be rather complete tracings of family trees showing how feeble-mindedness had persisted for generations. For a long time they were accepted at face value but now it is known that the techniques employed were not at all scientific. There was a lack of adequate testing, too much dependence was made upon subjective evaluations, and much of the evidence was mere hearsay. Today no scientific organization would take such books seriously.

Present-day studies indicate that roughly only about half of the cases of feeble-mindedness are hereditary. Some possible causes of nonhereditary feeble-mindedness are *endocrine deficiencies, brain trauma, congenital syphilis, brain inflammatory diseases, epilepsy,*

[5] Richard L. Dugdale, *The Jukes* (Putnam, 1877); and Henry H. Goddard, *The Kallikak Family* (Macmillan, 1912).

severe forms of common childhood diseases, and *extreme malnutrition* prior to or following birth. All of these may in some way damage the brain. Such damage may result in feeble-mindedness, or in some cases, insanity or psychosis. Persons who are psychotic usually have defects in the neural pathways leading to and from their brains but their intelligence potential apparently is not seriously impaired. In the case of the feeble-minded, however, there is a definite mental lack. In some cases, of course, it is possible for a person to be both feeble-minded and psychotic. A case in question would be a feeble-minded individual who develops paresis. In general, however, the problems are distinct and need to be treated differently.

A four fold classification is used in describing feeble-mindedness. The lowest category is that of *idiots,* those with mental ages of from 0 to 3 years. Their intelligence quotients [6] (I.Q.s) range from 0 to 24. Second in the classification are *imbeciles,* whose mental ages are from 3 to 7 and whose I.Q.s vary from 25 to 49; third are *morons,* whose mental ages are from 7 to 12 and whose I.Q.s are from 50 to 74; and finally there are *borderline* cases, whose mental ages are between 12 and 13 and whose I.Q.s are from 75 to 84. All these figures are rough approximations because even experts in the field are in some disagreement. In addition it should be stated that there are no clear-cut lines separating one category from another. An individual may be classed as an idiot by one psychometrician and as an imbecile by another. The classifications do, however, provide a useful measuring rod for comparative purposes.

The idiot is obviously the most helpless of the group. He cannot learn to read or to write. Usually he cannot feed or clothe himself or take care of his biological functions. He is almost completely helpless and needs almost constant care. For this reason the usual procedure today is to institutionalize individuals in this class.

Imbeciles can be taught to clothe and feed themselves and take care of their biological functions. Usually it is not necessary to institutionalize them. However, some students of human relations believe that imbeciles or even morons, even though they can be cared for at home, should be institutionalized because of the psychological

---

[6] Obtained by dividing mental age by chronological age, and then multiplying by 100. For all persons over 16 years of age, 16 is used as the chronological age.

effects they may have on other children. This view, however, is not held by many individuals who realize that persons in these categories do have an emotional life, and that the family situation means much to them.

Morons can learn to read and write, and can play elementary games with children; but they have much difficulty when abstractions are involved. They can be cared for rather easily at home, and many of them are able to perform menial jobs. In fact, some of them can become self-supporting in jobs not requiring too much imagination. They seem, in fact, to be rather well adapted to work on the assembly line. Frequently morons go to school and—with difficulty—are able to pass a few grades. In one case known to the present writer a person, technically classified as a moron, was graduated from one of our state universities. He studied almost constantly, and after this tremendous effort, finally was graduated with a "C" average.

The borderline cases are individuals who with effort can get along well in many of their activities. They are able to hold perfunctory jobs, and many get married and raise families. Obviously they have difficulty in school and are usually retarded one or more years.

Looking at Durkheim's classification of societies, it would seem obvious that feeble-mindedness is not directly related to the type of society. Brain damage has nothing to do with whether a society is *mechanistic* or *organic*. Feeble-mindedness is more of a social problem today than it was previously because people now define it as a social problem. It is a source of worry and conflict for families and for societies, and both want to do something about it. Institutions are set up for the feeble-minded. Specially trained people are employed, and special classes are given. In one possible way the present day *organic* society has more employment possibilities for certain forms of feeble-mindedness, such as morons and borderline cases. By this is meant that on the assembly line, where the task is of a routine mechanical sort, frequently a person of low intelligence can handle the work adequately.

Increasingly students of mental deviations are giving attention to a certain group of individuals who may be classified as *pseudo-feeble-minded*. These are individuals who have no organic impairment of their brains, but yet score very low on the standard intelligence test.

Their difficulty is emotional. It may be that because of some traumatic experience in a classroom they have formed an intense dislike of anything connected with school work. In addition some children are given tasks that are beyond their present capabilities, and as a result they form emotional blocs which interfere with subsequent performances. It would seem, therefore, that anyone who is classified as below normal on intelligence tests should be examined psychiatrically as well as medically to see if there are emotional factors which may be alleviated.

THE PHYSICALLY HANDICAPPED

In contrast to our comparative neglect of mental illness is our treatment of the physically handicapped, who are fitly recognized as a social problem. Each year millions of dollars are spent in an attempt to rehabilitate them so that they may lead useful, productive lives.

The Crippled

There are many kinds of cripples. There may be paralysis of the limbs, for example, or general loss of use of various parts of the body. Some people are crippled by poliomyelitis; others are born with clubfeet or congenitally dislocated hips; tuberculosis of the bone, osteomyelitis, rachitic deformities, spinal curvature, and amputations afflict still more. The social consequences of being crippled are many. One serious consequence is that a cripple has difficulty in obtaining many kinds of jobs; even some jobs on which a person's physical handicap would be undeterrent to successful performance are still not open to crippled people because of the attitudes of employers toward people with deformities. The increasing publicity given this situation may result in its being more clearly defined as a social problem and in its subsequent mitigation.

In terms of the individual personality, the individual who is crippled may readily develop an inferiority complex. This complex may take many forms. The individual may overcompensate for being crippled by driving a car at breakneck speed, or he may become aggressive in his personality. Perhaps a more typical reaction is to retreat and to try to avoid new situations whenever possible. This, of course, is a matter of debate.

Much is being done to brighten the outlook for crippled persons; there has been great improvement in artificial limbs; there are special devices that make it possible for the crippled to type, to operate machines, even to drive automobiles. But, aside from these mechanical aids, crippled people are being given a mental uplift, a higher morale; they are being encouraged to go into the world and to seek to be treated as normal individuals. An attempt is being made to educate others not to treat crippled people in a special manner. Persons who have physical afflictions prefer to be treated like anyone else. With effort they can frequently diminish the effects of their handicaps.

The Blind

Probably no other group of the physically handicapped so catch the sympathy of people as do the blind. It seems that everyone who has sight looks upon blindness as being perhaps the worst of physical afflictions. As a result, various charitable agencies have been, comparatively speaking, extremely generous with the blind. Blindness is defined as a social problem in our society. Although chances of some accident causing blindness are greater in our *organic* type society than was true in the *mechanistic* type of society, new operations and techniques of treating eye disorders show tremendous progress.

The Deaf

People who are unable to hear have not been given the attention nor the aid which the blind have received. Yet persons who are deaf have far more difficulty in social interaction than do the blind, and social interaction is the most typically human of all activities. Now that hearing aids are greatly improved new hope is held for the partially deaf. At one time persons were quite ashamed to wear a hearing aid, but eventually there will be no more stigma to the wearing of a hearing aid than is attached to the wearing of glasses.

Speech Defects

Perhaps less attention has been given to those suffering from speech defects than to either the blind or the deaf. In comparison with the amount spent on the blind, very little money is spent on speech defectives,[7] for as yet our society has not defined speech defects as a serious social problem. There is, however, a tendency to judge a man by his voice. A big, strong-looking man with a weak voice will not command as much respect as a small man with a powerful deep bass voice. Our society has been characterized as an extrovert society, one in which all are salesmen selling either wares or their personalities. To the extent that this is true, persons with speech defects obviously are at a disadvantage.

Although some speech defects, such as cleft palate and harelip, have a physiological basis, there is ample reason to believe that the chief speech defect, stuttering, is an emotional problem. Some of the Indian tribes, for example, had no word for stuttering since it was unknown among them.[8] In those societies speech was less emphasized than it is in ours. From a child's earliest moments, modern Americans talk to the child and encourage him to speak. But the child, even after he begins to talk at roughly the age of one year, has a limited vocabulary and must search for words. It sometimes happens that he will try to talk faster than the words will come to him, and this is entirely normal. Some of these children develop as stutterers, and some of them do not. There is reason to believe that those individuals who stutter do so because too much emphasis is given to their really normal speech hesitations. Persons who have speech defects are not aware of the fact until they are told so. Then they become afraid, and the effect is magnified. Thus, it can almost be said that persons stutter because they stutter. They fear that they are going to, and so they do.

[7] Edward M. Lemert, *Social Psychology* (McGraw-Hill, 1951), p. 158.
[8] Wendell Johnson, "The Indians Have No Word for It: Stuttering in Children," *Quarterly Journal of Speech*, XXX (1944), 330–337.

Girls are far less prone to become stutterers than boys. The reason for this is not known with certainty, but probably certain maturational factors are present. It is known that girls mature faster than boys and hence are better prepared for speaking at an earlier age. When boys lag behind girls of their age level, perhaps there are complicating emotional factors that produce stuttering.

Some speech pathologists say there is really no cure for stuttering, although some institutes have various techniques for treating it. These techniques of treatment center around getting the stutterer to forget himself as a person. He may be asked to talk with a strange accent, or in a singsong fashion, or he may be encouraged to count by striking his leg with his hand as he says words. Such techniques are effective in eliminating stuttering temporarily, but when they become so habitual that the stutterer doesn't have to think about them as he speaks, the stuttering returns and is complicated by having these new techniques incorporated into the stuttering pattern.[9]

Our *organic* type of society, with its attendant emotional problems, also helps induce speech defects and other mental complications. When the child is given a *mechanistic* type of home environment, and when no great attention is given to speech lapses, there is little likelihood that speech disorders will occur. However, very little research of a statistical nature has been done on speech defectives; and until this is done, little really accurate information will be available.

OTHER PROBLEM BEHAVIOR

Alcoholism

There are many theories as to the cause of alcoholism. Some of the oldest attributed alcoholism to hereditary factors. It was observed that alcoholism tends to run in certain families, and the conclusion was drawn that this tendency was inherited. It is now realized, of course, that such is not the case. There seems to be no hereditary propensity toward alcoholism. When one is reared in an environment in which there is alcoholism, he may be more likely to

[9] Johnson, *op. cit.*, p. 154.

become an alcoholic than would otherwise be the case. Of course there are some individuals who are so repelled by the observed effects of alcoholism that they are determined that they themselves will never become alcoholics. Yet alcoholism is a form of escape, and individuals may take to alcohol to escape the unpleasantness of their immediate situations. The present view is that alcoholism is a social product and nonhereditary. Social factors such as extreme disappointment in love, loss of a job, loss of a close friend or member of the family, disillusionment, and so on, may produce situations that will make a person more prone to alcoholism.

Our society certainly defines alcoholism as a social problem. With present-day, high-speed automobiles, alcohol definitely is a killer. It is known also that alcohol has definitely injurious effects on the human body.

Various institutes have been established to treat alcoholics; their treatments vary somewhat. One is *immediate withdrawal* or "cold turkey" treatment. In this, as the name implies, the individual's supply of alcohol is completely cut off, and he must undergo the pains of withdrawal. For the real alcoholic this period may be characterized as a living hell.

A second type of treatment uses the *aversion technique*. The alcoholic is given some sort of drug, such as antabuse, which makes him hypersensitive to alcohol; then if he drinks any alcoholic beverage he becomes violently ill and nauseated. The theory behind this treatment is that the fear of nausea will be greater than the desire for alcohol. This type of treatment has merit, but only when employed under the care of a psychiatrist.

An entirely new type of treatment which is receiving some attention is the use of a *special diet* for the alcoholic. The theory is that there is some dietary lack that produces the craving for alcohol. If this craving can be eliminated, then this person will no longer feel the need for alcohol. In some individual cases success has been recorded with this type of treatment.

By far the best known of the current treatments of alcoholics is that of *Alcoholics Anonymous*.[10] The members of this organization are

[10] See Joseph Hirsch, *The Problem Drinker* (Duell, Sloan and Pearce, 1949), ch. VII.

former alcoholics. They have regular meetings and all the members
are on twenty-four hour call from other members who feel the need
for their presence. This organization believes that cures depend upon
complete abstinence from alcoholic beverages. In addition, spiritual
factors are invoked. The persons are encouraged to have a belief in a
power greater than their own, and to call on that power to help them
overcome their craving for drink. Today virtually all communities of
any size in the country have chapters of Alcoholics Anonymous, and
their rate of cures is well above fifty per cent.

Perhaps the most promising approach, but the most expensive, is
psychiatric treatment. A criticism of the Alcoholics Anonymous,
of course, is that the treatment is completely symptomatic, that it
does not get down to the basic causes of the craving for alcohol. Since
this cause is not removed, the person can never again take even a social
drink. But with psychiatric care an attempt is made to get at the
causes of the craving for drink. Then the individual is encouraged
to face his problems realistically without the use of any kind of drugs.
The chief disadvantage of this is the high cost of employing a psychiatrist.

There seems to be no question that in our organic type of society
the rate of alcoholic addiction is going up. Apparently a complex
society makes for more social situations that are capable of producing
frustrations and hence the need for escape. In a number of primitive
societies, however, having a *mechanistic* type of organization, various
forms of alcohol are used; but in these societies the alcohol seems to
be used more in prescribed situations, and not as a means of escape
to the extent that it is so used in *organic* society.

In our society alcohol is increasingly becoming an almost indispensable adjunct of certain social gatherings. The ready availability
of alcohol, high-pressure advertising, and the widespread use of alcohol by the characters portrayed in movies have helped to make its
use a part of our culture. The obvious question is this: is our society
prepared to meet the challenge presented by the increasing consumption of alcohol?

Drug Addiction

There are numerous opinions concerning the nature of drug addiction. Some say that individuals take drugs largely in order to get a feeling of euphoria. Others hold that drugs are used to escape the withdrawal pains associated with the cessation of the medical use of drugs. And still others maintain that the drug addict is a definitely neurotic type whose addiction is symptomatic of a mental disorder. In any event, when the individual has become addicted to the drug, he has a terrific craving for it. If the drug is not available when the addict feels a need for it, he undergoes severe crises. He may sweat profusely, have nausea, cramps, headaches, diarrhea, and extreme insomnia.

Social factors have a close connection with drug addiction. From newspaper headlines and sensational magazine stories one would get the impression that most drug addicts are young boys and girls of fine homes who are forced to steal and to sell their bodies in order to buy drugs to meet their cravings. As a matter of fact the individuals who, according to the surveys, are most likely to take up drugs, are persons in the economically underprivileged groups—those discriminated against because of race, social class, or nationality.[11] Many Negroes, Puerto Ricans, and Mexicans, for example, have serious drug addiction problems. In these cases it seems likely that the individuals are seeking escape from unpleasant surroundings. Also there is evidence that the use of drugs may for a time give them feelings of status and prestige. They are one of the gang and have a certain spirit of bravado about their escapades and use of drugs.

The use of drugs is not directly correlated with our *organic* type of society. In England today, where addicts may register with the government and receive rations of drugs to keep them from having to work with the underworld, the rate is negligible. This is far different from the situation fifty years ago when drug addiction was a serious problem in England. In the United States, on the other hand, where

[11] See Mabel A. Elliott, *Crime in Modern Society* (Harper, 1952), p. 175. But Dr. Elliott points out that only a small fraction of the total number of addicts are apprehended.

it is illegal for a doctor to prescribe drugs for an addict, the problem seemingly is becoming greater.

In a family where the relationships are of the *mechanistic* nature, the chances of a person's becoming a drug addict are far less than in a situation where the social contacts are of an *organic* nature. When an individual is a member of a primary social grouping, he does not feel the need to engage in deviant forms of behavior in order to get acceptance. It is true, of course, that in some gangs one must engage in deviant behavior in order to remain in good standing.

The most serious drugs from the standpoint of treatment are *opium* and its derivatives, heroin and morphine. Opiate addiction is most difficult to treat because the body builds up a need for the opium. Then if opium is not forthcoming, the body is wracked with horrible physical torture. Opium tends to produce a feeling of pleasantness, well-being, relaxation, and in general, nonaggressive behavior. Also the person under the influence of opium is lacking in drive or ambition. For that reason one should be skeptical of reports of enemy soldiers, obviously under the influence of opium, charging viciously at our own soldiers; a person under the influence of opium would not react in such an aggressive fashion. An addict in an army would be more concerned about getting the drug than about fighting.

Another important drug is *cocaine*. It is not habit-forming in a physical sense because the body does not build up any need for it. The treatment of cocaine addiction seems less hopeless than that of opium addiction. Cocaine is a stimulant, and a person under the influence of cocaine may be aggressive. If troops are ever drugged, it is likely that cocaine and not opium is used. Cocaine is a problem among some of the Indians in Bolivia who use it to help them endure hard labor in the tin mines.

Another drug—one very much in the Sunday supplements—is *marijuana*. This, like cocaine, is not habit-forming in the sense that the body builds up a need for it. It is dangerous, however, because the person using it frequently has hallucinations and delusions. Under the influence of marijuana one may be in an automobile going eighty miles an hour, and then decide to get out and walk because the car is traveling too slowly. It is dangerous, too, because frequently it is a steppingstone to the use of opium.

In some ways the person under the influence of marijuana is similar to a person under the influence of alcohol. Cortical action is inhibited, which means that a person's actions become uninhibited. Sensational magazines play up stories of the wild sexual orgies that apparently take place as a result of the use of marijuana, but it would seem likely that the use of the drug is an excuse for uninhibited behavior and not necessarily the cause of it.

As is true with other drugs, marijuana seems to be used chiefly by persons in the less privileged economic classes. Its use is especially prevalent in Texas and California where there are sizable Mexican populations.

Minor Drugs and Stimulants

Another drug about which there have been many claims and counterclaims is *tobacco*. Tobacco has been accused of responsibility for everything from cancer to prostitution. Actually there is some reason to link tobacco smoking with lung cancer, but the enemies of tobacco have probably hurt their cause by their wild and frequently unfounded claims. There is also physiological evidence that an individual's mental functions are slowed by the use of tobacco.[12] Claims are made, too, that one's lung capacity is decreased by smoking.

The body builds up no physiological need for tobacco; the habit is social and psychological in origin. The person who uses tobacco craves tobacco as one who bites his nails craves to bite his nails.

---

[12] In the widely syndicated column of Dr. William Brady, published on June 19, 1953, by the Duluth *Herald*, the following statements are made: ". . . Breathlessness comes on earlier in the smoker and lasts longer. The heart pumps less blood after smoking. . . . After a single smoke, particularly a cigaret, mental efficiency is lowered an average of ten per cent, and this is most manifest in imagery, perception, and association—the chief essentials of thinking. Various investigators have found that the immediate effect of a smoke is lowered accuracy and lowered coordination of fine reactions. . . . Among the well-recognized effects of excessive smoking are chronic pharyngitis (smoker's sore throat); according to some physicians cancer of the bronchial tubes or lungs; tobacco heart characterized by undue breathlessness on slight exertion, palpitation and distress or pain felt in the area of the heart or under the breastbone; duodenal ulcer complex (all the symptoms of ulcer but negative x-ray picture); thromboangiitis obliterans—Buerger's disease—which leads to amputation of foot or leg in some instances; amblyopia (partial blindness); insomnia; headache; tremor." Permission to quote granted by Dr. Brady.

With present techniques of high-pressure advertising, there seems little likelihood that the consumption of tobacco will decrease within the foreseeable future. To many persons the use of tobacco is still a moral as well as a social problem. Certainly tobacco does not directly lead to any breakdown of morals as some of the more zealous supporters of anti-tobacco legislation maintain. It is reasonable to point out, however, that it is an expensive habit, a habit on which we spend as much money annually as we do in support of public education.[13] This is reason for questioning some of our values.

Coffee and *tea* are also minor drugs or stimulants. Some groups, such as the Mormons, disapprove of their use, but they are widely consumed in the world today. In the cases of those individuals who each day take twenty-five or thirty cups of tea or coffee, the practice can certainly become a vice. When a person feels that strongly in need of stimulants he probably is in need of psychiatric help. One sometimes wonders why it does not become a fad to consume fruit juices during rest periods, and at social gatherings, and in night clubs in place of beverages of questionable value. Will the day ever come when an ice cream bar will be as common at a night club as an alcoholic bar?

Begging

Begging is apparently a problem that has been with man since time began. We find instances of begging in virtually every culture in the world. Numerous attempts have been made to eliminate it: it has been made illegal, and states have provided relief for persons in need. Still begging persists.

Begging is a part of the cultural heritage of some people. In India, for example, begging is a profession; holy men travel about the country and depend upon gifts for their very existence. It also has been reported that in India some parents have blinded their children so that they could beg more effectively, but under modern leadership such practices in this oriental country are rapidly becoming a thing of the past.

[13] Harry Elmer Barnes, *Society in Transition* (2nd ed., Prentice-Hall, 1952), p. 836.

Some of the immigrants to the United States brought with them a pattern of begging.[14] As a result their children have frequently run into trouble with the law when caught begging in public places. In their own country there was nothing illegal about this activity, but our culture frowns upon it.

The individual factors making for begging are rather difficult to ascertain because each individual has his own reasons for his particular form of behavior. Some beg because they are desperate; but in this day of the near welfare state such a reason is less compelling. Apparently other individuals beg for psychological reasons. There are numerous instances of beggars who have left large estates. Apparently some beggars look upon their work as being the most degrading type possible, and psychologically they punish themselves by begging. This is true, for example, of a person of high social prominence who ends up as a beggar.

There are some who consider tipping a form of begging. Probably if people had a chance to vote on tipping, the vote against it would be considerable. Numerous attempts have been made at eliminating tipping on railroads and restaurants, but people largely continue this habit pattern. Often the persons who are the most vociferous opponents of tipping themselves tip more than is necessary. Even the persons who receive tips have frequently stated that they would prefer that tipping be abolished and their salaries raised to compensate for the loss. Many of the recipients of tips consider the custom of tipping rather degrading since it reflects the inferior position of the person receiving the gratuity.

Suicide

Among some peoples the phenomenon of suicide is unknown. When attempts are made to explain it to them they have difficulty in comprehending just what the term means. They cannot conceive of a person's ending his own life.

The eminent French sociologist, Emile Durkheim, classified suicides into three types: *egoistic*, *altruistic*, and *anomic*. The *egoistic* type of suicide occurs with individuals who are not strongly integrated into

14 Ruth S. Cavan, *Criminology* (Crowell, 1948), p. 111.

their society.   Their values tend to be more individual than is usually
the case, and when one of them feels that his life is no longer worth
living, he may summarily end it.   His chief obsession, then, is with
his own welfare.   *Altruistic* suicide occurs when society demands that
a person end his life.   In Japan, among some social groupings, when
a person brings dishonor to his family he is expected to commit
suicide.   His suicide is selfless and reflects the operation of a power-
fully integrated social organization.   On the other hand, the *anomic*
suicide is one which reflects a crumbling of the social organization.
When society is weakened by financial panic or other great distress,
social controls are loosened; a chaotic situation ensues, and an increase
in the suicide rate is one of its effects.

There are a number of differentials in suicide rates.   In countries
which are still largely agricultural in their economy, the suicide rates
are low.   But in countries which are highly industrialized it is found
that the suicide rates have increased markedly, with a very large
increase in the twentieth century.

Among racial groupings also there are differences in the suicide
rate.   Negroes in this country have much lower suicide rates than the
whites, but now that the Negro is increasingly settling in urban areas
his suicide rate also is increasing.   It would seem, therefore, that his
place of residence is important in determining the Negro's suicide rate.

In general there is a very high suicide rate in the central districts
of cities.   The reason doubtless is that in these areas are found the
cheap rooming houses, taverns, pool halls, pawn shops, and other
places that flourish on social and personal disorganization.   As the
student of suicide data proceeds outward to the more permanently
settled areas of the city he discovers that the suicide rate progressively
drops.

There are also differential suicide rates among religious groups.
It is found that Catholics the world over have the lowest rates of all,
Protestants next, and Jews the highest rates.[15]   The Jewish rate is
especially significant inasmuch as until the time of World War I the
Jews had the lowest suicide rate of any of the three great religious
groups.   Since the time of World War I, however, the Jewish cul-

---

[15] Maurice Halbwachs, *Les Causes de Suicide* (Paris: Alcan, 1930), *passim*.

ture has undergone many crises as a result of persecution; their increased suicide rate probably reflects this fact.

The comparatively low suicide rate among Catholics, in the European countries at least, perhaps does not reflect so much their religion as it does their place of residence. In Europe the Catholics are largely a rural people, and, as indicated above, rural areas characteristically have a much lower suicide rate than do urban places.

None of the suicide rates are too accurate because many suicides are never reported as such. Failure to report death as suicide is more common when there is a strong family organization to which suicide would bring dishonor. If a Catholic commits suicide, he is refused a Catholic burial; so, according to the suggestion made by Halbwachs, many Catholics hide the fact of a suicide in order to insure a Christian burial for the deceased.

There are marked differences in the suicide rates for various age groups, the rate increasing with each higher stage in the age brackets. As people grow older their health declines and perhaps their optimism also diminishes; depression may set in and this in turn may lead to suicide. It should be added, however, that suicide occurs among children and young people.

Concerning sex differentials, it is found that males in this country have a suicide rate three or four times higher than females. In part this may be because they are more effective killers of themselves. Some reports indicate that more women than men attempt suicide but that they are less successful in achieving it. Of course many women who attempt suicide may not actually have a desire to end their lives; they may merely wish to win sympathy by their dramatic act.

Divorced persons have much higher suicide rates than any other marital group. The widowed have the next highest rates, then the married. Single people have the lowest rates of all. After a person is divorced or widowed there is inevitably a great amount of personal disorganization which creates a propensity toward depression; this, in turn, may lead to suicide.

Persons who are socially isolated are the ones most likely to have various forms of mental abnormalities. For this reason, it has been suggested that the decline of the primary group with the consequent social isolation is an important factor in the growing suicide rate.

Suicide is a social problem in our society because our culture so defines it. It is against the mores and the folkways of American culture, and it is certainly against the religious beliefs of most Americans. This problem seems to be definitely on the increase, and if the present high suicide rates are to be counteracted, the approach must be societal rather than individual. The individual, after all, tends to be a reflection of his society.

Study Questions

1. Why is a particular condition a social problem in one cultural area and not in another?

2. What is meant by *mechanistic* and *organic* types of societies?

3. What are the chief types of neuroses?

4. What are the chief causes of feeble-mindedness?

5. Why would a speech defect be a more serious handicap in modern day American culture than it would be in some of the American Indian cultures?

6. What are the principal types of treatments for alcoholism?

7. Which of the drugs build up a physical craving in the human body?

8. Is smoking harmful?

9. Is tipping likely to be eliminated soon in our culture? Why?

10. What are the three types of suicide described by Durkheim?

Selected References

Barnes, Harry Elmer, *Society in Transition* (2nd ed., Prentice-Hall, 1952). An almost encyclopedic but interestingly written account of the general field of social problems.

Beers, Clifford W., *A Mind That Found Itself: An Autobiography* (Longmans, Green, 1908). This book gave much of the impetus for the establishment of the Mental Hygiene Movement.

Benedict, Ruth, *Patterns of Culture* (Houghton Mifflin, 1934). A classic in the field of cultural anthropology which gives the reader a wide perspective for examining societal definitions of social problems.

Cavan, Ruth S., *Suicide* (University of Chicago Press, 1928). Perhaps the best of the American treatises on suicide, but the statistics are out of date.

Faris, Robert E. L., *Social Disorganization* (Ronald Press, 1948). A provocative work in the sense that it critically scrutinizes theories still held by many students of human behavior.

Fuller, Richard C., "The Problem of Teaching Social Problems," *American Journal of Sociology*, vol. XLIV (1939). One of the most influential articles in print concerning the theory of social problems.

Gilmore, Harlan W., *The Beggar* (University of North Carolina Press, 1940). A well-written monograph containing many enlightening case studies of beggars.

Lemert, Edwin M., *Social Pathology* (McGraw-Hill, 1951). One of the best recent books on social pathology, especially noteworthy for the chapter on speech defectives.

Lindesmith, Alfred R., *Opiate Addiction* (Bloomington, Ind.: Principia Press, 1947). Probably the best social psychological work on this subject. Critical of many of the older views concerning nature of addiction.

Young, Kimball, *Personality and Problems of Adjustment* (2nd ed., Appleton-Century-Crofts, 1952). An important work emphasizing societal interaction within a general cultural framework.

6

Problems of Crime and Juvenile Delinquency

Crime and juvenile delinquency are human acts transgressing the regulations formulated, promulgated, and relatively enforced by society in accordance with its code of acceptable human conduct. As a violation of law, they are among the more serious of the pathological phenomena in the United States today.

CRIME

Correlated with an unmistakable social fact—that an outside agent coerces and controls man's relationships in the community—the problem of crime is a perplexing one. It becomes persuasively so as one considers the structure that has evolved around it: the apparent inconsistencies of legislation, of law interpretation and enforcement, of judicial decisions, and of legal penalties. It is, moreover, conditioned upon the elements of time and place. An act that may be a crime in Europe may not be one in the United States; and an act that may be a felony in Florida may not be even a misdemeanor in Vermont or Arizona. Consequently the problem of crime presents a kaleidoscopic pattern, a sociological phenomenon which, to this day, seems to have resisted adequate measurement and a comprehensive remedial program.

The Increase in Crime and Its Cost

Crime appears to have increased yearly since the Federal Bureau of Investigation began compiling official statistics. Bureau records for the nation show a rise of 1.5 per cent in 1950 in all *reported* offenses except robbery. Every five minutes someone was feloniously assaulted or killed. By 1952 major violations climbed above the two million mark, reflecting in all categories an overall rise of 8.2 per cent over the 1,882,160 estimated crimes in 1951. Major crimes increased 2.5 per cent during the first six months of 1953, as compared with the same period in 1952. The 1,047,000 crimes reported at the midyear 1953 represented a 9.0 per cent jump over the 1951 semiannual figures. Victims of killers numbered 6,470, and 54,000 persons were feloniously assaulted by rapists or potential killers. Over 29,000 persons were confronted by robbers using guns, other weapons, or simply physical force.[1]

Estimates of the annual cost of crime vary from one to twenty billion dollars; and there is no agreement upon the elements these estimates should include. Many crime-cost categories are ambiguous, often misleading. Even reliable authors fail to concur. One criminologist considers a 10-billion-dollar estimate as "extravagant" because it includes "many nebulous and mythical costs"; another maintains that 15 billion dollars is "quite possibly an underestimate"; whereas a third says the cost is probably between 10 and 18 billion dollars. There is, therefore, ample latitude for the discussion of this "gigantic crime bill." [2]

Among the chief reasons for the inconclusiveness of the estimates is the paucity of meaningful crime data. Although the Bureau's *Uniform Crime Reports* is the best source of information, the data for about 40 per cent of the urban and rural communities are not represented therein. In most instances, this neglect ostensibly reflects the failure, even apathy, of some of our law-enforcement agencies. Obviously, then, no complete criminal statistics for the

[1] Federal Bureau of Investigation, U.S. Department of Justice, *Uniform Crime Reports*, semiannual Bulletin, XXIV, No. 1 (1953), 1.

[2] Frederick A. Conrad, "Statistics in the Analysis of Social Problems," *Sociology and Social Research*, XXVI (1942), 540–541.

United States are available. Even prison statistics are merely summarized in the annual report of the Federal Bureau of Prisons. The
FBI refuses to vouch for the accuracy of data supplied by police
chiefs; but the Bureau makes available whatever data it has, hoping
that they "may throw some light on problems of crime and criminal-
law enforcement." [3]   Hence, caution must be exercised in interpreting
these data. What may appear as an increase or decrease in crime
may be only a variation in *reported* offenses, or a result of a reorganization or deterioration of police operations. Manifestly this renders
any crime picture incomplete. Likewise, an aggregate crime-cost
figure compiled from the available data can have little if any accuracy. The National Commission on Law Enforcement and Ob-
servance, which attempted the first comprehensive crime-cost study,
concluded: "We are of the opinion that no such aggregate figure can
be worked out with even approximate accuracy and are unwilling to
indulge in vague estimates which could, at best, be no more than
guesses." [4]

Detection and Apprehension

In addition to being challenged by the probability of having one
of the highest rates of crime in the world, Americans can find no
solace in a record showing that most crimes in the United States remain unsolved. The FBI, at the close of 1945, could announce
merely that a conviction was obtained in one out of seven of the
299,083 serious felonies; and 50 per cent of 970 murders reported by
162 cities were still mysteries. Police, in 1952, cleared by arrest only
one out of every four reported crimes. The proportion solved was
high in some categories, nine out of 10 homicides, for example; but
the clearance rate for all offenses as a group was weighted down by the
large number of larcenies in which only one out of five was cleared.
If these are excluded, the police unraveled one out of 2.9 of the more
serious offenses.

The clearance rate for crimes against the person is noticeably higher
than for crimes against property. This is not attributable solely to

---

[3] *Uniform Crime Reports*, XII (January, 1952), 68.
[4] Conrad, *op. cit.*, p. 541.

the situation—one in which the offender is usually observed by the victim—because the highest percentage of crimes cleared concerns murder, and in these cases the best witness is deceased; it can more probably be attributed to the fact that police concentrate effort on the more vicious crimes. For such crimes clearance ranges from 75 per cent for aggravated assaults to 93.1 per cent for murders. Over 78 per cent of rape offenses and 87.5 per cent of negligent manslaughters were cleared by arrest. Negligent manslaughters, to a large extent, involved traffic victims.[5]

Various detection and apprehension agencies may differ in reporting procedures; but even if there were uniformity in reports from all jurisdictions, still problems of analysis resulting from the apparent inadequacy of police statistics would remain. Generally, an offense is cleared by arrest when one of the perpetrators identified with the crime is apprehended and charged, although there may be certain technical exceptions. The number of persons charged in no way indicates the number of offenses cleared. This is true since the latter term pertains to offenses known, as distinguished from individuals caught. In addition, several persons may be detained and charged with the commission of a single crime, as in the case of the members of a gang being arrested for a warehouse burglary. On the other hand, the arrest of a lone bandit and his identification with five armed robberies would clear five offenses.[6]

Detection and apprehension problems are aggravated by many factors. On the surface, the police and the public, in some instances mutually suspicious and equally distrustful of each other, seldom see matters eye to eye. Policemen are expected to enforce what, in our day, may seem to be stupid or antiquated laws. Furthermore, the public does not always appear to desire total law enforcement. In some communities the police soon learn that a number of laws are *not* to be enforced; these often pertain to gambling, liquor, prostitution, and abortion. Concomitantly some individuals are *not* to be arrested. Police department educational standards and salaries frequently are low, apparently resulting in a low-grade police personnel. In 35 cities of over 100,000 population police departments have no

[5] *Uniform Crime Reports*, XXIV (1953), 44.
[6] *Ibid.*, p. 44.

formal education qualifications; some cities require merely that policemen be able to read and write English.[7]

Although inefficiency is usually the chief criticism leveled against
American police it is generally agreed that improvement in detection
and apprehension is a paramount need.   On the other hand, police
specialization has kept pace with criminal specialization, and progressively has forged ahead in armament.   Recent years have witnessed a
considerable decentralization of police forces and a definite trend
toward professionalism.   This indicates, among other things, a growing release from politics, increasing educational qualifications, and the
utilization of the contributions of science—radio, ballistics, radar, and
chemistry.   In the general pattern there is ample evidence of positive
progress.   Nevertheless, the plague of cynicism toward law enforcement remains.   This seems to be applicable especially to the interrelationships of crime and politics, and to commercial gambling.
Definitely more public support for law enforcement appears to be an
urgent need.

Problems of Conviction

President Taft said in 1909 that the administration of criminal law
"is a disgrace to our civilization."   A record of almost no reform in
American jurisprudence has stigmatized the past century.   By emphasizing, sometimes overzealously, the desirability of obtaining a conviction, the courts, practically unchanged since Beccaria's time (1738–
1794), have repeatedly incurred the accusation of producing injustice.
Too many of them are censured for being unbusinesslike and for
exhibiting scanty scientific knowledge.   Generally it seems that jurists
are unpredictable.   For identical crimes in the same locality one judge
granted probation to seven per cent of the culprits brought before
him, whereas another judge placed 40 per cent on probation.

However, despite the stress placed on securing a conviction, many
district attorneys conscientiously perform their duties.   Undoubtedly,
they have saved a considerable number of innocent persons who were
enmeshed in webs of damaging circumstantial evidence.   Most criminal convictions are obtained without legal trial; the defendants are

[7] Ruth Shonle Cavan, *Criminology* (Crowell, 1948), p. 416.

permitted "to make a deal" or plead guilty to a lesser charge, and thus "save the state money." The police may facilitate such "deals." This brings us to one of the weakest links in law enforcement— namely, the assumption or usurpation of court duties by the police in extracting "confessions." Numerous examples might be cited. Often brutal and sadistic techniques are employed. Foreign ob- servers refer to this "third degree" as the "American method." The continuance of such illegal activity constitutes one of the most serious threats and challenges to the administration of justice in the United States.

A strong selective factor is presumably operative in the conviction pattern, for high proportions of those judged guilty are young, male, uneducated, and, above all, poor. Attempts to discredit this ob- servation by the assertion that most persons in the United States are poor are invalid; the fact is that most persons are neither young nor male. Most of the individuals accused of crime are not finan- cially able to hire competent legal defense; annually thousands of persons having no one to defend them appear in court. Legal aid is a vital need as a weapon in combatting the apparent discrimination against the financially handicapped, in or out of minority categories; such provision would probably destroy once and for all the charge that, as a rule, American justice is obtainable only when citizens have the money to pay for it. It is largely on this financial basis that the upper-strata offender, the so-called "white collar criminal," is said [8] to escape both apprehension and conviction.

No social problem in the United States deserves more considera- tion and research than that which results in the conviction of in- nocent men and women. Numerous persons who have been in American jails, prisons, reform schools, and detention homes would undoubtedly agree with Arthur Train's statement early in this century: "The most presumptious of all presumptions is the presumption of innocence." A firmly rooted American tradition is that everyone is innocent until proved guilty; yet there are those in law-enforcement positions who subscribe to this principle neither in their words nor in their deeds. To the police, "once a thief, always a thief" is the more realistic philosophy, fallacious or not. Repentance and improvement

[8] See Edwin H. Sutherland, *White Collar Crime* (Dryden, 1949).

are words that have vanished from most police-desk dictionaries. Too many citizens erroneously believe that the police do not make an arrest unless the person arrested is guilty, and that officials do not prosecute unless guilt is present. They appear to be unaware that, unless the American tradition is reasserted and jealously guarded, the threat of an unjust conviction, imprisonment, and even death by execution is ever-present in their own lives.

Problems of Punishment and Rehabilitation

Punishment is a control device; its pattern has probably evolved through millenniums. An early manifestation of it was personal retaliation on the *lex talionis* principle, an eye-for-an-eye philosophy. Some primitive tribal customs embodied the expiation approach. Offenders were generally banished to pacify the gods, who might otherwise have chastized the tribe itself for the individual's crime. In Homeric times, when the trustee family exercised the greatest social control, the family itself could be punished for the wrongs of one of its members. With the advent of Christianity came the emphasis on punishment as a part of reformation, and on forgiveness for all sinners doing penance. During the Middle Ages, the sin of religious heresy was also a crime against the state. For many centuries the concept of punishment embodied the principle of deterrence. Publicly the offender was scourged, beheaded, or burned at the stake as a warning to others.

Traditionally, society seems to have assumed the attitude that the law violator must be made to suffer; hence, every law must embody a severe penalty to be inflicted on all offenders. In other words, punishing the convicted has emerged primarily as a means of social revenge; as such, it is more or less opposed to the avowed principles of rehabilitation, principles in which lip service, at best, is paid to a high social ideal. That is to say, the present objectives of punishment and rehabilitation are contradictory and appear to be mutually exclusive. It would appear to be easier to cut glass with soap than to rehabilitate a convicted individual after he has been shamed, degraded, and humiliated. Moreover, punishment often isolates the individual who, by nature, is a social being; it transforms him into a confirmed enemy of society; and often it tends to produce an anti-social *esprit de corps* among prisoners. Hatred of the criminal by society results in hatred of society by the criminal; and because of this mutual hatred, the gravest failure of punishment is that it renders rehabilitation impossible or difficult, particularly for those convicted of the more serious crimes. Consideration should be given, therefore, to such factors as society's perplexing demand for revenge, and the prisoner's personal disorganization, isolation, loss of status, and acquisition of the techniques of crime.[9]

A stronger argument is frequently advanced against capital punishment, which some criminologists feel is as out of date as burning witches or practicing astrological medicine. Its deterrent effect, they maintain, is nearly zero, since usually no one sees an execution except prison officials who presumably need no deterring. Most cases of capital punishment are for the crime of murder in the first degree. Kansas abolished the death penalty in 1907 and restored it in 1935. Its homicide rate from 1931 to 1935 was higher than from 1935 to 1940; and a similar trend characterized the bordering states which had the death penalty during the same period. Hence, homicide trends appear to be the result of social conditions, and occur regardless of the death penalty threat.

Who Are to Be Rehabilitated?

Not all criminals are alike. To some crime is a profession, a means of securing a livelihood. Such criminals are convinced that "only saps work"; in their vocabulary "slave" is the appellation for the workingman. The category of professional criminals includes the heist men, pickpockets, shoplifters, confidence men, criminal gangsters, criminal racketeers, and members of criminal syndicates. Most of these offenders have nothing but contempt for society and its laws; the prospect of the reformation of these criminals is extremely poor.

About 80 or 85 per cent of those convicted of crime are nonprofessionals, persons who rarely are guilty of daring violations. They seldom make front-page news or commit the technically-skilled crimes

[9] Edwin H. Sutherland, *Principles of Criminology* (Lippincott, 1947), p. 360.

characteristic of the professional culprits. This amateur or non-professional category includes casual violators of traffic regulations, "hit-and-run" drivers, alcoholics, some drug addicts, most youthful prostitutes, and others who seem to be impelled to commit crime by personal handicaps, unfortunate surroundings, sudden passions, neurotic ailments, and temporary amnesic lapses; it also includes those who run afoul of multitudinous laws of which they have no knowledge. White-collar criminals, business or professional men and women who violate the law in the regular performance of their occupations, would also fall into the nonprofessional category, but owing to their higher economic status and social roles, apprehension and convictions are difficult to secure, and hence, members of this group seldom appear for rehabilitation. Moreover, too often "Public Enemy No. 1" is hidden behind the screen of respectability, dignity, or even of high public office. As a result, people have an incorrect, stereotyped conception of the real criminals in American culture. From the standpoint of the social cost, the serious offenders may be quite different from the burglar, the robber, or the thief as we have known him in the past.

Types of professional and nonprofessional criminals cannot be distinguished by any measurable physiological or psychological traits. This statement is true despite the profound claims of the various typological schools, past and present. Criminologists are agreed that if a burglar, sex offender, robber, murderer, kidnaper, and embezzler were placed in the same room, and side by side, no one could distinguish one "type" of offender from the other. Moreover, if a group of law-abiding citizens, including university students and policemen, were added to the experiment, it still would be impossible to differentiate them from the others. The criminal type simply does *not* exist.

Rehabilitation for those in the nonprofessional category is not only indicated but has good promise of success. As a matter of fact, crime is usually incidental to the major personality problems of the neurotic, the psychotic, the feeble-minded, and the psychopathic; also to drug addicts, alcoholics, and prostitutes. Personal disorganization is the tragedy of too many of these unfortunate human beings. Unless they are given outside help and sympathetic treatment, self-adjustment is practically impossible; with such treatment adjustment can be expected.

Areas of Rehabilitation

1. *Probation.* The failure of imprisonment as a remedy for crime is chiefly responsible for the establishment of the system of probation —a form of court disposition of the defendant when guilt has been proved. Although probation is a nonpunitive method of treating offenders, it should not be interpreted as leniency or mercy; it seeks to accomplish the adjustment of convicted persons by returning them to society *under supervision,* at least for a period. Probation differs from classical penology in that it attempts to deal with offenders as individuals and not as classes or concepts. Its social principle is to keep them out of prison, with their families, and on their jobs. Further, since it tries to prevent suffering, it is not punishment; nor is it a *right,* but rather a matter of *grace.* Still, probation is granted in only about 30 per cent of the cases, although the proportion varies between about 70 per cent in Rhode Island and 10 per cent in North Dakota.

In this rehabilitation procedure the most important figure is the probation officer. He is supposed to make a thorough study of the case and the culprit before release is granted. Obviously, since the objective is to change the probationer's attitudes, the services of competent, professional officers is essential. Unfortunately, however, many probation officers are overworked, some carrying case loads three or four times the recommended maximum of fifty. Moreover, public opinion, as it seems to be crystallized largely by the press, appears to be against probation. Probably this opposition is rooted in the assumption that because it fails to satisfy the deep-seated desire for social revenge, probation weakens or destroys the usual incentive for prosecution, namely, that of securing a conviction.

2. *The jail.* Fishman's characterization of the American jail is not entirely invalid today. It is, he said,

. . . an unbelievably filthy institution in which are confined men and women serving sentences for misdemeanors and crimes, and men and women not under sentence, who are simply awaiting trial. With few exceptions, having no segregation of the unconvicted from the convicted, the well from the diseased, the youngest and most impressionable from the degraded and hardened . . . A melting pot in which the worst elements of the raw material in the criminal world are brought forth blended and turned out in absolute perfection.[10]

Certainly some jails have improved, but most of them continue to deserve the opprobrium of being called "the shame of America." In such an environment, what is the chance of successful rehabilitation? Jails actually contribute to crime in that much criminal behavior is nurtured there. In 1947 the United States Bureau of Prisons found, that of the 3,111 county and city jails it inspected, 75 per cent were unfit to house federal prisoners of any age. Only six jails throughout the nation could rate 80 out of a possible score of 100. In view of these facts, it should be clear that the typical jail cannot even pretend to control crime and delinquency. On the contrary, this instrument, which should be one of rehabilitation, appears to be a leading entry among the causes of crime. Instead of correcting and rehabilitating offenders, it tends to demoralize and harden them. Ellingston has said that the judge who sends anyone to jail to "teach him a lesson" is either cynical or ignorant.[11]

3. *The prison.* The prison is the chief custodial institution of our time. It is here that the convicted offender's rehabilitation is attempted when he is neither given probation nor sent to the city or the county jail. The term "penitentiary" designates a place of penance and reformation combined with physical punishment, but since the beginning of our prison system in 1798, a system indigenous to the United States, it appears that the principal stress continues to be placed on the custodial, punitive, and industrial aspects of incarceration. Concomitantly, rehabilitation efforts seem to be incidental. Nevertheless attempts have been made to humanize prisons. The "New Penology," which crystallized in the 1930's, seems to reflect a nationwide trend toward the acceptance of probation and parole, and with this has come a more sympathetic attitude

[10] Joseph Fulling Fishman, *Crucibles of Crime* (Cosmopolis Press, 1923), pp. 13–14.

[11] John R. Ellingston, *Protecting our Children from Criminal Careers* (Prentice-Hall, 1948), p. 186.

toward treating inmates as individuals rather than as groups.   Still nearly all prisons are built today for maximum-security custody, even though not more than 20 per cent of the convicts actually require this restraint.

Probably the basic approach to prison rehabilitation is the classification system current in most prisons.   Since the early days of penology prisoners have been segregated according to sex, age, indebtedness, and professional status; and they have been further distinguished from each other by grade, insignia, and clothing.   More recently, the clinic has been established.   Its experts diagnose, treat, train, and attempt to predict behavior.   Progress has been slow in the classification program.   One reason is the lack of public support.

Old-time prison officials tend to cling to a timeworn routine.   Many antiquated prisons, averaging almost 80 years in age, lack funds for renovation or innovations.   Even more disconcerting is the fact that specialists in human behavior seem confused and in disagreement among themselves as to what should be done.   Prisons are overcrowded.   Few of them employ a full time psychiatrist to assist in the process of rehabilitation.   Because of this and the continual processing of new arrivals, the average inmate receives no more than two hours of psychiatric consultation during his entire prison life.

Such is the status of prison punishment and rehabilitation.   Prisons operating on a fear-system basis forge bonds of alliance among convicts—a mere "consciousness of kind" which does not result in the type of synthesis sanctioned by the ideals of our society, but rather in the antithesis of these ideals.   Prisons may turn out good prisoners; but good prisoners are not necessarily good citizens.   Too many convicts returning to a free society (and 97 per cent do return) have uppermost in their minds the thought that "someone is going to pay."

The theory that the offender should be punished by being sent to prison is not based on an entirely valid premise.   Prison brings shame to one, indifference to a second, and prestige to a third.   It appears impossible to punish convicts and rehabilitate them simultaneously.   Prisonization (cumulative processes that interact upon the personality of incarcerated human beings), characteristic as it is of the prison community, hampers the rehabilitative efforts of even the most enlightened administrators.

4. Parole. Neither mercy nor leniency as such, parole frees the prisoner to serve his unexpired time outside the prison walls under the supervision of a parole officer; it is an administrative act, a continuation of punishment. A good parole officer should possess emotional stability, tact, energy, and mature judgment. Excellent men and women who so qualify may be found in almost every community and they could assist in any intelligent rehabilitation program for the offender. Supervision is the crux of successful parole.

Rehabilitation for the parolee is not an easy task. Parole officers face many difficulties in helping parolees adjust to a life which is the complete antithesis of that they knew in the prison community. The newly released prisoner has suffered; he is somewhat of a convalescent, a sick man getting well. Furthermore, both the officer and the parolee are handicapped by absurd restrictions that few people could live up to. Extraordinary hardships are still imposed on the parolee; he is not allowed to forget his past, and he is expected to prove that he is more exemplary than the average citizen.

Nothwithstanding the various handicaps surrounding the parole system it is more effective in rehabilitation than imprisonment; and, for that reason, a more generous granting of parole is indicated. However, the astounding thing is that probably the chief obstacle to the extension of either parole or probation is the prejudice, even hostility of the public, the press, and of some social scientists.

Does Rehabilitation Succeed?

Recidivism, or the amount of criminal behavior that is repeated, is a good test as to whether or not the correctional process has been successful. Despite the efforts made to rehabilitate the criminal, his behavior appears to become habitual, resolving itself into a pattern. More than half of all offenders commit new crimes. Numerous studies show that from 50 to 70 per cent of those who are delinquent during their youth, continue to live outside the law into adulthood; they are not deterred by serving sentences in either reformatories or prisons. According to Sutherland,[12] the general recidivistic rate tends to run as high as 60 per cent; in state prisons it is as high as 70 per

[12] *Op. cit.*, p. 584.

cent. This latter fact should not be surprising since the state prison
is the *last* institution to which the repeater is sentenced; that is to
say, the prison is essentially an institution for repeaters.

Reasons suggested for recidivism include the inadequacy of re-
formative and rehabilitative agencies, tempting social situations, the
persistence of criminal habits, isolation from law-abiding society, en-
during loyalties, criminal associations, and various emotional instabilities. Many convicts laugh at the rehabilitation process. They
know that rarely is one reformed in the sterile, repressive, unnatural
environment of a reformatory, a jail, or a prison. In the monotony
of prison life and routine they face the unending and inexorable
sameness of days, nights, people, and activities. It is not unlikely
that the effect of this tedium is dulling even to the most promising
inmates. It is probably not surprising therefore that there exists in
the United States today an Association for the Abolition of Peniten-
tiaries.

Until the basic system of punishment is changed, it is doubtful that
a full-fledged plan of rehabilitation can be instituted. Its achievement will be possible when the public and its legislators, on the one
hand, and the entrenched guardians of the law, the judges and
lawyers, on the other hand have been re-educated in a new philosophy
of human nature. Until these responsible persons can be revitalized
by the psycho-sociological comprehension of criminal conduct, until
they understand that the present correctional system in most prisons
creates a socio-cultural monstrosity repulsive to the soundest scientific
knowledge of crime and the criminal, genuine rehabilitation may remain a remote, unattainable ideal.

Supporting rehabilitation is the knowledge that man is not born a
criminal; that he is by nature, a social animal. Man is conditioned
both by his heredity and his environment. He is conscious of social
values. Until rehabilitation takes cognizance of the elements in this
frame of reference and considers all the factors of crime and the
scientific methods of how to remedy this antisocial behavior, its
procedure will fail. Moreover, regardless of the value of probation,
parole, incarceration, and vocational training, the offenders are still
prisoners sentenced to penal institutions, or, in the case of probation,
convicted persons with the constant threat of imprisonment hanging

over them. If society had set out to invent the most *ineffective* system with which to deal with criminals, it could have done no better than establish the jail, the reformatory, and the penitentiary.

In comparison with the past, however, there is today greater flexibility in dealing with offenders. Many prison administrators are intelligent, enlightened men who, if prisons were to be operated solely as instruments of retributive punishment, would refuse to accept appointments to administer them. But there are contradictory purposes in prisons and diametrically opposed philosophies among prison personnel, a conflict between those trained in custodial service and those trained in the science of human behavior. Between these two schools of thought stands the prisoner who, for the most part, receives the benefit of neither.

Contributory to the general confusion and ineptitude of rehabilitation are the phenomena of punishment and social stigma. For example, one offender may steal $25,000 and draw a *jail* sentence as a penalty; when the sentence is completed he may be welcomed back into the community by his friends and his crime is overlooked and perhaps eventually forgotten. Another offender may steal $500 and as a result of the judicial process, get a year in the state *prison*; when *he* has paid his "debt to society"—which he may do with even better grace than the jail-term offender,—he may find no welcome in his community except from his immediate family.

Any individual emerging from a prison finds a stigma attached to his name regardless of the triviality of his offense or of whether or not complete restitution was made. Most employers, including state and federal agencies, refuse him employment; he can no longer practice pharmacy, law, or medicine, and in many communities he cannot be a barber, sell automobiles, or even drive a taxicab; and he cannot run for public office, make bond, vote, or occupy any position of trust again in most states, unless he can secure a governor's pardon. Because he was punished in a prison he becomes a social pariah, an outcast often unable to secure insurance on his automobile, home, or even his life. This irrational, inhuman, inconsistent paradox is directly responsible in many cases for the collapse of the rehabilitative process. It penalizes an offender neither on the degree of his offense nor on the viciousness of his character but merely on the *place* in which he was punished.

Present-day publications are full of suggestions on how to reduce crime. Recommendations range from the proposal to abandon Beccaria's eighteenth-century penal philosophy and concentrate on the doer instead of on the deed, down to the proposal to provide more playgrounds and youth centers, and better lighting of streets. Confusion and dissipation of effort result here primarily from the failure of trained and experienced men to supply the public with leadership.[13]

Actually the problem goes much deeper than the lack of leadership. Leaders themselves are not in agreement. In many respects experts in the science of human behavior appear to be as apathetic as the general public. They are hampered by too much cross-purpose activity; and between theory and practice there is a tremendous lag and gap. Social scientists are far ahead of the practitioners, who seldom make use of their findings. On the other hand, the social scientists, while they are far ahead, do not constitute a group; they are individuals whose activities are not coordinated. Because these scholars have failed to present a sociologically sound program upon which most of them agree, the American press, which educates the general public, is only lukewarm to the philosophy of the juvenile court, probation, parole, rehabilitation, and to other enlightened devices of crime amelioration. An excellent opportunity as well as a challenge awaits the sociologist who can devise a program that offers a unified effort in applying a remedy to the problem of crime.

JUVENILE DELINQUENCY

Americans have been disturbed by predictions that the number of juvenile delinquents in the United States might rise to 750,000 a year by 1960. Most youngsters conform to society's rules and grow into good citizens, but too many others pursue the practices that lead to delinquent careers. They are the professional criminals of tomorrow.

[13] Horace S. Volz, "Let's Stop Fooling Around," *Federal Probation*, XII (1948), 18.

Society often looks biliously at the phenomenon of juvenile delinquency and at the apparent enigma of such questions as: Why does
one boy steal a car and another refuse to commit any depredation?
Why does one child become a gangster and another in the same
family become a pillar of the community? Why does one son of a
criminal follow in his parent's footsteps while his brother becomes a
clergyman? What are the answers to such inquiries?

The Bugaboo of Terminology

A very difficult problem to face in the study of juvenile delinquency is that of deciding upon an exact definition of the term itself.
No two authorities agree in this matter. In general, juvenile delinquency refers to the antisocial acts of children and of young people
under age. Such acts are either those specifically forbidden by law
or may be those that are legally interpreted as constituting delinquency, or as requiring some form of official action. According to
one expert, delinquency has many meanings. There are *legal* delinquents (those committing antisocial acts as defined by law), *detected*
delinquents (those showing antisocial behavior for example), *agency*
delinquents (those detected who reach an agency), *alleged* delinquents (those caught and brought to court), and the *adjudged* delinquents (those found guilty).[14]

Generally, "juvenile delinquent" denotes a child who has been
officially acted upon by the courts or police officers. The age covered
by the term juvenile varies in different states, ranging upward to six-
teen or twenty-one, with the majority of states considering individuals
as juvenile if they are over six and under eighteen. A Massachusetts
law defines a juvenile delinquent as "a child between seven and seventeen who violates any city ordinance or town bylaw or commits an
offense not punishable by death." Under this law nearly every child
within that age range is, or will be, a delinquent by definition. It
may be the son of a prominent minister, and his only offense may be
riding a bicycle on the sidewalk. Moreover, the complexity of delinquency is emphasized by the fact that morally it may mean one thing,
legally something else, practically a third thing, and statistically still

[14] Lowell Julliard Carr, *Delinquency Control* (Harper, 1941), p. 59.

a fourth.   It seems impossible to define the term in such a way as to satisfy all concerned.[15]

Incidence of Juvenile Delinquency

Juvenile delinquency, like adult crime, seems to be increasing; in fact, according to the final juvenile-court reports for 1952 to the United States Children's Bureau, juvenile-court delinquency cases rose 29 per cent between 1948 and 1952.   Increases appeared in Cincinnati, Cleveland, Columbus, Knoxville, Evansville, Indianapolis, Houston, Fort Worth, El Paso, Denver, and San Francisco.   Bureau Chief Dr. Martha M. Eliot reported to the Senate that while some 385,000 children were brought into court during 1952, the total number who encountered police action must have been around 1,000,000. Yet the total number of children 10 to 17 years old (the age group in which most delinquency occurs) increased no more than six per cent during this four-year period.   For one year, 1951 to 1952, the delinquency case load reported by the courts increased ten per cent; whereas the increase in the 10-to-17 age population group was only three per cent.   These figures indicate, then, that the increase in delinquency incidence continues to be considerably greater than that which might be expected from growth in population alone.[16]

Federal statistics also show that the increase in delinquency in less densely populated areas during the year 1952 kept pace with the average increase for the nation as a whole; it outpaced the national average for the four-year period 1948 to 1952.   Courts serving jurisdictions of less than 100,000 population handled 10 per cent more delinquency cases in 1952 than they did in 1951.   During the aforementioned four-year period the increase for these courts was 41 per cent.[17] These data have aroused interest on higher levels.   Near the end of 1953 a special inquiry group of the Senate Judiciary Committee, headed by Senator Robert C. Hendrickson, opened hearings on the incidence of juvenile delinquency.

[15] *Ibid.*, p. 58.   See also Oveta Culp Hobby, "Youth Is Your Business," *Newsweek* (November 9, 1953), p. 35.
[16] U.S. Department of Health, Education, and Welfare, *News Notes on Juvenile Delinquency* (October 13, 1953), p. 5.
[17] *Ibid.*

Handling the Juvenile Offender

Detection and apprehension of the juvenile offender are difficult tasks. The police receive little help from citizens in many communities, and practically none from citizens in the urban areas in which delinquency is concentrated. Thomas Gill, presiding judge of the Connecticut juvenile court system, told the Senate committee that parents should be advised to become an active part of their community if they wish to set behavior standards for their children. Moreover, he said, parents should find out if there is a neighborhood pattern of behavior and what that pattern is.

Law officers apprehend only a fraction of the juveniles they accost; that is to say, they settle more violations than they take into court. This is known as monitory justice. It is one of the factors that lead some criminologists to believe that sincere, however misguided efforts have been taken in behalf of the juvenile offender. Thus the juvenile offender is seldom fingerprinted or photographed by the police and his name is frequently deleted when his crime is reported by the press. Inasmuch, however, as the professional criminals are generally recruited from the ranks of juvenile delinquents, a reversal of this "protective" procedure seems to be in order. Juvenile fingerprinting proponents maintain that it is an accurate method of identification, that it protects the innocent, completes the records, and enables the FBI to include nationwide juvenile delinquency statistics in its *Uniform Crime Reports*. Moreover, this process, they say, may act as a deterrent to future offenses, and surely it constitutes no more of a stigma than going into a juvenile court or to a detention home.

Despite the fact that the majority of juveniles are released at the police station, at least 50,000 children are detained contrary to state laws in city or county jails each year. One western state forbids the detention in jail of children under twelve years old; but it was discovered in 1947 that in a period of nearly four years three of its local jails, all in the same county, had a record for the incarceration of children totaling 1,430 days. Only two states, Connecticut and New Hampshire, claim that they never jail children. Paradoxically, thousands of youngsters are yearly incarcerated in jails in communities having some of the finest juvenile detention facilities in the United States. Here they share the same degrading influences of which adults often complain.

Unwholesome environments for juveniles are not limited to jails. Detention homes mean different things to different children, depending upon their previous experiences. To some juveniles, detention means food and shelter; to others it means indiscriminate contact with fellow detainees; often it means a degrading experience. The latter is especially true where untrained personnel, without regard for the basic dignity of human nature and personality, treat all detainees as inferior persons. Finally, described as the weakest link in the rehabilitation process, detention usually means idleness.[18]

The juvenile court, since its inception in Chicago in 1899, has functioned on this basic premise, that the youthful offender is to be treated, not as a criminal, but as a child in trouble, whose parents or guardians are unable or unwilling to discharge their responsibilities to him. Nonlegalistic, this court is characterized by informal procedure, with great powers of discretion invested in its judge. Still, although much antiquated thinking regarding juvenile misbehavior has been abandoned, the handling of delinquent children continues to be largely punitive in character, and after more than a half-century of juvenile-court philosophy and practice, most people still believe that the juvenile court is a place where bad children are punished.

Limited courses of action are open to most juvenile courts or even to criminal courts in disposing of a child or adolescent who is not mentally ill or feeble-minded. These courses are: to return him to his home on probation; to refer him to such welfare services as exist in his community; to place him in a boarding or foster home; to send him to a private institution for children; or to place him in jail or in a correctional house—a juvenile institution, a reform school, or a prison. From the standpoint of rehabilitation, commitment to a reform school lowers appreciably any chance the youthful offender may have to change his ways. Some reform schools are merely junior prisons; by and large, they are more severe in treatment and discipline than some of the large state prisons. Witnesses to this are thousands

[18] Belle Boone Beard, "Detention: The Weakest Link," *Federal Probation*, XIII (1949), 18.

of adult convicts who have served time in both types of institutions. Sufficient evidence has been collected to show that reform schools are breeding places for crime. The judge who sends an offender there to remove him from a "bad" gang of six youths only places him in a gang of 400 to 500 members, more or less. Many children eventually are released from the reform school to finish the remainder of their sentence on parole. Here one encounters problems similar to those found in adult parole. Seldom is there a parole staff adequate either in numbers or in training for the child's post-institutional transition period. In some states no parole services are available for children; upon release they must fare as best they can without the proper supervision.

Present-day trends in handling juvenile delinquency problems are hopeful. More states are supporting intelligent programs. The Youth Authority, created and sponsored by the American Law Institute in 1940, is a step in the right direction. The procedure is to remand all convicted juveniles to a youth authority who, after careful investigation and diagnosis, decides the place of punishment and treatment. So far, however, only six states have adopted this program.

Community Responsibility and Juvenile Delinquency

Part of the responsibility for the high incidence of juvenile delinquency must be shared by the community. Delinquency cannot be prevented or controlled without community action. This action centers around the giving of adequate support to agencies and programs attempting to deal with the growing challenge of delinquent behavior. It may be that, outside the correctional school, the final solution of the problem of delinquency will be found in the local community. It is for this reason that every effort must be made to adjust the delinquent child through techniques and facilities that may be developed in the child's own community. Certainly, if the community wants the average child or youth who has passed through a correctional institution to follow acceptable paths upon his return to the community, it must provide him with the means socially to satisfy his inner feeling of "belonging"; it must encourage him to be a respected and useful junior citizen. Care must also be taken to find out whether or not the child's parents were responsible for his delinquency. Until delinquency areas are transformed into socially healthful communities, the best efforts of its parole officers will frequently be defeated. Local business and professional groups often have the leadership capable of understanding and controlling the incidence of delinquency; but they are discouraged by the apathy, even hostility, encountered from others.

An outstanding development in local community or area organization are the Community Council and its coordinating programs initiated in Berkeley, California, in 1919. Chief functions of these councils are: to secure cooperation among the various institutions, agencies, and groups concerned with child welfare; to integrate their efforts; to study conditions and resources; to educate the public regarding improvement conditions and programs; and to create social action to meet local needs. This organization is especially qualified to deal with the problem of juvenile delinquency.[19]

Many aspects of the social problem of juvenile delinquency demand immediate and serious consideration before any worthwhile progress can be made. The public, if its support is to be gained, must be better informed of the accepted scientific approaches to the solution of delinquency. Owing to the undue publicity given probation and parole failures, misconceptions of both are rife in the public mind. The press, movies, radio, and television continue to present an already apathetic public with a panorama of antiquated stereotypes and distortions in the field of juvenile delinquency and in law enforcement agencies as well. Moreover, to many parents and children a trip to the juvenile court clinic is a punishment process rather than a corrective treatment. Notwithstanding the major advances made in the thinking and philosophy exemplified by the youth authorities, too many offenders, when their corrective treatment and rehabilitation begin, have but one thought uppermost in mind: "How much time will I have to do?"

One encouraging sign for the future is the world-wide health and welfare program launched by the United Nations Social Commission.

[19] Martin H. Neumeyer, *Juvenile Delinquency in Modern Society* (Van Nostrand, 1949), pp. 308–310.

The commission plans include the prevention of crime and delinquency and the rehabilitation of youthful offenders.

Study Questions

1. What is meant by crime? Where did society get its code of "acceptable human conduct"?
2. Considering the data given in *Uniform Crime Reports*, can it be determined definitely that a "crime wave" is "sweeping" the nation? Give the reasons.
3. Apropos of the statement that detection and apprehension problems are aggravated by many factors, make a list of these factors.
4. Most of the individuals accused of crime are not financially able to hire legal defense. Explain and give the results of this phenomenon.
5. How important is the "white-collar criminal"? Who is the "real" criminal in our society?
6. The American tradition is that a man is innocent until proved guilty. Explain, giving the possible results of the continued abuse of this tradition.
7. Discuss Beccaria and the discipline which produced the philosophy inherent in classical penology.
8. What is the exact meaning of juvenile delinquency? What is the relationship of juvenile delinquency to the community?
9. In handling the juvenile delinquent, the law apparently recognizes only the child's chronological age. Why is it important to consider the mental age? Emotional age? Physiological age?
10. In your own region, city, community, neighborhood: Discuss the public apathy to probation and parole. Cite examples of the stereotypes and distortions in the field of juvenile delinquency.

Selected References

Barnes, Harry Elmer, and Negley K. Teeters, *New Horizons in Criminology* (Prentice-Hall, 1951), ch. II.
Caldwell, Robert G., "Why is the Death Penalty Retained?" *The Annals of the American Academy of Political and Social Science,* 284 (1952), 45–53.
Clinard, Marshall B., "Secondary Community Influences and Juvenile Delinquency," *The Annals of the American Academy of Political and Social Science,* 261 (1949), 42–54.
————, "Sociologists and American Criminology," *Journal of Criminal Law and Criminology,* 41 (1951), 549–577.
Conrad, Frederick A., "Statistics in the Analysis of Social Problems," *Sociology and Social Research,* XXVI (1942), 538–549.

Killian, Frederick W., "The Juvenile Court as an Institution," *The Annals of the American Academy of Political and Social Science,* 261 (1949), 89–100.

Lesser, Edith K., "Understanding Juvenile Delinquency," *Federal Probation,* XIII (1949), 56–62.

Lukas, Edwin J., "Crime Prevention: Who Prevents What?" *Federal Probation,* 12 (1948), 19–23.

Tannenbaum, Frank, "Social Forces in the Development of Crime," *Crime and the Community* (Ginn, 1938), pp. 25–28.

Tappan, Paul W., "Who Is the Criminal?" *American Sociological Review,* 12 (1947), 96–102.

Vold, George B., "Criminology at the Crossroads," *Journal of Criminal Law and Criminology,* 42 (1951), 155–162.

Young, Leontine R., "We Call Them Delinquents," *Federal Probation,* XV (1951), 9–13.

7

Rural Problems

As a society perfects a vast and efficient industrial system it is easy to minimize or forget the importance of farming and rural life. Agriculture provides man with food and fiber, but these things are not likely to excite the imagination. Industry, however, supplies all kinds of fascinating things that raise the plane of living. In a popularity contest industrial products would be likely to attract more attention than agricultural. Nevertheless, agrarian, or rural, society is of continuing importance to the whole society. The rural and urban segments of society are mutually interdependent and neither can be self-sufficient. In this chapter an effort is made to define and describe some representative social problems that prevail in rural society.

Certain problems—such as those relating to the amount, location, and fertility of soil—are as old as agriculture; other problems are of more recent origin. It will be seen that some of the present problems have assumed importance only as we have moved from an agrarian to an industrial society.

For more than a century cities and city influences have increased in importance in the nation. At the same time there has been a corresponding relative decrease in the extent and influence of the rural portion of the nation. During the last century the Industrial Revolution has transformed a once predominately agrarian country into the world's show case of industrial wonders. The social consequences of this very rapid and far-reaching transition have been very great. A social equilibrium satisfactory to many was permanently disturbed, and social values often shifted from the abstract to the material. The cities proved to be great magnets for many thousands of the rural born—they offered a level of living that farming districts seldom could equal. As a result many rural communities weakened or even disappeared. The advance of mechanized farming came to pose a real question as to the survival of the traditional family farm.

Many observers became alarmed over the possible demise of the family farm because they considered it to be not only a source of livelihood but also a way of life endowed with intrinsic good for the whole society. Champions of rural life are inclined to say that the ethical and social traits engendered by the farm family and other rural social institutions are highly worthy of being maintained; and they fear that rural society stands in some danger of being completely swamped by urbanization. This would seem a natural and inevitable consequence to the more extreme advocates of urban superiority who think that the rural areas must adapt to concepts of urban progress or suffer the consequences. Neither of the points of view to which reference has been made, is likely to prevail in an extreme form.

On the farm, the family works as a unit. It is a multi-bonded primary group whose members are closely united by many important social bonds and ties. The home and the business are one and the same. The farm family lives and works in intimate contact with nature. They deal with things that live and grow and have experiences that draw out an aspect of personality different from that engendered by machines or assembly-line specialization.

But despite the list of good things claimed for farm living that way of life involves a formidable array of problems. The farm has very poor holding power on its youth. Only a small percentage of those born on farms aspire to be farmers as a first choice of occupation, and because of the population loss, many churches, schools, and stores have closed and neighborhoods have vanished. Figure 7.1 shows graphically the relative change that has taken place in the size of rural and urban populations. Today the rural farm and nonfarm groups account for less than half the total population of the country.

In an effort to emulate industrial efficiency, large-scale commercial agriculture has grown apace and this makes uncertain the outlook for the family farm. Farms are becoming fewer and larger as a slow but rather steady concentration of land holdings continues. Rural areas

POPULATION OF U. S.

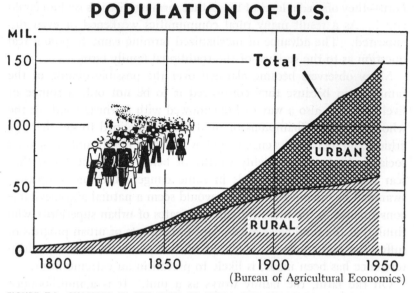

(Bureau of Agricultural Economics)

FIGURE 7.1: CHANGES IN THE SIZES OF RURAL AND URBAN POPULATIONS SHOWING THE RELATIVE DECLINE IN RURAL POPULATION.

are becoming "urbanized" as traditional rural cultural traits give way in favor of "modern" urban values.

Not all problems, even social problems existent in rural society, can or need to be discussed here. In order to promote insight into rural social problems generally, five specific areas are offered for consideration and analysis. These five were chosen because they are both important and representative. They are as follows: (1) problems of land tenure and the agricultural ladder; (2) problems arising from size of holdings and management systems; (3) social problems resulting from changes in neighborhood and community; (4) problems faced by the rural church and the rural school; and (5) problems resulting from differential fertility and migration.

PROBLEMS OF TENURE AND THE AGRICULTURE LADDER

In a rural society land is the prime source of wealth and also of social status. The high regard for land results partly from its income-producing quality; but it should be recognized also that the ownership of land involves intangible emotional values that go far back in the historical tradition of society. Land has always been a symbol of security—a constant in a world subject to change. As the source of food and fiber the land sustains life even when it yields no profits or provides no products for the great industrial systems. For the farmer the land is the seat of his business and also of his home; for him life and livelihood are not separated, nor are they usually even thought of apart. Moreover, for practical purposes, land is indestructible, and acquiring it is an investment for a lifetime and for generations to come.

Before the advent of the Industrial Revolution almost the sole source of wealth was the soil. Secondary production was negligible, and for the most part only those people who owned land possessed wealth or social position. Under the feudal system all land belonged to the king or prince and was parceled out to noblemen in return for an oath of loyalty and for maintaining a supply of fighting men at the call of the overlord. The feudal estates, or manors, were complete units of life. They were the only source of wealth, livelihood, and security for most people, since city life and urban crafts as yet embraced relatively few people. Eventually the feudal system broke down and individually owned farms gradually evolved from the manorial estates.

Exploration in the new world brought news to Europe of an abundance of good land. In the English Colonies and later in the new nation of the United States of America ownership of land conferred social status, provided a livelihood and income, assured a measure of security and sometimes was a requisite for voting. For many years ownership was the principal type of land tenure in the United States, but gradually as free land was exhausted in supply and as rural population increased, many other tenure categories made their appearance. Of particular concern to many agricultural economists, rural sociologists, and other students of rural life was the rapid increase in the number and the proportion of tenant operated farms which took place in this country during the closing decades of the nineteenth century and the first thirty-five years of the twentieth. This was generally thought to be caused by farm owners falling back into the tenant category. Hence it is not surprising that the "problem of tenancy" has been generally considered to be one of the principal rural social problems with which the nation was confronted.

Probably it is more fruitful of understanding, however, if the whole matter of land tenure is examined. Land tenure is one of the relationships between man and land. It is a legal and social relationship relative to holding land or the right to use the land. Everyone working on the land, managing land, or living from its income occupies some tenure position. Tenure classes arrange themselves in a vertical hierarchy depending on the extent of rights enjoyed. These tenure classes are also important criteria of status.

If land tenure denotes the conditions under which landed property is held, the *full ownership* category obviously occupies the top position because it carries with it the greatest security and the greatest degree of freedom to follow farming practices of individual choice. *Part-owners* and *mortgaged owners* may use their land under somewhat restricted conditions in that the other part-owner or owners or the financing agencies may be in a position to make certain requirements of the operator. The *renter* has use of the land for a stipulated period of time in return for the rent paid. The *sharecropper* has the right to live on the land and use certain facilities as long as he continues his working contract with the owner. Even the *wage hand* employed by the day or week has certain tenure status with more "land rights" than the outsider. Among the privileges accruing to sharecroppers and laborers are: housing, access to roads, access to wood lots, water supply and pasture for livestock.

Problems of Tenure and Tenancy

A number of social and economic problems are associated with the various types of tenure. These problems are not necessarily caused by the tenure status, nor are they necessarily inherent in it. Even the owners and independent operators are faced constantly with the problems of financing, marketing, crop failure or surpluses, and mechanization; but the present analysis deals mainly with those general social problems usually associated with farm tenancy and farm labor categories. Briefly these problems are: (1) low per capita income; (2) poor farming practices; (3) weak social institutions; (4) high mobility among farm families; (5) soil depletion; and (6) inadequate care of the land owner's buildings and other property.

These problems in their most extreme manifestations arise among tenants and sharecroppers operating under the short-term lease. Such farmers employ the most destructive soil practices. Outbuildings, fences, ditches, orchards, and gardens—and even the dwelling houses —are poorly cared for on farms which are rented for short periods. Soil mining and other adverse practices produce unsatisfactory relationships between landlord and tenant. In many sections the tenants and sharecroppers and the members of their families rarely participate in civic or community affairs and they are poor supporters of the basic institutions. School attendance is poor among the children of tenants and wage-hand families as is church attendance. Institutional ties, except within the family, are especially weak among the migratory farm group.

Tenancy, with "long-term" leases, sincere interest in the land and mutual appreciation and understanding between landlord and tenant, could be an almost ideal farming arrangement, but unfortunately this achievable ideal is seldom attained.

The Agricultural Ladder

The decline in the operation of the agricultural ladder is another of the tenure problems in rural society. The agricultural ladder is the term used to designate the various steps by which one rises or descends from one tenure class to another. It is the process by which the farm boy works up from a hired hand to become a farm owner. The main rungs in the ladder are farm laborer, tenant, part-owner, and owner. Sub-classification of these steps, of course, produces more rungs. A given case history might go something like this: laborer, share renter, cash renter, part owner, full owner. When land was plentiful and the capital outlay for operation was small, several years of hired labor might enable a young man to save enough to buy tools and workstock and become a renter. Then if all went well he might, through the exercise of diligence and thrift, eventually become a mortgaged owner, and finally a full owner.

In recent times many observers believe the operation of the agricultural ladder is slowing down. Relatively fewer of those who start as hired laborers eventually attain ownership. Many who move into the tenant class never move out of it. The day laborer or wage hand rung of the ladder is often only a temporary position held by farm youth before they move on to nonfarm employment.[1]

If one does not inherit a farm or have some outside assistance it is difficult to get into the farm business, at least as an owner-operator. When it is considered that a farm of the size generally styled a family farm may be valued at from $16,000 to $48,000 [2] and the investment in machinery alone may run from $6,000 to $10,000 per farm [3] it is not difficult to understand why few laborers can accumulate enough to start farming as an owner-operator. With the passage of time the per acre value of the most desirable land has gone up. Figure 7.2 shows the extent to which land prices have risen in recent years.

Even with capital in hand it may not be easy to find a good farm that is for sale. Much land is in large holdings and the owners are as much attached to it as are the small holders to theirs. Smith aptly points out that the planter is not a land agent and that he can hardly be censured for his unwillingness to sell his own holdings to those who wish to purchase a small farm.[4]

SIZE OF HOLDINGS AND MANAGEMENT SYSTEMS

Land tenure, operation of the agricultural ladder, size of holdings, and management systems are all interrelated, and in one way or another, each influences the other as a cause and each is, in turn, affected by all the rest. One cannot be considered without implications of

[1] Carl C. Taylor et al., Rural Life In The United States (Knopf, 1952), pp. 284 and 528.

[2] Sloan R. Wayland, Edmund des. Brunner, and Frank W. Cyr (eds.), Farmers of the Future: Prospect and Policies for Establishing a New Generation on the Land (Bureau of Publications, Teachers College, Columbia University, 1953), pp. 32–33.

[3] This is the estimated value of machinery per Mississippi farm according to an article in The Hattiesburg American (Mississippi), October 21, 1953.

[4] T. Lynn Smith, The Sociology of Rural Life (3rd ed., Harper, 1953), p. 318.

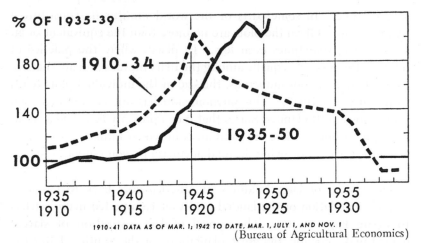

1910-41 DATA AS OF MAR. 1; 1942 TO DATE, MAR. 1, JULY 1, AND NOV. 1

(Bureau of Agricultural Economics)

FIGURE 7.2: INCREASE IN THE VALUE OF FARM LAND—VALUES OF FARM LAND, 1910–1934 AND 1935–1950, AS PER CENT OF 1935–1939

the others becoming clearly evident. A case might be made for the claim that size of holdings is of first importance among the above factors, and, in fact, size of holdings does exert a profound influence on both the prosperity and the problems of rural society. Smith has expressed the opinion that probably the most important single determinant of the welfare of farm people is the degree to which land ownership and control are concentrated in a few hands, at one extreme, or are broadly distributed among many farm operators, at the other.[5]

Size of holdings is the source of social problems whenever holdings become either too small to afford adequate income to those who own and operate them or so large that a majority of the persons who work thereon will fall into the category of agricultural laborers. In the vocabulary of rural sociology a Latin word, *latifundia*, describes large holdings and another, *minifundia*, denotes extremely small ones. Both are found often in the literature and will be employed from time to time in this discussion, though more often the terms "concentration" and "small holdings" are used. Subdivision of farms and concentration in land ownership are the polar processes by which farms become smaller and smaller or larger and larger with the pas-

[5] *Ibid.*, p. 297.

sage of time. In some parts of the world *minifundia* constitute a real problem. Often the plots are no more than the equivalent of an acre or two, sometimes even less. In places where the practice of dividing the property equally among the heirs prevails and alternatives for livelihood are not numerous, the size of the individual plots tends to become very small. This phenomenon has not yet reached such proportions in the United States that it can properly be called a social problem, although there are local areas in which farms are too small to provide a level of living deemed adequate by contemporary standards.

The system of large holdings in America goes back to Colonial times. Emulation of the landed gentry of Europe led many settlers to desire large estates. The spread of the institution of slavery helped make possible the great plantations of the South. Later the West produced its own version of the vast estates—the ranches. In recent times still another form of large holdings has developed. It is usually known as the corporation farm, used here to mean large acreages operated by a commercial producer of food or fiber. The concentration of large acreages into corporative "factories in the fields" has been encouraged by the demand for larger production, and has been made possible, to a large extent, by efficient and highly specialized farm machines.

Although concentration of land ownership and control is probably less pronounced in the United States than in most countries having extensive agriculture, the trend here is definitely toward fewer farms but larger ones. In 1950 the 5.7 per cent of the farms that were above 500 acres in size contained 53.5 per cent of all the land in farms. Between 1910 and 1950 the number of farms of 1,000 acres or more increased from 50,135 to 121,362, a gain of 142 per cent, whereas the total number of farms fell from 6,361,502 to 5,382,162, a loss of 15.4 per cent. Over the same period the proportion of land in these large farms rose from 19.0 per cent in 1910 to 42.6 per cent in 1950. This concentration of land ownership into the larger units went on during every decade of the forty-year period under consideration.[6]

In 1940 the average size of the farm in the United States was 174

[6] See, Bureau of the Census, U.S. *Census of Agriculture; 1950*, II, *General Report* (Government Printing Office, 1952), 774–775.

acres, and by 1950 this figure had risen to 215 acres. The interpretation of these changes in averages should be made with caution, however, since the inclusion of cropper units as farms by the Census invalidates some of the results. Sharecroppers decreased considerably in number between 1940 and 1950 and this factor alone made for a considerable, although undeterminable, part of the increase in the average size of farms. The data on the number of farms of 1,000 acres or more also are influenced by this factor, since a given census does not place a large plantation on which the labor is done by sharecroppers in the large-farm category. Rather it is counted as many small farms as there are sharecroppers on the place. If the labor system changes to some other basis at a subsequent census it then is counted as one of the large farms.

Concentration of land acreage is a subject much discussed by farm economists and farmers themselves. It is said that large holdings take vast acreages out of the potential market, and make it difficult or impossible for those who wish to buy land to find conveniently located tracts that are for sale, thus impeding the operation of the agricultural ladder. Smith contends that large estates make for development of a high degree of social stratification. Criticism of concentrated holdings is most pronounced in those cases where the owners are absentee landlords who live some distance from the farming operation and who therefore may be largely unaware of local conditions.

Farming Systems

Closely allied to size of holdings, and a part of the over-all consideration, is farming systems. Farming systems has reference to the type of farm organization or identifiable types of farms. There are numerous possible ways to classify farms, the classification depending on how finely lines are drawn. For present purposes the classification used is as follows: (1) the small farm, (2) the family farm, and (3) the large-scale farm. This is not just another way of saying that there are small farms, middle-sized farms, and large farms; there is more involved in a classification of farming systems than size in acres. Hoffsommer and his associates used six factors to measure the size of farms. They are: labor requirements, total acreage, acres in cropland, acres in major crop, amount of livestock, and capital invested.[7]

The small-scale farm.   Small-scale farms include those that are too small to provide the family with an adequate level of living, part-time farms, and "hobby farms"; in short, they are those farms that contribute some farm products to the agricultural pool but which do not completely support or employ the farmer or the farm family.   Rather than acreage alone it would seem that better criteria for this type of farming system would be: (1) number of days worked on the farm; (2) number of days worked off the farm; (3) real income from the farm (cash income plus value of food, "rent," and so forth); and (4) the proportion of the total gross income provided by the farm.   Thus a nursery or apiary of small acreage but necessitating the farmer's full time and providing his family a comfortable level of living would be considered, on this basis, not as a small-scale farm but as a "family farm."   The submarginal farm, or the farm so small or so unproductive as to fail to support the family, is an example of a small farm as here conceived.   Also included would be the suburban acreages of persons whose major employment is in the town or city.

The problem of the submarginal and the undersized farms is one of the real dilemmas of rural society.   Some of these farms are operated by people who have a long and strong tradition on the land and who by training and personal choice prefer farming over alternative occupations.   Yet on many of them, generation after generation, the fertility of the soil has been depleted by heavy cropping and erosion. Almost from sheer inertia, it would seem, families go on tilling such farms as they become increasingly submarginal.   Often scientific farming and soil conservation practices can restore the productivity of the land or convert it to a more profitable agricultural practice, but the process is a slow and costly one.

Another type of "small farm" is exemplified by one that is fertile enough but is simply too small to afford the farmer the income that he could readily earn in urban employment.   If no near-by land is for sale or rent or if he cannot accumulate enough capital to undertake expansion he must face a choice of lowered earnings or of leaving the farm.   The Columbia University Seminar on rural life estimated

[7] Harold Hoffsommer (ed.), *The Social and Economic Significance of Land Tenure in the Southwestern States* (University of North Carolina Press, 1950), p. 28.

that a well improved, advantageously located farm of 160 acres of good land has a value of from $16,000 to $24,000 and that from 240 to 320 acres would be required to produce a family income equivalent to that which could be earned in non-farm employment, without investment.[8] If the farmer does not feel reasonable assurance that the farm will be passed on to his children he may not consider the effort and expense entailed in expansion to be worth while.

The solution adopted by many farmers who find their farm income inadequate is to work part time off the farm. Some farmers find a happy balance between farm and nonfarm work and thus augment their income and still enjoy the satisfaction of living on their own farms. Others less fortunate find themselves unable to engage satisfactorily in two types of work. The peak season on the farm may conflict with off the farm work, and their farming operations may be too small to enable them to buy the machinery they would need to compete effectively with other farmers in the area.

It is sometimes found that the operator channels money from this nonfarm employment into the farm. This "subsidization" of farming from another source of income is not infrequent on what has been styled the "hobby farm." This refers to the "show-case" farms on relatively small acreages which many professional and business people maintain on the fringes of the cities. Many such units qualify technically as farms, although they are mainly places of rural residence and the farming involved comes closer to being a hobby than a source of livelihood. Every section of the country has experienced a mushroom growth of the small, semi-farms that line the highways and dot the countryside in the hinterlands of the towns and cities. The recent multiplication of this type of farm complicates the problem of evaluating the small-scale farm and makes a realistic count of rural-farm population even more difficult than it formerly was.

The extent of small-scale farms throughout the country is shown graphically in Figure 7.3. Here each of the counties has been shaded to show small-scale farms as a percentage of commercial farms.

The family farm. The literature of Rural Sociology and Agricultural Economics deals extensively with discussions, qualifications, and indexes of the *family farm.* Rather than array these numerous and

8 Wayland, Brunner, and Cyr, *op. cit.*, pp. 32–33.

imprecise attributes before the reader, a single simplified definition is offered. The term "family farm" is used to denote those farms that are the exclusive or major source of livelihood for a family, and on which most of the labor is supplied by its members.

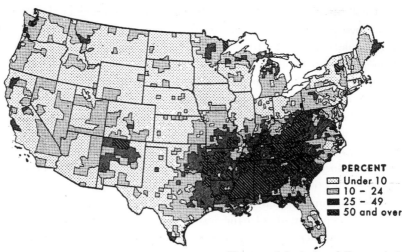

PERCENT
Under 10
10 - 24
25 - 49
50 and over

(Bureau of Agricultural Economics)

FIGURE 7.3: PROPORTION OF SMALL-SCALE FARMS IN THE UNITED STATES—SMALL-SCALE FARMS AS PER CENT OF COMMERCIAL FARMS

The size aspect of the family farm has received as much attention in the literature as have definitions. It is probably meaningless to try to express this in terms of acreage or labor requirements alone. The family farm is of sufficient size to utilize all available family labor but at the same time small enough to make it possible for the family members to provide the bulk of the labor required. Extra labor may be needed at peak seasons of planting, cultivation, and harvesting; but such occasional and emergency labor is not a reason for taking this unit out of the family-farm category.

A family farm may well be 40 acres or it may include a section (640 acres) or more. The size may vary with the number of persons in the family, their ages, the kind of farming engaged in, and the amount and kind of machinery employed.

The family farm has been a great American ideal and still remains so. Social values, status systems, the homestead acts, the Agricultural Extension Service and other agencies, and legislation have at once recognized and encouraged this ideal. But the family-farm system has been difficult to maintain, for the available supply of good, cheap land has been exhausted, farm consolidation has continued, and the attractiveness of urban employment has become stronger. This points up one of the most thorny problems in contemporary rural society, namely, "What should be the nation's policy toward the family farm?"

Those who advocate governmental measures favorable to the maintenance of the family-farm system contend that the family-operated farm is more than a means of making a living. They consider it an intrinsic good and believe that it promotes the qualities of thrift, patriotism, neighborliness, honesty, morality, respect for law, and self-reliance. Of course, the farm family has no monopoly on these virtues. But the farm youth form a homogeneous body of population steeped in the tradition and culture that buttress basic social values; and due to the pattern of differential fertility, the rural institutions leave their imprint on a large part of each new generation.

Opponents of legislative action designed to favor the operators of family-sized farms claim that it is class legislation and therefore wrong. They object to financing existing and proposed programs from general tax funds. It is said that prices of farm products are too high for the urban consumer and that family farms are partly responsible for the high costs. Statistics are cited to show that the unit or pound of food or fiber can be produced more economically by the large-scale mechanized commercial farms. The assertion is made that the family farm is outmoded and that it must give way to more efficient methods.

Large-scale farming systems. Although the family-owned and operated farm unit has been the American ideal the trend is away from family farms. As indicated above farms are tending to become fewer and larger. The tenant category has been depleted by a shift of many persons to farm-labor status or into nonfarm employment. The larger operating units use more day labor and waged or salaried skilled operators of machinery.

The category of large-scale farms includes such agricultural units

as: private forests and game preserves, large-scale grazing lands, plantations, corporate commercial farms, and chain farms. It is difficult to
characterize the type adequately. However, two examples are: farms
that produce food and fiber mainly for the commercial market; and
those where the labor is almost exclusively wage hands, croppers, or
"tenants."

Large holdings are significant because large acreages of cropland are
under a single management, and because on them mechanized agriculture has advanced most rapidly. To grow is a legitimate aspiration of any business venture; but just how big any one enterprise
should become is a continuing problem in a democratic society.
From the establishment of the R.F.D. to the 4-H Clubs, and from the
passage of the Homestead Acts to the establishment of the Federal
Land Banks the Congress has enacted a long series of laws designed
to help and encourage the owner-operator type of farmer. Nonetheless the long-term trend has been toward larger farming units; this
has been especially true since highly efficient machinery puts farming
on something approaching a mass-production basis, and whenever
large-scale farming appears to be economically more efficient than
the family farm, the latter is put in a bad light in the eyes of many.
The debate—family farm versus large-scale farming—may never get
full consideration, for if the family farm is unable to compete *economically* with the big mechanized unit, many of the former's real merits
may be overlooked.

CHANGES IN NEIGHBORHOOD AND COMMUNITY

An understanding of the concept of the social group is one of the
prerequisites for analyzing and understanding society. It is through
groups that social life is carried on and civilization is built. Most
of the values of life that man enjoys or for which he strives involve
other people. Association with other human beings is the essence of
the social group. Some groups are as simple and as transitory as two
persons engaged in conversation; others as complex and as permanent
as a nation.

The family group gives life to the child and sustains him wholly or partially until he is able to care for himself. Other groups are important in molding personality, conferring status, satisfying psychological needs, transferring culture from one generation to another, and initiating the children into society. A full treatment of groups would give detail and insight relative to many of those in which men participate and on which they rely every day of their lives. In this chapter only two groups of the many that might be considered have been chosen for treatment, namely the neighborhood and the community. They were selected because in them we find some of the most critically important aspects of social problems.

Few areas of social life reflect more dramatically the perplexities of a society in transition than these locality groups. Many patterns of neighborhood and community life, familiar and traditional a generation or so ago, may be completely forgotten or drastically changed today. Progress can be made only through change, but it needs to be clear, also, that problems frequently arise because of progress or change. Whereas life is enriched by the new, sometimes this is achieved at the expense of other social values. Generally speaking, in rural America, both neighborhoods and communities have undergone drastic change since the turn of the century. In the wake of this change have appeared numerous complications of concern to almost everyone.

Let us consider first the basic nature of the neighborhood and the community. The neighborhood is one of the primary groups, that is, a relatively small group whose members have intimate, informal, frequent face-to-face contacts. *Neighboring* makes the "neighborhood"; and neighboring may be defined as mutual-aid relationship plus intimate and informal social contacts. Mutual aid is the term sociologists use to describe those relationships of helpfulness between persons for which no pay or other reward is expected. Neighboring, then, as well as proximity of homes is a prime criterion of the neighborhood. The person who lives next door or the family who occupies the next farm may not be a neighbor. The neighborhood exists only when primary social relationships prevail within a given small area. Every person living in the locality need not be a member of the neighborhood, and some people have no neighborhood.

The community has similarity to the neighborhood in some respects, but is distinct from it in many ways. The community is larger than the neighborhood; and it includes both face-to-face and secondary patterns of social interaction. The community may embrace more than one neighborhood. It is large enough and complete enough to enable the individual to satisfy most of his basic needs within its limits. It includes all the basic social institutions, whereas the neighborhood may have only one or two institutions within its confines. The neighborhood bears much the same relationship to the community as the family bears to society.

The rural neighborhood has been weakened by the impact of the great social transition to which reference has been made. Frequently this change came about through an undermining of the old forms of social control. Superior means of communication have all but abolished the isolations of yesteryear. Rural youth have, in the main, the same aspirations as urban youth, and since the urban place and urban employment have so often afforded a higher level of living the great American cities are a magnet for a million rural people a year. Industry and commerce need population recruits, and the attractive opportunities of the cities assure continued migration. Figure 7.4 affords a summary of facts relative to the variation of levels of living by residence. If level of living is measured by such objective indexes as those used by the Bureau of Agricultural Economics, then the more rural the area the poorer the showing made. The "pull" factor of the city is, in part, made up of the attractive opportunities to possess those conveniences.

Rural society must deal with problems from two internal sources of change. Some of these arise within the neighborhood because human relations become increasingly impersonal and formal; and others develop because the community itself is weakened by the attrition of its members. Rural churches have closed their doors, rural schools have been moved away and rural stores have gone out of business because patronage shrank below a minimum needed to maintain these institutions. In many places it has become difficult for a community organization—a civic club, a co-operative, a 4-H Club, a Home Demonstration Club, or a community baseball team—to main-

Living Items	Counties with Farm Population of:				
	80% & over	60%-80%	40%-60%	20%-40%	Under 20%
 Births in Hospitals 1946	28%	47%	69%	81%	93%
 Hospital Beds per 100,000 Population 1946	45	131	231	359	432
 Physicians per 100,000 Population 1946	31	44	57	73	112
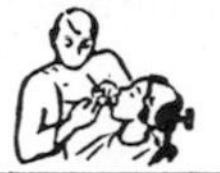 Dentists per 100,000 Population 1946	10	19	30	38	60
 Adults with 5 or More Years of School 1940	65%	74%	83%	86%	87%
 Adults Who Have Completed High School 1940	10%	14%	20%	23%	27%
 Farm Dwellings with Electricity 1945	19%	27%	44%	56%	68%
 Farm Dwellings with Telephone 1945	6%	17%	34%	36%	42%
 Farm Dwellings with Radio 1945	49%	61%	70%	73%	75%
 Farm Dwellings with Running Water 1945	7%	11%	21%	32%	47%

(Bureau of Agricultural Economics)

FIGURE 7.4: HOW LIVING DIFFERS IN RURAL AND URBAN COUNTIES—POSSESSION OF SELECTED LEVEL OF LIVING ITEMS BY PLACE OF RESIDENCE

tain adequate support. A terrible fatalism and depression accompanies the shrinking and weakening of a community.

Where the urban community is a going concern it attracts many of those from its rural hinterlands who desire identification with successful ventures. As a result many rural communities may almost be said to be laboring under an inferiority complex. This in itself is a great handicap. Anyone intimately familiar with the folkways and values of both urban and rural life knows that "rural" and "country" are often used as adjectives of derision. Most of the rural society's cultural heritage and many of its social contributions run the risk of passing to oblivion unless the fortune of urban acceptance smiles on them. The "square dance" was a dying recreational form until adopted by "smart" circles. Many of grandma's items of furnishing and art objects find sure repose in the attic unless up-graded to the status of "antiques."

In the societal realm the most serious problem is that of social control. The neighborhood makes an indispensable contribution in this area. Through no accident does a person obey the laws, discern right from wrong, follow the folkways and mores, and generally conform to the ethical, moral and social rules of society. He has to be taught these values and behavior patterns. If the results are to be satisfactory to society the training must begin early and must be thorough. Certain of this training must be gained outside the family. The play group and the neighborhood are the logical and necessary non-family groups for performing the function. If certain kinds of socialization are not provided by these groups the individual may sustain a life-long handicap. The great irony of the transition from a primary-group system to secondary-group ways of life is that, while the person may increasingly fancy himself a free agent, he actually becomes more and more interdependent with those about him.

As indicated above, the rural community and neighborhood are weaker and less important than they used to be. To some extent this is because the values for which people strive have changed, but it is also due to the fact that the alternatives for individual and social action have been multiplied. The nineteenth-century rural community was rather isolated due to lack of good roads and transportation. Everyone knew his fellow citizens and all were important to one another. Everyone knew from an early age what was expected of him and he also knew the punishments and rewards attendant upon his meeting or failing to meet these expectations. Recreational and social opportunities, though limited and simple, included almost everybody. The "box supper" or the community picnic were events of the year and brought an almost complete turnout of the community's population. All these things served to bind the people closer together with stronger social bonds.

With greater mobility, particularly that afforded by the automobile, it was possible for persons to spread their social activities over a much wider area. As transportation and communication improved, the neighborhood or community ceased to be the seat of or exclusive provider of social contacts. The tempo of life picked up. People's interests were extended. Help relationships became more and more contractual, and, mutual-aid relationships came to be considered, by some people, as quaint and impractical.

The sparseness of population necessarily accompanying agricultural pursuits makes joint action necessary if rural people are to enjoy institutional services and desirable social contacts. The weakening of the locality group multiplies the problems of rural people. Not only is there a lessening of social control and psychological security but many of the institutional services are lost. In many rural areas of the United States the farmers now must depend on fairly distant centers for churches, schools, and other institutions.

PROBLEMS OF RURAL SOCIAL INSTITUTIONS

Social institutions are patterns of behavior organized around what man considers to be his basic needs of life. They constitute the ground rules of a social order, and they reflect certain intrinsic social values of a group. Much of the order, predictability, and security that men enjoy are the endowments of their social institutions. All known societies possess the institutions, although their form and content may vary. Living together seems to lead men to the conclusion that a social life demands some sort of organized arrangements to define and regulate marriage and to care for children and other dependents (family); to train in the faith, belief, and ethics of the group (religion); to establish and maintain order and protection (government); to transmit knowledge to the on-coming generation (education); and to provide for production and exchange of goods and services (economy).

The family, religion, education, government, and economic organization are usually called basic institutions, the ones that are universal in human societies. The institutions of a society help to form its *ethos*, the character and nature of the social order being much dependent on them. In American society the rural population participate in the same social institutions as the general population. However, the needs and aspirations of various groups in the society help modify the organization and functioning of the institutions; even though rural institutions are the same as those elsewhere their services and needs frequently are different. Therefore, the social problems arising from the functioning of the institutions in rural areas may be and often are different from those in the city.

The Rural School

Any study of rural schools brings up a whole group of social problems rather than a single one. To be considered are such factors as physical equipment, size of enrollment, training of teachers, teachers' pay, the curriculum, financial support, and the question of consolidation or enlargement of districts.

By any realistic standard, numerous rural schools are inadequate for the needs and desires of the people they exist to serve. Some schools are overcrowded and understaffed; some lack transportation facilities or physical equipment; others have too few students or too short a term. Factors contributing to the inadequacy of schools include: a tax base that is too modest to afford adequate financial support; a "leave well enough alone" philosophy; too few students; and the difficulty of getting and retaining good teachers.

Some believe that the solution to the problem of the inadequate rural school is to abolish it entirely or at least to reduce the number materially. With something like 100,000 [9] one-room schools in this country, certainly it should surprise no one to find that many such schools are too small in patronage or facilities to meet reasonable educational standards. Undoubtedly the consolidation of some of these smaller units is indicated in the quest for efficiency of operation. However, consolidation in itself does not always solve the educational dilemma because, unless expertly planned, it may create social problems as well as solve them. Many citizens of the rural community oppose consolidation in principle, because they are afraid that the process will continue to take the school farther and farther away from the family, the neighborhood, and the community. What seems to be called for is a competent social survey in each case with consolidation carried on within community limits but with a cautious policy on consolidating across community lines.[10] On this matter social and institutional considerations deserve attention along with the economic.

The smallest and the largest of the open-country and village schools often have in common the problem of securing and retaining a full complement of adequately trained teachers. In some cases this difficulty is solved only when the rural school turns to the inexperienced teacher (new graduates), and the teacher who, for one reason or another, is a temporary (often only one year) employee. While there has often been a general "teacher shortage" since the war years, this shortage most seriously affects rural areas, for the city schools can almost always offer more in the way of prestige, pay, and specialization.

Among the other problems faced by rural communities in connection with their educational institutions are those of population distribution, those resulting from migration, and the necessity to train youth for life in both industrial and agricultural environments. Rural America has a high "dependency ratio," that is, a high proportion of children and aged to the more productive population group. The difference is significant in educational matters. Rural birth rates have been appreciably higher than those prevailing in the cities and the average of the number of children per family unit also runs higher.

[9] Lowry Nelson, *Rural Sociology* (American Book, 1948), p. 382.
[10] See Smith, *op. cit.*, p. 407, *passim*.

Even if the rural areas enjoyed the same per capita income and taxable wealth base as the cities, their educational responsibility would be greater and the financial requirement larger because of a higher proportion of children of school age in the population. But the problem is even more complex because rural America also has less than average financial resources. A rural school district may make a sacrificial effort in providing educational services and still find itself falling short of its urban counterpart.

Population distribution and migration often complicate difficulties of the rural school. Even though the birth rates are high the sparseness of population in some rural areas requires either an inadequate local school or transportation of the students over long distances. Local and long distance migration has been so heavy from some rural counties that it has caused the closing of schools because of lack of patronage. Migration also takes away income earners and taxpayers who are part of the potential support of the school.

As the rural youth approaches adulthood the urbanward migration starts in a trickle and soon grows to become a stream. Most of these youths have just come from the rural school system, but their energy and skills will be applied in other places. For the rural society this situation is a basic problem. Shall the educational program be oriented to farm life or to city life? Or, should the rural school try to do both jobs? Many of the rural schools also face the problem of whether the curriculum should be oriented toward college entrance or toward a terminal educational program that will prepare students for life and work immediately following high school graduation.

The Rural Church and Its Problems

The church has always been a part of the culture of rural America. It went with the pioneers out to the frontiers as the land was opened. While the population of the country was growing and denominations and congregations were multiplying, it was assumed that all went well with the country church. Actually, the rural church was among the first of our social institutions to feel the tremendous impact of the transition from a rural to an urban nation. By the turn of the cen-

tury the rural church was taking notice of its growing problems.
Church officials became concerned over the closing of many open-
country churches. In fact, the interest and concern created by the
rising problems of the rural church were partly responsible for the
development of rural sociology in this country.

Recent accurate and detailed statistics on rural churches are hard
to secure. However, weighing the data and avoiding extremes a
reasonable estimate would seem to be that there are about 20 million
rural church members. A large number of the rural churches are
small and this fact is a basis of one of the most serious problems of
this institution. When membership is very small the church is
likely to have a very restricted program, poorly trained ministers, inadequate financial support, and perhaps an inadequate physical plant.
Nelson states that the optimum ratio of population per rural church
is generally accepted to be 1,000. The actual ratio falls short of this
probably conservative optimum by almost one third, while the estimated average membership is less than 300 persons per church.
Under such conditions many local congregations are sure to fall short
of the objectives to which they aspire.

Perhaps of all the situations analyzed in this chapter the problem of
the rural church comes closest to demonstrating the relation between
social and personal problems. Many champions of the rural church
are determined to make a fight of it and are organized to combat any
further inroads on this institution. Ways proposed for remedying
the plight of the country church include various forms of inter- and
intra-denominational cooperation as well as church consolidation.
The union of congregations is one of the proposals for treatment of
the difficulty of the small, pastorless, limited-service congregation.
Another proposal calls on the denominational organization, particularly on the wealthier urban churches, to aid sister congregations in
the open country and villages.

Until the time of World War II there was a steady mortality
of open-country churches. An important factor, but not the only
one, in this trend was the attractions of the village or town church.
Although most church leaders lamented the closing of the small
churches, some observers approved the trend and, on occasion, spoke

out for church consolidation. The advantages claimed for the larger parishes are similar to those cited for school consolidation. The situation is not the same, however. Compulsory school attendance assures patronage for that institution. This is not so in the case of a church. When the open-country church gives way to the town church, the union does not necessarily take along the congregation. Indeed, frequently it does not. All the forces of social inertia and the latent rural-urban hostilities may be encountered. Sometimes such a consolidation leaves many farm people unchurched. The void left by any absent institutional service is a genuine social problem for a community.

If only from the point of view of the national welfare, the rural youth need to live in a community with vigorous social institutions. The social control and socialization provided by the church are therefore important. Surveys made in sample rural areas indicate that not much more than thirty-five per cent of the total population are on church rolls.[11] If most of the rural population were to participate in religious services there would not be many empty pews in the existing country churches.[12]

RURAL POPULATION PROBLEMS

Differential Fertility

Differential fertility denotes measurable differences in the birth rates of identifiable social groups. As indicated in Chapter 2 there is an inverse relationship between socio-economic status and the birth rate. Generally speaking the higher the socio-economic status the lower the birth rate. There are exceptions to this rule, but they are not important enough to concern us here. Another fertility differential prevails among the residential categories. Urban fertility rates are almost always lower than those prevailing in the rural areas. The difference becomes more pronounced the larger the urban place,

[11] See Lauris B. Whitman and William G. Mather, *The Rural Churches of Four Pennsylvania Counties*, Pennsylvania Agricultural Experimental Station, Progress Report No. 79, 1952, for a representative study.
[12] David E. Lindstrom, *American Rural Life* (Ronald, 1948), p. 239.

and the more remote a rural area is from an urban center the more pronounced the difference tends to be.[13]

The economic, racial, and religious groups which historically have provided the highest birth rates are concentrated in rural areas. Accompanying the high rural birth rates is a relatively low death rate. *Average* rural death rates are lower than those in urban districts, although some of the larger cities have lower mortality rates than do the country areas.[14] All these factors operate together to produce a large natural increase of population. Much of this reservoir of population is often "surplus population." The steady increase of population constitutes for the rural areas both its greatest asset and one of its most important social problems.

Migration

In view of the level of average farm incomes and the facts relative to natural increase, cited above, it is not surprising that there is a large volume of farm-to-city migration. In fact, this migration has been so heavy that, despite the excess of births over deaths the farm population has declined for a number of years. Of course many of those leaving farms move only short distances to rural-nonfarm areas, but large numbers find their way to cities of various sizes. Between the two world wars (1920–1940) the farm population sustained a net loss of some eleven million persons.[15]

This migration is selective by age, running heavily to young people (youths and young adults). Furthermore the fact that rural-urban migration is selective of females serves to produce an unbalanced ratio of women to men in both residential areas.

[13] T. Lynn Smith, *Population Analysis* (McGraw-Hill, 1948), pp. 208–209.

[14] John N. Burrus, *Life Opportunities: An Analysis of Differential Mortality in Mississippi* (University of Mississippi, Bureau of Public Administration, 1951), pp. 15–18.

[15] See Margaret Jarman Hagood's chapter on *"Dynamics of Rural Population,"* in Taylor *et al., op. cit.*

Social Problems Arising from Differential
Fertility and Migration

The brief presentation of the above facts serves to emphasize two points: (1) a disproportionately large share of our population comes from rural homes; and (2) a large proportion of the population born and reared on farms move to nonfarm employment and urban residence before attaining the age of 25. The problem aspects are readily apparent. Farm families shoulder far more than their *pro rata* share of the social responsibility and financial burden of sustaining and augmenting the nation's population. The population increment settles mainly in the cities, not on the farms. Migration takes away the farm youth just at those ages when they might begin contributing to rural society. This seems to be a social problem, and it is; but perhaps an even more serious problem would exist if they did not migrate.

The rural social institutions are hard put to provide for the youth of the rural districts many of whom will depart for the cities as soon as their elementary or secondary schooling is completed. Rural schools must meet the challenge for educating the large number of children. The average rural citizen, being of limited means, is faced with an extraordinary financial requirement to maintain the social institutions because the ratio of children to (productive) adults is high. The rural church may have many to whom it must minister but only a few who can contribute to its support. The rural family with many to nurture may do so only on a lower plane of living.

Study Questions

1. What basis, if any, is there for considering "rural social problems" apart from social problems in general?

2. What is the migration problem of rural America?

3. What do you consider to be the points for and against the family farm as an "ideal" for rural society?

4. Are social problems faced by rural people as numerous or as difficult as those faced by city people?

5. What factors should be taken into consideration when the *size* of a farm is discussed?

6. Can you think of some rural social problems that are not treated in this chapter?

7. Of the rural social problems that are discussed, which do you consider to be the most important? Give reasons for your answer.

8. Define the concept "neighborhood." Compare and contrast rural and urban areas as to neighborhood characteristics.

9. Define tenure. List the tenure categories. Why do rural sociologists disagree on how to classify tenure groups?

10. What is your idea of the outlook for trends in level of living for farm people for the next 25 or 30 years?

Selected References

Gillin, John L., Clarence G. Dittmer, Roy J. Colbert, and Norman M. Kastler, *Social Problems* (Appleton-Century-Crofts, 1952). Contains a chapter on "Social Problems of Rural Life."

Hertzler, J. O., *Social Institutions* (University of Nebraska Press, 1946). This is a standard source on the Social Institutions.

Hoffsommer, Harold (ed.), *The Social and Economic Significance of Land Tenure in Southwestern States* (University of North Carolina Press, 1950). Contains materials on many aspects of tenancy and related considerations.

Landis, Paul H., *Social Policies In The Making* (Heath, 1952). Chapter 2 has two short sections treating the merging of rural and urban culture and rural personality in an urbanized society. Differential birth rates in rural and urban areas are discussed on pages 524–527 in Chapter 24.

Loomis, Charles P., and J. Allan Beegle, *Rural Social Systems* (Prentice-Hall, 1950). Chapters 3, 5, and 6 provide material that may help the student to evaluate and interpret the social changes in rural society.

Nelson, Lowry, *Rural Sociology* (American Book, 1948). Chapters 5, 13, 14, 16, and 20 will provide the interested reader with materials for insight into rural society.

Ogburn, William F., and Meyer F. Nimkoff, *Sociology* (Houghton Mifflin, 1950). The chapters on culture, institutions and social change may prove useful to the beginning student in understanding some of the origins of social problems.

Reinhardt, James M., Paul Meadows, and John M. Gillette, *Social Problems and Social Policy* (American Book, 1952). Chapter 6 deals with problems of the rural community.

Smith, T. Lynn, *The Sociology of Rural Life* (Harper, 1953). A volume containing 1950 census data as well as a general presentation of facts and interpretation of rural life.   See Chapters 2, 3, 7, 8, 13, 14, 19, and 20.

Taylor, Carl C., *et al., Rural Life in the United States* (Knopf, 1952).   A number of well known persons have contributed chapters dealing with their own specialties.   See Chapters 3, 5, 16, and 30.

8

Urban Problems

As was pointed out in the first chapter, social problems may be studied from many points of view. Although there is no simple, clear-cut procedure for classifying communities around the world neatly into the broad sociological categories of "rural" and "urban," nevertheless this twofold approach to social problems helps bring into sharper focus certain important matters. *First*, it helps to emphasize the inter-relatedness of all aspects of society within the community at the same time that a wide range of types of social problems is reviewed. *Second*, it permits an enlightening comparison to be made between the patterns of problems that are presented in the discussions of the rural and the urban worlds, respectively. *Third*, this dual approach helps to bring out the fact that the urban problem pattern is more typical of some total societies, while the rural pattern is more characteristic of others. *Finally*, the rural-urban approach serves as a reminder that in any society that is undergoing either urbanization or ruralization the pattern of problems is likely to change throughout its entire configuration.

It has also been indicated that no given set of conditions characterizing a particular society or community may be assumed, in and of themselves, to constitute a social problem. Only on the basis of certain value assumptions can we say a problem exists or does not exist. And values are held only by persons—individual members of groups, such as families—even though most values originate in and are transmitted through the culture. From the latter point of view they exist in the culture, and are simply received or transmitted in various ways.

We are, however, most sharply aware of social-problem phenomena that are problems to *us*; that is, when the external, objective reality of society and the culture fail to yield us what we feel or believe *we* need and want.   In other words, each of us, in our own way, aspires to what we regard as the good life.   We recognize the existence of a problem when life strikes us as less than good in any particular respect.   In the presentation that follows, accordingly, the point of view taken wherever possible is that of the individual member of society in his various roles: as dweller, breadwinner, family member, and citizen in the urban community; as seeker after education, recreation, and other institutionalized services; as taxpayer and supporter of many munici-pal "housekeeping" functions; and as recipient of the benefits con-ferred by these same services.   To personalize urban social problems in this fashion involves the danger of over-simplification, but it should assist the reader in obtaining a clearer understanding of the nature and inter-relationship of the materials.

The ground covered in this chapter, in brief, is as follows.   First is a section relating our consideration of urban problems to the current international scene.   Next we glance around the globe for geo-graphical and cultural perspective, and take a quick look back through time to give historical perspective.   Then we consider several ap-proaches to the definition and appraisal of urban problems in our own contemporary society.   The most extensive section is a discussion of a number of problem areas arranged in terms of the major institutions of our culture, such as the family, education, and recreation.   After a brief consideration of some of the characteristics that seem to be in-herent in the city, and from some points of view are regarded as assets and from other points as liabilities, we conclude with a brief review of urban planning as an approach toward a better life for those who will be living in the cities of tomorrow.

THE CURRENT INTERNATIONAL SCENE AND URBAN PROBLEMS

Today the pervasive and overwhelming consideration that must be kept in mind in any comprehensive treatment, however brief, of urban problems is the existence of tension and distrust between the major military powers of the world.   "War or peace?" is certainly the supreme question of our time. The answer provided by history to this basic and ever-present question will have the most profound consequences and far-reaching implications conceivable for urban as well as for rural social problems.

This assertion is true because of two interrelated facts: *First*, the world society of today has evolved into a vast and complex rural-urban interdependence, on a scale and to a degree that has never before existed in the history of mankind on this planet. *Second*, the development of science and technology has delivered into the hands of the present generation of human beings a destructive force of unbelievably ghastly potency. The variety and the effectiveness of the lethal weapons now at the disposal of civilized man have been made possible by the improved technology in agriculture, which, by insuring regular and adequate supplies of food and fiber, has permitted greater specialization on the part of more people in industrial centers. At the same time, it is the concentration of life and power and machinery in cities that makes the new weapons the threat they are. If there were no targets more vulnerable than Frenchmen's Flat in Nevada or the Bikini Islands in the Pacific, the fearful significance of nuclear weapons, poisonous gases, and biologicals would be greatly reduced. The ever-present possibility of war is a major factor in the changes affecting American cities today.

To emphasize the rapidity with which the atomic scientists have produced bombs ever more and more destructive, let us see what has happened since 1945. The blast damage area—that is, the area in which brick buildings could be destroyed—of the uranium bomb in 1945 was seven square miles; by 1950, with an improved type of the same bomb, blast damage area had more than tripled—to 25 square miles; by 1953 an improved type of hydrogen bomb had quadrupled the area receiving the same destructive effect: its blast damage area was 100 square miles. The heat-flash area in which this last type of bomb was effective—that is, capable of searing a person's skin—was 150 square miles.[1] No wonder the ordinary civilian defense type of publicity, such as warning the urban householder to keep his medicine cabinet well stocked with first aid items, seems grotesquely

---

[1] Stewart Alsop and Ralph Lapp, "The Inside Story of Our First Hydrogen Bomb," *Saturday Evening Post* (October 25, 1952), p. 150.

outmoded. Most significant of all, however, is the realization that
scientific and technological progress toward maximal destructiveness
is no monopoly of the Western capitalistic countries.

Let us now amplify the first of the two key facts mentioned above.
For many centuries the kinds of goods and services that comprised the
level of living enjoyed by certain limited and privileged classes of society have been dependent on rural-urban and, broadly speaking, international exchange. Today, thanks to many things, but particularly
to the development of techniques for the efficient mass production of
an innumerable variety of goods, the "average" urban American family enjoys tangible benefits in its level of living that were inconceiva-
ble even to the elite of a century ago. But this miracle has been possible only because of an infinity of minute, individual inventions,
discoveries, borrowings, adaptations, diffusions, and communications
all over the globe. Take such commonplaces as the electric light, a
program of symphonic music over the table radio, the telephone, the
wrist watch, or a glass of pasteurized, homogenized milk, and trace
their evolution: the contributions of the inventors, scientific theoreti-
cians, and technicians from various nations, cultures, and races become apparent. Then trace back, from the finished product, to the
points of origin of the various raw materials from which the items,
and then the men and machines which contributed to its final form
and delivery to the consumer, were ultimately derived; a spot map
giving these points of origin for even so apparently simple an item
as that glass of clean, nutritious, hygienically safe milk, would show
many hundreds of thousands of workers, scattered widely over the
globe, as having contributed their infinitesimal shares in the elaborate
division of labor essential to so small an end product.

This is the modern miracle: that the good things of life can be
enjoyed by ordinary moderate-income people with such confident
regularity that they have come to be regarded as "necessities." Only
when the seamless web of organized society breaks down, through the
drastic disorganization of wars or total strike or natural catastrophe,
do we begin vaguely to realize our interdependence with the rest of
integrated humanity.

And nowhere is the interdependence, hence the vulnerability, of
the beneficiaries of this life-giving and life-sustaining network of hu-

man relations greater than in the modern metropolitan center, the "ideal type" of the urban community. The central supply of water, for example, constitutes a jugular vein which, if cut, can quickly bring paralysis if not death to the organism of the city. The same type of vital concentration is to be found in the sources of electricity, power, light, and heat, which make it possible to refrigerate perishable foods, operate fire-fighting equipment, and to carry away the wastes whose piling up would quickly clog the city; which permit hospitals to function effectively; and which run the various media of communication, means of transportation, and coordinating mechanisms without which the people of the city would soon be tied up like the fabled caterpillar who could get nowhere since his feet got in each other's way.

All these types of vulnerability, and many more, are basically dependent on just two conditions: first, close concentration in physical space of the people and "things" that make up the tangible culture traits and complexes of the city; second, differentiation and specialization of function operating in precisely coordinated patterns of interdependency. The larger the urban center the greater the vulnerability. Accordingly, as an increasing proportion of our population has concentrated in cities, and as large cities have become even larger, they have provided increasingly difficult problems of defense for our military intelligence and armed services, and increasingly better targets for an enemy.

THE CITY IN SPACE AND TIME

On the basis of a 1950 compilation of cities of the world estimated to have populations of 500,000 or more, Table 8.1 has been prepared.[2] This shows that major metropolitan centers are found in all parts of the world, but that the greatest urban concentration is in Europe.

The twelve largest cities of the world, with their estimated populations, in millions, were (in 1950) as follows: London, 8.7; New York,

[2] T. Lynn Smith and C. A. McMahan, *The Sociology of Urban Life* (Dryden, 1951), pp. 11–12, Table II.

7.8; Paris, 6.7; Tokyo, 6.7; Shanghai, 6.0; Berlin, 4.3; Moscow, 4.1; Chicago, 3.6; Osaka, 3.2; Buenos Aires, 3.1; Leningrad, 3.1; Yokohama, 2.6.

These summary data should be sufficient to remind us that the phenomena, including the social problems, of urban life are not confined to North American cities. In fact, there are four large cities elsewhere for every one found on our own continent. If this is kept in mind we shall be prevented from ethnocentric thinking regarding the problems of the urbanite in the twentieth century.

TABLE 8.1: CITIES HAVING ESTIMATED POPULATIONS OF 500,000 OR MORE, BY CONTINENTS, 1950

	NUMBER OF CITIES			TOTALS	
Continent	500,000–999,000	1,000,000–2,499,000	2,500,000 and more	Number	Per Cent
Europe	35	12	5	52	43
Asia	19	9	4	32	26
North America	15	5	2	22	18
South America	5	3	1	9	7
Oceania, Australia and the Philippines	—	3	—	3	3
Africa	2	1	—	3	3
Total	76	33	12	121	100

On the other hand we should not forget that, in terms of man's recorded history, cities have been with us for quite a long time, even though by geological standards this same period began only very recently. Although no dates on the earliest urban origins can be regarded as finally established, cities have probably existed in some parts of the world during at least the past 7,000 years, and possibly longer.

The earliest centers of urban civilization appear to have been the great and fertile river valleys or deltas of the Near, Middle, and Far East. These include the Nile in Egypt, with the cities of Heliopolis, Memphis, Sais, and Thebes; the Tigris-Euphrates in modern Iraq— ancient Babylonia and Assyria—with Assur, Babylon, Eridu, and Nineveh; the Indus and the Ganges in India; the Mekong in Indochina (Angkor); and the Yangtse and Hwang Ho (Yellow) in China. With the well-known city-states of Greece, such as Athens, Sparta, Corinth, and Syracuse, and the numerous urban centers established or taken over by the Romans we come to the actual forerunners of the modern Western city.

To stand, comprehendingly, in the presence of the surviving physical remains, to see a well-filmed reproduction, or to read a vivid historical account of these early cities is to appreciate more fully that some urban problems remain fundamentally unchanged: the need to obtain adequate supplies of good food and pure water; ample weather-proof, hygienic, and fire-resistant shelter; means for disposal of wastes; defense from the lawless within and enemies without; structures to house religious, recreational and educational materials and activities.

With the decline of the Roman power, new urban patterns came into existence. The Medieval period was marked by semi-rural fortress towns. Portions of old walled cities, such as Nuremberg, existed until they were destroyed by bombs during World War II. Only gradually did the relatively free, self-governing, and powerful cities emerge. In Italy, in such cities as Florence, Venice, Milan, Naples, and Genoa, and later in northwest Europe, increased manufacture and trade led to a renewal of city growth along with the decline of the feudal system. The Hanseatic League, which included such cities as Lübeck, Bremen, Hamburg, Danzig and Cologne, was perhaps the most famous urban organization of this period.

With the rise of modern technology—the use of the steam engine and machinery in manufacturing—the industrial center as we know it began to appear. New lands opened up to supply food, raw materials, and markets for the European city. London, as political, financial, and commercial capital of the new industrial empire, then became the first city of the world. It kept this position until World War II and the breakup of the British Empire; it was then replaced by New York, Washington, and other centers which together play the roles once monopolized by the British capital.

This quick historical review is intended only as a reminder that, regardless of how novel and unique we may regard modern urban problems, few indeed are the current worries which are without precedent. Except for such genuine novelties as traffic congestion and pollution of the air by the wastes from chemical industry, the basic problems have probably remained the same throughout history.

SELECTED APPROACHES TO THE DEFINITION AND APPRAISAL OF URBAN SOCIAL PROBLEMS

As has been pointed out above, the concept of social problems is inseparable from a theory of value, whether implicit or explicit, held and applied by some one individual. A portion of the universe, singled out as a distinct entity, is weighed in this evaluator's theoretic set of scales and found wanting. The several approaches to the definition and appraisal of urban social problems presented below differ in a number of respects, but perhaps most fundamental is the variation in the characteristics of the persons doing the evaluating.

First, to illustrate the process of problem definition by the "man in the street," the randomly selected urban adult, let us consider the approach of the social psychologist, Arthur Kornhauser, in his study, *Detroit as the People See It.*[3] Early in the course of one-hour long interviews with nearly 600 Detroit residents 21 years of age or older he asked the following questions:

.   .   .   .   .

3. Now, as you have come to know Detroit, how do you feel about the city? I'm interested in hearing any things that you think about Detroit.

4. Before we go into some other questions, now, and just speaking in general, would you say you like living in (around) Detroit or not?

5. What are the things you like most about living in (around) Detroit?

6. Now what are the main things you *don't* like about living here? [4]

In general, the unfavorable responses to Question 3 are very similar to the "things disliked," as reported for Questions 5 and 6. The spontaneous comments made showed that the highest percentages of unfavorable reactions were to the following: first, physical characteristics (such as climate, size, congestion, ugliness, dirt, smoke, noise); sec-

[3] (Detroit: Wayne University Press, 1952.)
[4] *Ibid.*, p. 179.

ond, intergroup relations (especially Negro-white); third, the city transportation system (municipally operated streetcars and buses); fourth, traffic, parking, need for expressways; and fifth, housing.

Behind these responses undoubtedly were numerous specific situations that would be defined by those questioned as social problems. But these Detroit interviews come even closer to asking for an informal specification of local urban "problems" through the following question: "7. What changes would you especially like to see made in Detroit?" [5] Though the order is transposed, the same five high-frequency categories are identified as those requiring some type of change.[6] These, then, appear to be the problem areas as defined by the spontaneous comment grass-roots approach in Detroit in the summer of 1951.

The Kornhauser study shows slightly different results, however, when the same respondents were confronted with a previously prepared checklist of the following fourteen items: schools, Wayne University, labor-management relations, activities of labor unions, activities of industrial companies, Negro-white relations, bus and streetcar system, city government, Detroit newspapers, housing needs, automobile traffic and parking, garbage collection and street cleaning, Police Department, spare-time activities.[7] The respondents were asked first to read over the entire list and then to "pick out the 3 things you feel it is *most important* to do something about in Detroit." Interestingly enough, three of the high-ranking spontaneously mentioned categories are again among the top five when the checklist approach is used: housing needs, Negro-white relations, and the bus and streetcar system. Detroit city government, which had previously come in for its share of critical remarks, moved up into fifth place on the basis of the checklist. But the item, "labor-management relations," which came in for only scattered spontaneous comment, drew top-priority problem appraisal from one of every 12 respondents when they were reminded by the checklist of this very important intangible among Detroit's problems. This twofold approach—through questions designed to elicit free and spontaneous evaluative

[5] *Ibid.*, p. 180.
[6] *Ibid.*, pp. 60–61.
[7] *Ibid.*, p. 187.

comment versus a formal checklist—may be employed with profit whenever the minds of Mr. and Mrs. Averageman are to be probed for the state of "public opinion" on current local community problems.

The second approach to the definition and appraisal of community problems to be considered here is that of the social worker, as exemplified by Joanna C. Colcord's study guide.[8] This volume follows the pattern of its pamphlet predecessor, *What Social Workers Should Know about Their Own Communities*, by Margaret F. Byington, in listing numerous suggestive questions under the various topics under which community problems are subsumed. The following quotation specifies the positive values that are intended to be furthered by means of Colcord's publication. In other words, here is an authoritative example of the value foundation on which the social worker might build his approach to the identification of urban social problems.

This outline contains suggestions for groups of persons desirous of securing a rounded picture of their own community, especially as to the provision which that community makes to conserve the health and safety and to promote the education and general welfare of its inhabitants. The outline is not intended as a guide to technically equipped surveyors engaged in making social evaluations of a professional thoroughness. It suggests rather the type of information that might be assembled and studied by intelligent citizens and citizens-to-be, in order to have a background from which to attack the problem of supplying community lacks and improving existing services.[9]

Selected chapter titles and questions from the respective chapters serve to illustrate more concretely how such values as health, safety, and welfare are employed by Miss Colcord.

In the fifth chapter, "Provision for Public Safety," Question 8 is: "Does your state law provide that all drivers of motor vehicles must be licensed? Under what age is driving prohibited? What tests are given before licenses are issued: (a) physical test, (b) examination by questions on traffic regulations, (c) driving test? By whom?"

Chapter 8, "Provision for Health Care," contains this question:

---

[8] *Your Community, Its Provisions for Health, Education, Safety, and Welfare* (2nd ed., Russell Sage Foundation, 1941).
[9] *Ibid.*, p. 11.

"What has been the infant death rate in your community for each of the past five years, by race? How do these figures compare with those of your state, of the nation?"

Another example of the value approach is taken from Chapter 16, "Special Provisions for Child Care": "Is any child-caring agency in your community prepared to offer emergency care, either in boarding homes or institutions, to children who need such care only for short periods?"

Although, as the author indicates, she has outlined

a descriptive and not an evaluative study, . . . a good descriptive study . . . [should enable the listing of] problems calling for further attention. Do answers to questions suggest that in certain fields there are gaps and uncovered areas in a community's equipment? Are there health and welfare needs of a community with which no existing agency, either state or local, seems prepared to deal? Or is more than one agency attempting to provide a specific service, without, so far as can be ascertained, a clear delimitation of function between them? [10]

Miss Colcord properly suggests that this outline and its questions could well be used by the inquiring student in his attempt to understand local urban problems, provided only that the social work approach meets his own needs.

The third approach to the identification of urban social problems is through statistical measures as employed, for example, by the psychologist, Edward L. Thorndike, and reported in *Your City*.[11] On the basis of nearly 300 measures collected for each of the 310 American cities that had 30,000 population or more in 1930, Thorndike arrived at a composite index called "G." This he defined as "A score or index based upon 37 features characteristic of a good community for good people to live in; such as infrequency of child labor, infrequency of homicide, frequency of home ownership, and per capita value of schools and parks."[12] When we look for Thorndike's value premises for selecting the crucial 37 items we find the following: "Among the three hundred items or features or traits there are thirty-

[10] *Ibid.*, p. 22.
[11] (Harcourt, Brace, 1939.)
[12] *Ibid.*, p. 198.

seven, all or nearly all of which *all reasonable persons* will regard as significant for the goodness of life for good people in a city." [13]

Thorndike's first value is health, as reflected in five death rates (reversed); for example, the higher the death rate for typhoid, the less is a given city achieving the value of health. The second value is "The educational opportunities provided by the public." The third value concerns "public provision for recreation," measured by two items. Fourth is a category of eight items which Thorndike calls "economic and 'social,'" such as the "infrequency of extreme poverty" and "the frequency of home ownership." Fifth is the value category of creature comforts: "ownership of automobiles and installations of gas, electricity, telephone, and radio (per capita in all cases)." Sixth is a measure of illiteracy (reversed) and circulation rates of selected periodicals. Finally is a miscellaneous category of six items including three death rates (reversed) and three measures involving value of public property. In spite of the arbitrary nature of Thorndike's procedure, and the very debatable nature of some of his pronouncements, his two brief final chapters, "Measure Your City" and "Improve Your City," provide the third usable approach, along with those of Kornhauser and Colcord, to the identification of urban problems in the student's own community.[14]

Perhaps it is clear by now that one may either set up his own value criteria for appraising social problems or, again probably on the basis of his own values, he may accept those proposed by others. In either case, the next step, once the basic value choices have been made, is one of means or methodology: what are the best (that is, most accurate, complete, accessible, etc.) yardsticks for converting the value criteria from subjective norms to objective criteria? Sometimes the investigator is faced not with a choice among several available good measures but with the unhappy choice of using available scales, with their known shortcomings, or else making up his own new scale, which may be practically impossible.

---

[13] Thorndike, *op. cit.*, p. 22. Italics added.

[14] In this connection the reader is referred to a related but a more refined quantitative approach, that of the sociologist, Otis Dudley Duncan, in his essay entitled "Optimum Size of Cities," published in the *Reader in Urban Sociology*, Paul K. Hatt and Albert J. Reiss, Jr. (eds.) (Glencoe, Ill.: The Free Press, 1951), pp. 632–645.

MAJOR INSTITUTIONAL PROBLEM AREAS

Various ways of approaching and identifying urban problems were dealt with in the preceding section. Now we shall point the finger specifically at those areas needing attention without actually presenting detailed supporting data on each one. Which of the problems considered deserves most extensive study on the part of the student can be determined only by a preliminary survey of the needs of his community judged in the light of the student's interests. The major institutional problem areas to be discussed are: economic life, housing, transportation, education, recreation, religion, health and government.

Economic Life

It is not possible to rank in order of seriousness the various problem categories now to be taken up, since this is always a relative matter, and depends on many things. But nobody would disagree that economic dangers and difficulties have been among the most serious ever faced by the urbanite.

What causes such economic dangers and difficulties to the members of urban families? Unemployment of the chief provider for the family, usually the father—due on the one hand either to ill health, crippling accident, or old age, or to economic causes beyond the individual's control—is the chief cause of such problems. Fortunately, out of great need sometimes comes great improvement: since the Great Depression of the early 1930's the governmental machinery of Social Security has been fashioned and put to work to help meet such economic needs.

In the upper half of Figure 8.1 are shown the numbers of individuals (in millions) of beneficiaries, rural and urban combined, who received Social Security payments of various types from 1942 to 1952; the lower half shows the amount of Social Security payments (in millions of dollars) for the various types of insurance and assistance. Practically all of the curves show upward trends for the period under examination,

FIGURE 8.1: SOCIAL SECURITY OPERATIONS, 1942–1952   ⟶

Old-age and survivors insurance: Average monthly number and amount of monthly benefits (current payment status). *Unemployment insurance:* Average weekly number of beneficiaries and average monthly amount of benefits paid under all state laws. *Public assistance:* Average monthly number of recipients and average monthly amount of payments under all state programs.

though there is variation in regularity and amount of rise. Most striking is the abrupt rise in numbers of aged beneficiaries and in amounts of payments to them.[15]

Though a post-World War II depression was widely and fearfully anticipated it has not materialized by 1954. But sooner or later, in one form or another, economic adjustments are bound to come: the spread of automation (automatic machinery) leading to technological unemployment; cutbacks of production (as markets become glutted) necessitating temporary layoffs; and prolonged strikes in the struggle for a guaranteed annual wage. Each of these situations spells diminished purchasing power for the urban worker, hence reduced trade, hence slower sales for agricultural products, and so on. It is in such situations that the contrast between the meaning of economic insecurity for the urban and the agricultural family is most clearly apparent.

Typically the farm family is sufficiently independent of the market and money economy to be able to count on good shelter and ample sources of food, come what may. But the urban family, dependent on money income for its minimum necessities, soon feels the pinch when income is cut off even briefly. For this reason the various forms or organized private and public assistance have been most fully developed in urban centers.

Housing

The concept of "adequacy," whether it be applied to food, clothing, housing, or any other item of consumption, is difficult if not impossible to define in generally acceptable terms. Housing, for example, which

[15] *Statistical Abstract of the United States: 1953* (Government Printing Office, 1953), fig. XIX, p. 242.

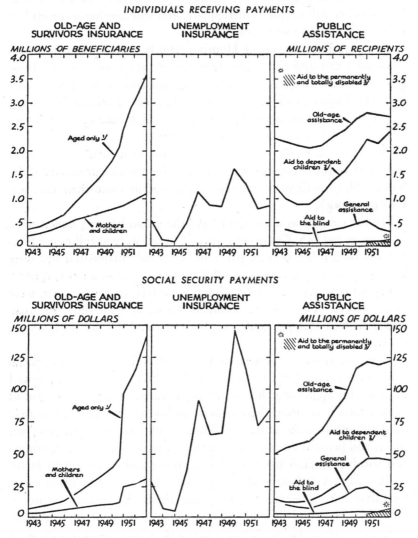

INDIVIDUALS RECEIVING PAYMENTS

OLD-AGE AND
SURVIVORS INSURANCE
UNEMPLOYMENT
INSURANCE
PUBLIC
ASSISTANCE

MILLIONS OF BENEFICIARIES

MILLIONS OF RECIPIENTS

Aged only ¹⁄

Mothers
and children

Aid to the permanently
and totally disabled ³⁄

Old-age
assistance

Aid to dependent
children ²⁄

General
assistance

Aid to
the blind

SOCIAL SECURITY PAYMENTS

OLD-AGE AND
SURVIVORS INSURANCE
UNEMPLOYMENT
INSURANCE
PUBLIC
ASSISTANCE

MILLIONS OF DOLLARS

MILLIONS OF DOLLARS

Aged only ¹⁄

Mothers
and children

Aid to the permanently
and totally disabled ³⁄

Old-age
assistance

Aid to dependent
children ²⁄

General
assistance

Aid to
the blind

¹ Receiving old-age, wife's or husband's, widow's or widower's, or parent's benefit. Beginning September, 1950, includes a small proportion of wife beneficiaries
under age 65 with child beneficiaries in their care.

² Children plus one adult per family when adults are included in assistance
group; before October, 1950, partly estimated.

³ Program initiated October, 1950.

one person, family, or culture defines as satisfactory in a minimum way, another will regard as inadequate, and still another as much better than minimally satisfactory.

The 1950 U.S. Census of Housing reports provide data by which the reader can appraise urban housing adequacy in terms of three types of criteria: first, does the dwelling unit contain a full set of the necessary facilities or is it lacking running water, a private flush toilet or private bathroom facilities; second, is it in a state of good repair, or is it run down, neglected or dilapidated to the extent that it fails to provide "shelter or protection against the elements," or endanger the safety of the occupants; and third, is there sufficient space for the household, or is there overcrowding (defined as more than 1.50 persons per room).

For the country as a whole in 1950 the urban housing deficiencies, in terms of the U.S. Census criteria just listed, were as follows: 3,602,-851 dwelling units, or 12.5 per cent, were not dilapidated but were lacking in one of the above essential facilities; an additional 1,853,775, or 6.5 per cent, were dilapidated; and 1,307,635, or 4.7 per cent, were overcrowded. These figures compare favorably with those for 1940 which showed 17.1 per cent, 11.5 per cent, and 5.8 per cent, respectively.

In recent years the American Public Health Association's special Committee on the Hygiene of Housing has been working on improved methods for appraising the quality of housing. Good and useful as these efforts have been, there is more to housing a family adequately than the shell of the structure alone. Sufficient sunlight, pure air, space, and privacy; nearby growing things, such as grass, trees, flowers and shrubs; freedom from the fumes, noise and confusion of heavy traffic or heavy industry—these are but a few of the additional factors that have a significant influence upon the quality of urban housing. The rural dweller rarely is concerned about such housing problems as these; the attractive features he is likely to have with little or no effort on his part, and the dangers he is likely to avoid with equal ease. In the past he was less likely to have electric power, running water, a completely equipped bathroom, and the other major items of household equipment that make for comfort, convenience, and safety in American housing. But with the spread of electric power and gas lines into many rural regions, these rural-urban differentials have diminished.

The biggest problem in urban housing in this country today appears to be those crowded, dirty, decrepit, rodent-infested sections commonly called "slums" or blighted areas, typically located close to the core of the central city of a metropolitan area. With enactment of the Housing Act of 1949, the importance of good housing was officially recognized; the same can be said regarding such closely related matters as housing research, low-rent housing and the re-development of blighted urban areas. How far we have yet to go to achieve the central goal of this Act can be seen from the fact that it aims to help assure "a decent home and a suitable living environment for every American family." Private enterprise is encouraged to contribute all it can, and governmental aid is authorized to assist where necessary and feasible. Our urban population continues to increase, however, in unprecedented numbers, and in attempting to meet our housing needs we shall have to run very fast indeed merely to keep from falling behind in the race with the stork. Unless present trends change drastically the prospect is that our shortage of good urban housing at moderate prices will continue for a long time to come.

Transportation and Traffic

With this topic we come to a problem that has grown prodigiously, and all within the present century. The mechanization of transportation for people and things has had a revolutionary impact on all phases of the city's structure, functioning, and modifications. Within the memory of persons now living it used to be necessary for horse-car passengers to get out and walk, or even to push, when the uphill going got too tough for the team of horses or mules that pulled the car. Today the most modest automobile manufactured can boast many times as much power to convey the lone occupant, the driver. Surface, elevated and subway trains, omnibuses, and the ubiquitous taxi and private automobile have made obsolete every American city street layout more than 25 or 30 years old.

The railroad, only a little over a century old, and the street railway both tended to increase the urban concentration. But, as Walter

Chrysler observed in his autobiography, development of the automobile brought the hitherto unattainable luxury of the railroad tycoon's "private car" within the reach of the ordinary man. And with improvement of the highway network, and multiplication of cars and buses, urban decentralization got under way. Though concentration of population in cities has gone on since this country began, the process of decentralization has continued for only a generation, now, and the end is by no means in sight. These associated processes—urban concentration of business and movement of the population to the suburbs—have made it necessary for limited access freeways and expressways to be built between, around, and through our major cities. Furthermore, the problem of providing economical parking space has by no means been solved. Partly as a result of this failure great new suburban shopping centers, housing branches of the major downtown establishments, are being built, close to the suburban market and in areas where parking space can be freely provided.

Meanwhile, most big cities suffer from chronic traffic congestion, which becomes acute at the peak hours of inward and outward flow. Discussion and debate are endless, but little drastic experimenting is being done to provide public transportation of such speed, comfort, and convenience as will woo the motorist from the use of his own car.

Education and Communication

The type of education which is carried on through formal instruction in the public, private, and parochial elementary and secondary schools during the youthful years is complemented, in part, throughout adulthood by the various means of mass communication. For this reason the problems of these two related areas are considered together in this section.

Three main troublesome problems exist today in connection with elementary and secondary public education in American cities. First are the problems growing out of the increased birth rate that followed the close of World War II. Second are the problems associated with getting and keeping a qualified teaching staff. Third are the problems rooted in what is taught, and how.

Between World Wars I and II the typical amount of schooling re-

ceived by the American soldier increased from the elementary to the
secondary school level. Therein lies one of the basic problems of an
educational machine which has never been provided with a physical
plant adequate to care for this upward shift of typical required schooling. To this type of deficiency has been added "more of the same"
in the form of a suddenly expanding generation of school-age youngsters.

Along with this expansion of need has gone a dwindling teacher
supply. While other segments of the economy have organized to
acquire a larger share of the total national income, the teaching profession has largely disdained effective techniques of group action.
Instead, the individual teacher has "pieced out" his meager income
by part-time and summer jobs to bring his level of living into closer
agreement with his standard of living. Often his wife, endeavoring
to capitalize on her better-than-average education, has sought work
outside the home in order to swell the total family purchasing power.
But the dissatisfactions and loss of self-respect deriving largely from
low salaries (usually involving compulsory three-month summer "vacations") have led many teachers to shift to other occupations.

This shift may have been encouraged in part by the vicious and
demoralizing attacks leveled at the schools in recent years by unscru-
pulous critics who claim the loftiest of motives. Along with the
lengthening period of compulsory schooling has gone, necessarily, a
decline in the influence of parents over the rearing of their children.
This two-sided process has gone further in cities, generally speaking,
than in rural areas where children, particularly in the high-school
years, are still economically functional for the family. As some of
the results of "progressive" educational methods have become more
clearly visible, the hue and cry against the schools has become deafen-
ing. More emphasis is demanded on such "fundamentals" as reading, writing, spelling, and arithmetic. In some cases question is
raised about the loyalty to American institutions on the part of
teachers and administrators who have the courage, education and
originality to indulge in somewhat independent thought. At the
moment the fanfare is about communists in the schools. It seems
likely, however, that if and when this contaminating epithet loses its
effectiveness to intimidate critical expressions by teachers, something

new will be tried; for every pressure group covets the schools' opportunity to indoctrinate the rising generation with its own ideology.
This seems sure to be a continuing problem.

In terms of ultimate social consequences, a problem closely related
to pressure group influence is that of sensational, irresponsible pander-
ing to public emotion through the mass media. This is not to say
that the newspapers, magazines, radio, television, and movies indulge
only or even mainly in venality. Rather, the contention is simply
that none of the mass media is geared to adult education. With the
minor exceptions of educational radio and as yet largely experimental
educational television, the mass media are engaged in business of
various kinds. The primary object of these business establishments,
obviously and necessarily, is to make money and thus to keep afloat
under highly competitive conditions. As a result the concern of the
educator for truth, balance, and accuracy of detail as well as perspective for the whole is largely absent from the products of the mass
media. They clamor for attention by emphasizing striking and exceptional detail. But incidentally they often build up, meanwhile, fan-
tastically inaccurate and stereotyped conceptions in the minds of the
public.

The rural dweller, exposed to urban media, is equally susceptible,
along with the urbanite, to these misconceptions—with the fortunate
exception that nobody in his right mind is misled by these means of
communication on matters about which he has intimate experience or
first-hand knowledge, such as his racial, religious, or ethnic background, or his occupation and economic interests; and for this reason it is discovered from time to time that the mass media do not
actually control the vote on election day. The problem is serious,
however, to the extent that issues increasingly involve citizens and
electors in matters about which their knowledge—or misinformation
—is largely dependent on what they have been able to put together
from mass media.

It should be pointed out, before concluding this topic, that there
are certain exceptions to the type of newspapers considered in the
above paragraphs to be typical. Almost any list of such exceptions
would include *The New York Times*, the *Christian Science Monitor*,

and the *St. Louis Post-Dispatch*; the reader may have in mind others
of their stature.

Problems of Recreation and Leisure Time

The recurrent Olympic games, and many of the types of contests
they feature—such as the javelin throw, the discus throw, boxing,
wrestling, the marathon race, short dashes, and relay races—originated
in the periodic festivals of the Greek city states some 3,000 years ago.
The theater, the stadium, the gymnasium, public baths, and the great
public spectacle known as the circus, flourished as standard leisure-
time institutions in the Greek and Roman cities of over 2,000 years
ago. The great Circus Maximus at Rome, for example, with its capacity of over 150,000 spectators, would dwarf all but the largest of
comparable modern structures. There is a long history, accordingly,
of the public recreational and leisure-time activities of a distinctively
urban nature.

But not all recreational activity requires vast numbers of people for
its justification: there is a tremendous variety of patterns of such
activity beginning with the simplest sandpile play of the pre-school
youngster through the advancing age levels to the vigorous activities
of young adulthood, and eventually to the safe and sedentary sports
of old people.

With the rise of the modern industrial city, packed with people,
characterized by soaring land values and generally by economic ex-
ploiters of the situation rather than civic-minded planners for the
health and joy of living of the present and future generations, space
for the active outdoor sports has often been sorely lacking. Only recently has the transportation revolution in America transformed this
problem into one of ample highways for the week-end exodus from
the city. Certainly there is still extensive urban need for play lots for
little tots, for softball and baseball diamonds, for football and soccer
fields, for tennis and basketball courts, for golf courses, parks, picnic
grounds, areas for sun bathing, swimming pools, and skating rinks, to
say nothing of such less demanding resources as zoos, museums, art
galleries and other public facilities for group or individual recreation.

While television, radio, the daily "comic" strip, as well as the neighborhood movie house provide relaxation and diversion for rural as well as urban populations, the fact that most American urban recreation is commercialized means that those segments of the population who are most in need are least likely to be able to afford good leisure-time opportunities. To help meet these needs various tax-supported and philanthropic programs of recreation, sometimes jointly operated with the public schools, have been developed in cities of all sizes throughout the country. With gradually shortened working hours for the urban labor force, needs for expanded and improved recreational facilities will constantly become greater.

Problems of Organized Religion

Just as the city, in a physical form, reveals by its visible features the focal points of a total society, so do the buildings in the city by their functions reflect the inner values of the city dwellers. Thus in all historical societies (prior to the twentieth century) the place of worship—whether church, temple, mosque, synagogue, or cathedral —has always held an important place, and often it was held in reverence. But in Paris, incident to the French Revolution of 1789, there was a brief attempt to abolish traditional Christian religion entirely and to replace it by the worship of Reason. With modern communism, apparently for the first time in human history, there has been a sustained and systematic effort to indoctrinate an entire people with atheistic beliefs. This effort, it seems, has been generally more successful within the urban than the rural portions of the U.S.S.R. and her satellites.

In a symptomatic way it is significant that throughout the world, in civilized cities today, the great temples of production—the mills, plants and factories—and the towering secular shrines—the skyscrapers, office buildings, department stores, theaters, auditoriums, and coliseums—all dwarf the religious structures. In other words, the basic problem of organized religion in our kind of society is its incompatibility with the secularism which tends to permeate the modern city. Religious centers there are today, as always: Jerusalem, Vatican City, Mecca, and Salt Lake City. But our concern here is rather with religion in the typically not-particularly-religious American city.

First of all, what organizations are involved in "organized religion" in the American city? Usually there will be not only local branches of the major denominations and faiths—Protestant, Roman Catholic, Greek Orthodox, and Jewish—and their numerous specialized related organizations (on the basis of sex, age, and interest, largely), but also unique local groups of many varieties (such as that of Father Divine in Harlem, or of the Prophet Jones in Detroit, or that founded by the late Aimee Semple McPherson in Los Angeles). Further, there are the inter-faith organizations such as The National Conference of Christians and Jews, the Young Men's Christian Association, the Young Women's Christian Association, the Young Men's and Young Women's Hebrew Associations, and the Catholic Youth Organization. Finally there are the community-wide organizations of professional religious workers and clergymen, such as local ministerial associations, and such bodies as a community council of churches, or a local branch of the National Council of the Churches of Christ in the United States of America, a body comprising some 30 denominations and representing approximately 35,000,000 members (1953).

The First Amendment to the Constitution of the United States guarantees that "Congress shall make no law respecting an establishment of religion, or prohibiting the free exercise thereof . . ." This assurance—that religious freedom was to be respected—was essential to secure ratification of the newly drafted Constitution. Religious differences were, in the eighteenth century, of such deadly seriousness that domestic peace might often have been shattered in the absence of this fundamental protection. Since then the proliferation of varieties has gone on to such an extent that denominational competition, duplication, and occasional conflict constitutes probably the greatest weakness of organized religion in this country today.

One of the problems created by this insistence on the importance of denominational differences is related to the fact of shifting currents of population within the city. As the congregation gradually moves away to locations remote from the original church neighborhood, these alternatives must be faced: (1) to stay on in spite of shrinking membership; (2) to dispose of the church property and relocate in a newer suburban development; or, (3) to open the doors of the church to members of racial or nationality groups other than those who initially predominated. The only course, often, has been to admit defeat by disintegration.

Partly consciously and partly through the operation of natural processes some denominations or organizations have developed specialized programs. For example, the Salvation Army and the Volunteers of America have, in the larger cities, emphasized programs of welfare and rehabilitation in the poorest and most blighted urban areas. The Unitarian and the Universalist churches, on the other hand, have tended to appeal to and to work primarily with the urban intellectual.

At the end of World War II, during which there had been an alliance between anti-religious communists and the—at least nominal—Christians of the West, there came a renewal of ideological conflict and of more widespread interest in the sources of our faith. Religious novels, such as *The Robe*, and non-fiction, such as Rabbi Joshua Loth Liebman's *Peace of Mind*, Bishop Fulton Sheen's *Life Is Worth Living*, and the Rev. Dr. Norman Vincent Peale's *The Power of Positive Thinking*, have all become best sellers. Films dealing with religious themes, such as *Martin Luther* and *The Robe*, have drawn tremendous audiences. And the evangelist, Billy Graham, recalls the days of Billy Sunday, with the large numbers he draws to his revival meetings in cities all over this country and abroad. Likewise, the radio and television programs of certain religious leaders, such as Bishop Sheen and the Rev. Dr. Norman Vincent Peale, have been extremely popular. Church membership appears to be increasing at a rate faster than the population. But whether this revitalization of religion is a temporary phenomenon, incidental to our desire to show how different we are from the materialistic and godless Marxists, or a rediscovery of the fundamentally mystical and spiritual values of religion really remains to be seen.

Problems in Urban Health and "Housekeeping" Services

The contemporary American city most of the time does a remarkably effective job through its various "housekeeping" services, of keeping under satisfactory control the hazards of urban living. Nevertheless, here are some questions of the type with which the citizen and city government should be constantly concerned. Is the water supply generous and safe for human consumption? Are sewage, garbage and other refuse disposed of in hygienically acceptable ways? Are foods tested and inspected at various stages to assure the consumer's safety? Are public eating and drinking establishments inspected to check on sanitary compliance and are their personnel given periodic medical examinations to minimize the spread of disease? Are rodents (mainly rats) which are potentially dangerous spreaders of disease and general health hazards kept within tolerable numbers? Are swimming pools kept reasonably clean? Is pollution of the air, through smoke and other contaminants, confined within reasonable limits?

Construction and maintenance of the private home and likewise the public habitation—the hotel—are regulated by ordinances designed to protect the health and safety of the resident and the remainder of the community. Diseases and conditions that constitute abnormal hazards or problems—such as tuberculosis, venereal diseases, contagious diseases (for example, diphtheria, scarlet fever, and smallpox), insanity, mental defect, dangerous or unhealthful industrial conditions—these and many more receive specialized attention for preventive as well as curative purposes. Dental problems, which have flourished in the most civilized places, are increasingly receiving city-wide preventive action by the fluoridation of public drinking water. Public health nursing and the assistance of the medical social worker are available in a wide variety of needy circumstances. Emergency ambulance services and hospital facilities, including a great variety of specialized skills and equipment, are within limits available to all.

Private physicians and surgeons, particularly the specialists in various medical fields, are generally much more numerous in cities than elsewhere. The equipment and skilled personnel for preventing or minimizing losses from fire and for providing emergency help in such catastrophes as earthquake, flood and tornado, are relatively most accessible in cities.

From this list of urban health and housekeeping services, which represents both cause and effect, it is possible to point the moral: just as the city intensifies for its inhabitants the hazards of hygienic living, so it must evolve efficient safeguards or perish.

Government and Political Institutions

With the increase in this country's population and its rapid urbanization and industrialization has gone a very great spread in the functions of government. This expansion has taken place in numerous fields, such as formal and informal education, health and sanitation, recreation, highways and transportation, and protection to persons and property. Thus the range of problems that are of concern to municipal government expands as there is recognition of need (a) for regulation or control of the person, family, corporation or other organized group, or (b) for the provision of public services in the interests of the common welfare.

But there are more basic urban political problems. These may be characterized as obstacles that obstruct the effective democratic functioning of the citizenry—the ultimate initiators and masters of their governmental machinery. Let us begin with a consideration of some of the problems of this type that stem from the high degree of geographical mobility that has characterized Americans for generations, and was even further intensified during World War II.

In order to perform the essential political function of voting, one must possess certain qualifications. First, there is usually a residence requirement prior to registration as an eligible voter, and without registration one cannot vote. Second, for certain elections in some states one must also be a property owner, and consequently migration between regions of the country, or between states, often serves to disfranchise the migrant in local elections. Even if the necessary conditions could have been met, the migrant may have neglected to inform himself concerning them. Being informed, he still may not have taken the trouble to comply. Often he has a feeling of uncertainty, impermanence, or strangeness in the new location. Or there may be simply a feeling of futility, of impotence, a sense of individual insignificance and inability to make one's weight felt.

Even if the migrant has completely cut loose from his earlier ties, and identifies himself completely with his new community, it still takes him some time to become sufficiently well informed to function effectively in a political way. He needs to learn about numerous governmental units, the issues, the officials or candidates, and the biases inherent but perhaps not clearly disclosed in his sources of political information—the local newspapers, both daily and weekly, the local radio and television news analysts or commentators, and so on. Without such knowledge the newcomer can hardly be well informed regarding what his own enlightened self-interest in the situation may be, or have a clear conception of what the common welfare may call for. Without these guides he certainly cannot know how best to vote when election day rolls around.

Even the short-distance changes of residence often entail, though to a lesser degree, the same type of temporary political nullification of the migrant. Most typical of such shifts is the residential movement outward—from the older, more densely inhabited portions of the central city within a metropolitan area—to the newer, less crowded, cleaner, and often socio-economically more homogeneous suburban residential areas. In such cases there is a tendency for one's political interests to be unequally split, his typical civic concerns focusing about the community of residence—where family, school, church, and recreational interests are centered—and the community of his work-a-day world suffering a severe civic neglect.

Frequently this type of suburban migrant is in the higher income brackets. By his moving he reduces the tax resources of the central city without proportionately reducing the need for many of the central city services, such as streets, lights, sewers, fire and police protection. The migrant's needs for other types of services, such as schools, churches, libraries, and hospitals shift from one area to another. But the physical structures in the central city which he and his family had earlier utilized may now become obsolete. Furthermore, such "successful" people are often among the better educated, the more vigorous and vocal, and in general may constitute potentially superior community leadership material.

Another type of population shift which has been going on for generations, and has yielded but dimly perceived political problems, is that from rural to urban places generally. In some of the states with heavy urban population concentrations, such as New York, Illinois,

Michigan, and Maryland, there has been a pronounced lag in the achievement of a corresponding adjustment in state legislative representation. According to one source, each of the following large cities was (in 1944) under-represented in its state legislature by from 9 to 20 per cent: New York, Chicago, Detroit, Los Angeles, Baltimore, and St. Louis.[16] The rural population in such states consequently exercises disproportionate political power with the result that state constitutional and legislative changes desired by substantial portions of the urban electorate may be long delayed or prevented.

A second broad spectrum of problems arises out of the great expansion of types of municipal services necessitated by urban population growth. A widely quoted study on this subject by the late Lent D. Upson, of Wayne University, reported almost 400 distinct functions performed by the municipal government of Detroit in 1941. For most citizens there is relatively little need to come into frequent close contact with members of the city government bureaucracy. However, the reader will have a clearer idea of the ramifications of government as a regulating mechanism in the large city if some details are supplied on that point. Here is a selection from Upson's list of functions of city government in Detroit that entail official inspections (possibly including some that [since 1941] have been discontinued, and almost certainly omitting others that have since then been added): general public construction, applicants for liquor licenses, buildings and plans, plumbing, boilers, electric wiring, smoke, signs, elevators, inflammables, refrigeration, oil burners, explosives, food, meat, milk, school children (medical and mental), sanitation, swimming pools, day nurseries, Negro housing, hairdressers and cosmeticians, retail liquor establishments, mattress factories, substandard dwellings, sewer construction, and paving construction.[17] Those who specialize in understanding and manipulating the formal and informal structures of city government are the persons who become really skilled in its use: the politicians. Hence, every so often newspaper headlines chronicle a scandal breaking into public view: someone not

---

[16] William Anderson and Edward W. Weidner, *American City Government* (rev. ed., Holt, 1950), p. 115.

[17] *Ibid.*, pp. 73–84.

only has succumbed to the temptation to trade on his political knowledge, but has been caught at it.

The operations of big government, in other words, have developed some of the same characteristics—in both challenging opportunities and demoralizing temptations—as big business. Under these conditions it becomes as difficult for the ordinary governmental civil servant as for the private organizational bureaucrat to remain totally incorruptible. And when political corruption has gone too far a reform regime is swept into power by the outraged citizens. Then when the vigilance of the citizens is again relaxed the curve of governmental honesty and efficiency may again show a decline. Without presuming to over-simplify the problem, or its solutions, let us suggest that the short ballot is probably one of the simplest and surest ways of making the administration of city government truly responsible and responsive to the electorate.

A third category of problems consists of those arising from the number, complexity, spread, overlap and general lack of coordination among the various agencies of local government that typically function within the standard metropolitan area: counties, cities, towns, villages, commissions, agencies, authorities, and special districts for such various purposes as schools, parks, housing, drainage and sewage disposal. The natural processes of urban growth, especially along the major transportation networks, result in gradual changes in land use over a period of time. Vestiges of such partially completed shifts may be observed in any American city which still displays the vitality of a growing, expanding entity. But too often the governmental structures that served well under earlier conditions linger on despite their being obsolete in the contemporary context. The "evils and inconveniences arising out of a chaos of areas and authorities . . ." such as seem all too typical is summarised by the text in city government previously cited as follows: the voters become confused; political bossism is facilitated; some local governmental functions drop entirely out of public sight; some unnecessary duplication of work is inevitable, while other functions are neglected; costs of local government become needlessly high; inefficiency results from failure to obtain maximum benefits from specialization of personnel; progress takes place unevenly; and, finally, development of a unified plan is impossible.[18]

VALUES AND COSTS INHERENT IN THE CITY

In the section just concluded we have been considering institutional aspects of urban life that always seem to function with some degree of adequacy but at the same time are always subject to varying degrees of improvement. Hence they were presented as suitable candidates for consideration as "urban social problem areas." We are now to undertake a different approach to problem aspects of urban phenomena, those features that are simply inherent in the sociological nature of the city, that may be regarded as either positive or negative features, or that carry both desirable and undesirable facets as opposite sides of the same coin.

"It Takes All Kinds"

American cities, because of the historical conditions under which they developed, may have carried to a totally unprecedented degree the heterogeneity of their populations. Since cities always have gained population by immigration as well as by births, they have always acquired persons of diverse racial and cultural backgrounds. But probably never has the range of diversity been so great, or on so large a scale, as has been true of American cities in the course of the past hundred years. As Maurice Davie pointed out, there are in New York City more Italians than in the largest city of Italy, more Germans than in any but the two largest German cities, twice as many Irish as in the largest city of Ireland, more Bohemians than in the largest Bohemian city, and the largest centers of Jewish and of Negro population anywhere in the world.[19]

So much for the fact of heterogeneity in the urban population. Does this condition carry with it any social problems? Almost cer-

[18] Anderson and Weidner, op. cit., pp. 173–174.
[19] Problems of City Life (Wiley, 1932), p. 11.

tainly the answer is affirmative, for under conditions of racial and cultural heterogeneity there are very likely to be tensions arising from majority- and minority-group relations. The fact that we may strive as good citizens to minimize the actual discriminations resulting from whatever prejudices exist should not blind us to the pervasiveness of such problems. We should also recognize that the problems are practically inherent in the nature of the city, and that our efforts at constructive action need to be based on a clear recognition of the "built-in" nature of this type of problem. If the problem at the time happens not to be acute, some type of accommodation has probably taken place. This brings us to a consideration of the types of adjustment that are most likely to become permanent and institutionalized.

APPRECIATION, TOLERANCE, AND ISOLATION

It has been pointed out that heterogeneity of the city's people and their cultures makes some type of adjustment mechanism imperative if mutual suspicion, distrust and tension, or even outright hostility and conflict are to be normally avoided. Probably the most typical adjustment is the maintenance of psycho-social isolation or distance. In the beginning, in the American city, one is a stranger. Relatives or friends may have contributed to one's migration to the city. But one cannot live forever with kinsfolk or friends, however kindly or hospitable. And when one moves to a new location he begins there as a stranger. Children, being generally less inhibited than their elders, are often the first to break the barriers of strangeness and establish contact and roles for themselves as members of the resident groups. Hence it is that as the children are assimilated, a social situation that originally was characterized by inter-cultural differences between families of adults may gradually be transformed into one involving mainly differences between generations within families. At any rate, the possible types of adjustment seem to be four, represented in Figure 8.2 by the positions lettered I, H, T, and A.

Perhaps, in the large city, the simplest or "easiest" way for members

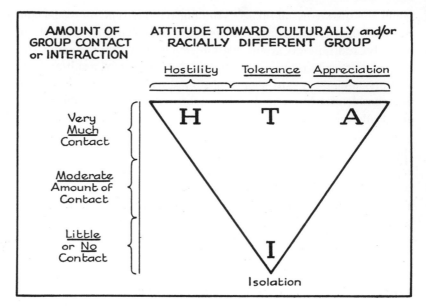

FIGURE 8.2: MODES OF INTER-GROUP ADJUSTMENT

of one group to adjust to those of another group that is culturally different or racially so, and the way most economical of emotions and nervous energy, is to maintain a low degree of interaction: psycho-social isolation, represented by "I" on the chart. With increasing amounts of contact or interaction (illustrated by moving upward from "I" in the chart) inter-group relations may become hostile, tolerant, or appreciative. Whereas these social relations may become stabilized in a continuing pattern of appreciative or tolerant interaction, or of psycho-social isolation, this is not so of hostility: somebody or something has to "give."

If relations (both type and frequency of contact) between members of racial or cultural group "X" and "Y" are represented on the figure by a point near "H," any of the following is likely to happen: (a) either X or Y will leave the locality or be driven out; (b) the amount of their interaction will become less and less (move toward isolation); (c) a favorable change of heart will take place, represented by a shift in the chart position in the direction of "A." Given the kinds of values commonly summarized under "The American Creed," unquestionably we are committed to extending the last type of adjustment whenever possible. Isolation represents the refuge of privacy for some; for others it is a major curse of the big city. Tolerance is perhaps a necessary step on the way to genuine "brotherhood." But hostility, as a standard reaction to the heterogeneity of our cities, plays directly into the hands of those who would divide and weaken and destroy us as a people.

Freedom, Anonymity, and Anomie

The city has always been looked on by non-city dwellers as the place where the functioning of group controls is at a minimum. From the point of view of the person who has been impressed by the overly restricting, inhibiting, repressive and coercive aspects of group pressures for conformity in the small town, the city is a haven in which individualism and non-conformity may flourish. This is true partly because the city, through large numbers, affords anonymity, and partly because people do not care what other strangers do. The upholder of the group ways, on the other hand, sees in the city a subtle, seductive and demoralizing force, hard to pin blame upon in any specific way, but nonetheless destructive, dangerous, and to be avoided.

Where people with drastically differing sets of mores live in close proximity, the least they can do to preserve a minimum of community harmony is to develop an attitude of "live and let live." In the course of time, however, out of the need for peaceful co-existence there may come not only a tolerance for the mores of the out-group nigh-dweller; there may come a relaxing of the requirements for stringent conformity to one's own erstwhile mores.

Another way of putting this type of shift is in terms of secularization: the gradual loss of the belief that certain consecrated days, places, persons and things—known as the sacred—are qualitatively different from other kinds of days, places, persons and things—known as the secular. Here is a pervasive, complex and fundamental problem, and it cannot be more than suggested here. But it should at least be recognized that one of the concomitants of increasing urbanization is this tendency for "open-mindedness" about the religious differences to change into an "empty-mindedness" regarding all religions.

And along with this type of conversion may disappear all feeling of solid confidence in any sure, absolute values. This loss of orientation to a stable set of group values is known as "anomie." Thus, what is known from one point of view as "emancipation" becomes, from another, simply aimless, rudderless drifting.

Specialization and Interdependence

The modern city exhibits a higher degree of specialization of skill, knowledge, experience, and functions than has ever existed in any human society up to this time. The classified section in the telephone directory of any large city gives evidence of this, showing, as it does the very many types of specialization among business, professional, and special-interest groups to be found in the city. Furthermore, under each type of firm it lists numerous specific occupational specialties. Under "building industry" or "business services," for example, will be listed numerous specialized firms. Such differentiation is possible only under urban conditions, for only a very large population will create a sufficiently large demand for the ultra-narrow specialty to enable its producer or distributor to exist economically.

But the greater the degree of specialization within a population the more inescapable is the interdependence of the various occupations comprising the total system. Hence, if any one of the numerous vitally essential specialty in-groups for any reason withdraws its services, efficient functioning of the entire complex system is impossible, and even the survival of the system itself may be placed in jeopardy. Perhaps most obviously crucial is the role of the transportation workers, and of those whose efforts supply the services indispensable to the maintenance of food, water, heat, power, ventilation, and light. Many other occupations contribute in one way or another to the long-range sustenance of the complex urban social organism.

Each of these occupational groups, from time to time, impressed by the high importance of its own services, is tempted to try to increase its share of the total economic product yielded by the entire economy. If we look on as outsiders we may say, "They are charging all the traffic will bear." If we are insiders, however, we may say, "We must improve our relations with the public, so that people will understand

why our services are essential and should be more amply rewarded."
This is why, in our type of free-enterprise economy, the balance is
constantly being altered, for nobody feels he is being fully rewarded
in accordance with his actual contributions to the total welfare. And
we all, in one way or another, attempt to increase the share and the
security of our "take" from the system. Some years ago, for example,
Reader's Digest conducted and reported on a series of studies in which
the honesty of rural and urban automobile mechanics, watch and
radio repairmen were compared. The larger the city, the greater was
the likelihood, generally speaking, of questionable or dishonest dealing by the repairman consulted. The findings are potentially so significant it would seem they deserve to be tested through much more
extensive research.

Inequalities of Wealth and Income, Philanthropy, and the Foundations

The city typically is characterized by wider variations in wealth and
income than exist in rural society. And the proximity of great wealth
and grinding poverty, such as is afforded by the big city, has long been
recognized as one of the most fruitful sources of friction, discontent,
and even rebellion and revolution. On the other hand there is a
possibly not unrelated fact: the city has also been the scene of the
great acts of penance and philanthropy on the part of those whose
wealth was great and overflowing. Here are a few examples: the
National Gallery of Art in Washington, D.C., which is housed in a
$15,000,000 building donated by Andrew D. Mellon; the Carnegie
public libraries in cities throughout the country; the Rockefeller financed University of Chicago; and the Pierpont Morgan Library in
New York City. With gifts of this type in mind some people deplore high corporate taxes arguing that they prevent those accumulations or concentrations of great wealth that permit the generous
private support of hospitals, colleges, universities, foundations, and
agencies devoted to education, philanthropy, and the development
of science. But others argue that society in general contributes so
much to the great surpluses of wealth that the governmental machinery
of society itself should function to redistribute much of this wealth

through the collection of taxes and the provision of public services, such as health, educational, welfare, and philanthropic services, and the subsidy of scientific research. There seems to be little question about the ends to be served by surplus wealth, but there is much disagreement as to the best means for achieving these ends: specifically, who shall have the power to decide just how the surplus is to be spent— the public official acting in accordance with legislative mandates, or the private philanthropist? At any rate, poverty and wealth, misery and felicity, the greatest heights of achievement and the greatest depths of depravity and degradation, all abound in the city, and probably no part can be fully understood without the other parts: urban society is an organic and integrated whole, with each part interrelated with every other.

PLANNING FOR THE GOOD LIFE IN THE CITIES OF TOMORROW

Our culture tends to implant in all of us definite conceptions and expectations regarding what it is right and proper for us to do. In the same way, the accepted modes of behaving in American life give us explicit expectations regarding what cities should do for themselves. Individuals, organizations, or corporations, it is assumed, should do the rest. Too frequently planning, as a long-range, rational process of adapting and manipulating means to ends, is regarded as proper and necessary in private life and business, but unjustifiable and even dangerous—"socialistic"—when the interest of the total public or of generations yet unborn is at stake.

In fact, unless the society is totally static—which it has never yet been in our society—planning by somebody is inevitable; the only alternative would be such total chaos as would render the term "society" inapplicable. The significant questions are, who is to do the planning, and for what purposes? The actual range of variation among cultures has been very great with respect to the ends sought through planning and with regard to the distribution of opportunity and obligation to plan for distant goals. For that matter, over the years city planning has taken a variety of forms in American culture itself, including William Penn's early checkerboard street system of Philadelphia and L'Enfant's familiar combination of the grid with thoroughfares radiating from the national Capitol and other places in Washington, D.C. The Chicago World's Fair of 1893 served to emphasize the visual and architectural aspects of city planning. Enactment of zoning laws and their enforcement for a time seemed to offer the short cut to urban planning salvation. The concept of the Master Plan next captured the imaginations of the planners as a device for bringing together in a single systematic formulation all aspects of physical planning within a city. Currently the metropolitan region—the central city together with all its peripheral communities —as an extremely complex but nevertheless interdependent entity is perhaps receiving most attention in the planning field. At midcentury more than ever before there is probably a recognition in this country of the need for more, better and more comprehensive planning in order to realize the potential benefits of city life.

But our tendency is to let things drift until they become so desperate as to demand drastic action. There is evidence of various kinds that American cities are close to such an extremity right now. As was emphasized early in this chapter, always lurking ominously in the background is the threat of atomic attack. But very much in the foreground are such problems as slums in the large cities, the gradual deterioration of non-slum areas, adequate public transportation, and adequate parking space and expressways. What must be done in the existing portions of our cities, and how best to do it, is a matter of increasingly widespread concern. But in addition there is urgent need to plan for the use of adjacent available lands not yet committed to any particular mode of utilization.

To conclude this chapter, let us take a brief look at the kinds of considerations that are likely to enter into planning for the city life of tomorrow.

First, it is necessary to ascertain the raw material potentially available for planned use. Where are the boundaries of such land? What is the area of the land included in the space under consideration?

What are its major topographical and subsoil characteristics?   (Top-soil characteristics are rarely very important for urban land use considerations.)

Second, it is equally essential to have certain information regarding the population which now occupies, and which it is anticipated within a given period will occupy, the area which is involved. This will include the various significant demographic, sociological, and economic characteristics of the population: such matters as age and sex distribution; frequency distributions showing the size of both completed and incomplete families; indicators of family levels and standards of living; and distributions of family incomes or economic standings.

The third type of consideration is this: what are the major functions to be performed in the available space for the present and anticipated population? Housing is sure to be one of the top priority functions. The needs of prospective apartment dwellers and of renters of single-family dwelling units must be provided for as well as those of prospective home owners. Close behind housing would come provision for the educational needs of the expected children of school age. Usually this will call for a coordinated arrangement of elementary and secondary schools. Then there are the various needs to be met by local community and neighborhood institutions: space and facilities to meet the recreational needs of children, young people and adults of all ages; provision for the anticipated religious needs of the population; shopping facilities of the type that are often needed within walking distance of the home, especially grocery and drug stores; health facilities in the form of some sort of local hospital or health center; library facilities and services appropriate to the needs of the population to be served; and all the essential urban services, such as fire and police protection, adequate supply of water, electricity and gas, and disposal of surface water and sewage.

The fourth type of consideration involves recognition of the fact that not all members of the labor force dwelling within the area being planned for can hope to find suitable employment strictly within that same area. Accordingly, the economic resources of the area must be considered most carefully. This consideration should not be exclusively in terms of the numbers and kinds of people for whom employment is to be provided; equally important are the industrial, commercial, and other establishments constituting potential places of employment for the labor force residing in the area. Attention should be given to their distance, direction from the residences, and to the influences of possible undesirable by-products (such as noise, smoke, dirt, poisonous gases, unpleasant odors, other wastes, earth-shaking vibrations, and railway or heavy trucking traffic) upon the area involved.

The final type of consideration grows out of the variety of needs for transportation and movement of people and things in relation to the area being planned: separation of traffic having local from non-local destinations; control of speed of local traffic to lower accident hazards; routing of non-local traffic; and maximum safety for children going to and from school.

The foregoing review hardly serves even to pose adequately the range of types of problems involved. At first glance it may seem to emphasize the physical and structural aspects of city planning at the expense of more distinctively sociological phases. The real concern, most certainly, is this: in what ways and how much is the quality of life likely to be improved for those people who are directly or indirectly affected by the planning activity? Finally, let us remember that the core questions of the "real concern" are for thoughtful people today what they were for the philosophers of Greece some 2,500 years ago: what does the good life really consist of, and how can it best be achieved?

Study Questions

1. Formulate your own criteria for evaluation of various urban problem situations. In sociological terms, what are the origins of your criteria?

2. Compare the nature and treatment of a selected problem in the ancient city, Greek or Roman, with its analogue in the modern American city.

3. Has fear of the atomic bomb's destructive power significantly influenced American urban development since 1945? Review and evaluate the supporting and opposing evidence.

4. What are the strengths and weaknesses of the public-opinion survey type of approach to the appraisal of local community problems?

5. Select the major city with which you are most familiar and trace some

of its most important economic interrelationships. What are the greatest
threats to the economic welfare and security of its inhabitants?

6. How have the characteristic recreational patterns of urban dwellers
with various characteristics (age, sex, marital status, educational level,
economic status) been changed by the impact of television?

7. What currently appears to be the top priority health problem in your
own community? What is the evidence for this conclusion? Has the
situation changed materially since 1900? Since 1920? Since 1940?

8. Compare the proportions voting in the last few local and national
elections. What are the most significant similarities and differences?
Are there important implications for reform in local political institutions?

9. Can you identify some notable novels of the 1920's or 1930's which
deal with the social psychology of city life? What themes are emphasized? Have new trends appeared in comparable fiction since 1940? Implications?

10. In what ways is urban planning either consistent or in conflict with
basic values in American culture? What are your overall conclusions?

Selected References

Colean, Miles L., *Renewing Our Cities* (Twentieth Century Fund, 1953).
Brief but enlightening review of the current problems of American
cities and what is being done about them.

Dahir, James, *Communities for Better Living* (Harper, 1950). Practical
and encouraging little book which first poses some of the problems
of unplanned urbanism, then reviews significant constructive efforts.

Davie, Maurice R., *Problems of City Life* (Wiley, 1932). Standard urban
sociology text emphasizing four major problems: housing, health,
education, recreation.

Drake, St. Clair, and Horace R. Cayton, *Black Metropolis* (Harcourt,
Brace, 1945). Study of the Negro community in Chicago com-
bining social anthropological and sociological approaches.

Gallion, Arthur B., in collaboration with Simon Eisner, *The Urban Pattern: City Planning and Design* (Van Nostrand, 1950). Stresses
need for "clearer realization of democratic responsibility for the condition of our urban environment." Excellently illustrated.

Lynd, Robert S., and Helen M. Lynd, *Middletown in Transition* (Harcourt, Brace, 1937). Sequel to the same authors' famous case study,
Middletown; shows impact of the Great Depression upon life in a
small midwestern city (Muncie, Indiana).

Mumford, Lewis, *The Culture of Cities* (Harcourt, Brace, 1938). Provocative historical interpretation of the modern city's problems;

regiona. planning approach as a solution. Excellent annotated bibliography.

National Resources Committee, *Our Cities: Their Role in the National Economy* (Government Printing Office, 1937). Findings and recommendations of the Urbanism Committee with thorough digest of urban problems. Effective use of graphic materials, especially maps.

Pearse, Innes H., and Lucy H. Crocker, *The Peckham Experiment: a Study in the Living Structure of Society* (London: George Allen and Unwin, 1944). A strikingly original socio-biological attack upon some of the central problems of urban life: the Pioneer Health Centre at Peckham, England. Emphasizes the family-within-a-community as a unit improvement of health, socialization, recreation, and morale of individuals.

Woodbury, Coleman (ed.), *The Future of Cities and Urban Redevelopment* (University of Chicago Press, 1953). Comprehensive study of the total complex of issues and factors that must be adequately dealt with if our cities are to be substantially transformed.

9

Domestic and Family Problems

All human beings have their biological and cultural beginnings in the family group. The family as an institution represents the standards of society governing the relations of the sexes, it provides for the nurture and socialization of the human infant and instills in the child the fundamental elements of the culture. The child grows and matures in a group which is characterized by a bond of affection between father and mother, parents and children, and among the siblings themselves. The family is the nursery *par excellence* of mankind.

The emphasis in this chapter—as in this book—is upon problems. The preceding paragraph must not be taken to mean that the author considers that all is sweetness and light in the family group. He wishes it were so, but it requires only everyday observation on the part of anyone to realize that it is not. In spite of the strength of the bond of affection in the family group, there are many families in which there are severe tensions, and the clash of personalities at times may be bitter. Disagreements among family members are by no means uncommon. Parents may disagree with each other on many important matters, and children may not get along with parents or among themselves.

In some families, unfortunately, the tensions become so great that the ties of husband and wife are broken by divorce or separation. Moreover, death may remove one parent or the other before the children have matured and broken homes may result. Fortunately, as will be pointed out later, the prolongation of life which has been achieved in recent years has robbed the orphanages of most of their former volume of business. But, of course, there comes the inevitable time when the married pair is separated by the grim reaper.

In addition to the problems arising out of the clash of personalities in the normal (unbroken) family, and the break-up through divorce, separation, or death, there are difficulties growing out of the changes constantly taking place in any society. The family inevitably undergoes changes within itself as the norms or standards of family life are modified. Moreover, the family must adapt to the other institutions in the community. Some of the changes that have taken place in the size, the form, and the function of the family will be briefly sketched. This involves first a rapid backward view.

HISTORICAL BACKGROUND

The family and its institutions as they exist in the United States are the heritage of a long period of historic development. Its roots are in the monogamous system of the Greco-Roman world, and in the patriarchal pattern of both the Hellenic and Hebraic cultures. The father in the ancient patriarchal order had virtually complete authority over his wife and children. In the Greek family before the reforms of Solon (621 B.C.) the father had the right to sell his children, boys and girls alike, and if he cared to do so, could condemn a newborn infant to death from exposure. He was to decide the baby's fate the seventh day after birth, and the decision was governed by whether or not the infant had some deficiency, or whether the father thought he was getting too many daughters. The father alone held the family property. His wife's dowry became his property, as did any earnings which she might make. Before his death he would designate a guardian for his widow. She would not even be given legal control over the children; they would likewise be subject to the control of the guardian. Title to the family property passed to the eldest son.

The family in ancient Rome was similar to that of Greece in its extreme patriarchal authority. The father was the sole owner of the family property and had power of life or death over his children. If he discovered his wife had committed adultery, he was free to kill her at once. The wife in Roman society, nevertheless, was accorded a position of dignity in the family considerably above that of the Greek woman. She was mistress of her household and attended public and social events with her husband. By contrast the Greek wife was practically a prisoner in her own home, seldom seen outside her door.

The Hebrew family was entirely patriarchal in organization. Wives and concubines were subject to the authority of the husband and were apparently looked upon at times as his property. If the wife was guilty of adultery, the husband could put her to death. The father had complete authority over his children—even that of life and death during the early historical period. Later on in the history of the group, fathers were forbidden to burn their children on the altars of Moloch.[1]

Christian Influence Upon Marriage

The early Christian church had to be content with giving its blessing to marriages contracted and approved by the secular laws and customs of the times. Gradually, however, the church gained complete control over the marriage ceremony, a ritual which was regarded as one of the seven sacraments. This concept of marriage as a sacrament was negated by Martin Luther, who argued that marriage was a temporal, worldly concern and primarily something for the state to regulate. In England, too, after the Act of Supremacy (1534) separated the English church from the dominance of the Pope, the institution of marriage became a "civil rather than a religious contract, but in a public and formal rather than a private and informal contract. The state succeeded in imposing upon that civil contract the condition of publicity, a task which the English Church earlier attempted but failed to accomplish." [2]

[1] Leviticus, 18:21.
[2] Helen I. Clarke, *Social Legislation: American Laws Dealing with Family, Child, and Dependent* (Appleton-Century, 1940), p. 54.

The American Experience

The family in Colonial days was strictly patriarchal in the matter of authority. The members of the family lived and worked as a little commune. The rigors of pioneer life in the New World required the utmost contribution of all members of the group, young and old alike, if they were to survive; there were no laws and no moral scruples against child labor, even of the very young. To a very large degree, each family was responsible for supplying itself with the necessities of life, including the growing of its food, the spinning and weaving of cloth and manufacturing it into clothing, the building of its own house, and so on. The economic bond was strong since it was so closely related to survival. Like the family in seventeenth-century Britain, the New England family was ruled by the father whose powers were those of a despot. Children were sometimes treated with what today would be considered brutality. Discipline was the watchword; filial obedience the great virtue.[3]

Beginning with the nineteenth century and coming on down to the present time, the family has undergone a steady but gradual transition from the patriarchal to a more democratic, equalitarian form. The individual has been largely emancipated from the absolute control of the group. Many of the bonds which earlier combined to hold the family together have been loosened. For instance, the manufacture of cloth and clothing, and the growing and processing of food, have largely been removed from the home. Education of the young is institutionalized outside the home. Family worship in the home has declined and recreation is no longer "home-made."

Observing these historic developments, Burgess and Locke were led to characterize the changes as a transition from "an institution with family behavior controlled by the mores, public opinion, and law to a companionship with family behavior arising from the mutual affection and consensus of its members." [4]

[3] The best single source of information on the early American family is A. W. Calhoun, *A Social History of the American Family* (Cleveland: The Arthur H. Clark Company, 1917), vol. I.

[4] Ernest W. Burgess and Harvey J. Locke, *The Family: from Institution to Companionship* (2nd ed., American Book, 1954), p. 22.

The American Family at Midcentury

During the century and a half following the attainment of national independence American society underwent remarkable changes, and these changes had much to do with the modifications in family life that were noted above. From the narrow, thinly populated Atlantic coast, the boundaries of the nation were pushed rapidly westward to the Pacific Ocean. The population grew rapidly partly through a very high birth rate, but largely as a result of the immigration of millions of people from Europe. The nation changed from a dominantly agricultural society to an urban-industrial one. Notably rapid was the growth of urbanization during the second quarter of the twentieth century. Farm life was transformed from a self-sufficing to a commercial economy.

With this drastic shift from an agricultural to urban-industrial society, went a change in values. The roles or expected behavior patterns of family members underwent modification. The father-husband in his role as breadwinner spent the working day away from home. Like as not the wife-mother might also be employed outside the home. In the home, because of the absence of the father, her role as the seat of authority was greatly enhanced. Children after leaving school also were employed outside the home, usually being away from early morning until evening. The employed children were financially independent of the parents and sought associates outside the home during their leisure hours. Thus, little time was spent in the family circle—a marked contrast with the practice in an agricultural family, which traditionally lived and worked as a unit with a minimum of time spent away from home.

The American family today is predominantly an urbanized family. It is urbanized not only in the sense of residing in towns and cities, but in the value system that governs its existence. That value system exalts the interests of the individual over those of the family as an institution. It makes the family a means rather than an end in itself. It makes possible and justifies the sharing of hitherto exclusively family responsibilities with the school, the church, even with such private organizations as the American Legion or Kiwanis Club, and the recreational and other services provided by the community. It encourages would-be parents to use foresight and prudence in bringing children into the world. Birth-control clinics are condoned, if not promoted, and planned-parenthood organizations flourish. Children are regarded as individuals in their own right; the parents' responsibility to the child is as important as the child's responsibility to the parent. Filial obedience is no longer the primary virtue of children that it was in a pre-urbanized society. Whether the family resides on a farm, in a small town, or in a metropolis, these values tend to prevail in our time. Differences in the degree of acceptance and practice of the urbanized ways of life do exist among various groups, but they are becoming progressively less marked.

The object of this abbreviated survey of the historical background of the American family is (a) to focus attention on the changes that have occurred, and (b) to provide a bit of background for the understanding of some of the problems which the modern family faces. We have noted the change from a family system in which statutes, rights, and obligations were rigidly defined and enforced, and where the group was more important than the individual, to one in which there is, in general, greater elasticity and flexibility, less rigidity and discipline over the individual; to a system indeed, in which the individual has become the dominant interest, and the group-institution a lesser interest. This transition has placed much greater responsibility on the individual in running his own life. He depends less upon the controls that formerly were exercised by the group, and more upon those that are self-imposed. His goings and comings are not made under surveillance of the family. He chooses his own associates—and, what is very important, his future spouse—without primary consideration of the family. In short, the type of family which in earlier times encompassed so largely the life and activity of the individual, has given way to one which shares with many other community institutions and agencies the function of providing for the wants of the individual, both material and nonmaterial.

SIZE OF FAMILY

One of the more pronounced changes in the family in recent times has been the marked rise in size. This rise during and since World War II reversed a long downward trend. Even more striking and significant is the fact that the birth rate has been maintained at a high level long beyond the period predicted by the experts. It is common observation that following wars the birth rate rises. Following World War I the birth rate in the United States rose from 22.4 per thousand in 1919 to 24.2 per thousand in 1921. Then came a gradual and steady decline to a figure of 16.6 in 1933. There was a slow rise after 1933, but the natural increase in population during the 1930's was only about half that of the 1920's. It appeared to skilled observers around 1940 that the nation had reached a plateau in its population growth. The average size of family, it was pointed out, had gradually declined. As measured by the fertility ratio (children under 5 per 1,000 women aged 16–44), there was a steady decline in each census from 976 in 1800 to 329 in 1940. But the ratio rose to 472 in 1950.

The upsurge in the birth rate during the 1940's was accounted for at first largely by the unprecedented number of marriages and the resultant first and second births. The large increase in the number of marriages was due first to the fact that many marriages had been postponed during the 1930's and the war years of the 1940's, and secondly to the extraordinarily large number of persons in the population becoming of marriageable age—those born in the high birth-rate years of the 1920's. War-induced prosperity and selective-service policies deferring married men and fathers also contributed to the rising trend in the marriage rate.

It was freely predicted, however, that the rise in the birth rate would in all probability not mean an increase in the size of the family. Pointing out that the persons of marriageable age during the late 1940's and early 1950's would be those of the low birth-rate years of the 1930's, the population students foresaw a decline in the number of marriages, therefore in first and second births, and a possible sharp decline in the birth rate. It was not expected that the average number of children per family would rise. The population, however, has not behaved according to expectations. While the number of first births has declined steadily since 1947, there has been a continuing rise in second, third, fourth and even fifth births. The ratio and percentage change from 1940 to 1950 are shown in Table 9.1.

Another important development is that the increase in the urban birth rate has been greater than that in the rural rate. While as a

TABLE 9.1: BIRTH RATES BY RACE, AND BIRTH ORDER,
UNITED STATES, 1940 AND 1950

	Birth Rates		Per Cent Change
Race and Birth Order	1950	1940	(— means decrease)
All Races	106.2	79.9	32.9
First	33.1	29.2	13.4
Second	32.0	19.9	60.8
Third	18.5	11.0	68.2
Fourth	9.2	6.5	41.5
Fifth	4.9	4.1	19.5
Sixth and seventh	4.8	4.9	−2.0
Eighth and over	3.6	4.4	−18.2
White	102.3	77.1	32.7
First	33.0	29.2	13.0
Second	32.2	19.9	61.8
Third	17.9	10.6	68.9
Fourth	8.5	6.0	41.7
Fifth	4.2	3.7	13.5
Sixth and seventh	3.8	4.2	−9.5
Eighth and over	2.6	3.5	−25.7
Nonwhite	137.3	102.4	34.1
First	33.8	28.6	18.2
Second	30.3	19.6	54.6
Third	22.9	14.1	62.4
Fourth	15.3	10.5	45.7
Fifth	10.4	7.8	33.3
Sixth and seventh	12.6	10.4	21.2
Eighth and over	12.0	11.3	6.2

Source: Adapted from Table B, "Births by Age of Mother, Race, and Birth Order," *Vital Statistics—Special Reports*, vol. 27, No. 13 (U.S. Department of Health, Education, and Welfare, November, 1953).

general rule, the urban birth rate is lower than the rural, the difference in rate between the two segments of the population is less than
formerly. We are accustomed to think of large families on the
farms of the nation, but large families in the cities in the past have
been the exception rather than the rule. This condition is now
changing, and comparatively large families are more and more a feature of urban societies.

It is becoming plainly apparent that the average size of family in
this generation is larger than that of the preceding one. This fact is
bound to affect the way of life of millions of people. It is our concern here to deal with "problems" that arise from this demographic
fact.

Housing

Until the rise in size of family, America was becoming an apartment-
dwelling population, as far as the large cities were concerned. These
apartments were designed for couples and at most for small families
of around four persons. Housing in the urban slums, of course, had
to accommodate larger families with the result that overcrowding was
a common condition there. The housing of the large number of new
families that came into being with and after the war had to be arranged on a "temporary" basis, one involving the use of prefabs,
quonset huts, and trailers. The "villages" near the universities where
so many of these new families were concentrated consisted almost entirely of this type of house, as also the veterans' housing provided by
cities for G.I. families not in universities. It would be interesting to
know what proportion of the present young population has spent its
childhood in quonsets, trailers and prefabs. It would amount to a
goodly number.

But what of the future? What kind of houses will the young families need and want? It is well to keep in mind the fact that the nation's population is more and more urban each year; it is not to be expected, however, that the cores of the large cities will or can increase
very much in total numbers. It is true that houses are being vacated
by older people, whose families are reared and who are themselves
willing to move into apartment houses or to small houses in the

suburbs; and the normal deaths of older people leave many houses vacant each year. But these houses made vacant will not be sufficient to accommodate all the new families; many must go into the "greenbelts" around the core cities, or into smaller towns.

Suburban dwelling is expanding rapidly around not only the large but also the smaller cities. This is the new frontier of home development. This is where new homes are being built, and also new business houses, new schools, new churches, and all the other construction associated with modern community life. Only in the suburbs may new families find space for individual houses and room for children to be out of doors without being on the street. To obtain such space is one of the major reasons why families are establishing themselves in the rural-urban fringe.

However, the advantages of space and fresh air are offset to some degree by certain disadvantages. One of these has already been implied; namely the great cost of new schools and other public places in which institutional life can function. Another disadvantage is that commuting to work is ordinarily necessary for the breadwinners and any other members of the family. The cost of schools and transportation is greater as the average size of family rises. By 1960 the school population aged 5 to 17 years will number an estimated 40,000,-000, compared with 32,000,000 in 1954,[5] and most of this eight million increase will be in the cities and rural nonfarm population. Truly, the housing and care of this increased child population arising in such large part from the increase in the average size of family, is a major problem.

Economic Security

Time was when parents desired many children in order that they might have someone to care for them in their older years, and to contribute to the family income. In America, a half century ago, children were expected to get jobs after reaching the age of 12 or 14 years. Today, however, children remain in school until they graduate from high school, and increasing numbers attend college. The period of

[5] Bureau of the Census, *Current Population Reports,*" Series P-25, No. 85 (Government Printing Office, December 7, 1953).

the child's dependency upon its parents lasts until the age of 18 and, in case of college education, until the age of 22 or more. This means a heavy drain upon the family financial resources, and the more children there are, the greater the financial burden.

The family is most vulnerable from an economic point of view during that phase of the family cycle that is sometimes referred to as the "elementary school" phase. This is the period when the oldest child has not yet reached the age of 14 years. Obviously the more children there are in this phase, the greater the hazard in case of unemployment of the breadwinner. Children who have reached the age of 14 can frequently do something to contribute to the family income: if the family lives in the city, there are small jobs which enterprising boys or girls may obtain to earn small sums; and if the family lives on a farm, there are always tasks to be performed which young hands can do.

In any case, however, the family with young children usually has not been able to accumulate a surplus against the eventuality of the unemployment, sickness, or death of the breadwinner. The larger family which in its later phases may be able to enjoy economic welfare and security beyond that of the smaller one, finds itself in a precarious stage while children are young. This is a period when public assistance is most likely to become a necessity. It is also the period when the household is most in need of a high income but when in reality the breadwinner is likely to be somewhat short of reaching his maximum earning power.

In some countries "family allowances" have been provided to equalize the economic welfare of large families with that of the smaller. The plans provide a certain monthly or weekly allowance for each child up to a maximum total amount. The justification for the policy lies in the fact that an employer makes no distinction in the level of wages between an employee with no dependents and one with dependents, no matter how many there may be. The wages are the same, but the needs of the families vary widely. The family allowance is graduated to take account of the variation in the need as indicated by the number of dependents. Thus, large families are more nearly able to provide opportunities for their children comparable to those enjoyed in a small family.

Managing Household Finances

It is at this stage of the family cycle that the responsibility of the wife-mother in budgeting expenditures and in making wise purchases is most crucial. All too often, the family finances founder on the rock of poor household management. All too often, also, the people who have the larger families fall in the low-income brackets, and in addition, have less education than those with higher incomes. Thus, the problem of improving household management is not easily solved. Social workers assigned to assist families who fall on the welfare rolls may be very helpful in assisting the housewife in budgeting the family income. Home demonstration agents have been working for years with farm families in efforts to raise the level of managerial skill. But in the long run, the efforts of those engaged in adult education programs must be supplemented by courses in financial management offered to students in schools, especially at the high-school and college levels.

Significance of Size of Family from Standpoint of Personality Growth

The change in the size of the family not only has important consequences from an economic point of view; it means a considerable difference in the relation of the family members themselves. Frequently the large family has been glorified as a model, where the income is adequate and the parents are otherwise competent to rear children into wholesome adults. It is a moot question, however, whether better adjusted personalities develop in a small or in a large family. The potential contacts among individuals is greater. But it is the *quality* of contacts which is of supreme importance in the shaping of personalities. If the home is characterized by economic adequacy, by mutual affection among the family members, and the environment is kept wholesome and stimulating, certainly the desirability of a large family can scarcely be questioned.

We have indicated but a few of the implications of the changing size of family. The recent trend to larger average family size may be only temporary. However, the present generation of children is being reared in households somewhat larger than those in which their parents were reared. The implications for housing, income, home management, and the rearing of children are of very great importance.

BROKEN FAMILIES

We are now ready to consider some problems arising out of the break-up of the parental pair, and its impact upon the parents and children. Since some data are taken from the United States census reports, it is important to know the exact meanings of certain words as defined by the personnel of the Bureau of the Census.

What is a family? It would not occur to most individuals to ask such a question, but to the student of population who is faced with the necessity of classifying various kinds of kinship groups, it becomes a very difficult and complicated problem. For instance, does a child-less married couple constitute a family? What about a widowed mother and her bachelor son for whom she keeps house? Or a spinster sister and her bachelor brother who occupy the same dwelling? Or a widowed father and his unmarried daughter—or son? Also, how many generations are counted in the "family"? Are the grandparents part of the family with whom they live? And then there are the situations characterized by a married son and his wife living in the household with his or her parents. Are they part of the "family," or a separate family unit?

The Bureau of the Census has had to face and answer these questions before it could set in motion the machinery of tabulating the decennial census enumerations. It is well to note the following Census definitions because so much of the data on marriage, divorce, and family or household comes from this source:

Family. A family . . . is a group of two or more persons related by blood, marriage, or adoption and living together; all such persons are regarded as members of one family. . . . If the son of the head of the household and the son's wife are members of the household they are treated as part of the head's family. A lodger and his wife who are not related to the head of the household, or a resident employee and his wife living in, are considered as a separate family, however. Thus, a household may contain more than one family. A household head living alone or with nonrelatives only is not regarded as a family. Some households, therefore, do not contain a family.

Household. A household includes all the persons who occupy a house, an apartment or other group of rooms, or a room, that constitutes a dwelling unit. . . . A household includes the related family members and also the unrelated persons, if any, such as lodgers, foster children, wards, or employees who share the dwelling unit. A person living alone in a dwelling unit or a group of unrelated persons sharing the same dwelling unit as partners is also counted as a household . . .

Quasi household. A quasi household is a group of persons living in quarters not classified as a dwelling unit, for example, in a house with at least five lodgers, or in a hotel, institution, labor camp, or military barracks.[6]

The census also makes a distinction between "primary" and "secondary" families. A primary family "comprises the head of a household and all (one or more) other persons in the household related to the head. All other families are 'secondary families.' "

In 1950, of the American people 14 years old and over, 87.6 per cent were living in "primary" families. In "quasi households" there was 4.8 per cent of the population, while 4.3 per cent were classified as "primary individuals" (mainly single-person householders), and 2.6 per cent as "secondary individuals" (mainly lodgers in households in which they are nonrelatives). A small percentage of people (.7 per cent) lived as "secondary families," as, for example, a lodger and his wife who were not related to the head of the household.

Among the major crises in the lives of many men and women is the break that comes in the husband-wife association. This is a critical problem whatever the cause of the "break," since it involves the necessity for a new adjustment. It is critical not alone for the husband and wife, but also—perhaps even more critical—for any children that may be involved. These breaks in the relationship of man and wife may be due to death, to divorce, or to the more informal "separation." The latter may be recognized in law, but may also be the result of informal agreement of the individuals to "live apart." In American

[6] Bureau of the Census, *U.S. Census of Population, 1950,* II, *Characteristics of the Population,* Part 1 (Government Printing Office, 1952), xiii.

society—or western European society for that matter—the normal, recognized relationship is that of the husband and wife living together with their children or with other related individuals. The exception of the "normal" is the "broken family."

The extent of the problem of broken homes is indicated in part by the statistics on marital status from the 1950 census of population. Of some 84 million persons male and female aged 14 years or older, who were ever married, about 13.5 million or about one sixth were either separated, widowed, or divorced. (Table 9.2 and Figure 9.1.)

TABLE 9.2: PROPORTIONS OF PERSONS EVER MARRIED LIVING IN NORMAL AND BROKEN FAMILIES BY SEX AND COLOR IN THE UNITED STATES, 1950

Color and Sex	Total Number	Normal (Per Cent)	Broken * (Per Cent)
U.S. Total	84,093,320	83.9	16.1
Male	39,216,210	89.2	10.8
Female	44,877,110	79.3	20.7
White	76,119,120	89.2	10.8
Male	35,611,710	90.1	9.9
Female	40,507,410	80.7	19.3
Nonwhite	7,974,200	72.8	27.2
Male	3,604,500	80.7	19.3
Female	4,370,700	66.2	33.8

Source: *U.S. Census of Population*, 1950, Special Report, P-E No. 20, *Marital Status*. The data are estimates based upon a 3⅓ per cent sample of the population of the United States.

* "Broken" includes the following census categories: divorced, widowed, and wife (or husband) absent, separated.

The following points should be observed from this table: There is a higher percentage of "ever married" females than males in the "broken" column: of the 13.5 million persons in this category, nearly 70 per cent are women. This higher proportion for women is due to two factors; the greater tendency of divorced or widowed males to re-marry, and the much greater tendency of women to survive their husbands. There is a much greater proportion of nonwhite persons in broken family situations than of white persons. The "nonwhite" group is composed mainly of Negroes, and the high percentage of broken family situations among them is evidence of their, as yet, incomplete acceptance of the mores of American family life. It is not necessary to recount the historic circumstances back of this simple statistic; most students are aware of the tragic demoralization of the Negro culture resulting from the forcible transplantation from Africa to America, from slavery, and from the lower-caste status of the post-

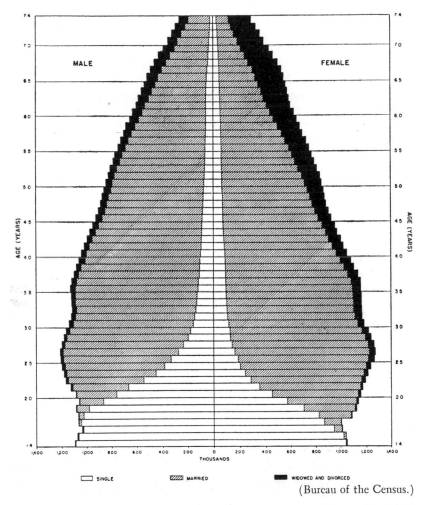

(Bureau of the Census.)

FIGURE 9.1: MARITAL STATUS OF PERSONS 14–74 YEARS OLD BY SINGLE YEARS OF AGE AND SEX, FOR THE UNITED STATES, 1950

slavery era.[7] Note that sex differences in the nonwhite group are much more marked than in the white group, with over a third of the nonwhite women widowed, divorced, or separated.

Death is the main cause of the broken home, accounting for around two thirds of all cases. (Table 9.3.) Divorce ranks second as a cause; separation is the least significant on a numerical basis. The rural farm population differs somewhat from the total population in this respect, and there also are some marked differences between whites and nonwhites. These differences are shown in Table 9.3 and will be discussed in the sections to follow.

TABLE 9.3: NUMBERS AND PERCENTAGES OF DIVORCED, WIDOWED, AND SEPERATED PERSONS, 14 YEARS OLD AND OVER, FOR THE UNITED STATES, NONWHITE AND RURAL FARM, BY SEX, 1950

Area, Color and Sex	All Spouses from "Broken" Families (Number)	Separated (Per Cent)	Widowed (Per Cent)	Divorced (Per Cent)
United States	13,499,040	15.0	66.8	18.2
Male	4,216,080	20.3	54.1	25.6
Female	9,282,960	12.6	72.6	14.8
Nonwhite	2,170,590	37.2	51.2	11.6
Male	694,650	45.9	40.3	13.8
Female	1,475,940	33.2	56.3	10.5
Rural farm	1,209,450	13.5	75.0	11.5
Male	481,320	16.9	65.8	17.3
Female	728,130	11.2	81.1	7.7
Rural farm nonwhite	230,880	31.9	62.4	5.7
Male	80,940	38.6	54.1	7.3
Female	149,940	28.3	66.8	4.9

Source: see Table 9.2.

Divorce

As we pointed out earlier in this chapter marriage was regarded as a sacrament during the period of the Middle Ages when the Christian church had undisputed control over the marriage ceremony. This

[7] E. Franklin Frazier, *The Negro Family in the United States* (University of Chicago Press, 1939) gives an authoritative study of the Negro family.

meant that divorce was practically impossible. Annulment was granted by the church when it could be proved that the marriage had not been consummated, but, in general, the situation was such that persons once married were married for life.[8] There are many people in the United States today who look upon marriage in the same manner, and consequently regard divorce as an evil. On the other hand there are people who regard their marriage vows so lightly that they run to the divorce courts on the slightest provocation.

Divorce in most cases is accompanied by severe unhappiness and painful readjustment. Nevertheless, it is possible to consider divorce as a desirable alternative to the perpetuation of an intolerable family situation. The courts have come to look upon divorce as a means by which people of incompatible temperaments, or those who otherwise find themselves in an unhappy partnership, may be legally separated in order that they may start life anew.

The rate of divorce has been rising over a long period of time. In 1870 there were only 3.1 divorces for each 100 marriages. By 1945 the number of divorces reached the high rate of 30 per 100 marriages. (See Table 9.4.) By 1950 the rate had fallen to 22.7, but in the succeeding two years, it rose again. The usual explanation of the high rate of divorce in the 1940's is that there were many hasty marriages incident to the departure of men for the armed services, and for all of the couples involved there was a long period of separation. Oftentimes, the newly married wife of a soldier whose spouse had left immediately for war service found herself after a while becoming interested in some other man. Undoubtedly the high divorce rates during the war and shortly after it were the result of the disruptions incident to the shifting about of population, and particularly of the prolonged separations resulting from sending the troops abroad.

Legal grounds for divorce. The real grounds for persons seeking divorce from each other are often quite different from the grounds stated in the petitions, for the reason that the courts must decide cases on the basis of the permissive grounds stated in the statutes of the various states. These statutes may not indicate the real reasons which

[8] The student will recall from study of the history of England during the reign of Henry VIII that the difficulty the king experienced in getting a special dispensation from the Pope to annul his marriage with his first wife resulted in the establishment of the Anglo-Catholic Church of England.

are involved in all cases. A list of these sanctioned grounds for divorce and the states which recognize each one is provided in Table 9.5. Adultery is the only basis for divorce on which all state laws are agreed. The others vary from state to state. States differ widely also in the period of residence necessary before a divorce can be ob-

TABLE 9.4: TRENDS IN MARRIAGES AND DIVORCES IN THE POPULATION OF THE UNITED STATES, 1870–1952

Year	Marriages		Divorces		Divorces per 100 Marriages
	Number	Rate	Number	Rate	
1870	352,000	8.8	10,962	0.3	3.1
1875	409,000	9.1	14,212	0.3	3.5
1880	453,000	9.0	19,663	0.4	4.3
1885	507,000	8.9	23,472	0.4	4.6
1890	570,000	9.0	33,461	0.5	5.9
1895	620,000	8.9	40,387	0.6	6.5
1900	709,000	9.3	55,751	0.7	7.9
1905	842,000	10.0	67,976	0.8	8.1
1910	948,166	10.3	83,045	0.9	8.8
1915	1,007,595	10.0	104,298	1.0	10.3
1920	1,274,476	12.0	170,505	1.6	13.3
1925	1,188,334	10.3	175,449	1.5	14.7
1930	1,126,856	9.2	195,961	1.6	17.4
1935	1,327,000	10.4	218,000	1.7	16.4
1940	1,595,879	12.1	264,000	2.0	16.5
1945	1,612,992	12.2	485,000	3.5	30.1
1950	1,693,257	11.2	385,144	2.6	22.7
1951	1,621,159	10.6	409,268 *	2.7	25.2
1952	1,562,579	10.0	437,438 *	2.8	28.0

Source: National Office of Vital Statistics, *Vital Statistics of the United States,* 1949 (Government Printing Office, 1951), Parts I and II; and *Monthly Vital Statistics Reports,* vol. 1, No. 13 (1952).

* Estimated by the author.

tained. Nevada has become notorious as a divorce mill state where one spouse may take up residence for a period of six weeks and receive an absolute decree of separation. Other states, hoping to provide adequate opportunity for reconciliation, will grant the plaintiff an interlocutory decree providing for separate maintenance and other considerations, and require a waiting period of say, six months, before issuing a final decree.

TABLE 9.5: LEGAL GROUNDS FOR DIVORCE RECOGNIZED BY THE VARIOUS STATES

Grounds	States in Which Accepted	Number of States
1. Adultery	All states	48
2. Desertion	All except La., N.Y., N.C.	45
3. Cruelty	All except Ala., Md., N.Y., N.C., Vt., Va.	42
4. Alcoholism	All except Md., N.J., N.Y., N.C., Pa., Texas, Vt., Va.	40
5. Impotency	All except Calif., Conn., Del., La., Idaho, Iowa, Mont., N.J., N.Y., N.D., S.C., S. Dak., Vt., W. Va.	34
6. Felony conviction	All except Conn., Del., Fla., La., Maine, Mass., Minn., Miss., Neb., N.J., N.Y., N.C., S.C., Ohio, Vt., Wash., W. Va.	31
7. Neglect to provide	All except Ark., Fla., Ga., Ill., Ky., Iowa, La., Md., Minn., Miss., N.J., N.Y., N.C., S.C., Oreg., Pa., Texas, Va., W. Va.	29
8. Insanity	(Most states specify a time interval of from two to six years.) All except Ariz., Ark., Fla., Ga., Ill., Iowa, La., Maine, Mass., Mich., Mo., N.H., N.J., N.Y., Ohio, Pa., R.I., S.C., Tenn., Va., W. Va., Wisc.	26
9. Separation	(Most states specify a time interval of from two to five years.) Ariz., Ark., Idaho, Ky., La., Md., Mich., Minn., Nev., N.H., N.C., R.I., Texas, Utah, Wash., Wisc., Wyo.	17
10. Imprisonment	Ala., Conn., Del., Mass., Mich., Minn., Miss., Neb., N.H., N.M., Ohio, Vt., Va., Wash., W. Va., Wisc., Wyo.	17
11. Pregnancy at marriage	Ala., Ariz., Ga., Iowa, Kans., Ky., Miss., Mo., N.M., N.C., Okla., Tenn., Va., Wyo.	14
12. Bigamy	Ark., Colo., Del., Fla., Ill., Kans., Md., Miss., Mo., Ohio, Okla., Pa., Tenn., Wisc.	14
13. Indignities	Ariz., Ark., Fla., Mich., Mo., Ore., Pa., Tenn., Wash., Wyo.	10
14. Violence	Ala., Ariz., Ga., Ill., Ky., La., Maine, Mich., Tenn., Wisc.	10
15. Drug addict	Ala., Colo., Maine, Mass., Miss., N. Dak., R.I., W. Va.	8

**TABLE 9.5: LEGAL GROUNDS FOR DIVORCE RECOGNIZED
BY THE VARIOUS STATES (continued)**

Grounds	States in Which Accepted	Number of States
16. Fraudulent contract	Conn., Ga., Kans., Ky., Ohio, Okla., Pa., Wash.	8
17. Absence	(Most states specify a time interval of from one to seven years.) Conn., Mich., N.H., Ohio, R.I., Tenn., Vt.	7
18. Infamous crime	Ala., Conn., Del., La., N.C., Va., Tenn.	7
19. Relationship within prohibited degree	Fla., Ga., Miss., Pa.	4
20. Felony before marriage	Ariz., Mo., Wyo.	3
21. Loathsome disease	Ill., Ky.	2
22. Other grounds *	Del., Fla., Ky., La., Miss., N.H., N.Y., Ohio, R.I., Tenn., Vt., Va., Wyo.	13

Source: *The Book of the States*, 1952–53 (Chicago: Council of State Governments, 1952). Data furnished by the Womens' Bureau, U.S. Department of Labor. See also, Earl Lyman Koos, *Marriage* (Holt, 1953), pp. 332–333.

* Other grounds include underage, insanity at time of marriage, joining a religious sect not believing in marriage, "Enoch Arden" laws, other gross misbehavior, etc. There were 12 other grounds listed.
Total number of different grounds, 33.

Characteristics of the divorced. The divorced persons are predominantly in the younger age groups. An analysis of the 1950 census data revealed the modal age to be from 35 to 50, with one fourth of all divorced males and 30 per cent of divorced females under 35. Another way of stating the problem is to compute the divorce rate by duration of marriage. Jacobson found, for example, that the divorce rate was highest for those who had been married for a shorter time than five years, and that as the duration of marriage increased the divorce rate declined steadily.[9]

Since it is among the younger families that divorce is most frequent, the likelihood of minor children being involved is very great. On this point, Jacobson found that in 421,000 divorces in 1948, about 313,000

[9] Paul H. Jacobson, "Differentials in Divorce by Duration of Marriage and Size of Family," in Robert F. Winch and Robert McGinnis, *Marriage and the Family* (Holt, 1953), p. 522.

children under 21 years of age were involved.[10]   That it is a critical experience for children is readily appreciated.   It is especially serious in communities where the mores are strongly set against divorce, and where divorce is looked upon not only as a tragedy, but as an unnecessary—even irresponsible—step for married people to take.

As pointed out by Burgess and Locke, the crisis of divorce may be different for "educated and sophisticated" persons, at least superficially.[11]   The writer knows of a case in which two couples, thought of by the community as happily married, rather suddenly found themselves facing divorce because one of the two men had fallen in love with the other man's wife and she with him.   Three minor children were involved in one family and two in the other.   The situation was discussed quite rationally both by all four adults and by them with the children.   The eldest of the five children involved was 13 years old. It was hardest for her to adjust, but she went with her mother who entered one of the universities after her divorce and did graduate work.   She finally made a professional career for herself.   The transition to this new life must have been difficult for all concerned, but at least, on the surface, it was made with a degree of rationality and emotional maturity that seldom characterizes such adjustments.

Reducing the divorce rate. The rate of divorce existing today raises serious questions as to ways of reducing it.   In this matter, the students of the subject stress prevention of unhappy marriages by better preparation of young people for the responsibilities of marriage and family life.   A vast amount of research has been done aimed at finding certain criteria which might guide young people in the wise selection of mates and thus help to ensure happy marriages.[12]

Other approaches to the problem of reducing the divorce rate include the following: (1) legal reform; (2) family counseling; (3) individual therapy, for those cases in which pathological persons are involved.   Legal reform has two aspects.   First is the proposal to make divorces more difficult to obtain, and the other is to establish uniform divorce laws for all the states.   It would seem to be futile to try to get

[10] *Ibid.*, p. 523.

[11] Burgess and Locke, *op. cit.*, p. 638.

[12] The pioneer study and the most widely known is by E. W. Burgess and Leonard S. Cottrell, Jr., *Predicting Success in Marriage* (Prentice-Hall, 1939). See also the bibliography, Earl Lemon Koos, *Marriage* (Holt, 1953), pp. 406 ff.

the individual states to approve uniform standards as regards such things as length of residence, and the admissible grounds for divorce. In any case, persons who are bent upon getting a divorce will go to extreme legal lengths to obtain it, even if it means residence in a foreign country. Also with little likelihood of attainment is a uniform federal law which would be acceptable to all the states. And after all is said and done, how potent are the legal strictures against divorce in keeping couples together in a state of unhappiness? It is difficult to prove that the degree of strictness of the laws is an important factor.

A possibly and potentially much more important attack on the problem can be made through family counseling agencies. However, William J. Goode calls attention to the following limitations of this measure:

1. Now and for decades to come, there will be few . . . experts to take care of the flood of cases. A conservative estimate of the number of cases would be no fewer than 1,500,000 each year, for the number of actual divorces will fluctuate about the figure of half a million a year.
2. A large proportion of the cases will not come to any counseling organization.
3. Those who do come will be a select group, composed of white-collar classes, those dedicated to self-help, and in general those whose cases are more amenable to therapy.
4. While the experts are attempting to help the proportionally small number of cases with which they can deal, nothing is being done about the society itself which produces individuals unable to be happy in marriage . . .[13]

Goode goes on to assign only limited value to individual therapy, inasmuch as it is applicable only in those cases in which one of the individuals can be helped by psychiatric and similar treatment.

It is often emphasized, and must be underscored here again, that much more research is needed on the factors that produce tension that develop into the break-up of families via the divorce or separation route. Only with a richer body of knowledge available can family counseling, courses in education for marriage and family life, and the

---

[13] William J. Goode, "Social Engineering and The Divorce Problem," *The Annals of the American Academy of Political and Social Science* (November, 1950), p. 87.

prediction of success in marriage be placed upon a substantial and factual basis.

Separation

Reference again to Table 9.3 reveals the following statistical facts regarding "separation" among American people as of 1950: (1) persons "separated" made up 15 per cent of all persons living in broken-family situations; (2) among nonwhites (who are overwhelmingly Negroes) the proportion in this category was 37.2 per cent—46 per cent for the males and 33 per cent for the females; thus the nonwhite group was much more concentrated in this category than the whites.

The reasons for the existence of this class of broken families—in addition to those resulting from divorce and death—is that "divorced" and "separated" represent two very different status situations. "Separated" persons may not re-marry. Unless the situation has been recognized by a court, the responsibility for maintenance of the family may be avoided by the husband.

It is sometimes called the "poor man's divorce," since it costs nothing for a couple to agree to separate and go their respective ways. Little information is available regarding "separated" persons, as compared with that regarding the divorced and widowed. As a means of effecting permanent separation where both parties are agreed to the arrangement, it may be as satisfactory as if it were legally sanctioned. However, since in separations of couples there is usually property as well as children involved, a court decree governing the responsibilities and rights of the respective parties is, in the long run, the most satisfactory arrangement.

Widowhood

The normal family may be "broken" not only by the divorce or separation of the husband and wife, but also by the death of one or both parents. Fortunately the gradual improvement in health conditions and the rising expectation of life make it possible for husband and wife to have a longer period of married life together, with larger proportions of married couples reaching the "empty nest" stage of the family before the death of one or the other. According to the Metropolitan Life Insurance calculations, "at the beginning of the century, marriages were broken by the death of the husband at a rate of about 28 per 1,000 per year. The reduction in mortality since then has brought this rate down to 18 per 1,000 . . . Currently, about 660,000 marriages are broken by death each year. In two thirds of these families the wife is the surviving spouse. Fifty years ago the corresponding proportion was close to one half." [14]

Two thirds of all persons in the United States in 1950 who were living under broken-family conditions were classified as "widowed." (See Table 9.3.) There was a considerable difference, however, in the proportions of men and women in this category. Of the total number of slightly over 9 million widowed persons, 6,736,000 were women. In 1940, there were only twice as many widows as there were widowers. The reasons for the larger numbers of widows are in the main as follows: (1) women are on the average two or three years younger than their husbands; (2) women have a longer life expectancy, and consequently tend to outlive their husbands even if they are of the same age; and (3) men are more likely than women to re-marry.[15]

Thus, from a statistical standpoint, the problem of the widowed is largely a problem for the aged woman. It is perhaps fair to say, however, that from the standpoint of individuals the adjustment of a surviving husband is a more serious matter than that of a surviving wife. Many aged widows can live in separate quarters and care for themselves, whereas an aged widower is likely to need someone to cook for him, and provide him with general care. Moreover, the aged mother is more likely to be invited to live in the family of a son or daughter, because she can be very useful in the household and pay her way in services rendered in the home. In many cases of broken families, the grandmother has been able to help tide children over the

[14] Metropolitan Life Insurance Company, *Statistical Bulletin*, 34, No. 9 (September, 1953), 1 ff.

[15] The greater tendency of men than women to re-marry after being divorced is also generally assumed. There is little data on the question. However, information is available from 14 states. In 1950, in these states, about one fifth of all marriages were cases of remarriage. See *Vital Statistics-Special Reports*, vol. 37, No. 5 (December 16, 1952).

difficult period of adjustment. Many an American war widow with her child or children went back to the parental roof for at least temporary refuge. Of course, in these cases, the role of the grandfather was also often important. But in the second half of the twentieth century many grandmothers of advanced years are caring for children born during the hectic years of war and postwar years—children who suffered the loss of one or both parents through death, divorce, or separation.

The problem for many aged widows and widowers is one of loneliness. Though not a common thing as yet there is some evidence of a trend among aged people to counteract this loneliness by forming associations among themselves. Many of the Townsend Clubs formed during the depression of the 1930's continue to carry on, with greater emphasis on gatherings for sociability than for political discussion. Little attention has been given in the past to the development of community facilities of any sort for the aged. However, most of the states are taking note of the growing number of their "senior citizens" and are developing policies to cope with the problems they present. Living arrangements constitute one of the most urgent of these problems.[16]

To sum up, widowhood is as inevitable as death to one or the other of the married pair. It is far more likely to be the lot of the wife than of the husband. The lengthened expectation of life has greatly reduced the chances of dependent children surviving the death of a parent. War, of course, has been a cause of orphanage. In many such cases grandparents have taken on the burdens of rearing a second family. The problems of aged widows and widowers are the problems largely of the aged in general. Since the aged parents are not commonly quartered with their children in present-day America, the extra-familial care of the widowed aged is a responsibility which is coming to be accepted more and more by the community, State and Nation.

[16] For a discussion of social organization for the aged, see, Irving L. Webber, "The Organized Social Life of the Retired: Two Florida Communities," *The American Journal of Sociology*, LIX, No 4 (January, 1954), 340 ff. This number also contains eleven other articles on problems of "Aging and Retirement."

CONCLUSION

In this chapter we have reviewed some of the problems of the family in mid-century America. We pointed out that in the two thousand or more years of evolution of Western society, the family, too, has undergone many changes. Once the center, not only of those activities having to do with reproduction and the nurture of infants, but also of the many economic, educational, and social activities, the family in the twentieth century has surrendered many of its one-time functions to institutions and organizations outside itself. Today the central fact about the American family is that it is dedicated to the goal of making a happy life for its members through companionship and mutual affection of parents and of children.

Today the family shares with the church, with the school, and with numerous other local organizations and institutions within the community, the problems of rearing children and of supplying the basic necessities of existence. This steady transfer of functions to the larger community has created many problems of adjustment. The very fact of this transfer implies the growth of a vast number of organizations and institutions which form so prominent a feature of contemporary American life. The number of organizations in even a small community may run to a hundred or several hundred. Such organizations have to be supported by individuals all of whom are members of families. Some families, more than others, participate in these organizations, and for high participating families, the calls upon the members in time, effort, and also in money are very exacting. Many a person may be heard to complain that he or she never has time or opportunity to spend an evening at home. Thus the growing complexity of modern society has many implications for the role of the family in the community.

Realization of this growing complexity has led many people to fear that the family may decline and lose its real significance as a stabilizing force in our civilization. It is too early for any man to pass a judgment as to the consequences of this trend, but it is well to keep in mind that the bond that holds the family together, is, in the last analysis, the bond of affection. This bond might possibly even be strengthened by the opportunities a rich and varied community life offers the members of the family to enlarge and multiply their contacts outside the home. They may thus escape temporarily from any annoying frictions that develop, and return regenerated and fortified with better perspective and greater appreciation of their home and family ties. Certainly there is no real evidence to support the hypothesis that family ties are weaker today than they were in some past time. On the contrary, there is reason to think that they are actually stronger. Much has been said about what is wrong with the family; too little, possibly, has been said about what is right with it. The outlook for the American family as a source of happiness for its members is today more promising than it has ever been.

Study Questions

1. Describe and evaluate the program of the Home Economics Extension Service in training rural housewives to handle finances more effectively.

2. Write the history of the changes in divorce laws of your state since the adoption of its State Constitution.

3. Should the laws governing divorce be made more strict? Discuss arguments pro and con. Is a federal uniform divorce law desirable? What are the arguments for and against?

4. Should the United States consider following Canada's lead in establishing a system of family allowances? Give reasons for and against.

5. With the rapid growth in population more and more families must find places to live outside the built-up areas. Discuss the implications for satisfactory family life of suburban residence and of commuting to work.

6. Discuss and evaluate the various explanations for the rise in the birth rate—demographic, economic, social, and military.

7. Is a small or a large family to be preferred? Poll the class or other sample of students for opinions as to the optimum number of children they consider desirable, in general and for themselves.

8. Juvenile delinquents come in greater proportion from broken homes. What explanations may account for this fact?

9. Since the management of household finances is so important, how do you account for the comparatively low enrollment of girls in courses in household management?

10. Interview a number of veterans who married before entering mili-

tary service. What problems of adjustment did they have during military service and after returning home?

11. Interview a number of people at various age levels regarding their attitude toward divorce. Try to determine whether the attitude of the community is changing and in what direction?

12. A question not discussed in this chapter but which may be dealt with in class discussion is one dealing with that portion of the population that never marries. What are the problems of single men? Of single women?

Selected References

Baber, Ray E., *Marriage and the Family* (rev. ed., McGraw-Hill, 1953). A long-time favorite textbook, with good coverage of "problems."

Burgess, Ernest W., and Harvey J. Locke, *The Family* (rev. ed., American Book, 1954). A standard textbook on the family in general. The seven chapters in Part IV dealing with "Family Disorganization and Reorganization" are especially valuable for purposes of this chapter.

Christensen, Harold T., *Marriage Analysis* (Ronald, 1950). Emphasizes factors important in establishing stability in family life.

Hill, Reuben, *Families Under Stress* (Harper, 1949). The standard work on the problems of young families resulting from the war.

Konarovsky, Mirra, *The Unemployed Man and His Family* (Dryden, 1940). How economic crisis may affect family relations.

Koos, Earl Loman, *Marriage* (Holt, 1953). Readable with much personal history documentation. Chapters 15–18 deal with family disruption and adjustment problems. Excellent bibliographies in each chapter.

Landis, Judson T. and Mary G., *Building a Successful Marriage* (Prentice-Hall, 1948). Emphasis is on the considerations that help to obviate unhappiness and failure.

Locke, Harvey J., *Predicting Adjustment in Marriage* (Holt, 1950). Factors and characteristics of persons and situations associated with success and failure in marriage.

Skidmore, Rex, and Anton Cannon, *Building Your Marriage* (Harper, 1950). A book excellent for the abundance of illustrative experience documents.

Winch, Robert F., and Robert McGinnis, *Selected Studies in Marriage and the Family* (Holt, 1953). A carefully chosen group of "readings." Chapters 7, 8, 9, and 10 deal with relationships among family members; Chapter 18 is on family dissolution.

Waller, Willard (as revised by Reuben Hill), *The Family: A Dynamic Interpretation* (Dryden, 1951). Chapter 22 on adjustment after bereavement, and Chapters 23 and 24 deal with adjustment after divorce.

Economic Problems

Economic problems are among the most serious ones that must be faced by a sizeable portion of the American people. Certain conditions in the economic aspects of life persist to such an extent as to constitute problems for the total society. It is these situations that are of particular concern to the sociologist. Historically, these problems have been poverty, dependency, low levels of living, insecurity, unemployment, and, more recently, problems related to fluctuations in the business cycle. A considerable part of the study that has been made of these problems has been concerned with the magnitude of the situations and the plight of the individuals who are directly concerned. Few of the researchers have attempted to view the problem from the standpoint of the total societal structure. In this chapter, an attempt is made to relate difficulties in the operation of the business and economic system both to the individual and to the society in general.

In order to comprehend fully the problems that are apparent in the economic order of the United States, the student must be cognizant of the nature of the system which has been developed in this country. This is necessary because societies possessing economic systems of a different type are not faced with the same problems as those currently existing in the United States. For example, a simple, agricultural economy is not likely to have severe depressions due to an oversupply of goods which cannot be sold on the open market. Most likely, crises in that type of economy result from the operation of some natural phenomena, such as a failure of the crops brought on by drought, flood, or pestilence.

THE CAPITALISTIC SYSTEM

There is much talk presently about capitalism, communism, democracy, facism, Nazism, totalitarianism, and socialism. Each of these terms is descriptive either of an economic or a governmental system. In some cases, it is very difficult to separate one from the other. In all of them, government is used to some extent as a regulatory device in controlling the operation of the economy. There are many arguments as to the proper function of government in regulating the economic aspects of a society, and many of the conflicts of ideologies which exist in the modern world center around this issue. Although no modern society has developed an economy completely unregulated by government, the system of the United States traditionally has been one in which government regulation has been kept to the minimum necessary to prevent widespread human suffering that might result from the free operation of economic forces. This kind of economy is designated most frequently as capitalism or as a free-enterprise economy.

The basic principles of a capitalistic economic system are freedom of enterprise, private property, freedom of exchange, and freedom of contract. Freedom of enterprise means that the responsibility of making economic decisions regarding production, distribution, and consumption is placed primarily upon the individual. Private property is the right of the individual to possess objects (goods, commodities, land, and so forth) and to use them as he pleases so long as such use does not violate the established law. Freedom of exchange is the right to transfer goods and services without duress between individuals or groups of individuals for what is considered by the parties concerned as an adequate payment for the things which are transferred. Freedom of contract means that the individual is not restricted in his right to enter into agreement with his fellowman and to expect that the agreement will be honored by all parties concerned. In a capitalistic economy, these principles are subject to a minimum of restriction by the authority of the state.

The motivations that keep a capitalistic economy in action are profits, interest, wages and salaries, and rent. They provide the incentive needed to make society dynamic, and they keep the economy in operation at a high level of activity. Without these motivations, the economy would stagnate and disintegrate.

The principal mechanism that regulates the operation of a capitalistic economy is competition among sellers in a free market. This factor keeps prices in a reasonable relationship to costs and also protects the ultimate consumer by assuring him a fair price and acceptable quality in the goods and commodities which he purchases. In areas in which economic competition does not obtain, such as in the case of public utilities and monopoly, governmental action has been used to maintain prices related to costs, to establish a reasonable margin of profit, and to assure an acceptable quality or, in the case of monopoly, to restore a competitive market.

PROBLEMS OF THE BUSINESS CYCLE

A free enterprise system such as is outlined above does not operate on an even, level plane. Instead, it proceeds through periods of intensified activity to periods of slack activity and again to intensified activity. The peaks of production and the depths of business stagnation have become known as prosperity and depression, respectively. "Boom and bust" is another phrase which has been used to describe these movements in business activity. The tendency of the economy to fluctuate in business intensity is more properly designated by the term "business cycles." This phenomenon is of extreme importance to the people of the United States. Individually, it means that during periods of depression thousands of persons suffer losses of goods and possessions which they have spent a lifetime in acquiring. Other thousands are forced into the depths of poverty and must undergo the social evils associated with that condition. The business cycle, therefore, tends to make the problems of individual economic security of much greater magnitude than they would be otherwise. For the society as a whole, these fluctuations in business mean that during depression periods the nation is greatly weakened in its ability to deal with foreign affairs, and domestic problems become greatly intensified. In the struggle between ideologies now taking place in the world— communism versus capitalism—the former might be able to gain an upper hand in a depression period. Desperate people are usually much more susceptible to new and strange ideologies, since these tend to hold out hope that the immediate difficult situation may be alle· viated by their adoption. In this sense, a "boom and bust" economy represents a threat to our democratic American way of life.

Business Fluctuations in the United States

Evidence seems to indicate that the phenomena of business cycles have been a part of the economy of the United States since its beginning, even though they were not recognized as such until later years. People were cognizant of financial depressions and periods of prosperity, but they did not attribute any cyclical movement to them. Apparently they assumed that the economy operated at a fixed level from which unusual national and world events might cause an abrupt change. Thus financial panics and unusual prosperity were merely considered deviations from a normal level of economic activity and were related to national and international events, but not necessarily to each other. Attention was focused on crises, panics, and depressions, but industry, commerce, finance, and general business were not conceived as moving in cycles. However, as statisticians began to deal more and more with economic phenomena, they reached the conclusion that business does not operate at a fixed level only to be thrown into panics and depressions from time to time and more or less suddenly.[1] The statistics instead demonstrated that business and industry proceed in a series of more or less rhythmic cycles or waves. These wavelike movements may be observed in the production of basic materials such as pig iron and coal, in the volume of manufactured products, in the quantity of freight transported by railroads, in wholesale and retail commodity prices, in fluctuation in wage rates, and in other business activities. Similar observations may be

[1] Frederick Garver and Alvin H. Hanson, *Principles of Economics* (rev. ed., Ginn, 1937), p. 348.

made on the stock market in the prices of stocks and bonds and in the volume of sales of securities. The movement of loans, commercial-paper rates, call-loan rates, bank clearing, liabilities of business failure, deposits, and reserves also follow a pattern indicative of the existence of cycles. It appears, therefore, that the entire scope of business activities moves in cycles and that the component changes are somehow related to one another.[2]

A survey of American business activity since 1790 indicates that there has been a series of wavelike movements in which the economy has risen to a level of prosperity only to subside once again into crisis and depression. Figure 10.1 graphically presents these movements in American business activity since 1790. A study of this graph shows that twenty-two periods are identified as depressions and twenty-one periods are identified as years of prosperity. These periods bear names which generally indicate the factor believed to be the basic causation in the situation. Thus, the periods of prosperity have names such as "Bank Credit Land Boom," "Mexican War Prosperity," "Railroad Prosperity," and so forth. "Embargo Depression," "Succession Depression," "Rich Man's Panic," and "Secondary Postwar Depression" appear among those used to specify periods of reduced business activity. The most interesting feature of the cyclical movement of business, which is evident in Figure 10.1, is the much greater intensity and magnitude of the depression period (Secondary Postwar Depression) of the 1930's. The prosperity period beginning around 1940 also assumes greater proportions than any other similar period in the country's history.

The Phases of the Business Cycle

Economists and statisticians who have closely analyzed the phenomenon of the business cycle have identified several different phases through which business passes in the course of a complete cycle. Most business cycles appear to have four distinct stages, which have been identified as (1) prosperity, (2) crisis, (3) depression, and (4) recovery. These stages are presented schematically in Figure 10.2. Some writers add a fifth stage which may or may not be a part of a

[2] *Ibid.*, p. 349.

1790–1829

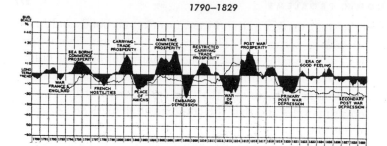

1830–1869

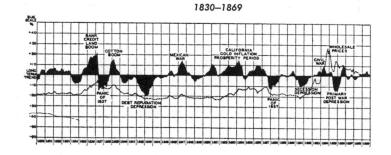

1870–1909

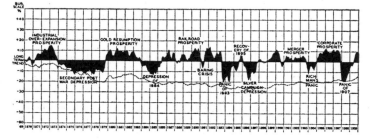

1910–1954

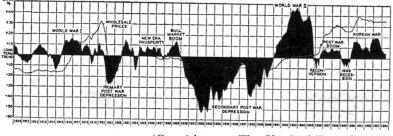

FIGURE 10.1: AMERICAN BUSINESS ACTIVITY SINCE 1790

complete business cycle.[3] This stage is most often called "financial panic" and may happen in any part of the retraction period. It does not always occur; however, many economists observe conditions in a considerable number of the cycles which they feel can rightfully be designated as "financial panic." The economic characteristics of the various phases of a business cycle are presented below.

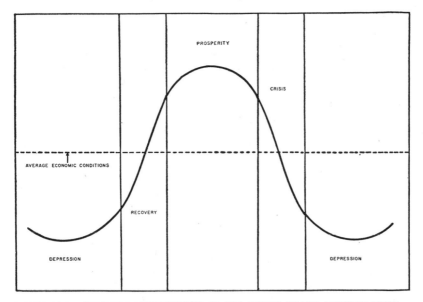

FIGURE 10.2: SCHEMATIC PRESENTATION OF THE PHASES OF THE BUSINESS CYCLE

Prosperity. This is a period of generally intense business activity. Unemployment is at a low ebb and expansion is evident in every part of the economy. There is much money in circulation and individual savings are high. This phase is characterized by increases in profits, in wages, in the volume of bank credit and its rate of circulation, in employment, and in demand for capital equipment. Prices tend to rise at a more rapid rate than costs with the result that greater profit margins prevail. Expansion occurs as people enter into business and manufacturing under the motivation of the greater profits

[3] Albert L. Meyers, *Elements of Modern Economics* (rev. ed., Prentice-Hall, 1946), p. 350.

which are now to be had. A considerable part of the expansion that takes place, however, is accomplished through bank credit. This expansion continues until eventually the supply of goods catches up with the demand, with the result that the market becomes very competitive. In many sections of the economy surpluses begin to appear. Inventories swell until orders from retailers to wholesalers and from wholesalers to manufacturers have to be reduced. When this point is reached, the cycle enters into the next phase. Of course, the transition is gradual and it is not possible to determine the exact day and hour at which prosperity enters into a crisis phase.

Crisis. During this phase of the cycle, businessmen see the wide profit margin that prevailed during most of the prosperity period gradually narrowed until it becomes a loss margin. At this point, there is a great struggle to remain solvent and to stay in business. Merchants and manufacturers are caught with large stocks of high-cost merchandise and products on hand. Therefore, orders to manufacturing companies and, as a result, to basic industries are further reduced. This means that men are laid off in these enterprises and that unemployment rises. Prices continue to fall, and businessmen dump their stocks on the market for whatever they can get for them, largely because they need capital with which to liquidate the heavy indebtedness they incurred during the prosperity period, and partly because they fear that prices will decline still further. The very fact that goods are dumped on the market serves to drive the price level further downward. There are many bankruptcies during this period because many firms cannot meet their heavy indebtedness. The values of the things which were purchased through borrowing have declined sharply; debt, however, remains of the same magnitude as when incurred and has increased tremendously insofar as the burden which it represents is concerned. In general, this is a period of business uncertainity and turmoil with bankruptcy and failure being imminent on every hand. Finally the crisis leads into the next stage which is a slump into a period of low level of business activity designated as depression.

Depression. In this stage, those firms and enterprises that had the ability to absorb their losses during the crisis period continue to operate; other firms which were unable to meet their indebtedness or which were unable to compete have now closed their doors or resorted to bankruptcy. In the period of the depression prices are at rock bottom, money is scarce, unemployment is high, and business moves at a fraction of its pace during the prosperity phase. Most of those factories which are able to continue operation do so at a very reduced capacity. Wages and salaries sink to low points as the great numbers of unemployed compete for the few remaining jobs. Oddly enough, goods are plentiful on the shelves of merchants; but the purchasing power of the people is so small that it is difficult for the merchants to sell these goods at any price. Gradually, however, the great inventories are diminished. They are either sold at a fraction of their cost, they are destroyed, or they spoil with the passing of time. When inventories are depleted new orders for goods are placed with manufacturers, and the economy gradually moves into the next phase.

Recovery. A gradual revival of business activity is characteristic of this phase of the business cycle. After the high-cost inventories are worked off, merchants place new orders with manufacturers for goods to replace them. The cost of these new goods is in keeping with current prices and other business indices; therefore they can be sold at a profit even though the selling price is low. New orders to manufacturers lead to an increase in the level of their production. Operations are stepped up to higher proportion of capacity, and men are hired to produce the additional goods. With increased employment, consumer purchasing power increases, and the movement upward commences in earnest. The recovery phase is then in full operation. Finally, the plants are again operating at near full capacity and business is once again intense. When this occurs, the cycle has been completed, and the prosperity phase has been entered upon once again.

Duration of Cycles

The length or duration of the depression period is of great significance for it indicates the extent of financial loss and economic setback which is incurred. If the period is not too long, the transition can be made without causing intense human suffering and deprivation. In a long-enduring depression period, such as that of the 1930's, human suffering and deprivation become acute, and a problem arises in regard to the continued existence of the state itself. Mass unemployment, greatly increased poverty, bank failures, bankruptcies in great numbers, widespread loss of property and possessions through mortgage foreclosures, declining production—all these constitute a situation which, if prolonged indefinitely, reaches a point where it becomes intolerable, and something must be done to relieve the conditions that prevail. In the United States in the 1930's, such action took the form of the election of Franklin D. Roosevelt to the Presidency, and the inauguration of the "New Deal."

Wesley Mitchell has made a study of the duration of business cycles in the United States in the last century which provides considerable insight into this aspect of the phenomenon.[4] In all, for the period 1854 to 1938 21 complete business cycles have been recorded. The average duration of the business cycles of this period was approximately 48 months. The longest cycle—that occurring from December, 1870, to March, 1879—was 99 months. The shortest complete cycle was the one which lasted from April, 1919, to September, 1921, a period of only 21 months. This is the only business cycle completed in less than 30 months. Eight of the cycles required 30 to 39 months; six 40 to 49 months; one 50 to 59 months; two 60 to 69 months; and three 70 months or more.

To the individual the duration of the various *phases* of the cycle is of much more interest than the duration of the cycle itself because his economic security and well-being are directly related to them. Mitchell has divided the business cycle into two different phases which he calls months of expansion and months of contraction. Expansion is roughly equivalent to recovery and prosperity; contraction to crisis and depression. Mitchell's data show that between 1854 and 1938, the United States experienced 550 months of economic expansion and that the average length of the periods of expansion was 26 months, although there was considerable variation. For instance, one period of expansion (April, 1919 to January, 1920) lasted only nine months. At the other extreme, the period of expansion from March, 1933 to May, 1937 lasted for 50 months. Among the remaining periods of

---

[4] Wesley C. Mitchell, *What Happens During Business Cycles* (National Bureau of Economic Research, 1951).

expansion, five lasted 10–19.9 months; eight 20–29.9 months; four 30–39.9 months; and two 40–49.9 months.

During the same period, the United States underwent 451 months of economic contraction, the periods of which averaged approximately 21 months, slightly longer than the average period of contraction. As for expansion, there was also considerable variation in the duration of the contraction periods. Two of the latter persisted only eight months while one, that from October, 1873 to March, 1879, lasted for 65 months. The short periods of contraction occurred between October, 1860 and June, 1861, and from August, 1918 to April, 1919. Of the others eleven lasted 10–19.9 months; four 20–29.9 months; two 30–39.9 months; and one 40–49.9 months.

Theories of Causation

Interest in the causes of business cycles has been intense for a considerable period of time, but most of the important systematic explanations have been developed only in the last half century. The earlier widespread acceptance of Say's "Law of Markets," which states that supply creates its own demand, indicated that attention was focused on problems of production and distribution rather than on business cycles. Certainly the world depression of the 1930's served as a stimulus to research into the causation of business cycles, and many of the more plausible theories resulted from this increased interest. The following discussion is merely an introduction to some of the principal theories.

Overproduction and underconsumption theories. These are perhaps the oldest and most persistent theories of causation of business cycles. They are the ones with which the average individual is most likely to be acquainted. In general terms, these theories point out that during the prosperity phase of the business cycle a great expansion in capital-goods industries occurs. This expansion is financed from current savings and from expanding bank credit. Because of the fact that consumer goods are a long time in the processes of production, prices tend to rise as money income increases. Consumers with increased income bid against one another for the existing stocks, and this in itself leads to price inflation. Of course, an increase in

prices is an incentive for further investment and expansion. When
the productive processes are complete, the final volume of consumers'
goods resulting from the expansion that has taken place is greater than
the capacity of the economy to absorb it. Therefore, the market is
glutted, prices fall, profits are reduced or entirely wiped out, manufacturers cut down on output, and a general depression follows.[5]
This situation obtains because the propensity to consume fails to
increase sufficiently to create a demand for all the consumers' goods
produced by an expanded industry. Thus, underconsumption is a
fundamental part of these theories.

Monetary theories. A number of economists hold that cyclical
changes in total spending stem chiefly from the amount of money in
circulation.[6] They state that the main kind of money in a credit
economy is bank deposits, and that the action of banks in expanding
and contracting the money supply is the main cause of fluctuations
in business activity. This means that business cycles are believed
to result from changes in the amount of money in circulation. Variation in the supply of bank credit is an important element in the variation in the amount of money available and, in most of these theories,
is assumed to play a key role in causation of business cycles. The
interest rate is also an integral part of monetary explanations of variations in business activity. Low interest rates stimulate the expansion
of inventories by business firms, and this, in turn, leads to a cumulative expansion of production, incomes, and spending. This expansion is reinforced by continued borrowing from banks, until the banks
bring the process to a halt because eventually they find themselves
short of reserves. As a result, banks are forced to increase interest
rates and to curtail credit. Such a procedure stops the expansion
which is underway, and businessmen are forced to reduce inventories;
and this, in turn, produces a sequence of falling production, income,
and spending. The economy then moves in the direction of recession until the situation has been modified and the reverse movement
can begin again.

"Business economy" theories. These theories emphasize the inter-

[5] D. Hamburg, *Business Cycles* (Macmillan, 1951), p. 250.
[6] Robert Aaron Gordon, *Business Fluctuations* (Harper, 1952), pp. 316–320.

dependence of the various parts of a business economy. Maladjustments inevitably occur because of the role of uncertainty in planning
for the future and the inevitability of mistakes. These maladjustments spread throughout the system and bring about a general decline
in business activity. Eventually, however, the maladjustments are
corrected, and the economy enters into a recovery phase. The process
then tends to repeat itself. "Business economy" theories, therefore,
hold that business cycles are an inherent part of the economic system.
Such theories emphasize that production depends on profit-making
and profit-expectation, that profits depend on a balance in cost-price
relationships, that uncertainty exists in planning for the future, that
mistakes are inevitable, and that all parts of the economic system are
interdependent in such a manner that maladjustments in one sector
rapidly spread throughout the whole system.[7]

Investment theories. Another group of ideas that have been put
forth in explanation of fluctuations in business is concerned with the
role of investments in the business process. There are many variations of these theories, but they all find the basic causation of business
cycles in the role of investments. Apparently they differ in their
explanations of the causation involved in bringing the investment
boom to an end. These explanations are lengthy and difficult to
summarize in a few sentences. Some of the more important of them
are—"shortage of capital" theories; theories that emphasize "partial
over-investment" and the role of innovations; theories that are concerned with the interaction of investment, income, and consumption,
and the dependence of investment on the behavior of the final product; and theories dealing with "oversaving" and "underconsumption." [8] All of these have been advanced to explain why the investment boom inevitably comes to an end and a process leading to depression commences. They are too detailed to elaborate here, but
the essential idea has been presented; that is—the business cycle can
be explained as a result of fluctuations in investments. A period of
prosperity that results from expansion of investment inevitably comes
to an end, and the process leading to depression commences. Ap-

[7] *Ibid.*, p. 308.
[8] *Ibid.*, pp. 321–341.

parently, the phenomenon of investment itself has within it the conditions that bring the boom to an end and start the downward movement in business activity.

Agricultural and meteorological theories.   Advocates of agricultural and meteorological explanations consider the phenomena of nature to be the ultimate cause of business cycles.   The principal idea in these theories is that agricultural production is subject to fluctuations that initiate changes in the rest of the economy.   Agricultural variables are thought to obey laws of their own and to be the underlying causes of cyclical changes in business activity.[9]   Since man does not have control over all of the factors in agricultural production—such as rainfall, storms, and temperature—he is unable to prevent fluctuations in production.   Basic causation for these agricultural cycles has been traced to variations in rainfall, phases of the planet Venus, the appearance of sunspots, solar radiation, and so forth.[10]   These phenomena of nature are found to have a high statistical correlation with agricultural cycles.   In brief words, these theories hold that fluctuations in agricultural production are the underlying causes of business cycles, and that these fluctuations follow a law of their own which is based in phenomena of nature.

Secular stagnation and a mature economy.   Perhaps the most important ideas relative to the business cycle that have been developed in recent decades are those of J. M. Keynes and his associates.   These have to do with the theory of secular stagnation and a mature economy.   Simply stated, the Keynesian theory is that highly industrialized economies such as that of the United States are "mature" in that no great opportunity for further expansion exists.   As a result of this situation, the annual rate of investment is too low to provide a national income high enough to maintain full employment.   The propensity to consume does not increase of its own accord to an extent necessary to make up for the inadequate annual rate of investment.   The secular stagnation idea is that the above-described situation tends to become a permanent condition; that is, the economy no longer moves in a clearly defined cycle, but levels off at a point below that necessary to provide full employment.   Therefore, depression tends

[9] Gordon, *op. cit.*, pp. 347–351.
[10] *Ibid.*

to become greatly prolonged even if not a permanent situation. This is a rather gloomy outlook to which the Keynesian school offers the solution of deficit spending and public works as a means of taking up the slack caused by the lack of sufficiently high annual rate of investment and the failure of the propensity to consume to increase sufficiently to offset that lack.

Social Consequences of the Business Cycle

Not much scientifically verified information is available concerning the *social* changes that occur as the economy moves through the different phases of the business cycle. Nevertheless, observation indicates that the pattern of life prevailing during a period of prosperity differs considerably from that in a period of depression. Certain phenomena have been studied and have been found to have definite correlations with the business cycle. Phelps and Henderson, after reviewing the research on the subject, conclude that certain social phenomena increase in intensity with prosperity and that others increase in intensity with depression.[11] Social phenomena that increase in magnitude during prosperity phases of the business cycle are found to be alcohol consumption, birth rates, crimes against the person, divorce and desertion, immigration, employment, income, industrial accidents, labor liberalism, marriages, maternal mortality, migration, strikes and labor disputes, tuberculosis death rates, and wage scales. Those that increase with depression are arrests, business failures, church attendance, crimes against property, housing deficiency, illegitimacy, lynching, malnutrition, pauperism, poor-relief, sickness, suicide, restrictions in standards of living, transiency, and unemployment. Phelps and Henderson further conclude that the research which has been done indicates that attitudes and interests, crime in general, death rates in general, ill health or lowered vitality, infant mortality, mental disease, mobility and redistribution of the population, changes in social institutions, tuberculosis, and war and revolution are associated with the business cycle but in an undetermined manner.[12] It is the opinion of the present author that not enough

[11] Harold A. Phelps and David Henderson, *Contemporary Social Problems* (4th ed., Prentice-Hall, 1952), pp. 299–301.
[12] *Ibid.*, p. 299.

research has been done toward verifying the hypotheses suggested by Phelps and Henderson to accept them as factual knowledge. Actually much of the interest in social correlates of the business cycle existed before the onset of the depression of the 1930's, and much of the research done during the depression was not oriented toward determining cyclical correlations over a trend period. Most of it was concerned with the analysis of a particular situation at that time, and made little attempt to relate changes in the business cycle to the social phenomena that were being observed. Nevertheless, there is considerable evidence to support the contention that certain of the above-listed social phenomena have a direct relationship to the changes that occur in the business world. For instance, considerable research has been done which shows that birth rates, marriage rates, and divorce rates are influenced by the movements of the business cycle.

An examination of trends in birth rates in the United States over the last half century indicates a close correlation between economic conditions and the phenomenon of reproduction. Maurice Hexter studied the relationship between birth rates and the business cycle in the city of Boston, Massachusetts, from 1900 to 1921 and found a definite relationship to exist. He found a correlation coefficient of −.410 between birth rates and unemployment and of +.705 between birth rates and wholesale prices.[13] Since the movement of wholesale prices and the volume of unemployment are good indicators of cyclical trends in the economy, these correlations suggest a very close causal relationship between the business cycle and rates of reproduction. They mean that birth rates tend to increase during periods of prosperity and to decline during periods of depression. Further evidence of a relationship between birth rates and the business cycle can be found in the trends in births since the study of Hexter was made. For example, in 1915, the birth rate of the United States was 25.0 per 1,000 persons. However, in 1933 in the depths of the Great Depression the birth rate reached an all time low of 16.6, and the rate remained low during the existence of depression conditions. Not until the advent of the prosperity phase which com-

[13] Maurice Beck Hexter, *Social Consequences of Business Cycles* (Houghton Mifflin, 1925), pp. 136, 161.

menced around 1940 did the birth rate rise to such a magnitude as recorded in 1915. In 1949, the birth rate was 23.9 per 1,000 persons. These facts appear to support the hypothesis that rates of reproduction are related to fluctuations in business activity. Apparently birth rates tend to rise during periods of prosperity and to decline during periods of depression.

The fluctuation in birth rates as noted above probably is influenced to a considerable degree by the marriage rate. This latter measure also shows a direct relationship to fluctuations in business activity. Dorothy S. Thomas, in studying the relationships between marriages and the business cycle in Great Britain from 1854–1915 found that, on the whole, a significant correlation existed between the two phenomena.[14] This was a positive relationship; that is, the marriage rate rose during periods of prosperity and declined during periods of depression. Hexter arrived at a similar conclusion in his attempt to correlate movements in marriage rates and wholesale prices between 1900 and 1921 in Boston, Massachusetts.[15] He found a correlation coefficient of +.469 between the occurrence of these two phenomena. An examination of trends in the marriage rate in the United States since 1920 further suggests a relationship between marriages and the business cycle. The marriage rate in 1929, which was a peak year of prosperity, was 10.1 marriages per 1,000 population. In 1932, in the most severe year of the depression phase that followed, the marriage rate stood at an all time low of 7.9 marriages per 1,000 population. The highest rate recorded to date was that of 16.4 registered during 1946, which was a year of prosperity and which followed immediately the end of World War II. The rate has continued relatively high during the years of prosperity that began in 1940. At no time after that year has it fallen below 10 per 1,000 population.[16] The data definitely show that marriage rates are related to business fluctuations. During periods of prosperity, the marriage rate rises, and it declines during periods of depression.

The divorce rate also appears to be affected by fluctuations in busi-

[14] Dorothy Swaine Thomas, *Social Aspects of the Business Cycle* (Knopf, 1927), ch. III.

[15] Hexter, *op. cit.*, pp. 150–157, 161.

[16] Marriage rates are from *Vital Statistics of the United States, 1949,* Part I (Government Printing Office), Table LIX.

ness activity. Although the long-time trend in the United States has been rather consistently upwards, decreases in the divorce rate have occurred during periods of depression. In his study of Suffolk County, Massachusetts, between 1900 and 1923, Hexter found that divorce rates were not as sensitive to changes in economic conditions as the birth rate and the marriage rate.[17] Thomas, in her study of England and Wales between 1857 and 1913, arrived at the conclusion that there was no connection between the business cycle and fluctuations in the divorce rate.[18] However, Ogburn and Thomas in analyzing the relationship of divorces to the business cycle in the United States between 1867–1906 found a correlation of +0.70.[19] This correlation is high enough to mean that a significant causal relationship exists between business fluctuations and divorces. Examining the trends in the divorce rate in the United States since the period of the study by Ogburn and Thomas, one finds other indications that this rate is related to changes in business and industry. For instance, in 1932, the divorce rate (number of divorces per 1,000 population) declined to 1.3, which represented the lowest rate since World War I.[20] This year, of course, was the depths of the depression that began in 1929. On the other hand, the highest rate that has been recorded was in 1946 which was a year of prosperity following the end of World War II. The rate at that time was 4.3 divorces per 1,000 population. Since that year, the trend has been gradually downward. These data strongly suggest that in the United States divorce rates are affected by the economic conditions prevailing. They appear to increase with prosperity and to decline with depression.

In the business cycle, inflation (higher prices) accompanies the prosperity phase and deflation (lower prices) occurs in the depression period. This fluctuation of prices seriously complicates the problem of individual economic security. Particularly is this true for persons who retired during periods of deflation or for those who have money incomes that do not respond readily to the changes occurring

[17] Hexter, op. cit., p. 159.

[18] Thomas, op. cit., p. 91.

[19] William F. Ogburn and Dorothy S. Thomas, "The Influence of the Business Cycle on Certain Social Conditions," *Journal of the American Statistical Association*, XVIII (1922–23), 334.

[20] Divorce rates are from *Vital Statistics of the United States*, 1949, Part I, Table LXII.

in the economy.   Both the retired persons with fixed incomes and the salaried people whose incomes enabled them to live comfortably during a period of deflation often find that they are reduced to a poverty level through inflation.   This is well illustrated by the changes in the purchasing power of the dollar since 1935.[21]   A dollar which valued 100 cents based on the 1935–1939 average as measured by consumer prices was worth only 52.7 cents of actual value in 1952. The same dollar as measured by retail food prices valued only 43.1 cents in 1952.   Another example of inflationary pressures accompanying the prosperity phase of the business cycle can be found in the indexes of retail prices of food.   In 1929, this index (based on 1935–1939 as 100) was 132.5, a figure which declined to 84.1 in the depression year 1933.   In 1940, prior to World War II, the retail food index was 96.6, and rose to 159.6 in 1946 at the close of that conflict. By 1951 it was 277.4, and it continued to rise thereafter.

Still another factor affecting individual economic security arising from deflation and inflation is related to debt.   Persons who incur long-term debts during periods of inflation when money is cheap often find the burden unbearable during a deflation period when money becomes scarce.   The purchasing power of money fluctuates, but the magnitude of the debt remains the same.   Therefore, long-term debts incurred in periods of prosperity and cheap money may have to be paid off during periods of depression and scarce money, and this, of course increases manyfold the burden which the debt represents.   As a result, many debtors are forced into mortgage foreclosures because they can no longer make payments on their loans. This occurred on a large scale among farmers during the depression of the 1930's.

Needless to say, if people living on fixed incomes retired during a period of inflation, they reap an advantage if a period of depression ensues.   Salaried persons also find their economic positions strengthened during deflation periods because prices tend to decline more rapidly than their incomes.   Furthermore, debts incurred during periods of deflation are more easily paid off during periods of infla-

[21] The indexes that are used in this discussion are from the *Statistical Abstract of the United States,* 1953 (Government Printing Office, 1953), Tables 337 and 339.

tion and cheap money.   Therefore, the debtor has his economic position strengthened because the debt does not represent nearly so great
a burden during the period of inflation as it did during the deflation
period when it was incurred.   Of course, these advantages obtain
only if the salaried person and debtor are able to retain their positions
and their source of incomes and are not forced to join the ever-increasing numbers of the unemployed.

There are other social correlates of the business cycle which are
well established.   Unemployment and poverty have direct causal
relationships with the conditions of business and industry.   Both
of these phenomena increase with depression and decrease with prosperity; since, however, unemployment and poverty are significant
social problems even in periods of economic prosperity, they are given
separate treatment in the following sections.   It seems evident that
the migratory tendencies of the people are also affected by fluctuations
in business activity.   The trend of the rural-urban movement apparently is altered by changes in the economic world.   This is suggested
by the fact that one of the few times in which the movement of people
to farms exceeded the movement *from* farms was in 1932—the worst
year of the depression of the 1930's.   Also, it seems certain that
transiency must become of greater magnitude during depression and
of less magnitude during prosperity.

The changes that occur in the social life of a people as the economy
moves through the various phases of the business cycle need to be
investigated thoroughly in their many aspects, for knowledge concerning the relationships between changes in business activity and
trends in social phenomena would aid much in the planning of action
to offset the disastrous effects of prolonged depressions.   It also
could be of importance in the attempt of the government and of the
business world to bring the business cycle under conscious control.

UNEMPLOYMENT AND POVERTY

Unemployment and poverty are social problems, and they are always present within the society.   Even in periods of economic pros-

perity between one and two million workers in the United States are without jobs. Of course, many people live under conditions of poverty regardless of the general circumstances prevailing in the business and industrial world, but unemployment and poverty do vary in degree according to the status of the economy. During the depression phase of the business cycle, both of these social problems become of great significance; but even during periods of intense economic activity and general prosperity society has not been successful in completely eliminating them.

Unemployment probably became a problem when specialization in the productive processes began to develop. In the stage of development in which an individual produced the things which he consumed there could not have been much unemployment. However, as specialization in the productive process occurred, the worker was separated from the ownership of the productive tools he used, and a money economy was created in which goods were not produced for direct consumption but for sale to others at a profit, the phenomenon of unemployment became of ever greater significance. At the present, millions of workers may be unemployed due to factors in the economy over which they have absolutely no control. This is particularly true of highly urbanized, industrial societies.

Poverty as a social problem is as old as the history of man. The phenomenon appears in all types of societies and in all parts of the world. It should be kept in mind that poverty is a relative concept; what constitutes a condition of poverty in one society might be above the level of living expected in other groups.

Unemployment

Unemployment can be defined as a condition in which the individual is able and willing to work, but is unable to find a job. This concept differentiates unemployment from other forms of idleness, such as that resulting from illness, disability, or voluntary withdrawal from the labor force. The extent of unemployment in the United States varies considerably from one period of time to another. In 1952, a year of prosperity, 1,673,000 persons were unemployed. This circumstance is considered normal because this figure represents people in the process of changing jobs, and those temporarily out of work. In 1933, a severe depression year, the number of unemployed rose to between 13 and 15 millions. One estimate by the American Federation of Labor gives 15,700,000 millions unemployed in March, 1933, out of a potential labor force of 50.5 millions.[22] This means that about 30 per cent of the entire labor force was unemployed in March of that year. Table 10.1 gives data relative to the annual average amount of unemployment in the United States in 1929–1952. These figures show that the proportion of the labor force that was unemployed during this period ranged from almost 25 per cent in 1933 to 1.2 per cent in 1944. This 1933 figure means that one out of every four workers was without a job in that year. Since 1942, the country has maintained a high level of employment reflecting the prosperity the nation has experienced since early in World War II. The figures presented in Table 10.1 show that the proportion of the labor force which is unemployed during periods of prosperity is between one and five per cent. They further demonstrate that during depression periods the proportion of unemployed in the labor force is likely to be somewhere in the vicinity of 25 per cent, or one fourth of the entire working population.

Three main types of unemployment prevail in the American society: (1) seasonal, (2) cyclical, and (3) technological.

Seasonal unemployment. By seasonal unemployment is meant that which results from the effect which changes in the seasons have upon a particular industry. Practically every form of economic activity goes through periods of fluctuation in production and sales resulting from seasonal variation in weather. Seasonal unemployment is very much evident in farming, food-processing industries, lumbering, transportation, and the building trades. Other enterprises in which seasonal unemployment is significant are mining, canning, automobile manufacturing, clothing manufacturing, and shipping. Seasonal unemployment causes considerable loss of income and creates hardships on the worker and his family; however, it can be foreseen, and the worker can make necessary plans to cope with the situation when it does occur.

[22] *The Recovery Problem in the United States* (The Brookings Institute, 1936), pp. 612–613.

Cyclical unemployment. Cyclical unemployment results from the depression phase of the business cycle as described elsewhere in this chapter. A study of Table 10.1 shows the extent to which unemployment results from the business cycle. From 1931 to 1940, the proportion of the labor force unemployed was 15 per cent or more. In 1933, 25 per cent of the labor force were without jobs. In direct contrast, the proportion of the labor force which was unemployed

**TABLE 10.1: AVERAGE ANNUAL UNEMPLOYMENT
IN THE UNITED STATES, 1929–1952**

Year	Civilian Labor Force	Number Unemployed	Per Cent Unemployed
	(in thousands)		
1929	49,180	1,550	3.2
1930	49,820	4,340	8.7
1931	50,420	8,020	15.9
1932	51,000	12,060	23.6
1933	51,590	12,830	24.9
1934	52,230	11,340	21.7
1935	52,870	10,610	20.1
1936	53,440	9,030	16.9
1937	54,000	7,700	14.3
1938	54,610	10,390	19.0
1939	55,230	9,480	17.2
1940	55,640	8,120	14.6
1941	55,910	5,560	9.9
1942	55,410	2,660	4.7
1943	55,540	1,070	1.9
1944	54,630	670	1.2
1945	53,860	1,040	1.9
1946	57,520	2,270	3.9
1947	60,168	2,142	3.6
1948	61,442	2,064	3.4
1949	62,105	3,395	5.5
1950	63,099	3,142	5.0
1951	62,884	1,879	3.0
1952	61,293	1,673	2.7

Source: *Statistical Abstract of the United States,* 1953, Table 206.

dropped to a low of 1.2 per cent in 1944, a period of prosperity. Cyclical unemployment presents an extremely serious problem because it is completely beyond the control of the individual worker. He can do little to prevent its occurrence, and can do only a minimum amount of planning to meet such a condition. Therefore, a lifetime of effort embodied in savings and accumulations of property can be lost during a period of prolonged unemployment resulting from external forces operating in the society over which the individual has no control. Unemployment is one of the most serious social correlates of the business cycle. When a situation prevails in which one out of every four workers is unemployed such as in 1933, the very existence of the nation itself is threatened.

Technological unemployment. Technological unemployment is that which results from the displacement of workers by the introduction of machines with which one man can do the work formerly accomplished by many. The basic idea, a debatable one, is that the introduction of machines into an economic operation eliminates more jobs than are created in the production, distribution, and servicing of the machine itself. Many examples are cited by persons who support this hypothesis. For instance, they point out that the combined harvesters and threshers gather the wheat with a relatively few workers, whereas the older method of harvesting and threshing by cradle-scythes and flails required large numbers of laborers. In the South, the example of the cotton-picking machine replacing hand labor is often cited as a case of technology creating unemployment. Many other examples in industry and business could be given. However, the role of technology in creating unemployment is not completely accepted by many other persons, and they have considerable evidence to support their case. When one observes the tremendous industries which have been developed around a new technological development and the millions of jobs created either directly or indirectly, the arguments supporting the idea of technological unemployment do not appear so strong. The invention of the automobile destroyed employment in the wagon-making industry, in the harness-making industry, and in the blacksmith shops, but literally millions of new jobs were created in the manufacturing, distribution, and servicing of this new mode of transportation. It may be stated, therefore, that technological unemployment does not assume the critical importance of cyclical unemployment.

Nevertheless, there is a problem associated with the introduction of labor-saving machines, one that arises out of the lack of spatial mobility on the part of workers and their families, and the difficulties met in learning new skills or in changing trades. Therefore in a given locality technological employment may exist because machines have destroyed the demand for the existing skills and services of the workers in the particular area. Yet, thousands of new jobs may have been created elsewhere in the nation in the production, distribution, servicing, and operation of the machines. However, these new jobs require different skills and trades from those required by the jobs that were eliminated. As a result, technological unemployment may be very real to the worker in a local area, even though in the overall operation more jobs are created than are eliminated. New jobs created hundreds of miles from the worker's usual place of residence, which require different skills and trades do little to relieve the difficulties of the unemployed worker in the local area. The introduction of labor-saving machines combined with the difficulties of spatial mobility of the labor force and of learning new skills and trades, therefore, creates technological unemployment in a localized area.

Poverty

Poverty may be defined as a condition in which the individual cannot command the minimum of goods and services considered by the society in which he lives as necessary for health and physical efficiency. This definition, of course, reflects the fact that poverty is a relative term. A mode of living that constitutes poverty in one society may approach or exceed the average or anticipated level of living of another group. Poverty in the United States, therefore, must be judged in terms of the standard of living (or that which is considered a minimum use of goods and services) of the American people. Weaver concludes that the number of persons in the United States who are living at a poverty level varies from 12 to 15 per cent of the total population.[23] Data on the money income of families in the

[23] W. W. Weaver, *Social Problems* (Dryden, 1951), p. 640.

TABLE 10.2: MONEY INCOME OF FAMILIES IN THE UNITED STATES,
1951, BY RACE AND RESIDENCE

Money Income	Total Families	By Race		By Residence		
		White	Nonwhite	Urban	Rural Nonfarm	Rural Farm
			(Percentages)			
All Families	100.0	100.0	100.0	100.0	100.0	100.0
Under $500	4.4	3.7	11.7	2.8	5.0	11.3
$500–$999	4.7	4.0	12.6	2.9	5.6	12.0
$1,000–$1,499	5.3	4.6	12.5	3.5	6.5	12.2
$1,500–$1,999	6.1	5.5	12.3	4.6	7.3	11.5
$2,000–$2,499	7.6	7.2	11.7	6.6	8.3	11.5
$2,500–$2,999	7.8	7.5	10.1	7.5	8.6	7.5
$3,000–$3,499	9.9	10.1	8.0	10.0	11.9	7.0
$3,500–$3,999	9.8	10.2	5.6	10.6	9.5	6.3
$4,000–$4,499	9.2	9.6	4.8	10.1	8.9	5.3
$4,500–$4,999	6.4	6.7	3.2	7.4	5.7	3.0
$5,000–$5,999	10.8	11.4	3.9	12.4	10.1	3.9
$6,000–$6,999	6.8	7.3	2.0	8.2	5.0	2.8
$7,000–$9,999	7.5	8.2	1.0	8.9	5.5	3.9
$10,000–$14,999	2.4	2.6	—	3.0	1.4	.7
$15,000 and over	1.2	1.3	.3	1.4	.7	1.2
Median Income	$3,709	$3,859	$2,032	$4,071	$3,365	$2,131

Source: *Statistical Abstract of the United States*, 1953, Tables 323 and 324.

United States in 1951 as presented in Table 10.2 indicate that 14.4 per cent of all families had money incomes of less than $1,500.00. Although money income may not be an exact means of measuring level of living, it probably is a fairly good indicator of living conditions which exist. At the present level of prices, it seems justified to assume that any family with less than $1,500 income per year is living at a poverty level. Certainly the 4.4 per cent of American families with less than $500 income annually must be classified as living in poverty. The same statement applies almost equally to the 4.7 per cent with $500 to $999.99 annual income, and the 5.3 per cent with annual incomes of between $1,000 and $1,499.

If the figures on annual money income of families in the United States are examined on the basis of the characteristics of the families concerned, the phenomenon of poverty is found to be more prominent among certain elements of the society than among others. Table 10.2

shows that poverty is more prevalent among nonwhites in the population than among whites: only 12.3 per cent of white families had money incomes of less than $1,500 compared to 36.8 per cent of the families among the nonwhites; and only 3.7 per cent of the white families had incomes of less than $500.00, while 11.7 per cent of the nonwhite families were in this category.

If the figures relative to money income of families are analyzed according to residence, one finds that poverty is greatest in the rural-farm areas, lowest in the urban localities, and intermediate between these extremes in the rural-nonfarm places. (See Table 10.2.) Thus, 9.2 per cent of the urban families had incomes of less than $1,500.00 as compared to 17.1 per cent of the rural-nonfarm and 35.5 per cent of the rural-farm families. The figure for the rural-farm families is probably misleading because many farm families depend upon goods produced on the farm for home consumption rather than upon a money income. Nevertheless, it seems likely that poverty exists to a greater extent in rural-farm than in the other residential categories. The high proportion of Negroes in the rural-farm population would serve to support this contention. Rural-farm nonwhites had a median income of only $966.00 in 1951 as compared to a median of $2,457.00 for the urban nonwhites. Rural-farm whites had median incomes of $2,351.00 as compared to $4,200 for urban whites.[24]

Poverty continues to exist in the American society probably as a result of faulty social organization. It seems evident that the United States possesses the basic resources to allow for an adequate level of living for all of its people. The fact that the nation has large surpluses in agriculture and is often faced with overproduction of industrial goods while at the same time from 10 to 15 per cent of the people are living at a poverty level is indicative of the problem which exists. Therefore, the business cycle also constitutes a hindrance to the elimination of poverty from the society.

[24] *Statistical Abstract of the United States, 1953,* Table 324.

CONCLUSION

The most serious economic problem facing the people of the
United States is the business cycle. This phenomenon, per se, is
not pathological; however, it becomes a serious difficulty when the
depression phase is of such severity and length as to cause widespread
human suffering over a prolonged period. Such an occurrence took
place during the 1930's. Depressions of that intensity place great
strain upon the government and even threaten the existence of our
political institutions. Millions of citizens suffer great economic
losses which mean that the accumulations of a lifetime are often
wiped out. The pattern of life also is modified considerably as reflected by changes in the birth rate, the marriage rate, and the divorce
rate. Changes also occur in practically all other phases of social
behavior; however, the exact nature of these changes has not been
scientifically determined. Unemployment and poverty are greatly
intensified during the depression phase of the business cycle.

The American people have done much to prevent the recurrence
of severe and prolonged depression periods. The banking system has
been reorganized, and bank failure and subsequent loss of funds on
the part of citizens are, theoretically, no longer possible. Measures
have been taken to provide economic security to the individual worker.
The Social Security Act of 1935 was designed for this purpose. This
Act provides for a weekly payment for a period of several months to
workers who lose their jobs and thus helps to reduce the severe economic consequences of unemployment and to allow the worker time
to seek other employment without suffering deprivation and poverty
in the period of transition. Another feature of this legislation is the
provision of a pension for workers at the age of 65 years. There are
many other important features of the Social Security Act which are
designed to lessen the possibility of prolonged depression. In 1951
and 1954 this Act was modified and coverage was extended to almost
the entire working population.

Still another form of regulation that has been built into the economy of the United States is the system of farm-price supports, which is designed to prevent severe economic losses among farmers as a result of sharp drops in prices of agricultural products. Also buying and selling on the stock market have been regulated in a manner to prevent such over-speculation as brought on the crash of 1929. These and many other governmental actions have been taken to provide additional regulation of the economy in those areas in which control by competition among sellers in a free market operate in such a manner as to cause widespread and prolonged human suffering.

Although additional regulatory measures have been provided in the economy of the United States by means of governmental action, these controls have as yet to face a severe test. The big question in the minds of the American people is whether or not the legislative controls will actually be effective in preventing depression of the sort which was experienced during the 1930's. Practically no person hopes to eliminate business fluctuations entirely. The most that people expect is to be able to contain the fluctuations so that prolonged human suffering and deprivation will not occur during the depression phase. There is considerable confidence that this objective has been accomplished by the legislative action adopted during recent decades. However, only time will tell.

Study Questions

1. Name and explain the principles that are considered basic to a capitalistic system of economy.

2. What motivations and regulatory mechanisms operate in a capitalistic economy? Discuss the role of legislative action as a regulatory mechanism.

3. Explain the concept of the business cycle. Identify the various phases of the business cycle and briefly describe what happens in each of them.

4. Discuss the history of business fluctuations in the United States and comment on the duration of the periods of contraction and expansion.

5. Name and briefly explain the various theories that have been advanced in explanation of the phenomenon of business cycles.

6. Explain how the movements in the business cycle affect birth rates, marriage rates, and divorce rates.

7. In what ways do inflation and deflation accompanying the business

cycle make the problem of individual economic security more complicated?

8. Discuss the extent of unemployment in the United States during the various phases of the business cycle.

9. What are the main causes of unemployment?   Explain each of them.

10. How prevalent is poverty in the American society?   Explain what is meant when it is said that poverty is a relative concept.

Selected References

Brookings Institution, *The Recovery Problem in the United States* (Washington, 1936).   This analysis provides a general picture of the world economic situation out of which developed the depression in the United States in the 1930's.

Colt, C. C., and N. S. Keith, *28 Days, A History of the Banking Crisis* (New York: Greenburg, Publisher, 1933).   This book gives a detailed history of the events that led to the banking collapse in the United States in 1933.

Douglas, Paul H., and Aaron Director, *The Problem of Unemployment* (Macmillan, 1931).   A good discussion of the extent and types of unemployment in the United States during the first quarter of the twentieth century.

Garver, Frederic B., and Alvin H. Hansen, *Principles of Economics* (Ginn, 1937).   Chapter 21 presents a good description of the relationships between costs and prices during the various phases of the business cycle, as well as information relative to other economic phenomena.

Gordon, Robert Aaron, *Business Fluctuations* (Harper, 1952).   This book provides up-to-date information and data relative to business fluctuations in the United States and gives explanations of the various ideas regarding causation of these phenomena.

Hamberg, D., *Business Cycles* (Macmillan, 1951).   This study presents detailed discussions of the various theories of causation of business cycles.

Hart, Albert G., *et al.*, *Debts and Recovery* (New York: The Twentieth Century Fund, 1938).   A study of changes in the internal debt structure of the United States from 1929 to 1937.

Hexter, Maurice Beck, *Social Consequences of Business Cycles* (Houghton Mifflin, 1925).   An analysis of social correlations of the business cycle in Boston, Massachusetts, from 1900 to 1921.

Mitchell, Wesley, *What Happens during Business Cycles* (New York: National Bureau of Economic Research, 1951).   A very detailed analysis of the occurrences in business during the various phases of the business cycle with a valuable section on the duration of the different phases.

Ogburn, William F., and Dorothy S. Thomas, "The Influence of the Business Cycle on Certain Social Conditions," *Journal of the American Statistical Association*, XVIII (1922–1923), 324–340. An analysis of the relationships between fluctuations in business and changes in certain social phenomena.

Phelps, Harold A., and David Henderson, *Contemporary Social Problems* (4th ed., Prentice-Hall, 1952). Chapter 12 gives a summary of social correlates of the business cycle as indicated by a review of the research on the subject.

Thomas, Dorothy Swaine, *Social Aspects of the Business Cycle* (Knopf, 1927). A study of sociological aspects of the business cycle in Great Britain from about 1850 to 1915.

Industrial and
Labor Problems

All areas of human relations have been affected by the Industrial Revolution and twentieth-century industrialization. In some of these areas the individuals, organizations, and institutions most affected have attempted to understand their specific problems and have made notable progress in solving them. But in the industrial-labor area, where remarkable success has been achieved in solving material and technical problems, human-relation problems, while not wholly ignored, have been relegated largely to a secondary role. The conflict between employers and employees, between the owners of the tools of production and those who operate them still goes on; and it will continue to be a problem until both sides admit that they have a common interest and direct their research to the solution of their human-relations problems with the same energy as has already been applied in solving the problems of production.

What are the major problems of the employer and the employee? From the point of view of the worker the foremost is insecurity. The fear of want, the loss of individual identity, the loss of self-sufficiency, the loss of ownership, family instability, unemployment, industrial accidents and disease, and old age all combine to haunt the industrial worker as he attempts to find security in our complex, ever-changing industrial society. In his search for security, he has turned to an economic organization for workers—the union. The union in its effort to give greater security to its members is almost constantly in conflict with the employer. The employer sees labor as just one of the factors of production, whereas the worker and his union contend that labor is a *special kind* of commodity, a human commodity. This divergent approach produces disagreement, conflict, and industrial warfare. When conflict develops, each side employs weapons, devices, and techniques to enhance its position in seeking a temporary solution. This conflict has been a feature of Western society for many years.

ROOTS OF OUR INDUSTRIAL AND LABOR PROBLEMS

Few, if any, of the social problems with which we are concerned have originated during this century. Most of them go back many decades or even centuries. In general, social problems do not develop instantaneously, nor are their true dimensions seen or understood merely by observing their present manifestations. This sociological truism is nowhere more applicable than in the crucially important industrial and labor problems. A review of their historical backgrounds helps one greatly in obtaining the needed perspective.

The Industrial Revolution

Richard Arkwright applied water power to a group of James Hargreaves' "spinning jennies" in 1769. During the same year James Watt provided a counter stroke and condenser for the steam engine. They thus unconsciously set in motion the factors that produced the most significant, determinant, and dynamic force in modern civilization—the Industrial Revolution. Although Arkwright is frequently referred to as the "father of the factory system," Watt, Savery, Newcomen, Macadam, Telford, Kay, Hargreaves, Stephenson, Cartwright, Whitney, Fulton, and Howe—all contributed inventions and techniques equally important in giving momentum to the Industrial Revolution.

Power-driven machines soon destroyed the home as a unit of production, forcing fathers, sons, and other family workers to leave the household and perform their tasks in factories. This destruction of the home as a basic unit of production launched a revolution in human relations that altered every basic institutional structure serving man in Europe and America. The introduction of power-driven machines not only started the trend toward the complex, highly specialized mass production of the modern world, but also almost destroyed the old consanguinal type of family. It altered man's concept of religious values, redefined the functions of our governmental and educational institutions, and gave rise to a multitude of problems between government and citizens, labor and capital, employers and employees, and consumers and producers. In brief, industrialization is a major factor in every one of the important current social problems confronting American society.

The Disintegration of the Consanguinal Family

Industrialization brought about major dislocations in our basic institutional structure. A brief review of some of the problems that have accompanied the disintegration of the old type of family as it attempted to adjust to rapid industrialization illustrates this.

The early American family was large, sometimes including 15 or more children and had a close-knit or clannish organization. Young people usually married in their middle teens under the guidance of Christian mores, which dictated family and parental responsibilities. The family whether working in a small handicraft shop adjoining the home or on acres surrounding it—produced basically for home use. The father managed the farm or other business and the mother managed the home and the children. Each member of the family except the younger children was responsible for some part of the "family business." The members of the family worked together and played together. They shared alike in fortune and misfortune.

Injury or illness was a family responsibility. If a son was badly injured while helping a neighbor the family assumed full responsibility for his care until he was well again. If an older married son suffered the misfortune of a bad crop year, illness, or unusual financial obligations his need became a family responsibility. If a married son or daughter died and left several young children the family assumed responsibility for rearing the orphans; and, when the parents grew too old to work, they were provided for by the sons and daughters.

In its organizational structure and values, the early American family resembled the English, French, German, and Scandinavian families during the latter part of the eighteenth century. This consanguinal type of organization implied responsibility for the children, the ill and injured, the old and infirm—all members unable to fend for themselves. These implied family responsibilities were fully sanctioned by society and assumed—more or less—the position of universal mores within these countries.

Cultural Lags

As power-driven machines gradually destroyed the basis of domestic production and forced the workers into factories, the cohesive bonds that held the consanguinal family together began to disintegrate. Accompanying power-driven machines, factories, and rapid industrialization was a high incidence of industrial accidents and illnesses. Safety devices for the protection of the workers from the hazards of industrial employment were notoriously absent. Yet workers who were injured in factories, regardless of the cause, were considered as the responsibility of the family and not the factory. And, because of societal sanction of the concept of family responsibility, and the prevailing atmosphere of laissez faire, the family attempted to fulfill its defined societal role.

During the early part of the nineteenth century the European worker families and particularly those in France and England were the first to feel the disharmony, strain, and stress created by lack of balance between the "cultural lead" (brought about by the introduction of power-driven machinery, the economic philosophy of laissez faire, and the accompanying industrialization) and the "cultural lag" with respect to family organization and responsibility. One of the first maladjustments was the displacement of skilled craftsmen. Not only did machines reduce the demand for their products but they also made it possible to employ women and children in manufacturing. The results were low wages, frightful—and often brutal—working conditions, and incredibly unsanitary slums to live in for those who *did* find employment, in addition to widespread unemployment. These led to sporadic and violent attempts by the masses of workers to demolish the machines which they believed were responsible for the destruction of their former way of life and were the primary cause of their growing unemployment.

The uprooting of factory workers from their former kinship organizations, the crowded, unsanitary slums, and the dependence upon cash wages created conditions that made it almost impossible for the worker family to continue the old socially sanctioned practice of caring for the injured and aged. Old emotional beliefs, attitudes and values were so entrenched, however, that the masses of workers believed these misfortunes were the concern of the family. In Europe, it was not until the last decades of the nineteenth century, when the problem became extremely acute, that the inherent social contradiction was recognized and means of closing the gap put into operation.

Political Answers

Toward the end of the nineteenth century the governments of England, France, and Germany enacted legislation to cope with industrial accidents, occupational diseases, and such problems, thereby forcing industry to assume partial responsibility. However, in the United States, it was not until the second decade of the twentieth century that a number of states enacted effective legislation to protect the industrial worker. Furthermore, it was not until the Great Depression of the 30's that our federal government enacted legislation designed to correct some of the dislocations brought about by our industrialization.

Modern programs of workmen's compensation, old-age assistance, old-age and survivors insurance, unemployment compensation, aid to dependent children, and the like—these are merely partial answers to problems created by industrialization. In the past, industry as a whole consistently refused to accept its share of responsibility for the social problems it had created until industry itself was in dire need of assistance. Likewise, as organized labor increased its economic and political power, it also refused to accept its share of responsibility.

Similar examples of cultural lags and the resulting social problems created by industrialization can be found in our governmental, educational, economic, and religious institutions. The shift of population from the rural areas to urban centers of production, and the change from primary, face-to-face, relations to secondary, contractual association have brought about tremendous changes in our society. Not least of them has been man's quest for security and guarantees against want.

INSECURITY

Freedom from Want

Man's life has been filled with insecurities, but in the past most of the uncertainties were products of nature—not of man. Our preindustrial ancestors accepted it as a matter of fact that success or failure, happiness or unhappiness was an ordained pattern to which man must fashion himself. To them, life was either a great adventure—a testing-ground where they showed their mettle—or a mere process of vegetation and decay. Twentieth-century industrialized man, unlike his courageous ancestor, is now being nurtured in a tradition that happiness and security are both birthrights, and that freedom from want and freedom from fear may be found in mass organization. The belief that material things—such as higher wages, pension plans, unemployment insurance "side benefits," higher prices, mass production, and higher profits secured through mass organization—will partially, or perhaps completely, solve man's quest for security is nowhere more evident than in the area of industry and labor.

Loss of Identity and Self-sufficiency

As the Industrial Revolution destroyed man's former way of life, his hunger for stability and security increased. Preindustrial man was individually and economically self-sufficient. Through years of arduous apprenticeship, the individual was taught a trade which, besides enabling him to support himself and his family, gave him a sense of individual worth. Inwardly the craftsman took pride in his creative ability and the quality of the product which he fashioned with his own hands. Although there were few, if any, economic guarantees associated with his craft or occupation he felt secure because he owned his tools and could perform services for which he received pay and which society thought desirable.

Modern industrial man lacks individual self-sufficiency and is economically dependent. In 1830, approximately four of every five Americans owned their means of making a living; that is, they *made* their living. One hundred years later, approximately four out of every five Americans had no independent means of making a living and were dependent for their livelihood upon property, tools, and equipment owned by someone else; they *earned* their living. This transferal of the ownership of capital goods from the majority to a small minority has destroyed the foundation of American individualism. Preindustrial man was personally identified with his work and his product—modern man has few opportunities for personal identification with the product on which he works.

Loss of Ownership and Family Stability

With the workingman's loss of the tools of his trade has come a decrease in the percentage of individuals owning farms, land, and small businesses. This loss of ownership and proprietorship by the masses of American workers has further weakened the flimsy base upon which their economic and psychological security rests. The lure of property ownership was one of the great forces that expanded our frontiers from the Atlantic to the Pacific Ocean; its protection and promotion has been a cornerstone in our democracy. Stability and security are not characteristics of a society in which the property aspirations of its citizenry are blocked. The modern family—fragmentary in its organization, with the small conjugal unit—has not been able to afford the emotional, affectional, and economic security that characterized the large consanguinal family. As indicated elsewhere in this volume, the instability of our modern family is evident in our high divorce rate and the rapidly rising incidence of juvenile delinquency. Of all our basic institutions, none has been more thoroughly affected by industrialization than the family.

Unemployment

Not least among the insecurities of modern propertyless, nonproprietary, and toolless man is his quest for a steady job; for his hopes, fears and expectations center fundamentally in the security of his job. In fact, his only property claims are the wages or salaries (and sometimes a small pension) which he receives from it. Since the worker survives only by means of work, full employment is imperative. But full employment was not easy to maintain during the first half of this twentieth century; and during the second quarter, unemployment has varied from approximately 15,000,000 during the depression of the 1930's to less than 1,000,000 during World War II.

Politicians, as well as social scientists, know that unemployment and underemployment increase the insecurities and instabilities of the workers and of society. Industry also knows that workers without jobs soon exhaust their unemployment compensation and savings; that loss of income means a decrease in consumption of goods and services; that every curtailment of the consumption of goods and services leads to a decrease in the demand for goods and services; that a decrease in the demand for goods and services leads to a decrease in the demand for labor to produce goods and services, and that any decrease in the demand for labor inevitably means unemployment. The forcing of the worker and his family to a lower level of living as the result of unemployment places an additional social and financial burden upon society. It comes in the form of increased malnutrition, more illness, the spread of slums, higher rates of crime, poorer educational training, and more heavily taxed facilities in the ameliorative institutions. Full employment is imperative for a secure and healthy industrial society.

Illness and Accidents

Another insecurity that faces the worker is that of industrial accidents and illness. Each year some 2,000,000 or more workers receive disabling injuries while gainfully employed, and approximately 100,-000 suffer occupational diseases. Statistically, about one in every thirty employed workers has an industrial accident each year, and about one out of every hundred accident is fatal. Each year since the end of World War II approximately 90,000 industrial workers have received injuries resulting in permanent impairment. Although industrial safety has become a must in every large enterprise, the problem of industrial accidents is serious. Aside from human suffering, the economic loss in man-days of production exceeds from two to ten times that caused by strikes and other types of work stoppage. Professor Glenn W. Miller of Ohio State University has estimated that approximately 45,000,000 man-days of employment were lost in 1947 through industrial accidents. He also estimated that an additional 190,000,000 man-days would be lost in subsequent years from the physical impairments resulting from these accidents.[1]

The incidence of industrial accidents varies considerably. Industrial man is most frequently injured in manufacturing, trade, agriculture, and transportation. He is least often injured in mining and quarrying, railroads, and public utilities. Timbering and logging cause the highest rate of disabling injuries, while the communications industries cause the fewest.

We know less, statistically, about the incidence of occupational diseases than is known about industrial accidents. Diseases and illnesses arising out of the work environment are not as easily attributed to industrial conditions as are accidents. Accidents are sudden in occurrence, usually observable and explainable, and usually require immediate attention. Diseases on the other hand develop slowly, are not readily detected, and the causes are not always easily identified. The occupational diseases resulting from poisoning and inhalation of dust and gases are the easiest to identify. Because these hazards are known to exist, precautionary measures are usually taken to safeguard the workers.

Old Age

The problem of economic insecurity harrassing millions of industrial workers is most acute for the aged. Many of the older members of our industrial labor force have spent most of their productive years

[1] See Glenn W. Miller, *Problems of Labor* (Macmillan, 1951), pp. 301–320.

earning wages and salaries so low that little, if any, savings have been accumulated to assist after they are forced to retire. Potential economic dependency in old age is not only the fear of the older workers, but of most of the middle-age group as well. The decreasing purchasing power of the dollar, inflated prices, and high taxation have made it almost impossible for industrial workers to accumulate sufficient economic wealth to sustain them during their old age.

Statistically, the proportion of persons 65 years or over in the United States almost doubled between 1900 and 1950. Conservative estimates indicate that by 1975 we will have almost 20 million persons in this age group. One of the most challenging social and economic problems of the last half of this century will be finding ways to adjust our industrial society to the needs of an aging population. In the first half our society did not succeed too well in its dealings with the problems of old age. Prior to the depression of the 1930's, little or no effort was made by the federal or state governments to assist the aged; whatever help they received was given by the family or community.

The federal social-security program, launched in 1935, attempted in its old-age and survivors-insurance program to increase the economic security of the older workers by a payroll-financed annuity plan with the hopes that it would keep the annuitant off the relief rolls.[2]

The cyclical prosperity that followed the economical pump-priming experiments of the late 1930's, coupled with the unusual period of World War II, brought full employment, and this made possible the employment of many of the older workers. But as the inflated, war-expanded economy began to adjust to peace-time economic activities, the older members of our industrial labor force found it more difficult to secure jobs or to keep those they had. Our profit-motivated industrial organization is not geared to the slow pace of the older worker. After a worker passes 45, loss of job can be critical because industry is prone to hire the younger worker. As the labor supply increases, the older worker has greater difficulty in securing employment. The more unemployment, the more acute the problem of the older worker

---

[2] The program was expanded in 1939 to include survivor benefits and further liberalized in 1950 and 1954. Slightly more than 50,000,000 persons in the civilian labor force are now covered by old age and survivors insurance.

becomes. The older workers are among the first to feel an economic recession, and to be afflicted by the panicky fear of economic insecurity.

The thought of the future, with the prospect of old age, subsequent unemployment and economic insecurity, produces as a by-product a latent morale problem among industrial workers. The average worker in our highly complex industrial society needs no great wisdom to interpret the significant events in his work career and those of his fellows; nor is it difficult for him to predict his probable plight when old age and retirement policies force him from his job. He knows that full employment—except for the short war periods and the cyclical prosperity—has been but a rare and fleeting thing compared with long years of recession and depression. The thought that old age is likely to bring to him a similar period of deprivation, misery and hardship, cannot fail to affect the morale of every industrial worker. Every thought, expectation, action and habit of the employed industrial worker is influenced to some degree by the precariousness of his way of life.

LABOR-MANAGEMENT RELATIONS

The existence of unequal relations between men is, in all probability, as old as man himself. Throughout history, relations such as master–slave, lord of the manor–serf, and master craftsman–apprentice, in which some individuals held a dominant position over others, have existed. With the coming of the factory system and industrialization, new terms evolved to denote these positional roles: employer-employee, and manager-worker. As the factory system utilized a greater number of mass-production techniques and the size of the business enterprise increased, the relations between the worker and the employer became depersonalized, fragile, and sometimes hostile. The rapid growth of industrialism in the twentieth century further widened the cleavage into bitter economic conflict.

The factors underlying this conflict are many. Some of them—such as the loss of individual identity and self-sufficiency, the loss of ownership of property and the tools of production, the instability and frequency of unemployment, and the fear of want, particularly in the later years of life—have been enumerated. These and other factors have combined in such a manner that today two of the groups that make industrialism possible—the owners of the tools of production and the operators of the tools of production—are almost continuously engaged in conflict. At times this breaks out into open warfare with hard and fast lines drawn between the two groups.

Labor's Approach to Management

The average industrial worker must seek, from sheer necessity, the most advantageous conditions when he sells his manual labor or services. In reality, this is his only property, his only saleable commodity, and his only means of a livelihood. To him advantageous conditions usually consist of: (1) a wage or salary that will enable him to maintain his family in health and decency, (2) employment stability and job security, and (3) reasonable protection against the physical hazards of industrial accidents and occupational diseases.

The twentieth-century industrial worker has learned much from the short but vivid history of the industrial worker, the daily experiences of his fellow associates, and from his own intimate industrial experiences. He knows that when disagreement or conflict arises with the employer regarding wages, hours of employment and the like, his individual bargaining power is greater and more effective if he and his fellow workers bargain as a cooperative cohesive group. This modern industrial worker, to the disgust, bewilderment and fear of some employers, is unlike most of his nineteenth century predecessors in that he is well aware of his weak economic bargaining power when dealing as an individual with management. This knowledge of strength through unity, gleaned from a sordid history of economic exploitation by industry, is the foundation stone upon which the American labor movement has been built.

Another important factor conditioning labor's approach is that mass production, mass machines and endless, repetitive assembly lines are synonymous with monotony, fatigue, and mental frustration—the personal by-products of industrial employment. Thus, labor's approach to its relations with management is conditioned by what is seen through a social lens fabricated out of labor's bitter experiences.

Management's Approach to Labor

Probably the most important factor influencing management's approach to labor is the nature of the modern industrial corporation. Only a small proportion of industrial workers are employed in enterprises that are owned and operated by the same individuals; the majority of them are employed by corporations that are owned by thousands of stockholders. The major interest in the corporation on the part of most stockholders is the return they receive in dividends. Few of the stockholders of America's vast industrial empire have much concern about the operation or policies of the corporations. They are absentee owners with a marked degree of apathy toward corporate affairs.

Thus the control of corporate affairs is vested in a small group of hired administrative officials known as managers. These hired managers who direct and control industry are highly dependent upon the profit-and-loss showing they make to the board of directors and stockholders. Their jobs and their reputations are less dependent upon the quality or durability of their product, their labor policies, or their public relations policies than upon profits. Because they are hired employees, they must inevitably expend their major efforts in seeking the economic welfare of the company.

Management—under the inexorable dictates of the profit-and-loss statement—must continuously strive for the production of goods and services at a low cost per unit. Thus labor, along with the other factors of production, must be considered from the point of view of cost, utilization, efficiency, and productivity. Management, by necessity, must consider labor as just *one* of the factors that enter into the total production process.

Common Grounds

Although each side approaches labor-management relations from opposite or, at least, sharply divergent points of view, the basic assumption upon which each acts is essentially the same.   This is that each individual or group in pursuing self-interest promotes the best interest of society.   Labor's demands for shorter hours of employment, higher wages, industrial safety measures, and the like are but simple expressions of this basic assumption.   Management activities, in its unceasing efforts to lower the cost per unit of production in order that the stockholders may enjoy higher returns from their investments and thus ensure management's continued control of corporate affairs, are also based upon this principle of self-interest.

While self-interest has inevitably led to labor-management conflict, both groups are becoming increasingly aware of their mutual interdependence.   They are aware that each is essential to the other for the survival of both.   They recognize—although it is not usually explicitly stated to the public—that neither can force conditions or settlements upon the other that would endanger the latter's welfare or existence.   Both are essential and inseparable in our capitalistic economy.

Areas of Conflict

Disputes between those owning the tools of production and those using them originated in the guild system in medieval times.   They then revolved mostly around the relationship between the master craftsman and the apprentice.   From the decline of the guild system in the fifteenth century to the end of the Great Depression of the 'thirties, the economic environment in central Europe and the United States was highly favorable to the owners of industry and antagonistic toward associations of craftsmen and workers.   As the economic institution increased in importance and changed to meet the demands of a dynamic society, the conflict between management and labor became more intense.

The first major area of conflict developed when the factory system replaced the domestic system; the conflict grew out of the unemployment that followed technological changes.   The attempts, previously mentioned, by French and English workers to destroy the machines they believed responsible for their unemployment afford one of the earliest examples of industrial conflict over the right of the worker to a job. The subsequent frequency of unemployment growing out of technological, seasonal, and cyclical causes has made this right to a job the major objective and aspiration of every industrial wage earner. It has become the main issue of conflict between those who own and control the tools of production and those who use them. There are, however, several issues which, while varying in intensity with time and place, have consistently complicated labor-management relations. In addition to the right to a job, the industrial worker has sought and fought management for: (1) wages that will enable him to maintain a standard of living of "health and decency"; (2) moderate and reasonable hours of employment; (3) a work environment conducive to health and safety; (4) adequate compensation for accidental injuries and occupational diseases; (5) protection against "company-town" exploitation, the withholding of wages, job and employment racketeering, and substandard workers; and (6) contributions toward financial security in old age. These are the major issues over which management and labor have fought their conflicts of the past. Most of them, in all probability, will remain the areas of conflict throughout the twentieth century.

Management's Weapons

During the early part of the nineteenth century American workers began to feel that they had common interests that were opposed by the employers, and they formed associations of skilled craftsmen to bargain for them. The employers were antagonistic. They felt that theirs alone was the prerogative of determining wages and the hours of employment. Modern industrial warfare revolves around this identical issue. Trade unions feel that their common interests are opposed by management; management believes that labor and the unions are encroaching upon the prerogatives of owners and managers. During the many years that this conflict has been in progress, the employers and their associations and the employees and their unions have invented and used many devices and weapons to further their respective interests.

Management's attitude toward the right of workers to organize has varied from industry to industry, with advances in mass production, and with changes in customs and laws. Not all employers have held the same attitude toward unions, nor employed the same techniques in dealing with the attempts of their employees to organize.

From about 1800 to the time of World War I management and employers were generally violent in their opposition to unionization. The weapons and devices they employed were equally violent, and frequently bloodshed resulted. The economic philosophy of laissez-faire capitalism had little or no tolerance for labor's attempt to seek a voice in determining its wages or hours of employment. Whenever laborers joined together in craft associations to further their participation their employers branded them as conspirators and brought them into court.

Court action. When American craft associations made their appearance in the early years of the nineteenth century, with demands that employers agree to joint determination of wages, a new and precedent-shattering process—collective bargaining—emerged. Many of labor's demands were defeated by the sheer economic power of employers. When, however, some of the craft associations proved almost equal to the employers in strength, the employers frequently resorted to the courts, bringing charges of conspiracy against the associations; conspiracy in that they planned to improve their own status and to harm the employer by demanding higher wages. They accused the associations of violating common law, not statute law. Although the craft associations were not found guilty in every case, they were often convicted and punished. When, however, in 1842, Chief Justice Shaw of the Massachusetts' highest court held that no conspiracy existed unless the end sought or the means by which it was accomplished were unlawful, organized labor groups were greatly benefited in their attempts to bargain for higher wages.

Around the middle of the nineteenth century, employers found that court injunctions and damage suits were as effective as, or more effective than, the old charges of conspiracy. Such activities as striking and picketing were alleged to be harmful to employers and their property. The courts concurred and issued orders for the strikers to cease and desist. Such injunctions were usually based upon such legal concepts as invasion of private property, destruction of property, disturbance of the peace, and appropriation of property without due process of law. Whenever it was shown that unions had violated these concepts, the courts rendered their decisions in favor of the employer.

When labor organizations became interstate in character, the employers tested union activities under the Sherman Anti-Trust Act of 1890, and the courts frequently found that certain union activities prevented or impeded the flow of goods in interstate commerce. They held that the unions were combinations in restraint of interstate trade and therefore subject to penalties under the anti-trust law. This attitude of the courts is typical of that usually exhibited through almost the entire history of the American labor movement—except for a brief period following the depression of the 1930's; the judiciary has generally shown itself ready, willing, and able to lend a hand to management and employers in their opposition to organized labor and unions.

Employers' associations. Equally as important as the courts as weapons against organized labor has been the employers' associations. These emerged during the second half of the nineteenth century. Some of them are still in existence. The employers' associations were organized to combat unions in those industries in which there were many independent companies; they were, in reality, unions of employers. The primary purpose of employers' organizations today is to promote the special interest of their respective groups; but they devote much of their attention to labor-management relations. As a rule they are most effective pressure groups. Maintaining offices in national and state capitals, they spend vast sums of money in lobbying activities designed to influence legislation in their behalf. The enactment of the Taft-Hartley Act is thought by many to represent one of their most successful promotions.

Blacklist, yellow-dog contract, and spy systems. The early trade associations devised all sorts of methods to oppose organized labor. The blacklist, the yellow-dog contract, and spy systems were among the methods developed by them. Whatever effective means of combating labor was found was widely used by members of the association. The blacklist consisted of the names of laborers—and particularly labor leaders—who were considered undesirable by the employers. These lists were circulated widely among members of the trade associations and allied employers. Individuals whose names appeared on them were almost sure to be denied employment. Although legislation has outlawed them or at least restricted their use, they are still employed in some industries.

The yellow-dog contract required the employee, as a condition of employment, to refrain from organized labor activities and from membership in a labor union. It was widely used by trade associations and employers. These contracts usually contained clauses stating that if the worker became a union member he automatically forfeited right to his job. While state laws were passed to make such contracts illegal, the Supreme Court of the United States held that to deny the employers these rights would be taking their guaranteed liberties from them.

In order to ferret out the undesirable employees, the labor leaders, and the plans of the unions, employers established spy systems. Detectives were employed to pose as laborers and to join the unions. Many of these men were secured from Pinkerton, a private detective agency. Among union members, these men were identified by several derogatory names, but they were most frequently called "Pinkertons." These spy systems were very effective in maintaining the blacklists and in assisting employers to combat union activities.

The closed non-union shop and the non-union shop. In a closed non-union shop no union men were allowed to work. The blacklist and the yellow-dog contract enabled the employer to hire only non-union employees and the spy system was effective in finding those who were undesirable. In the non-union shop, union men were allowed to work, but the employer refused to recognize any union as a bargaining agent. In the non-union shops the employers often favored the non-union employees in matters of promotions, vacations, and lay-offs.

Local law enforcement. Certain industries—particularly mining and lumbering—were noted for their "company towns." Frequently the entire local law-enforcement agency was employed by the company. In such cases the sheriff and municipal police were quick to escort labor organizers and undesirable employees out of town and to keep employees from organizing labor unions. Some employers by giving political and financial support "bought" the support of local law-enforcement agencies, which then stood ready to defend the interest of the employers. In other instances, where the local law-enforcement agencies were indebted to the employer, members of the managerial staff were frequently appointed as deputy sheriffs or special police. Although these practices have declined in importance, many employers still rely on such techniques as safeguards against unionization and industrial violence.

In the early period of American industrial-labor relations the resort to rioting and fighting in which many hundreds of persons were killed was not uncommon. Management and the employer generally held the upper hand and received the backing of the courts, but despite this, unionization grew with the rise of political democracy and the changing concept regarding the rights of the common man.

The early years of the twentieth century found America's industrial empire expanding to meet the needs of a growing population at home and of the warring countries of Europe. Better educational opportunities, mass communication, and political democracy were bringing America's heterogeneous segments into closer understanding. Judges and the courts less frequently branded concerted action as a conspiracy in violation of common law. Management and employers became more tolerant of labor and unions. With the entry of the United States into World War I, the federal government—realizing the necessity for industrial harmony—established it as a policy that workers should be allowed to join unions. Thus, for the first time, unions were given national recognition. The war-expanded economy together with almost full employment, greater profits, and governmental sanction of unions, tempered management's opposition to labor into tolerance. With tolerance came new, less explosive, and less obvious methods and devices designed to combat unionization.

The company union. The policy announced by the government to the effect that workers should be allowed to join unions did not specifically state the type of union. Trade associations and the larger employers were quick to see the advantages of a company-dominated union over an independent union. These advantages would be: (1) it would satisfy government policy; (2) its membership could be restricted to the employees of one firm; (3) its small dues and initiation fees would hinder the accumulation of a strike fund; (4) the officials of the union would be employees of the company and subject to company pressure; and (5) company-dominated officials and a weak treasury would hinder the growth of a strong bargaining union. The company union did, in fact, prove to be one of the most effective weapons against independent unions during the war and postwar period.

The open shop. During World War I the "American way" concept that all persons should be left freedom of choice gained wide acceptance. Strange as it may seem this philosophy developed into another device for management's use in its opposition to independent unions. As interpreted by management and the trade associations, the "American way" implied that no one should be required to belong to a union; each worker should be free to make his own choice. They thus advocated what is called the "open shop."

The open shop offered the employer the advantage of taking no position for or against unions as such. Union and non-union men could work side by side. If the employer could maintain an open shop, the chances were favorable that an independent union would not achieve dominance over his labor force and thus endanger his disciplinary control.

Personnel policies and welfare activities. Besides the attempt to substitute company unions for independent unions, management established personnel departments and welfare programs with the intent of making their employees contented and of putting a stop to the union movement. Usually these policies and programs were not built around the major needs of the workers; they were of a paternalistic nature. Management established lunch rooms, recreational facilities, bathing and dressing rooms, summer camps, and gave vacations with pay. Personnel departments frequently placed a premium on athletic directors and the "hail fellow, well met" extrovert.

By the use of injunctions to harass the more active independent unions, by fostering the weak, deceptive company unions, by the open shop, and by paternalistic personnel policies, management made serious inroads into the independent labor movements.

Management found less necessity for continuing its programs of company unions and personnel policies as the depression weakened the independent unions. Usually the company could withstand the demands of the weak independent union without the assistance of a company union. With the advent of the New Deal and its friendly attitude toward unionization, management found the federal courts less favorably disposed toward some of its tactics. Besides guaranteeing the workers the right to join labor unions if they chose to do so, legislation guaranteed the workers and union leaders the right to organize. In the closing days of 1932, Congress passed an act that put restrictions on the use of injunctions in labor disputes. As a result management found it more difficult to deal with unions. After the passage of the Wagner Act (1935) with its provisions against unfair labor practices by industries engaged in interstate commerce, management revamped two of its former weapons to be used against unionization: personnel management departments and employers' associations.

Personnel departments were reorganized with specialists in industrial relations replacing the athletic directors. Emphasis was placed on selecting the right man for the right job, eliminating unsatisfactory working conditions, and establishing principles to govern promotions, wage policies, discipline, and hours of employment. Savings plans, pension plans, and hospitalization and sickness insurance plans were promoted by management through its personnel departments. Some employers established profit-sharing plans that enabled the employee to participate in the profits of the company, while others encouraged their employees to invest regularly in company stock, or gave shares of stock as bonuses. All of these policies were designed to promote efficiency, to provide means by which employees could improve their economic position without union membership, and to instill a sense of partnership or ownership in the employee's mind. Management hoped that these activities would tend to wean employees away from independent unions and minimize grievances against the company.

Accompanying the changes in personnel policies was a change of tactics by the employers' associations. Prior to the New Deal, management had more or less relied on Congress and the courts as allies in their opposition to independent unions. The changed policies of Congress and the federal courts under the New Deal forced the employers' associations into greater pressure-group activities. As long as the Wagner Act was law, the large industries that were engaged in interstate commerce were handicapped in their contests with organized labor. Thus, one of the major goals of the employers' associations became the modification or elimination of certain sections of the Wagner Act. After some ten or twelve years of continual pressure on Congress and vast expenditures for lobbying, plus an assist from irresponsible labor groups, management succeeded in having the Wagner Act modified by the Taft-Hartley Act of 1947.

In summary, during and after the Great Depression the weapons and devices employed by management against organized workers changed from overt, strong, and sometimes violent opposition to toleration and more subtle tactics, and to a gradual decrease in the intensity of opposition. But there was little or no change in the basic philosophy of opposition—only a change in tactics.

Labor's Weapons

In its attempts to secure higher wages, shorter working hours, better working conditions, and protection against industrial accidents and diseases, labor has met many difficulties. Faced with a problem too big to handle individually and feeling that they had common interest, American workers, during the closing years of the eighteenth century, began to unite into small craft associations. From these small organizations the American labor movement has grown into a group of organizations having almost 17,000,000 members, and great political and economic power. Labor has used many weapons and devices in its attempts to secure what it considers to be its fair share of the fruits of production; the independent labor union has been the major device.

Labor unions. The first craft associations in the United States were formed by skilled workers in the large eastern cities during the closing decades of the eighteenth century. However, it was not until the European wars at the beginning of the nineteenth century and our own War of 1812 made it difficult, if not impossible, for the United States to secure manufactured goods from abroad that attention was turned to manufacturing. The result was the emergence of a definable wage-earning class. And coincident with this development was the springing up of new worker organizations in the large manufacturing cities in the east. The business recession that followed the Napoleonic wars seriously affected trade unions and many passed out of existence. These early, uncoordinated, local unions were followed in the second quarter of the nineteenth century by attempts to organize union groups on a city-wide, county-wide and even nation-wide basis. The financial panic of 1837 with its subsequent depression and unemployment took its toll of local, county and nation-wide unions; union members turned their efforts toward organizing producers' and consumers' cooperatives and cooperative communities such as the well known Brook Farm venture in Massachusetts and the New Harmony colony in Indiana. Slightly before 1850, unions shifted their emphasis back to improving the status of the worker. The decade prior to the Civil War was notable in that several unions formed national organizations. By 1860, the seeds of an economic organization for workers had taken root firmly; and organized labor was becoming recognized as a part of the American pattern of life.

During and immediately after the Civil War there was greater expansion of union activities. In 1869, Uriah Stephens, a Philadelphia tailor, and others organized the Noble Order of the Knights of Labor. The Order had the broad aim of replacing our competitive society by a cooperative one which would give all workers their share of the wealth they created. This was to be achieved primarily through educational and political methods rather than through collective bargaining; strikes were to be employed only as a last resort. With an estimated membership of 10,000 in 1879 the Order grew rapidly and claimed over 700,000 members by 1886. Internal conflict led to its decline; in 1890 the Knights reported only 100,000 members and they ceased to exist in 1917.

In 1881 the Federation of Organized Trades and Labor Unions of the United States and Canada was organized. Then, in 1886 this organization merged with the newly organized American Federation of Labor. Led by Samuel Gompers, the Federation adopted policies almost directly opposite to those of the Knights of Labor. It included only craftsmen and tradesmen; instead of devoting effort to building the cooperative movement, it worked for immediate beneficial goals of its members; the strike was used frequently as a weapon, and a high degree of local autonomy was maintained. Under the able leadership of Gompers the American Federation of Labor met the challenges of competing labor organizations and an ever-growing industrial society. By the death of Gompers in 1924 the labor movement was left without positive leadership; it faltered and union membership declined until 1933.

While the craft unions met the needs of our nineteenth and early twentieth century society, there were many unorganized industrial workers. Although attempts were made within the American Federation of Labor to take advantage of the opportunity to organize industrial unions, the leaders, particularly William Green, were not too receptive. After several national conventions, heated debates and one well-publicized fight, John L. Lewis, the leading proponent of the industrial-type union, and ten union groups were expelled in 1936 from the Federation. Mr. Lewis formed a new organization, the Congress of Industrial Organizations, which by 1938 had increased its membership to about 4,000,000. The C.I.O brought a more liberal and broader point of view to the labor movement.

After the split between the A.F. of L. and the unions that united to form the C.I.O., competition between them became keen. Both unions grew by leaps and bounds, with the C.I.O. gaining the larger share of members; the industrial expansion accompanying World War II brought new millions into union membership. Following the war unseasoned leadership, unwise policies, and frequent strikes produced public resentment and resulted in the enactment of laws sharply restricting the activities of organized labor.

The strike. Of all the weapons used by organized labor to accomplish its ends the strike is the most favored and the one most frequently used. The strike emerged during the early years of the labor movement and has continued, with modification, to be an effective tactic in bargaining with management. The strike usually takes the form of refusal by all union members to continue working for an employer who has violated a contractual agreement, or who has been unfair in dealing with union members, or who refuses to bargain with respect to union demands. The workers do not quit or surrender their jobs; they refuse to enter the plant and work. In a *sit-down strike*, however, the workers report daily for work, enter the plant but refuse to work. A *stay-in strike* is somewhat different. The workers refuse to work—and they remain in the plant continuously. Food is usually stored in the plant previous to the strike or it is slipped in by union members. Another type is the *slow-down strike*. In this type of strike the workers report to work but deliberately slow down, or reduce their daily output.

More complicated is the *sympathetic strike*, one that is not directed against the immediate employer, but rather is called to assist another allied union group. The assumption is that the employer of the sympathetic strikers will put pressure on the employer of the original striking group to bargain with his striking employees. The Taft-Hartley Act of 1947 prohibited sympathetic strikes.

The *wildcat strike* may take any of the foregoing forms, but it is distinguished from the other types in that frequently it is unofficial; that is, it lacks approval from higher union officials. Usually a "wildcat" strike is unplanned, local in its area of influence, and of short duration. Some unions, not wanting to call an official strike, have had their members take "holidays" or "periods of mourning." A final type, the *jurisdictional strike*, has done much to create an unfriendly attitude toward organized labor. This type of strike is not between employers and their employees, but between unions. It arises out of a disagreement as to which union should have jurisdiction over certain jobs. Naturally, as new industrial processes are developed, new types of jobs are created, and this leads to disagreements among unions as to which shall have jurisdiction. But it is difficult for the public to understand why they should be denied goods and services while the unions settle the issue. This is one of the unfair labor practices prohibited by the Taft-Hartley Act.

The strike, regardless of its form, has one purpose—to stop production. The assumption behind this tactic is that the employer will be more willing to compromise or to reach an agreement over the issue involved when he is compelled to cease production.

Picketing. This tactic usually accompanies the strike. The striking union members, to gain public support for their cause, or to prevent nonunion workers from taking over their jobs, assemble around the entrance of the plant. They carry placards which usually state that this particular plant is "unfair" to organized labor; shifts in the picket line are established so that it is maintained during the strike. Frequently handbills giving the union's position are circulated. Although most picketing consists only of walking or parading with placards, some picketing activities have led to mob violence, destruction of property, and death. The strike and picketing were developed early in the labor movement, but they remain as effective tactics in assisting unions in their bargaining with employers.

Violence. Although deplored and denounced by organized labor, violence, destruction of property by dynamiting, and the employment of hired thugs have been and are still used by the workers against employers and their property. Violence is resorted to usually during prolonged and bitter strikes.

The boycott. There are two types of boycotts, the primary and the secondary. The *primary* boycott consists of concerted action on the part of union members and their families in refusing to purchase goods and services from employers whom they consider unfair to organized labor; the *secondary* boycott arises when not only union members and their families but also other groups—such as their friends, fellow townsmen, and merchants—join in the refusal. Frequently union groups honor the boycott by refusing to transport or handle the products of employers who are called unfair. This technique originated during the latter part of the nineteenth century, and the name is said to have been derived from the first victim, a Captain Boycott. The secondary boycott is prohibited by the Taft-Hartley Act.

The union shop. Under this type of agreement the employer may hire any worker, but all non-union employees must join the union within a specific period of time, usually thirty days. The union is recognized as the bargaining agent and the provision requiring non-union workers to join, enables the union to maintain its control over a majority of the employees. Although this type of agreement was used prior to 1933, it had its greatest success in the decade proceeding World War II. The Taft-Hartley Act with its many restrictions significantly reduced the effectiveness of the union shop.

The closed shop. This type of agreement is the most cherished by union members for it assures them the greatest amount of security.

In the closed shop a worker must already be a union member to get employment. The union is recognized as the bargaining agent, and the agreement assures that there will be no discrimination against union members. Prior to World War II a large number of closed-shop agreements were made with employers. The Taft-Hartley Act prohibits the closed-shop agreements.

Collective bargaining. The major purpose of all union organizations is to engage in collective bargaining with employers. The other tactics and weapons previously enumerated are designed primarily to assist the union in its bargaining activities. Collective bargaining is the process of negotiation between the employer and the duly appointed representatives of the workers in an attempt to settle issues of common interest arising out of the employer-employee relations. Labor has learned from experience that its bargaining power is considerably enhanced by having union organizations that are independent of influence or control by the employer.

Although the foregoing partial list of weapons and tactics used by employer and employees in their conflicts is impressive, it would be far from correct to assume that all employers and all union groups are constantly employing these weapons and tactics. By far the vast majority of employers and workers settle their differences and conflicts peacefully through collective bargaining.

TOWARD SOLUTIONS

It was stated earlier in this chapter that the individuals, organizations, and institutions most concerned with the industrial-labor relations have not always possessed the ability to solve their problems. While there is considerable pessimism today on the part of some labor and management groups regarding their future relations, there is also growing evidence that the solution to many of these problems can be found.

Early attempts at understanding some of the basic problems of industrial relations centered around psychological tests and vocational guidance, studies of fatigue and nutrition, and investigations of economic incentives, wage rates, bonus plans, and department quotas. None of them proved consistently fruitful. In 1927 Elton Mayo, Head of Harvard's Department of Industrial Research, and his associates began the now famed social experiments in the Hawthorne Plant (Chicago) of Western Electric Company. The fundamental objective of the researchers was to learn "What makes workers work?" Stuart Chase in his book, *Men at Work*, describes this search and discovery of the mysterious unknown Factor X.

What was this X? . . . It wasn't in the physical production end of the factory at all. It was in the girls themselves. It was an attitude, the way the girls now felt about their work and their group. By segregating them into a little world of their own, by asking their help and cooperation, the investigators had given the young women a new sense of their own value. Their whole attitude changed from that of separate cogs in a machine to that of a congenial team helping the company solve a significant problem. . . . They had found stability, a place where they belonged, and work whose purpose they could clearly see. And so they worked faster and better than they ever had in their lives.

A factory . . . may be regarded as performing two major functions: producing goods, and creating and distributing human satisfactions among the people under its roof. . . . A great deal of study has been devoted to the former by engineers, accountants, efficiency experts . . . Very little study had been devoted to the social function, the "creating and distributing of human satisfactions," until the Hawthorne experiment came along. . . . They found that the two functions were so closely connected that they could not be separated. . . . If the human organization of the factory is out of balance, all the efficiency systems in the world will not improve the output of goods. . . . Underneath the stop watches and bonus plans of the efficiency experts, the worker is driven by a desperate inner urge to find an environment where he can take root; where he belongs and has a function; where he sees the purpose of his work and takes pride in achieving it. Failing this, he will accumulate frustrations and obsessions, and ever so often break out in violent conflict. . . .

For their neglect of the human function of production, managers have paid a high price in strikes, restricted output, revolts, and a vast sea of human waste.[3]

The Hawthorne experiments and the publication of the findings by Roethlisberger and Dickson did much to stimulate social science

[3] Stuart Chase, *Men at Work* (Harcourt, Brace, 1945), pp. 12–27. Reprinted by permission of Harcourt, Brace and Company, Inc.

research in the field of industrial relations.[4] Management however
in general, refused to accept the findings of "impractical" academic
men. Then, at the outbreak of World War II, the War Manpower Commission established a Training within Industry (T.W.I.)
program to assist in maintaining high production rates. Realizing
that high production could be maintained only through the proper
handling of the human relations within industry, the T.W.I. developed a program designed to provide training for foremen, office
supervisors, plant superintendents and executives in handling problems of human relations. Almost a half-million supervisory personnel were trained in the new methods and techniques of handling the
groups under them. The success of this program did much to create
on the part of management a more favorable opinion of social scientists.

The Yankee City Volume IV *The Social System of the Modern
Factory* by Warner and Low, with its vivid story of a strike and an analysis of the factors involved, added to the accumulated store of knowledge concerning the factory as a social system.[5] This accumulation,
consisting of theory, research, and applied knowledge, has now been
systematized and integrated into university departments of personnel
management, industrial relations, and industrial sociology. Management has gradually realized that the problems of labor relations require trained specialists just as do those of technological production.
Farsighted industrialists are insisting that men employed for personnel
positions secure special college or university training in industrial relations, and particularly in the human organization of production.
Management is likewise appropriating ever larger sums for empirical
research in these areas. Labor unions, too, are cooperating with the
social scientists in an attack upon these problems.

If the evidence of the past is any guide, the future of human-
relation problems in industry justifies optimism. Since the 1930's,
the most significant development has been the striking increase in
the awareness on the part of the public, the government, the employer, and the worker of industrial and labor problems. Awareness

    [4] F. J. Roethlisberger and William J. Dickson, *Management and the Worker*
(Harvard University Press, 1939).
    [5] W. Lloyd Warner and J. O. Low, *The Social System of the Modern Factory*
(Yale University Press, 1947).

must come before understanding; but only through understanding can successful solutions evolve.

Study Questions

1. Why is it important to view the problems of the employer-employee from a historical perspective?

2. Do you think mass, formal organizations can solve social problems as effectively as primary, face-to-face, organizations? Why?

3. Which of our basic social institutions has suffered most from the impact of the Industrial Revolution and particularly of twentieth century industrialism? Why?

4. Of the many insecurities now facing the industrial worker, which is likely to cause the most concern in the last half of the twentieth century? Why?

5. In your opinion is the life of the worker today less or more secure than it was in 1776? Why?

6. Do you think the economic experiments of the New Deal effectively solved the unemployment situation existing prior to World War II? Why?

7. Of the various tactics and weapons used by employers and employees in industrial warfare, which do you think are most acceptable from the point of view of the public? Which are least acceptable?

8. What, in your opinion, will be the future of employer-employee relations? Explain.

9. Do you think the labor movement will ever again have the privileges it enjoyed under the "New Deal"? Why?

10. Do you think the conscientious application of social-science research and its findings could solve some of the major problems in industrial relations? Why? How? Examples?

Selected References

Bakke, E. Wright, and Clark Kerr, *Unions, Management and the Public* (Harcourt, Brace, 1948). An excellent exploration of the critical issues in the field of industrial and labor relations.

Chase, Stuart, *Men at Work* (Harcourt, Brace, 1945) and *The Proper Study of Mankind* (Harper, 1948). Unsurpassed for their graphic style which has placed important social-science research in industrial relations on the level of the lay reader.

Mayo, Elton, *The Human Problems of an Industrial Civilization* (Macmillan, 1933), and *The Social Problems of an Industrial Society*

(Harvard University Press, 1945). Mayo's books are exceedingly important for their interpretation of the social forces operative in industrial society.

Miller, Delbert C., and William H. Form, *Industrial Sociology* (Harper, 1951). The first book by this title. Excellent for its integration of new research materials into the frame of reference of industrial sociology.

Miller, Glenn W., *Problems of Labor* (Macmillan, 1951). This is probably the best review of current labor problems in the United States.

Moore, Wilbert E., *Industrial Relations and the Social Order* (Macmillan, 1947). One of the first texts in the field of industrial sociology.

Roethlisberger, F. J., and William J. Dickson, *Management and the Worker* (Harvard University Press, 1939). One of the first attempts toward an understanding of the human organization in industrial plants.

Selekman, Benjamin M., *Labor Relations and Human Relations* (McGraw-Hill, 1947). A valuable analysis of labor relations, particularly of the role played by the union leaders.

Walker, Charles R., and Robert H. Guest, *The Man on the Assembly Line* (Harvard University Press, 1952). A provocative study of new workers in a new automobile assembly plant.

Whyte, William F. (ed.), *Industry and Society* (McGraw-Hill, 1946). One of the pioneer texts in industrial and labor problems.

Problems in Education

Nearly one fourth of the American people are in school during the regular sessions. In the autumn of 1953, for example, the enrollments included 23,369,000 public and 3,417,000 private and parochial grade-school pupils, 6,421,000 public and 818,000 private and parochial high school pupils, and 2,500,000 college students. This total of almost 37,000,000 enrollment may normally be expected to grow as the higher birth rates since the 1940's increase the number of children and youth in the nation.[1]

In addition to these millions formally enrolled in schools, there are many thousands more who are in correspondence courses, night schools, lecture series, occupational study groups, and other varieties of informal education. If the growing numbers of these part-time students are added to the millions of full-time pupils, the total is doubtless equal to one out of every four persons in the total population.

These millions of learners represent a far larger proportion of the people than at any other time in American history. Only a generation or two ago schooling was generally expected for children from the age of six years to perhaps the fifteenth or sixteenth year, but only small percentages of the population completed high school or college. Now compulsory education laws, the pressure of public opinion, and requirements for obtaining jobs are keeping nearly all youths in school, often against their own wishes.

These pressures upon children and youth to go to school have not been uniformly applied throughout the nation. Consequently, even today about ten million adults in the United States have had less than

[1] "A Fourth of a Nation," *Newsweek* (August 31, 1953), p. 50.

five years of schooling. Four million native whites, three million Negroes, and three million foreign-born whites make up these ten million adults who are described as "functionally illiterate," those who cannot read and write well enough to make much use of these skills.[2]

Today throughout the nation programs of education are being extended toward both younger and older persons. Nursery schools and kindergartens are rapidly increasing, both those supported from tax funds and those provided by gifts and fees. Various types of schooling for adults have similarly increased. Education is no longer exclusively for young people or for the privileged groups in American society.

THREE DILEMMAS OF THE DEMOCRATIZATION OF EDUCATION

The accepted theory in this country—namely that in a democracy education is for all—and, moreover, the great expansion of American schools have resulted in many conflicts in theory and in practice. These conflicts provide contemporary education with some of its most significant dilemmas.[3]

The First Dilemma: Scholarship or Entertainment?

As the number of students increases, the proportion of those able and willing to do hard and rigorous study tends to decrease. Are high schools and colleges to reject these thousands who would like to have diplomas but who are bored or even emotionally upset by continued intellectual effort? If they are not to be eliminated by giving them failing grades, they must be given something to do that will increase their "school spirit" and protect them from boredom and frustration. To meet the needs of these "non-scholars" modern schools provide a variety of extra-curricular features; such as, athletic

[2] *Literacy Education*, Circular No. 376, U.S. Department of Health, Education and Welfare, June, 1953.

[3] L. J. Elias, "Democracy Hands the College a Dilemma," *Association of American Colleges Bulletin*, 34 (December, 1948), 486–492.

teams, fraternities and sororities, dances and parties, and clubs of many types. If these are not available, the students sometimes strike or riot in order to create some "excitement."

The primary purpose of these extra-curricular activities is to butter the dry bread of academic endeavors with enough fun to permit it to be swallowed with a minimum of effort by those who have little genuine interest in the educational work of the school. These scholastic sideshows tend, however, to overshadow the training, the primary work of the school. To many students school would be delightful if it were not for conscientious teachers and the labors of study. In fact, pessimists say that only a small percentage of American students fail to rejoice over an unexpected holiday or the illness of a teacher (that decreases learning without reducing the amount of credit for the class). Those who really enjoy academic work are often contemptuously described as "grinds," "book-worms," "eager beavers," or by other even less attractive epithets.

If teaching is the function of schools—as nearly all agree, at least in words—should it be overshadowed by recreational activities? What is to be done with the thousands of students who reject learning of almost any type? If they are not entertained, they leave school at the first opportunity. Is it better to abolish the "side shows" or to continue them in the hope that those who are being entertained may derive benefit from the unavoidable contact with teachers and learners?

The Second Dilemma: Selection or Non-selection?

Formerly one of the accepted functions of the school was to select for promotion and social approval those most adept in its work, whether this work were algebra or typing, law or bricklaying. But should many of the millions who now crowd American schools be given inferiority feelings by receiving failing grades? Some students are so frustrated by the pass or fail system that they become delinquents or neurotics.

One solution to this problem is to give a passing grade to all students, regardless of the quality or quantity of their work. By this plan a student is promoted on the basis of time elapsed or of attendance at class. This is chronological promotion, although it is sometimes erroneously described as "social" promotion. But, if everyone receives a passing grade, diplomas will soon lose their significance and will become only certificates of attendance, as, indeed they actually are at some schools. Then high school and college diplomas will be without economic and prestige value.

Some propose a compromise to lessen the unfortunate consequences of either failing some or passing all of those enrolled in a class. They suggest that in the elementary schools all students be given passing grades and that in the high schools all except a few of the most incompetent should be promoted. In colleges or universities and especially in vocational or professional schools, however, they believe that only the capable and the industrious should receive diplomas. The policy of passing all students, often accepted in the elementary school, has become increasingly prevalent in high schools. Will it reach the college level? Will college diplomas then become certificates of attendance?

The Third Dilemma: The Best, the Average, or the Poorest?

If the American schools are to be all-inclusive, as is the present tendency, should not the course of study and the teaching methods be adapted to the lower levels of student abilities? Only in this way will the least gifted be protected from early defeatism in our highly competitive society. On the other hand, if the gifted are relatively neglected, they will develop poor work habits that will be serious handicaps in later life. For example, a problem student in one of our colleges who confessed that he had bought no books and done no studying, explained that he had made satisfactory grades in high school by only listening "while the teacher tried to beat it into the dumbbells' heads."

If instruction is directed toward the average student (now the general practice) both the best and the poorest are somewhat neglected. This difficulty can be avoided by small classes and individual instruction, but the financial cost of such a plan would be almost prohibitive. Segregation of the gifted and the slow learners has often been tried but without very favorable results. Another plan is to devote some colleges and perhaps some secondary schools to the instruction of superior students only. Such, in fact, is the policy of a number of the endowed colleges. The following is quoted from a letter addressed to prospective students and to those adults who might be persuaded to give the college financial support. The excerpt expresses clearly the aristocratic concept of education.

> Ours is a day of leveling off. Some have called it the "century of the common man." Such a phrase suggests that the common denominator for our day is the average man. This accent makes for mediocrity. . . . This college is a fort standing against the mediocratization of life. . . . The average civilization, like the average man, is not good enough. The victory in history, as well as in life, is to those who have a *sense of excellence.*

Europeans, faced by these dilemmas arising from the democratization of education, have chosen through a system of rigid selection to restrict their secondary schools and colleges to the training of the relatively gifted. In their opinion the American schools are just "play schools" with low standards and ideals of accomplishment.

THE SCHOOLS AND THE SOCIAL CLASSES

Closely akin to the dilemmas brought about by the democratization of American education is the problem of the relationship of the schools to the class structure. From one point of view, students may be roughly categorized as coming from lower, middle, or upper-class families. Should teachers and administrators accept, reject, or try to modify this division of persons into social classes, perhaps more accurately called socio-economic levels of living?

Acceptance of Class Divisions

According to some observers, many American schools after giving only verbal allegiance to the ideals of democracy proceed to arrange curricula, teaching procedures, and even extra-curricular activities in such a way as to continue the present socio-economic status of the student. The higher grades and the majority of school "honors" go to the privileged few. The children from lower-class homes are often trained by repeated failures and rejections to accept an inferior status in the school and in later life.[4] In such schools, exclusive clubs, sororities, and fraternities tend to dominate "social life" and to control student activities, with the possible exception of athletics. Even teachers and administrators, many of whom are "social climbers" from the upper lower class or the lower middle class, often seem to favor the students from "the better families."

Attempts to Modify Class Divisions

On the other hand, in some schools much time and effort is devoted to eliminating or weakening class distinctions among students. In these idealistic schools, teachers and administrators endeavor to develop friendships across social class lines and to give special encouragement to the less privileged in order to promote what the Italian sociologist Vilfredo Pareto described as "the circulation of the elite." In this process the "best" of the underprivileged are permitted or helped to rise toward the top of the social pyramid, while the "poorest" of the upper groups are gently but firmly helped to accept roles in life less important than those of their parents. Schools with such purposes, it should be noted, are rarely approved by the presently successful families.

Perhaps the majority of American schools operate in such a way as to modify somewhat the class situation. Usually no open attack is made upon discrimination against the children of under-privileged families. Externally the class pattern of the community is accepted. But indirectly "the circulation of the elite" is aided by impartiality in grading and promotion, free lunch and textbook programs, emphasis upon simplicity in dress, reduction of the incidental expenses for student activities, curbing of the "organized snobbishness" of fraternities and sororities, scholarships based in part upon financial need, educational benefits for veterans, and similar methods.

The problem of how to keep a society from developing rigid social stratification is not necessarily one for the schools to solve, but in the

[4] A. B. Hollingshead, *Elmtown's Youth* (Wiley, 1949).

United States it has been left largely to them. The results have often been disappointing to those who believe strongly in the democratic ideal of equal rights to all and special privileges to none.[5]

INEQUALITIES IN FINANCIAL SUPPORT OF SCHOOLS

The mere location of the residence of a pupil has a marked influence upon his opportunities for having an adequate school building, a well-trained teacher, and necessary transportation and supplies. In general, school funds are more available in those areas where the proportion of children and youth in the total population is lower. For example, the rural areas have a large percentage of people of educable age but they also usually have low incomes from taxation.

The inequalities are often very marked. In the school year 1947–48 Arkansas and Mississippi spent less than $100 per pupil in average daily attendance, while New York and New Jersey spent more than $250 per pupil. Moreover the differences in taxable income in school districts within the same state may be as high as 100 to 1.[6] These inequalities, however, are often partially overcome by various forms of state equalization funds, allocated generally on the basis of the number of pupils in actual attendance.

Similar differences exist as between localities and states in the buildings provided, in teachers' salaries, and in other requirements for a modern school. Separate schools for racial minorities are often especially handicapped by inequalities in financial support; these differences, however, are now generally decreasing. The Southern states have far less funds for schools, even though they devote a larger percentage of their tax income to educational purposes than states in other sections of the country.

Perhaps the most neglected children in America in term of opportunities for education are those of the thousands of migratory workers who supply the seasonal demand for labor in orchards, can-

[5] W. Lloyd Warner, Robert J. Havighurst, and Martin B. Loeb, *Who Shall Be Educated?* (Harper, 1944)

[6] T. Lynn Smith, *The Sociology of Rural Life* (3rd ed., Harper, 1953), pp. 431–439.

neries, market gardens, farms, and factories, and of the thousands of highly mobile families who answer the calls for highway and construction workers. Many tenant farmers and "share-croppers" also have high rates of spatial mobility. The children of such families are often in school for only a few weeks or months before their parents move on in search of employment. Unfortunately no feasible plans have yet been developed to give even moderate educational advantages to these children of migratory workers as they move from one school to another, from one state to another, even from one section of the country to another. Possibly the cooperation of local, state, and federal agencies and funds could reduce appreciably the educational handicaps of these children of migrants.[7]

Federal Aid to Education

In the opinion of many persons, inequalities in the financial support of the public schools while regrettable are still unavoidable inasmuch as they arise primarily from the differences in income and wealth found in different communities and states. Others, however, believe that the inequalities should be overcome by large grants from federal funds used to provide a minimum of schooling for every child and youth, regardless of where he may live. Federal aid to education, however, is vigorously opposed by those who fear that it would reduce local control of schools and ultimately might end in a nationally controlled school system.

Private and Parochial Schools versus the Public Schools

There are also violent differences of opinion concerning the use of tax funds to assist, directly or indirectly, in removing similar inequalities among private or church-supported schools that now enroll about twelve per cent of the elementary and secondary school pupils. Some hold that adequate schooling should be provided for all boys and girls, regardless of whether or not they are enrolled in the public schools. Others believe that if tax funds are spent upon non-govern-

[7] President's Commission on Migratory Labor, *Migratory Labor in American Agriculture* (Government Printing Office, 1951).

mental schools, the historic principle of the separation of church and state will be imperiled with harmful social consequences.

Religious instruction. Some parents are so anxious for their children to receive religious instruction that they prefer to send them to church affiliated schools. Others wish the public schools to release the pupils from academic duties to go elsewhere to receive training in religious matters or even to permit religious instructors to come to the schools to teach the pupils. The latter plan, however, has been declared unconstitutional by the U.S. Supreme Court in the now famous "McCollum case." The schools may still legally provide non-controversial religious and ethical training; instruction of this type, however, is likely to be colorless and not very significant to the pupils. A third group holds that training in religious beliefs is primarily a function of the home and the church and prefers that the public schools devote all their efforts to other types of instruction.[8]

STRUGGLES FOR CONTROL OF THE PUBLIC SCHOOLS

Some years ago Joseph Stalin is reported to have said, "Education is a weapon, the significance of which depends upon who holds it and against whom it is aimed." According to this point of view, the school is an agency for changing men's minds and its work is closely akin to propaganda. This view of the purpose of schools has been vigorously opposed in the United States. Americans have generally believed that schools should enlighten and inform, but should not attempt to indoctrinate or to compel conformity in thinking.

Many observers have noted in recent years a weakening of support of the slogans "Keep politics out of the schools" and "Keep the schools out of politics." But the protests against politics in the schools have served to reduce or even to eliminate open attempts by political parties to control the public schools. Nevertheless ideological or power groups are frequently endeavoring to direct school policies and programs, often by indirect methods of control.

[8] Henry H. Hill, "Public Education Must Be Secular," *The Atlantic Monthly,* 190 (October, 1952), 75–77.

Ideological Power Groups

Among those that may attempt to affect public-school policies in various ways are such groups as pro-labor and "Big Business," ultra-conservatives and radicals, nationalists or isolationists and internationalists, those who wish to use tax funds to help church-supported schools and those opposed to such use, those who desire expanded school programs and those who prefer lower tax rates, and the advocates of "Progressive Education" and their opponents. ·

With few exceptions these ideological or point-of-view groups have exercised little long-time control over the schools. Any success gained by a group tends to arouse their ideological opponents, who in turn lead the public in neutralizing the temporarily dominant point of view. This neutralizing process is not likely to continue, however, if the general public should ever give up its present attitude of at least mild opposition to any special interest becoming very powerful in school affairs.

Personal Power Groups

In many smaller communities, however, power groups have often been quite successful in the control of the expenditures for schools, in the selection of teachers, in the location of new school buildings, in the determination of tax rates, and similar matters. The motivation of such groups is rarely ideological—more frequently it is "the will to power" for ego-satisfaction or monetary gain. Publication of recent studies of the operations of these financially or personally interested power groups may arouse the general public to resist such attempts to control the schools.

In a very real sense the struggles for democracy and intellectual freedom in America center around the schools. Dictators from either the right (fascist) or the left (communist) cannot long remain in power unless they obtain control of the schools. Would-be dictators will, consequently, make every effort to gain this control in the early stages of their fight for power.

GROUPS FOR AND AGAINST PUBLIC SCHOOLS

In conflicts over the public schools, many Americans are neutral or unconcerned, but others habitually take sides for or against the schools. Traditionally Americans are zealous for tax-supported schools as a means of public enlightenment, as a way of giving opportunity to the underprivileged, and as a bulwark of democracy. This is still the attitude of a large number of people, perhaps of the majority. On the other hand there are probably increasing numbers of people who are ready to attack the public schools whenever circumstances permit. Some of these have already been mentioned— those working for lower taxes, the supporters of private and parochial schools, and those frustrated in their attempts to gain control of the public schools.

Some persons are unfriendly to the public schools because though they have no children in school they yet have to pay taxes for their support. A few others are eager to attack asserted deficiencies in the schools in order to attract favorable attention to themselves, perhaps as "super-patriots." Others fear that public education will result in greater political and economic power for racial and cultural minorities and similar underprivileged groups.

A large group of opponents has grown from those whose own experiences in the public schools were frustrating or embittering. Some of these were disillusioned when the schools failed to provide a ladder to personal success. Others bear grudges because of low grades, harsh discipline by teachers, failure to obtain social recognition by fellow students, and compulsory attendance.

Perhaps a larger group consists of those who blame the public schools for the social ills of contemporary society. A well-to-do business man complains, "This country is in a poor way. Men won't volunteer for military service. Crime and juvenile delinquency are continually increasing. What has happened to us? It must be the schools!" This tendency to use the schools as a scapegoat whenever undesired or harmful social changes manifest themselves is now apparently on the increase. It will be reduced by more knowledge of the complexities of the causes of social disorganization and by the realization that, although the schools have a strong influence upon their pupils, they are not all-powerful for either good or evil.

Finally, it should not be forgotten that some persons are antagonistic to education in general, especially to higher education. They express their scorn in such terms as, "only a teacher," "long-haired professor," and "brain-truster." They are less critical of natural scientists than of social scientists and other scholars, doubtless because the work of the natural scientist has more demonstrable value—both economic and military. This opposition to education and to the highly trained has been aptly called "the revolt of the primitives." To this revolt probably can be attributed much of the strength of current attacks upon public education in the United States.

CONFLICTING PHILOSOPHIES OF EDUCATION

The American schools are, quite logically, the focal point for conflicting philosophies concerning the functions of education. These philosophies can be designated with fair accuracy as perennialism, progressivism, and essentialism.[9]

Perennialists

The *perennialists* emphasize religious and ethical principles which they believe to be right at all times and in all places. To them the most important duty of the schools is to teach values and principles of conduct that are not subject to change. Perennialists are generally moral absolutists—what is good is good, regardless of circumstances. The founders of most of the early schools in America were some variety of perennialists. Some perennialists today emphasize the values of religious and ethical instruction; others emphasize the superior values of "the great books"—that is, the traditional classics.

[9] Clifton L. Hall, "Conflicting Philosophies of Education" in William Van Til *et al., Great Human Issues of Our Times* (Nashville: George Peabody College for Teachers, 1953).

Progressives

Only during the past half-century have *progressives* markedly affected American education. They are chiefly followers of the philosophers William James and John Dewey, who emphasized "pragmatism," the testing of ideas by their practical consequences in the lives of men. The progressives have tried to make the school responsible for every phase of the child's development and well-being. They have emphasized that education is a social process and that a student's classmates may be more significant to him than his teacher. Progressives are generally experimentalists, holding that schools should provide more opportunities for significant experiences and that teachers should avoid any type of compulsion to influence children to learn previously ascertained facts.

Essentialists

During the past fifteen or twenty years the *essentialists* have made vigorous attacks upon the doctrines of the progressives. To the essentialists the school is primarily a place for intellectual training in such matters as the three R's, history, science, and literature. They oppose turning the school into a child welfare center. Instead they wish the school to transmit "the cultural heritage" and to prepare for progress those pupils capable of intellectual development. The purpose of the school is to provide children an opportunity to climb upon the shoulders of our wise ancestors and contemporaries in order to see farther.

In each of the schools of educational philosophy summarized briefly above there are sincere, honest, and capable men and women. When carried on with tolerance and perspective, their controversies have contributed to progress in American education. But sometimes their controversies have not been distinguished for either tolerance or perspective.

Liberal or Vocational Education?

Somewhat akin to the conflict over the philosophy of education is another disagreement over whether secondary schools and colleges should emphasize liberal courses or vocational training. In the past liberal education predominated, having its roots far back in the Greek and Roman schooling considered suitable for free men (Latin *liber* = free). Today the liberal curriculum is planned to enable a man to escape prejudices that bind him to his idols in the family, the community, and the nation. "Ye shall know the truth, and the truth shall make you free." Among the subjects emphasized are foreign languages, science, literature, history, and philosophy, but the primary goal is the development of the power of independent thinking and of objectivity in the pursuit of truth.

Vocational training, on the other hand, is aimed toward economic efficiency, toward ability to make a comfortable living rather than to live a thoughtful life. Its advocates point out that liberal education is chiefly suited to those with capacity for abstract thinking, to those with some wealth and leisure, and to those who enter the traditional professions of medicine, law, and the ministry. They claim further-more that vocational efficiency adds to the welfare not only of the individual but also of the community and the nation. Finally they insist that training in a trade or one of the newer professions also has an important liberalizing influence.

In contemporary United States the ideals of liberal education gen-erally predominate in the older and the church-affiliated under-graduate colleges, while vocational training is emphasized in tax-supported colleges and professional schools. Most of the public high schools attempt to provide both liberal (college preparatory) and vocational (trades and occupations) courses.

General education. A moderately successful attempt to com-promise the conflict between the advocates of liberal or vocational training is the development of *general* education on the college level. In a general-education plan a large part of the freshman and sopho-more years in college is devoted to giving the students greater per-spective about himself and the world around him, often using a modification of the materials and methods of instruction emphasized in the liberal arts colleges. After this period of cultural and per-sonal development the student can proceed either to a vocational objective or to further study in the arts and sciences. The advocates of general education claim that their plan gives most of the advantages of liberal education without undue use of the student's time, and that such a scheme gives a sense of cultural unity and perspective not provided in the diversity of vocational courses. Its opponents attack it as a watered-down version of liberal education (1) that will later be largely repeated in the junior and senior years for those going into arts and sciences and (2) that takes valuable time and effort from those who are going into vocational training.

QUANTITY AND QUALITY OF TEACHERS

One of the recurring problems of American schools is the scarcity of competent teachers. The shortage is becoming acute as higher birth rates result in increasing enrollments. The reasons for this shortage of teachers vary from time to time, but at least four are constantly present.

Low Pay

Except in a few states, classroom teachers are generally poorly paid. In spite of their investment in time and money for college training they often receive less pay than the school janitor. Many of them would get more income if they were given the wages of a fully-employed carpenter or truck driver. Financial advancement is also quite limited except for those who leave classroom teaching for positions as supervisors, principals, or superintendents. In general, classroom teaching has not offered a promising future, but some recent pay scales are offering strong inducements for continued service and training.

Lack of Freedom

Teachers, especially in small communities, are often subject to a great deal of surveillance. Their conduct, in and out of school, their personal habits, and even their beliefs are constantly under critical observation. The teacher's freedoms are also often restricted by frequent and bitter controversies over school policies and practices.

School teaching is not a suitable occupation for anyone who wishes to "live his own life."

"Discipline"

The task of dealing firmly but kindly with thirty or forty squirming children or an equal number of restless adolescents cooped up in one room is not one for the weak-willed or the faint-hearted. Many would-be teachers are so appalled by the problem of mere control of pupils that they give up the idea of joining the profession. Others quit after the first year of misery and defeat. "Teaching is no bed of roses."

Lack of Prestige

In Europe a teacher enjoys a social prestige far higher than his relative income, but in the United States his prestige is only a little higher than his relative income, unless perhaps he is a college professor or a school administrator. College students who believe themselves capable of competing with the best do not wish to enter a second-class profession, although many of them will accept teaching positions—almost as a last resort. This low social status of the teacher based on the idea that he is unable to make a living at anything else, especially affects the supply of men classroom teachers.

As a consequence of such factors as have been briefly described above the supply of any kind of trained teachers has been inadequate, while teachers of superior ability are quite scarce. Several studies indicate clearly that college students who plan to teach school make lower than average scores on intelligence tests and make lower grades on other comparable examinations. It is too frequently true that "he who can, does; he who cannot, teaches."

THE TEACHER'S CONFLICTING SOCIAL ROLES

One of the ever-present problems of education is the conflict in the social roles of the teacher, who is often expected to do at one and the same time things that it is virtually impossible to harmonize. For example, the teacher must be ever ready to praise, even for the slightest improvement, yet he is also expected to be ever ready to correct for errors of fact, thinking, or conduct. Actually, reward and penalty are supplemental means of controlling behavior—but immature pupils can hardly be expected to understand this.

Departmental Loyalty

Another conflict in the teacher's roles is the result of his tendency to identify himself with his subject-matter rather than with school or community welfare. This "departmental pride" is especially noticeable in high schools and colleges. It increases the teacher's loyalty to the fellow teachers in his subject-matter field and his zeal in teaching his own classes, which he assumes to be the most significant and important in the whole curriculum.

On the other hand, this emphasis upon the role of instructor of *one* field of knowledge may bring the teacher into conflict with other members of the faculty, who in turn may feel that their own subjects and their pupils should receive paramount attention. Occasionally this rivalry takes the form of competition for the study time of the pupils, each department demanding the lion's share for its own subject. (Sometimes the pupils react to such excessive demands by failing to work well for *any* department.)

Excessive loyalty to one subject-matter field may also confuse and disorientate immature pupils, who cannot place in proper perspective the conflicting claims and demands of his several teachers. This, in turn, prevents the pupil from seeing that all knowledge is consistent and is a unified whole rather than conflicting fragments. Education should help to lessen rather than to increase the segmentation of American life that results when each individual or group strives for its own interests and advantage without regard for interrelationships or the need for cooperation.

Pupil or Subject-Matter?

The teacher also is involved in the conflicts that sometimes arise between the requirements of the course of study and the personal needs of the pupils. This conflict is eloquently described in the following often quoted report:

I have taught in high school for ten years. During that time I have given assignments, among others, to a murderer, an evangelist, a pugilist, a thief, and an imbecile.

The murderer was a quiet little boy who sat on the front seat and regarded me with pale blue eyes; the evangelist, easily the most popular boy in school, had the lead in the junior play; the pugilist lounged by the window and let loose at intervals a raucous laugh that startled even the geraniums; the thief was a gay-hearted Lothario with a song on his lips; and the imbecile, a soft-eyed little animal seeking the shadows.

The murderer awaits death in the state penitentiary; the evangelist has lain a year now in the village churchyard; the pugilist lost an eye in a brawl in Hongkong; the thief, by standing on tiptoe, can see the windows of my room from the county jail, and the once gentle-eyed little imbecile beats his head against a padded wall in the state asylum.

All of these pupils once sat in my room, sat and looked at me gravely across worn brown desks. I must have been a great help to those pupils—I taught them the rhyming scheme of the Elizabethan sonnet and how to diagram a complex sentence.[10]

This tragic story illustrates one of the familiar dilemmas of the teacher, "Which is more important, the boy or the book, the child or the curriculum?"

An Anthropologist's Analysis of the Teacher's Roles

The distinguished cultural anthropologist, Margaret Mead, has given quite a penetrating analysis of the teacher's conflicting roles in American society. According to her, the teacher's roles are partially revealed by a study of the persons by whom children are reared in different cultures.

In some societies children are generally brought up by grandparents or other elderly kinfolk, as in old China or among some of the North American Plains Indian tribes. In such peoples the child's training is oriented toward the past and gives him a cultural tenacity and conservatism that often survives conquest or economic disaster.

[10] Naomi John White, "I Taught All," *The Clearing House*, XII (November, 1937), 151. Quoted by permission.

In contrast, among many peoples the child's nurse and teacher is another child—an elder child, probably a sister or brother—who has just experienced childhood with all of its fears and frustrations. The child-nurse, as among the Samoans or the Balinese, tends to give the growing child a means of self-expression and a richness of culture that carries even into adult life many of the joys and interests of childhood.

In America and in many other places, however, the children are reared by their parents—by young adults to whom life is full of serious purpose and struggle for success. Parent-training looks toward the future, toward a new and changing world, a world of conflicts and dangers that can be overcome only by continual striving for efficiency and attainment.

The good teacher of today, according to Miss Mead, approximates each of the types of child-rearing: "the grandparent who has seen the whole of life, the parent who is living it day by day, and the child or nurse who is the custodian not of the child's future so much as of the child's immediate past." The teacher who resembles the grand-parent-nurse may be found most frequently among the instructors of the classics or upon the staff of a college-preparatory school. The one who is most similar to the parent-nurse, who neglects the past in order to make desperate preparations for the future, teaches children of immigrants or of those struggling for a higher social status. Teachers in nursery schools, kindergartens, and the early elementary school are more like the older child-nurses in their emphasis upon the here and now and upon self-expression.

By this analogy Miss Mead infers that the better teachers are those who can fulfill three somewhat conflicting roles: (a) that of presenting to the child his cultural heritage and the wisdom of the past, (b) that of preparing him for future usefulness in a rapidly changing world, and (c) that of aiding him in enjoying the present by greater self-development and richness of experience. Miss Mead recognizes the teacher's difficulty in following these three roles even in a slowly moving world, but she finds that cultural change, both material and non-material, is so speedy that "the modern teacher becomes not more but, in a sense, less fitted to teach the longer she teaches."

Miss Mead's analysis is valuable in portraying the complexity of the teacher's roles, requiring him at one and the same time to be an older child, a young adult, and a grandparent. As if these were not enough, she points out that the teacher must not only change himself with the changing times but he is obligated to prepare his pupils to be ready for the yet dimly-foreseen future—"a readiness to use unknown ways to solve unknown problems." [11]

Grim Picture of the Teacher's Roles

A witty but somewhat exaggerated picture of the conflicting roles of the teacher has been given by the journalist, Robert Quillen, creator of the newspaper character, Aunt Het, who thus describes the situation in an American small town:

One o' my girls had her heart set on bein' a school teacher, but I talked her out of it. Teachin' school is too much like bein' a preacher's wife. It's a high callin', but people expect you to give more'n they pay for.

You take the teachers here in town. The only difference between them an' the Christian martyrs is the date an' the lack of a bonfire.

They was hired to teach an' they do it. They teach the younguns that can learn an' entertain the ones that fell on their heads when they was little. But that ain't enough. They're supposed to make obedient little angels out o' spoiled brats that never minded nobody, an' wet nurse little wildcats so their mothers can get some rest, an' make geniuses out o' children that couldn't have no sense with the parents they've got.

But that ain't the worst. They've got to get up plays an' things to work the school out o' debt; an' sing in the choir an' teach a Sunday school class; an' when they ain't doin' nothin' else they're supposed to be settin' a good example. [12]

The Teacher as "a Forgotten Man"

Teachers are only human—although pupils often find this hard to believe—and wish to achieve recognition and approval for their efforts. They wish the ego-satisfaction of success, perhaps of fame. But actually the teacher, like the wise parent, must strive to make himself unnecessary. His greatest success is achieved when his pupils

---

[11] Margaret Mead, *The School in American Culture* (Harvard University Press, 1951).
[12] Quoted by permission of Mrs. Robert Quillen.

begin to learn upon their own initiative, to improve without his
guidance, to grow without his stimulation.

This endeavor to make his own services less needed is one of the
distinguishing marks of the teaching profession, as was pointed out
by George Herbert Palmer when he noted that among the requirements for superior teaching is the willingness to be forgotten by the
pupils.[13]   But this lack of recognition for even the best efforts of the
teacher is one reason why the ambitious are loath to assume his
varied and conflicting social roles.

HOW FREE SHOULD THE SCHOOLS BE?

In totalitarian countries the schools are strictly controlled by the
masters of the state, but in a democracy there often arises the question of how much freedom should the schools and the teachers be
permitted to have.   An individual's answer to this question depends
in large part upon his beliefs concerning the social role of the school
and of the teacher.

In spite of many divergencies of opinion there is a fairly general
consensus on some aspects of the freedoms of the school and of the
teacher.   For example, the American schools do not have the freedom openly to attack democracy.   They are not free to isolate themselves from the people of the community.   They are not free to
dominate the lives of children and youth.

Teachers, it is generally agreed, should be permitted to think for
themselves but should not be allowed to use their authority to pros-
elyte or to convert impressionable young people to views greatly contrary to those of the community.   Freedom to express unorthodox
views is usually granted to teachers, provided they are "temperate in
speech" and conventional in conduct and provided their pupils are
considered to be mature enough to form their own opinions.   On the
other hand, the freedom of teachers in matters of personal behavior is
likely to be severely restricted as long as they are believed to be
potential models for the boys and girls under their supervision.

[13] *The Ideal Teacher* (Houghton, Mifflin, 1908).

Perhaps it should be noted here that the amount of freedom given to schools and to teachers varies greatly from time to time. "Heresy-hunting" often follows a period of considerable tolerance of unorthodoxy. The extent of freedom changes with alterations in the "intellectual climate" of the nation. In times of fear and dissension, almost anyone with a book in his hand is looked upon with suspicion.

THE SIGNIFICANCE OF NON-SCHOOL EDUCATION

According to general academic custom, *education* and *schooling* are often assumed to be almost identical in meaning. In any broad conception of education, however, schooling is only a small part of the process of learning that begins at birth or earlier and continues until senility or death. Perhaps more significant than the schools in that part of learning known as *socialization* are family rearing and example, community backgrounds, play or recreation groups, and the numerous agencies of mass communication. Other very significant sources of socialization are advertising, work experiences, law enforcement, and religious instruction.

All of these types of education are of some concern to the American people, and most of them are subject to at least a small amount of regulation by governmental agencies or public opinion. The schools, however, are far more often a source of deep concern and an object of strict regulation. Doubtless this is good for schools, at least in the long run.

For reasons not clearly understood the American people as a whole consider the learning obtained at school to be far more significant in one's life development than that obtained elsewhere. A single inept sentence or controversial paragraph in a textbook may result in legislative investigation, removal of the offending book from the approved list, and possibly the downfall of those responsible for its adoption. Yet the boys and girls who barely comprehend this objectionable paragraph go unhindered from school to newsstands, "fun-shops," and drug, grocery and book stores to purchase comics, "pulps," "slicks," and books that are pornographic, obscene, and contributory to juvenile delinquency and crime.

Similarly, teachers are generally looked upon as significant models of conduct and must at all times be examples of good behavior for children and youth. In reality, however, teen-agers are often scornful of teachers as "goody-goodies" or worse, while they hysterically worship and imitate the demi-gods and demi-goddesses of the movie and television world. An insignificant teacher who affects the lives of 30 or 40 pupils is peremptorily dismissed for any improper conduct, while the front pages of the newspapers carry lurid stories of the drunken brawls, hasty divorces, and sex misconduct of Hollywood's heroes and heroines who number their youthful followers by the hundreds of thousands. In fact, the press agents of the amusement world are alleged to exaggerate the misconduct of their patrons for their "publicity value," heedless of the effect of such examples upon impressionable and undiscriminating boys and girls.

A few years ago the president of the United States defended the tax collectors on the ground that at least 90 per cent of them were guiltless of any misconduct. But any superintendent of education or college president who defends his teachers by claiming that not more than 10 per cent of them have committed crimes would very likely lose his own job for condoning *any* mis-conduct. School-teachers and school books, like Caesar's wife, must be above suspicion.

At school, boys and girls must be carefully supervised at play to prevent accidents, moral contagion, and delinquency. Out of school, however, boys and girls are often left to manage their own affairs, perhaps upon the basis of a rationalization that they must learn by experience to take care of themselves.

A strange blindness seems to affect the American people concerning the effects of non-school education. Whatever goes into human experience is very likely to come out again in behavior, whether these experiences take place at school, in a back alley, at a movie, or in front of a television set in the home. Perhaps the underemphasis upon the significance of training outside of the school is a cultural lag, arising in part from our difficulty in tracing cause and effect in human behavior. Possibly greater knowledge of how people learn to be good or bad citizens, of the lasting effects of glamorous models even when they are not in the flesh, and more accurate evaluation of the anti-social and non-social results of training outside of school will result in no lessening of concern over schools but in a marked increase in social control over non-school education. Then the schools will receive effective aid from many types of outside influences instead of the harmful stimulation and example that often largely counteract the work of the best teachers. Many times the present task of the schools is to teach pupils to swim upstream against a flood of contrary influences. Small wonder that the schools so often fail to make any significant impression upon those who come within its doors!

THE SCHOOLS AND SOCIAL CHANGE

One of the continuing problems of institutionalized education is its relationship to social change, planned or unplanned. In a static culture this is a minor problem, but in a rapidly changing and somewhat disorganized society it is a major one, constantly requiring adjustment.

Aloofness

In early America the academies and colleges looked toward the past and emphasized the classical tradition, especially ancient languages and philosophy. The schools were almost apart from life, and the more socially significant types of education were carried on outside the school. This was the foundation of "the ivory tower" concept of education that still has its adherents who insist that schools and colleges should remain aloof from the controversies and problems of a changing society.

Neutrality

According to another concept, the schools should attempt to bring the pupils up to date by transmitting to them as far as possible the common cultural heritage in our diverse and multi-cultured society. From this point of view the school's emphasis should be upon such subjects as mathematics, literature and composition, history, and the natural sciences. After pupils are thus given an adequate background for their own thinking, they can more wisely plan for the future, or better choose among the possible alternatives. The school itself, however, should be strictly neutral concerning social or political policies. It should sharpen the weapons for social conflict and the tools for social change, but it should take no part in the struggles themselves. Until relatively recent years this policy of neutrality has been generally accepted as a suitable guide for teachers and school administrators.

Orientation to the Future

During the last half century, however, the movement known as progressive education has been emphasizing the "reconstruction of experience" of the child. According to this concept, the school is not a place where pupils go to acquire knowledge but to carry on a way of life in "an ideal community in which pupils get practice in cooperation, in self-government, and in the application of intelligence to difficulties or problems as they may arise." [14]   This, it is obvious, is education for the future, primarily by orienting the pupils toward the days ahead and by training them to expect social change. The advocates of this policy represent a minority of teachers and school administrators, but their influence is probably increasing.

Reform

According to a fourth concept, the schools should do more than prepare their pupils for social change—they should actively participate in building "a better social order." According to its advocates, the average man has proved that he is too selfish and too ignorant to improve his social surroundings. Consequently, the schools as representatives of the unselfish and the well-informed should foresee

[14] Boyd H. Bode, "The Confusion in Present-Day Education," in William H. Kilpatrick, *The Educational Frontier* (Appleton-Century, 1933), p. 19.

needed reforms and indoctrinate pupils in support of the necessary changes in social-economic goals and policies. There are several variants of this emphasis upon indoctrination, but they have in common the policy of consciously guiding the pupil toward the betterment of society. The abuses of this policy in fascist and communist countries have limited its growth in America, but many teachers still believe that the school should be an agency of social guidance, perhaps an agency of social reform.

All four of these educational objectives, as already briefly summarized, may appear beneath the surface in any one conflict concerning the relationship of the school to some particular social change. Many teachers will say, "It's none of our business." Others will offer to "do the research" and provide the proper background of information, provided they are excused from "taking sides." Some will insist that change is necessary and will "help get ready" for it. A few will attempt to lead the community in the "intelligent" direction. These conflicting points of view constitute a problem both for teachers and for American society.

SCHOOLS AND THE FUTURE

For a century American advocates have been claiming almost miraculous powers for the public schools. More buildings, more teachers, and more money would make America nearly utopian in democracy, efficiency, and proper conduct. But three major obstacles prevent the schools from having such significance.

In the first place, much—no one knows exactly how much—of the life of the individual is determined by the genes he received from his parents. His capacities are limited by his hereditary background, even though training is necessary for the development of these capacities. In the second place the personality traits of the child may be largely formed even before he enters school. The earliest years are perhaps the most significant—and the school is late upon the scene of personality development. Finally, the tremendous impact of non-school training may neutralize or even destroy the effects of the individual's experience with teachers, textbooks, and schools.

At present many Americans are disillusioned about the public schools because the schools have claimed too much for themselves and have perhaps attempted to do too much. One result of this disillusionment is the readiness with which some attack the schools without even waiting to evaluate the situation.[15] There is evidence that a period of deflation of the social significance of schools may develop before a more accurate and realistic appraisal can be made.

But whatever the future of the American schools—elementary, secondary, or collegiate—their role will be an important one. Never before has a nation attempted such mass education. Its minimum contributions will include more general knowledge of the world and its affairs, greater economic efficiency, trained leaders, and at least the possibility of discriminating followers. These contributions alone are enough to entitle the schools to adequate personal and financial support.

Study Questions

1. How would you decide each of the three dilemmas facing the schools as a result of mass education in the United States?

2. Do you think the public schools are effective in reducing socio-economic class differences in America? Defend your answer.

3. Why do Americans strictly control schools and teachers, while almost ignoring other powerful educative influences?

4. Would the raising of teachers' salaries greatly increase the quality of teachers? Explain.

5. Are you a perennialist, a progressive, or an essentialist in your philosophy of education? Clarify your position.

6. Why do you favor or oppose federal aid to education?

7. What are some of the power groups that make efforts to control the American schools?

8. Do you believe that teachers and schools should be leaders in movements for social reform or improvement? Explain.

9. Why have American schools been over-rated as an agency for personal and national improvement?

[15] David Hulburd, *This Happened in Pasadena* (Macmillan, 1951).

Selected References

Barzun, Jacques, *The Teacher in America* (Little, Brown, 1945). A keen discussion of the problems of teaching on the college level.

Cook, Lloyd Allen and Elaine F., *A Sociological Approach to Education* (McGraw-Hill, 1950). A well-written analysis of the social aspects of education, especially of school and community relationships.

Harvard Committee, *General Education in a Free Society* (Harvard University Press, 1945). An influential statement of the purposes and values of general education.

Hollingshead, A. B., *Elmtown's Youth* (Wiley, 1949). A significant study of youth and the schools in a small American city.

Mead, Margaret, *And Keep Your Powder Dry* (Morrow, 1942). An anthropologist gives a thoughtful and stimulating analysis of American schools and culture.

———, *The School in American Society* (Harvard University Press, 1951). A valuable discussion of the teacher's social roles.

Roucek, Joseph, and Associates, *Sociological Foundations of Education* (Crowell, 1942). A group of sociologists present the contributions of sociology to education.

Van Til, William, *et al.*, *Great Human Issues of Our Times* (Nashville: George Peabody College, 1953). A misleading title but excellent discussions of some of the leading issues in contemporary American education.

Waller, Willard, *The Sociology of Teaching* (Wiley, 1932). The classic statement of the teacher's part in education.

Warner, W. Lloyd, Robert J. Havighurst, and Martin B. Loeb, *Who Shall Be Educated?* (Harper, 1944). A thought-provoking treatment of the significance of socio-economic class upon American education.

13

Problems in Government
and Politics

Politics is man's most exciting game; men spend a considerable part of their lives in its various aspects, either as active, or as passive participants. No aspect of human life can be understood without a knowledge of the role played by government and politics in resolving man's ever-recurrent conflicts in ideology and social action. The distribution and control of power is the central problem of politics. Politics itself is the quest for power; and all political relationships are power relationships, actual or potential. This quest for power is carried on in all informal and formal groups. Consider the problems raised by "politics" in every family on such issues as the granting of favors, or the distribution of property. But our present consideration of this problem is limited to those "political" phenomena related to organs to which have been granted, in some legalized form, the power of government; and only the activities of individuals or groups in a state and its subdivisions and their attempt to gain power to bring about social changes are dealt with. Political activities used to achieve this end range from the voting procedures, or the refusal of the people to vote, or to no action whatever, to violence, murder, and terror. They come into play at all levels of government, local, state, and national. In the municipality, the county, the state, and the nation, by fair methods and foul, the struggle for political power goes on incessantly.

POLITICS, GOVERNMENT, THE STATE, AND LAW

Power, the core of the political struggle, may be compared to energy in physics.[1] In politics, it is the ability to act, the exercise of authority, the exerting of influence or the attainment of ascendancy. Political power, especially, is the ability of the government to impose decisions (the result of political processes) on the society under its control. Government imposes its decisions through the formal machinery available to it—the courts, the army, the taxing power—and also through influence exerted by acceptance and interpretation of ideologies. Thus the techniques of power may be classified as follows: (1) sheer force; (2) intimidation; (3) insinuation; (4) fear; (5) persecution; (6) conquest; (7) "divide and rule"; and (8) emotional appeals such as the deification of leaders, an appeal to unity, and the use of the flag, national hymns, historical traditions, and other symbols.[2]

The decisions arrived at by the government are the results of the political processes; they may come through revolutions, violence, or by periodic elections. The latter procedure is favored in the United States. In this country, in fact, we consider politics as a peaceful process whereby the conflicting interests of the numerous groups seeking to influence the governmental power are reconciled. Sometimes the term "state" is used as a designation for government. But government and the state are different concepts. The former is the organization or machinery through which the state formulates and exercises its will. This machinery includes not only the central organs, but all the levels of local agencies through which the state exerts its control, and also the instrumentalities for the expression of its will. Government is the sole possessor of the legal authority to employ coercion in enforcing its will.

There are innumerable definitions of the state. Sociologically speaking, it is an autonomous group, whose organization centers in the institution of government; its central machinery exercises coercive

---

[1] Bertrand Russell, *Power* (Norton, 1938), p. 12.
[2] Athan P. Allen, "Non-Symbolic Instruments of Power," in Roy V. Peel and Joseph S. Roucek, *Introduction to Politics* (Crowell, 1941), Ch. 4.

control over the mass of members and it has the voluntary cooperation of some of them. The goals and activities of the state are never static; rather they are constantly expanding or contracting from the interplay of various conflicting social forces. From this point of view, the state is an arena in which numerous struggling groups are seeking the favors of its directors, all aiming to influence, in varying degrees, the exercise of its power. The state regulates and arbitrates the ceaseless conflicts among interest groups.

The ends of government may be stated as follows: (1) external security; (2) internal order; (3) justice; (4) general welfare; and (5) freedom.[3] All these goals can be summarized by the term "common good." But what is "common good" and how this should be achieved is continuously debated within the framework of political ideologies.

It is hard to define law, for there are several schools of thought on this subject. In primitive societies, law was closely related to other means of social control. Primitive law lacks the rigid formalism that characterizes our codified law. If law is defined as the explicit command of the state, it cannot be easily found in primitive society. But as Malinowski has pointed out, the rules in primitive tribes, the working of which were essential for the maintenance of such institutions as the family, are comparable to our law.

Positive law is a command issued by the state and enforced by its authority; it is a general rule of external action enforced by a sovereign political authority. According to this theory there can be no legal restriction on the law-making power of the state; neither can any authority other than the state make a law. Sociologically speaking, law is one distinctive feature of social control and is sharply differentiated from other social controls such as public opinion, the mores, and the folkways. Law creates rights and defines duties; the language of law is the language of command. The task of legislation is the speculative construction of law in terms of ends, keeping all the while a circumspect eye cocked toward prevailing customs as the only source of obedience to satisfy the imperative of that legal demand.

[3] Charles E. Merriam, "The Ends of Government," *American Political Science Review*, XXXVIII (1944), 21–40; see his *Systematic Politics* (University of Chicago Press, 1945), for a more extensive discussion of this field.

It is in the field of application and interpretation of law that the political influences count most. The coercive power of all law derives from its enforcement by the state and its agencies, particularly the police and courts. (How this can be done is exemplified by the power exerted by Tammany Hall and other political machines in the United States.) On the other hand, social control is also exerted by the non-observance of many laws by the mass of the citizens.

While legislation is the plan to accomplish certain generalized aims, the government's function is to administer its operation. The carrying out of governmental programs has been given the title "public administration." Whatever the forms of the services offered to the people, one definite trend is discernible; the state has been assuming a greater and more important role in the field of special services. The details vary according to the conditions, reaching peaks in times of war, but persistently rising even in times of peace.

Problem Aspects of "the Ends of Government"

There is some disagreement among both theorists and administrators as to exactly what activities may be considered as social services. One group considers the control of private business and the conduct of such projects as those organized by the Tennessee Valley Authority to be social services; and others consider that the maintenance of law and order does not fall in the category. To the latter such a function is inherent in government and is not to be classified as a special service. "The ends of government," listed above, should be recalled in this connection. The problem presented by the endless arguments is, of course, how these general aims are to be interpreted or achieved. External security can be debated from the standpoint either of aggressive military policy or of pacificism. Is internal order maintained "properly" by issuing injunctions against strikes promoted by John L. Lewis or should it be maintained by leaving all labor disputes to private agreements? Is justice served by outlawing the communist and fascist parties? Is general welfare promoted by providing for a compulsory military service? And is freedom a "freedom" when the American-born Japanese are deprived of their constitutional rights and interned? All services of the government are, in fact, thrown into the area of conflicts when projected into the field of ideological debates and practical application. How far should the government collaborate with business enterprises, or grant them protective tariffs? How far has America's "general welfare" been benefited by granting public assistance to the American railroads since 1814? Highway construction, vital to the motor-carrier industry, remains one of the heaviest expenditures of state and local government. With federal aid, indeed, these expenditures amount to untold millions of dollars each year. Public assistance to the aircraft industry periodically runs into the hundreds of millions of dollars. Subsidies to the merchant marine for ship-building and operating expenses are other additional heavy drains on the Treasury. Collectively all of these are governmental problems of a high magnitude.

Democracy and Political Problems

In the United States, all social problems are defined in terms of a conflict of values, within the framework of what is vaguely known as "democracy." The term "democracy" may refer to a form of government, a form of the state, or a form of society. To be more exact, it is all of these things. In the first two of these meanings, it is purely a political concept and describes something rather definite. In its other sense, as a form of society, it is less exact; and there is, accordingly, a wider range of disagreement as to its meaning. Historians and students of politics most frequently regard democracy in one of its political senses; whereas sociologists, psychologists, and the mass of people generally think of democracy in its broader sense, as a form of society.

Democracy as a form of state signifies a commonwealth in which the exercise of sovereignty lies with the majority of the population. As a form of government, a democracy may be either pure or representative. In the first case the people formulate and express directly the will of the state; Switzerland's communal election is a good example of this. In the second they choose representatives to whom they delegate their powers.

To so restrict the meaning of democracy is unnecessary. It may be considered as a form of the state rather than as a form of government. In this sense, as long as the ultimate power in the state is recognized as residing in the mass of the population, any organization of the government having the people's sanction is democratic. According to this criterion, the United States is a democratic state, although it is, in general, ruled by a small group of persons to whom the masses delegate their authority.

The concept of democracy as a form of society is harder to define. It involves a type of social organization in which each individual may participate in group activities free from all restrictions that are not indispensable for effective functioning of the group. In addition, group policy must ultimately be determined with the consent of the majority of the members of the society.[4] Such a definition places the individual in a minority position and society as a whole, which determines the social policy and consequently part of the behavior of the individual, in the majority position.

The very essence of democracy is found in every form of social life, and it includes a social atmosphere, an attitude of mind, a philosophy, and a whole culture. The core is provided by a profound "faith in the capacity of man as a rational and human creature to achieve the good life by rational and humane means."[5] Thus, in the United States we believe in the dignity of the individual, his worth, and his right to the fullest development and happiness. Furthermore, we emphasize equality, especially equality of opportunity for the development of the individual's talents and capabilities. Other salient characteristics of democracy are the emphasis on freedom and the ceaseless search for truth. The basic control in such a democratic society is public opinion, in the formation of which we all participate.

MacIver approaches this point somewhat differently by insisting that democracy is not a way of governing, whether by majority vote or otherwise, but primarily a way of determining who shall govern and to what ends.[6] The only way in which the American people can determine who shall govern them is by referring the question to public opinion and accepting on each occasion the verdict of the polls.

[4] See Harry Elmer Barnes, *History and Social Intelligence* (Knopf, 1926), p. 394.
[5] Carl Becker, "Some Generalities That Still Glitter," *Yale Review*, XXIX (June, 1940), 667.
[6] R. M. MacIver, *The Web of Government* (Macmillan, 1947), *passim.*

Apart from this activity of the people, he asserts, there is no way of distinguishing democracy from other forms of government. Any kind of government, he concedes, can claim to rest on the "will of the people," whether it be oligarchy or dictatorship or monarchy. One kind of government alone rests on the constitutional exercise of the will of the people. But MacIver refuses to concede that the practical business of government consists in nothing more than the adjustment of conflicting special interests among different groups among the general public. In this respect one of the first problems is, historically, that of checks and balances.

THE PROBLEMS OF CHECKS AND BALANCES

Fear of concentration of power in the hands of one person or a group of persons induced the revolutionary leaders in America, conscious of the abuses of power against which they had successfully taken up arms, to seek to protect all future generations by incorporating into the Constitution salutary checks against tyranny. Since the American Revolution had been directed mainly against the abuse of executive tyranny, a solution was sought in the principle of the balance of power. The doctrine of the separation of powers itself is not exactly stated in the Federal Constitution, but it is assumed that it exists from the structure provided in the document as a whole. Ever since 1789 the system of checks and balances has been accepted as an outstanding and commendable feature of our fundamental law: the President checks the Congress, the Congress checks the President, the Courts check both of them, and they, in turn, check the Courts. The conflict between the advocates of strong government and the proponents of weak government that grew out of the struggle with the mother country and out of the clash of economic interests, was won by the latter, or at least they built these checks and balances into the structure of America's government. These checks and balances have remained to the present day, although the alignment of forces is not the same as at the time of origin.

The Founding Fathers never contemplated the development of

party politics; American political parties grew up outside the Constitution. They present such a striking contrast to those of Europe that some specialists regard them as a "distinct contribution to human institutions."

Many other values are in conflict in the political and governmental arena. Very important, for example, is the fact that people want government to perform certain functions for the common welfare, whereas the political party wants to perform functions for its own welfare. This objective of the political party is displayed most obviously in the patronage system, in which persons are selected not because they can best administer the institutions of a state but because they belong to the "right" party. The secret of the successful American politician is his clairvoyant opportunism. The essential mode of the American government is log-rolling, or give and take. The politician has to talk about ideas, or occasionally have them, but their power of appeal is much more important to his success than their economic and social soundness. He does not merely compromise; he incorporates into his policies the specific desires of as many articulate groups as he can. On his gold chain expediency hangs as the master key. This holds of course for "the great succession" as well as for those of whom less is heard. Politicians have always traveled light in intellectual and ideological baggage, ready for the change at the station, not being sure what train was coming next.

PROBLEMS OF THE TWO-PARTY SYSTEM

An outstanding characteristic of American political life is the relative continuity of the political order. We have had no deeply situated movements, no parties with objective chances to change the whole political structure. For a hundred and fifty years our parties have argued over symbols and about issues as to who got what *within* the general system. There has been no relatively successful "third party" which questioned the system within which certain men got what there is to get. Likewise there is no indigenous political theory that would proceed from such a movement. The American political opportunist politician has been contained for the most part in the two-party system.

Voting, in our society, is largely non-logical. Since three out of every four voters belong to the same parties as their fathers, environment is probably the most persistent influence. Economic motivation is largely indirect, serving principally to help create the "ideological atmosphere" in which the individual's political views develop. A political party, however, is a vast combination of groups which often have violently clashing interests. To coalesce these interests of diverse backgrounds into an effective political instrument calls for a leader with a broad national outlook and a genius for making party combinations tolerable. Our two-party system makes almost inevitable the rhetoric of vacuity rather than the ideology of particular social strata. The patronage party needs few ideas; definite ideas only estrange some elements of the diverse voting public. The more variegated the public to which they must appeal for support, the more generally empty of decisive (deeply antagonistic) contents the political programs will be. Many theorists praise such a system because it blunts and attenuates the difficulties it reflects. In such a set-up, however, a compromise is no temporary expediency on the road to some end. It is the prime principle of the going concern. In such a system the greatest politician is the man who can find the slogan that will disturb the fewest and attract the most. The big compromises in a two-party state tend not to be public, that is, between two parties in a public forum, but secret. They occur within the party formations. Even those between the parties tend to take the form of non-publicized or perhaps even non-publicizable deals.

The compromising party is, thus, different from the compromised party. The first means, ideally at least, that two groups, each representing definite and antagonistic interests, integrate policy as best they can in order to realize all the existing interests possible. How well they succeed in this depends in large part upon the depth of the articulated antagonism. Party managers minimize the public discussion of fundamental policies, while politicians solve them by means of the personal contact and the private integration. The compromised party is everybody's friend.

The danger of the two-party system is that it may turn into a one-

party state. If the parties get too close together, through their compromises and their common attempts to win everybody in a variegated
public, there may be no real oppositional group. The tangle of compromises within and between the two parties may become so thick
and sticky that the opposition is eliminated as an effective organization. When only one of two parties has a chance to win power, or
at least office and patronage, and when the publics to which it must
appeal are variegated, such principles as the parties stand for tend to
be the same, or at least so similar as to leave little choice. The differences are not in ideological principle or policy, or even in interest,
but in patronage and slogans.

In a situation of heavy compromise and many concessions, there
is a danger, very real today, that one party take the responsibility for
the acts of a government while not really having the power of decision.
Not having the power, it will try to get it; and the technique is, once
more, more compromise. It therefore may "sell out" those who
were decisive in voting it in. Then the idea of parties as representatives of definite interests becomes a fiasco.

The two-party system is doubtless a convenient system for people
already contented. It works best where there are no real divisions in
the recognized interests of the various segments in the population, or
where there are non-political outlets for economic antagonisms.
When the economic organization of a society does not readily permit
this, the political system of the two-party state may come effectively to
represent only one sector of interests. This leaves large segments of
the population without organized representation. Both parties are
expedient fixers, and the "integrating ideas," which the master politicians seek, unite small articulate power groups, or patches up their
loudest complaints; it does not even acknowledge quite fundamental
disintegration.

The system is one reason, but probably not a major one, for the
relative lack of class-consciousness in America. The consciousness of
economic interest does not, of course, follow automatically from the
structural fact of its existence. Political agitation that appeals to
specific strata is a major factor in the development of class consciousness. In the two-party state this is not likely to occur. The barter,
balance, and concessions of the parties, along with a near monopoly

of the media of mass communications, hide the contradictions of the social structure and for a time make them endurable.

The two-party system is not, however, as different from the multiple-party system of prewar France, Czechoslovakia, and the northern European countries as might be supposed. Yet, in these European countries, compromise was more public; more extreme and definite policies found public and organized expression. The whole apparatus of the coalition of parties was more flexibly geared to shifts in political opinion. The two-party system compromises variegated interests and principles within each of the parties, and the public stand that is finally taken is less definite and clear cut. The machine, by its size and organization, makes for inflexibility; it may remain rigid for some time after public shifts of conviction have occurred.

The two-party system has not remained unchallenged. Never for very long has it existed in pure and undefiled form. In the South the one-party state is common; and there have been many third-camp movements, parties, and jeremiads. Sometimes the third parties have affected presidential elections and even the determination of policy. In many state contests, third-party men have won; and beyond question principles first advocated by third-party elements have later been adopted by the major parties. If a policy attracts votes, the other parties adopt it—and that is likely to be the death of the third party. The more "radical" such vote-getting programs are, the more diluted their adopted forms and their translations into government policy become.

Party "Spoils"

The victorious party in America considers itself entitled to award public jobs to its supporters. The privilege of making the awards—ranging from contracts for public construction to concessions for operating soda stands in the public parks, or jobs in public administrative offices—is granted to a selected group of party leaders. Lawyers, especially, are favored with appointments as masters in chancery, receivers, trustees, and to other judicial functions. Urban political machines give construction contracts for public works to contractors in return for help in defraying campaign expenses. Corruption in

the purchasing departments of municipalities periodically makes headlines in our newspapers, as does the graft involved in the purchases of
real estate for public purposes. These practices are, in turn, related
to control over the bonds that public contractors and officials are required to furnish to insure their fidelity. Other dishonest sources of
revenue to party leaders are tax concessions or exemptions granted by
public officials, or payments for concessions sold to members of the
underworld.

Pressure Groups

Because the victorious party can distribute favors and jobs to its
followers, numerous groups aim persistently to influence the machinery of government. In Europe prior to World War II the various
"pressure groups" could, as distinct political parties, press their demands. In the United States the two-party system permits few clear-
cut stands to be taken by either of the two major parties on a question
of doubtful importance or one of a local, class, or ideological nature.
Although stands are taken to a certain extent by the formation of
other parties, all important decisions must be achieved either through
the federal government or through the party organization of the forty-
eight states. Hence many organizations try to influence the legislative
programs or the governmental actions, in the lobbies of the legislative
halls, before the electorates, and in the discussions where public opinion plays so large a part. Whereas some of these organizations are
formed for a specific purpose (the American Farm Bureau Federation,
the Grange, the American Bar Association), others assume these
functions as a part of more general activities (the National Educational Association, the Brotherhood of Railway Engineers, the American Medical Association). Many of these groups maintain head-
quarters in Washington, seeking to influence congressional committees as well as individual Congressmen; or their representatives appear
before administrative bodies and officials. The same is true in state
capitals; here pressure groups prominently endorse candidates, make
campaign contributions, canvass voters, or "work on" the platform
committees of party conventions. Stuart Chase has maintained that
American democracy will be torn apart, to be followed by the im-

position of a dictatorship similar to that now prevailing in Russia and to the one that prevailed in Nazi Germany, unless self-interested farm, labor, and business pressure groups are curbed and the general interest made paramount in the nation's economic and political processes.[7]   According to Chase, the chief culprits in prewar times were the big three: business, labor, and the farmers, each fighting for selfish interests.

There are also the activities of specialized producers, professional and occupational groups, reformers, and governments-in-exile.   Their strategy and tactics are: (1) get the "right" Congressman elected; (2) turn the "heat" on Congressmen already elected; (3) influence an administrative agency to interpret bills the "right" way; and (4) fight the constitutionality of unfavorable bills through the courts up to the Supreme Court.   A few lobbies operate intermittently; others work all the time.

THE PROBLEM OF THE BUREAUCRACY

The terms "bureaucrat" and "bureaucracy" are in bad favor with large numbers of people in this country who tend to associate the terms with waste and extravagrance and even regimentation, and hence build up a feeling of hostility toward what is really an essential factor in our government.   This feeling is most often one of prejudice based largely on a lack of information as to the process of government. Government today is big business and millions of personnel are required to carry this business on.   Of the hundreds of thousands of employees in the various bureaus of the federal government, a large proportion are career men and women who have become specialists in their particular fields, and who work year after year under the nominal direction of an appointed "top man" whose tenure depends upon politics and whose term is usually short.

The much-criticized bureaucracy is here to stay; the only real question is whether we shall have good bureaucracy or a bad one.   In any case, it will be a big one.

[7] Stuart Chase, *Democracy Under Pressure* (New York: Twentieth Century Fund, 1945).

Those who are most vocal in abusing bureaucracy are wont to exclaim—what we want is not more government in business, but more business in government. These people assume that the job of managing a private business is identical with that of running the government; that all private business is well managed, and that everything in government would be perfect if the functions of government were entrusted to men who have shown skill in private business. It is true that the administrative ability of efficient business men is needed in government; but it is not necessarily the only important qualification and it is not necessarily the most important.

Probably the most valid accusation leveled against governmental bureaucracy is one that many years since ceased to have much relevancy—the opportunity it afforded those who were in control of the government to appoint political friends—with or without competence —to positions in the government service. This so-called "spoils system," however, is no longer the menace to good government it once was; for, beginning in 1883 with the Pendleton Act, Congress has established a merit system, civil-service examinations, tenure of office, and the like, all tending to produce the following favorable results: [8] (1) the system removes the demoralizing influence in the service which is brought about by the partisan scuffle for office; (2) it very largely prevents the assessment of officeholders for political purposes; (3) it requires of the civil servants loyalty to the government rather than loyalty to a party; (4) it gives the employees security of tenure, without which no technical or professional officer can do his best work; (5) it elevates the civil service to a profession; (6) it makes possible a high degree of specialization within the service.

CONSTITUTIONAL PROBLEMS

Since the United States Constitution is the "supreme law of the land," all political argument is sooner or later based on appeals to the "constitutionality" of this or that proposed legislative measure

[8] C. O. Johnson, *American National Government* (3rd ed., Crowell, 1947), p. 398.

or governmental step. Basically the debate is merely an ideological aspect of the struggle for power between those who want to grant more power to the federal government and those who would reduce its power.

Nearly all critics of the existing order in the United States recognize that present trends are toward collectivism; they differ in that they either favor or oppose this trend. The conservatives advocate economic individualism—"free enterprise" and a restriction of governmental intervention in business. On the other hand, there are those who view individualism as outmoded; they contend that it is no longer just to *all* the people of the country and that adherence to it does not result in maximum production. They start with the premise that our complex modern society is basically collective and interdependent; hence, today's problems, set in such a framework, can be met effectively only by means of government action, by the more liberal interpretation of the Constitution.

LOCAL GOVERNMENT AND ITS PROBLEMS

The functions of local government are becoming highly technical. The role of the amateur is inevitably yielding to that of the expert, and paralleling this trend there has been tremendous expansion in the varieties and quantity of governmental activity. Recreation, city planning, and airport operation are examples of the newer municipal functions. Even those functions that once were wholly local, but which have recently been assumed by the national government, still have important local aspects. Consequently the locality often retains a responsibility in them, in its own right, as well as in its capacity as an agency of the central government. The locality, politically speaking, is made up of articulate human beings who are intent on solving their particular problems through the governmental machinery. Hence the selection of mayors is often accompanied by bitter political maneuvering, since these executives prepare the budget and have increasing power of appointment. Their decisions, whether made openly or behind the legal scenery, are of considerable importance to

every citizen. Certain projects, such as improved schools or better
public health, only now and then arouse a considerable interest.
When, however, vested interests, such as those of banking or of real
estate are involved, the circle of interest is narrowed. At any rate, in
virtually every municipality there has grown up either a formal or an
informal organization to give expression to the special interests of the
various groups concerned. The formal method is usually to elect a
council by wards, or to have a "complaint bureau" if elections are at
large; the informal method is through the party machinery. In
Chicago, for example, the party precinct leaders are the humanizers or
the facilitators between the party and the governmental machinery.
The price exacted for such services is always the same—party loyalty
and corrupt municipal politics.

The power of the political machine in American cities is considerably strengthened by the heterogeneity of the population, which
makes agreement on a really concrete platform difficult. It makes
rather for campaigns based on irrelevancies, such as national party
labels or the number of jobs given to a particular nationality group or
race. The greatest success in ridding American cities of machine
control has been in places where the responsibility is clearly defined.
But the whole problem is enormously difficult, and there is no one
solution. The difficulties confronting those seeking honest government can be exemplified by the history of the Pendergast machine of
Kansas City.[9] Pendergast put up the usual false front of the political
boss about being honest and loyal to his friends, but he was bottom-
lessly dishonest and completely ruthless. During his reign Kansas
City was one of the most wide-open and corrupt cities in America, a
center of vice, crooked gambling, and crime. Racketeers from all
over the country congregated there and were welcomed by Pendergast's special lieutenant in charge of crime, a gangster named Johnny
Lazis. Pendergast kept 50,000 "ghost" names on the padded registration lists, and in addition to voting the dead, the absent, and the
imaginary, used strong-arm methods to prevent many citizens from
voting. In the "Bloody Election" of 1934 several people were mur-
dered and many beaten up. There was also the fantastic insurance
scandal in which Pendergast collected $440,000 out of a promised

---

[9] M. M. Milligan, *Missouri Waltz* (Scribner, 1948).

bribe of $750,000, for using his influence in settling a long-standing legal dispute between a score of insurance companies and the State of Missouri. Like Al Capone, Tom Pendergast finally went to prison for income tax evasion.

THE SOLUTION OF POLITICAL PROBLEMS

Since politics is of such supreme importance to all citizens, there has never been a period in the history of the United States during which numberless proposals were not made for its improvement. In the first place, as mentioned above, specialists in political democracy define democracy as a form of government in which the people, in the long run, control policy. If the definition is accurate the question of responsible citizenship immediately becomes an acute issue.

Responsible Citizenship

If citizens are to have a clear concept of their political institutions, they must have fairly clear notions about various systems of government. To this end, at all levels of the formal educational system instruction should be offered in the dynamics of political processes, with greater stress placed upon political realities than upon fictional and legalistic aspects. Citizens can meet daily issues with which they are faced only if proper, realistic backgrounds are provided for them during the course of their formal schooling.

Reorganization of the System

There are only two means of reaching political decisions and translating them into action. One way is that of a totalitarian tyranny in which some individual or group at the top makes the decisions, and the citizens at the bottom obey—or suffer the consequences. The other way of reaching decisions is, as in the United States, by a system of proposal, discussion, and, in case of disagreement, compromise. The outstanding characteristic of our system is that it recognizes that men always will have differences but it permits those differences to be harmonized by sane discussions and compromises. Our system, indeed, sees value in differences of opinion, provided that each citizen practices tolerance for the opinions of others. As Thomas Jefferson once said: "Difference of opinion leads to inquiry and inquiry to truth. . . . We value too much the freedom of opinion, not to cherish its exercise, even where in opposition to ourselves."

Reorganization of Congress. Several times in its history the Congress of the United States has been largely reorganized.[10] The "great revolt" of 1909–11, headed by young George Norris, broke the power of Uncle Joe Cannon and his dictatorial Rules Committee in the House.[11] In 1917, the Senate, after a campaign that started in 1845, was able to adopt a closure rule, by which two thirds of the Senate can stop a filibuster; but rarely is this maneuver successful.

Some concerted attempts to streamline the Congressional system culminated in the Reorganization Act of 1946, the result of a year's work by a joint committee headed by Senator LaFollette and Congressman Monroney. The resolution creating the Committee, however, restricted the scope of its work, especially in regard to "rules"—that is, it was almost forbidden to consider the problem of the filibuster. But the witnesses before the Committee spared no effort to emphasize the nature and importance of this very problem. In due time the La Follette Committee reported, and on August 2, 1946, a Reorganization Act, including most of the recommendations of the Committee, was passed.[12]

The Reorganization Act reduced the number of standing committees in the House from forty-eight to nineteen and in the Senate from thirty-three to fifteen. The overlapping of committee fields was largely eliminated. The work is now divided among a larger number of subcommittees which can be set up or discontinued with

[10] David C. Coyle, "Reorganizing Congress," *Virginia Quarterly Review*, XXIV (1948), 13–28.

[11] Republican "Uncle Joe" Cannon, as the presiding officer of the House, developed an authority which was second only to that of the President of the United States. His arbitrary use of this great power led to his overthrow in 1910, although the Speaker still retains a power of great prestige and significance in the United States party system.

[12] See Estes Kefauver, *A Twentieth Century Congress* (Efficiency Books, 1947), and Monroney's appraisal of the results of the measure in the *Congressional Record*, July 26, 1947.

comparative ease, and the main committee can coordinate and direct their work.   There also was improvement in the operation of committees, such as requiring a quorum for approving a bill, helping witnesses prepare their testimony, and keeping conference committees from writing bills of their own.   (But the requirement proposal that hearings should be open—not secret—was entirely refused by the House Appropriations Committee.)   The Legislative Reference Service in the Library of Congress, set up in 1915 to provide information for committees and members, was strengthened; and the Legislative Drafting Service, a group of expert lawyers who draft bills, was enlarged.   Although the standing committees were granted larger staffs, this reform has been partly offset by the appointment of unqualified persons to positions which should be filled by experts.

A bill requiring registration of lobbyists was enacted into law, but this law has failed to deal effectively with the master-minds who work underground.   In addition, the law may be easily evaded by lobbyists who do not devote "a major portion" of their time to lobbying.   The main defense against doubtful use of the "right of petition" is generally efficiency and adequate information services, to help give the hard-pressed legislator the possibility of knowing what he is voting on.

The Legislative Budget was reduced to an absurdity, since the Congress refused to appropriate funds, provided in the Reorganization Act, for a study by the Comptroller-General of the economy and efficiency of the administrative agencies.

In summary, the committee system has been much improved, but it is still short of real streamlining, and is still handicapped by the practice of having seniority chairman; the expert staff services have been improved; lobbyists have been listed.   But the real reforms are yet to be accomplished.   Coyle believes that the committees or the party caucus should choose the chairmen "for usefulness, not for their value as antiques."   Congressmen and Senators should be paid around $25,000 a year, for personal income, in addition to an allowance for a sufficient office staff.   "A properly equipped and properly paid Congress would cost each of us about five cents more per year, or the price of one newspaper, in which the news might be much better if Congress were able to do a bang-up job." [13]

[13] Coyle, *op. cit.*, p. 20.

The work load of Congress needs to be reformed further, although the accumulation of private bills has been largely taken care of. The Reorganization Committee recommended that each member should have an assistant in his Washington office—mostly to keep the constituents off the Congressman's neck. Much time is wasted in both houses by roll calls. Whenever a member of either house wishes to delay action on a bill he can raise the question of a quorum being present. In the House of Representatives, particularly, this is a dilatory tactic (a sort of filibuster), for it requires a calling of the roll to establish the fact that a required number of members is present. The only way to prevent the time-consuming roll call (a roll call in the Senate requires ten minutes; in the House forty-five) from being taken is affirmative action on a motion to adjourn. To save time on roll calls it has been proposed that electric voting machines be installed.

Another big problem is how to attain a more efficient relation between the Executive agencies and Congress. Some believe that much would be gained if cabinet members and agency heads would appear before each house at regularly scheduled "question periods" both to explain their own programs and to answer questions raised by members of the house. Such a meeting of minds between executive and legislative departments would do much to bring public opinion into closer relationship with government. It is also proposed that each executive department and important agency should have an office on the "Hill," headed by an assistant-secretary or assistant administrator, to cooperate with committees and keep contacts with requests from constituents. A suggested Constitutional change would make all elective terms four years. This would relieve members of the House of Representatives of half their campaigning, would, by altering the present practice of electing only one third of the members of the Senate every two years, allow the voters to change the whole Senate if they preferred to do so, and would increase the probability of having the President and the majority in both houses belonging to the same party.

Improvement in public administration. Although continuous steps have been taken since 1853 to introduce the merit system into governmental administration, students of the problem have been urging that the President be authorized to place within the classified service nearly all of the federal employees. Attractive salaries should be paid to the specialists, and these specialists should not be required to take the routine "assembled" examinations. Although "non-competitive" examinations are provided for, the very system, unfortunately, is not too practical in all respects. Many students of personnel problems believe that the English system giving candidates general rather than specialized examinations is better since it allows the selection of all-round men who can easily learn the practical duties of office assigned to them, rather than of "over-specialized specialists."

Improvements in local government. The vitality of local public opinion and interests represents something very real to the American people. Hence the frequent emphasis laid upon "reform." The need for reform in municipal service found expression in the formation of the National Municipal League in 1894; from then to the present the alteration of reform and machine control has characterized most of our local units. More recently the League has widened the scope of its interest to include county and state governments. Greater emphasis has been laid upon sound and skilled administration and rather less upon reform. This new emphasis has helped develop a number of professional and research associations, among them the International City Managers' Association, the Civil Service Assembly, the Public Welfare Association, and the Public Administration Clearing House; as a result of their activities former extravagant and corrupt practices in local politics are less and less in evidence today.

The recent professionalization of local governmental services must not obscure the fact that, historically, the American people have always attached great importance to local self-government as a political educator. The federal government is remote from the average citizen, but the local government offers him the possibility of seeing the relationship between what bothers him, or what he wants done, and what can be accomplished through the local means. In the final analysis, most professional politicians will express a grudging but respectful recognition of the importance of public opinion, in shaping policies all the way from the local government on up to the national level.

The Importance of Citizenship and Public Opinion

How far the politicians are able to make decisions consistent with the voice of the people will always remain unknown. How much the voice of the people should be listened to is an ideological problem which, theoretically, has been settled in favor of the people; but that the power of public opinion has its limitations has been more than aptly demonstrated by the students of public opinion. In the world of today the dominant governmental systems are clearly divided into two groups: the totalitarian systems in which the decisions are made *for* the people, in various ways, by a few key men who pay hardly any attention to the voice of the people since they themselves manipulate it; and the more democratic systems which, in theory at least, assume that important decisions depend on public opinion and that day-by-day activities of government in some way or other reflect that opinion. Since a continuous series of referenda is practically impossible, public opinion must express itself through representatives of the people. The people express their opinions chiefly at the polls; but, in part also, through forums, letters to newspapers and to their representatives in Congress. Unfortunately there are other forces—ward bosses, lobbyists, and pressure groups—that too often *seem* to express public opinion, but actually defeat it.

In theory, the functions of a democratic government are to be exercised in the interest of the citizenry, and are intended to promote their welfare. But the democratic state is dependent for its operation and preservation upon a well-instructed citizenry. Democratic government can be no better that it is made through the intelligence, education, and mores of the people. Free, public, universal education is therefore of fundamental significance; it is a political as well as a social necessity. But here it is necessary to pause. Education? Yes. But who is to determine the *type* of education? Education and politics are inevitably complementary. The people may determine the nature of the education to be given and thereby determine the ideology of the state. On the other hand, the state, once in being, may control education to the end that the people will support the existing government. It is well known that some governments may and do, subtly or forcefully, shape the civic concepts in the minds of the people. Only an alert intelligent citizenry can preserve freedom.

Study Questions

1. What is the meaning of democracy in the political sense?
2. Explain each of the following: the state; government; politics; and law.
3. What are the basic ends of government?
4. What are the outstanding characteristics of politics in the United States?
5. What are the least effective features of America's electoral system?
6. Outline the differences between the various concepts of democracy.
7. What are the main weaknesses of the two-party system as indicated in the party platforms?
8. Outline the techniques used by pressure groups and lobbyists.
9. What are the sociological aspects of public administration?
10. What are the possibilities of improving politics in the United States?

Selected References

Arnold, Thurman W., *The Folklore of Capitalism* (Yale University Press, 1937). A study of the semantic aspects of law, government, and economics; American subservience to "magic words."

Binkley, Wilfred E., *American Political Parties* (Knopf, 1942). A brilliant analysis of the American two-party system.

Curti, Merle, *The Growth of American Thought* (Harper, 1943). An able and scholarly effort to summarize the various trends in American thought.

Elliot, William Y., *The Need for Constitutional Reform* (McGraw-Hill, 1935). A suggested program for overhauling our governmental system.

Gabriel, Ralph H., *The Course of American Democratic Thought* (Ronald, 1940). A history of American social and political ideologies.

Griffith, E. S., "The Changing Pattern of Public Policy Formation," *American Political Science Review*, XXXVIII (June, 1944), 448–59.

Morgenthau, Hans J., "The Evil of Politics and the Ethics of Evil," *Ethics*, LVI (October, 1945), 1–18.

Roucek, Joseph S., "Political Behavior as a Struggle for Power," *Journal of Social Philosophy*, VI (July, 1941), 341–61.

———, "Ideology as a Means of Social Control," *American Journal of*

Economics and Sociology, III (October, 1943), 35–45; III (January, 1944), 179–92; III (April, 1944), 357–70.

Swisher, Carl Brent, *The Growth of Constitutional Power in the United States* (Chicago University Press, 1946).   A convenient review of the great landmarks in constitutional interpretation.

14

Problems in Health and Medical Services

To estimate the importance of good health for the individual or for society is impossible. The state of one's health looms always as a tremendously important factor to every person, because on it depends, at least in large measure, the attainment of such desirable personal qualities as physical efficiency, bodily comfort, a sense of well-being, and happiness. Nor is the matter of health any less importance to the group as a whole. There is good evidence to show that a healthy citizenry is a major factor in social progress and that no society made up largely of physically unfit persons can be very successful in achieving many of its goals.

At least since the time of the classical Greeks the role played by positive physical health and a sound mind in attaining both personal and social efficiency has been recognized. Today these factors may be even more important and, at the same time, somewhat less certain. As societies have changed and become increasingly complex, greater and greater demands have been placed upon the body and the mind of the individual; and these demands have placed both his physical and mental well-being in somewhat constant jeopardy. Furthermore, without soundness of both mind and body, the individual of today is robbed not only of the ability but also of much of the real opportunity to participate efficiently and effectively in the affairs of his society.

THE IMPORTANCE OF HEALTH TO THE INDIVIDUAL

Considered from the economic viewpoint alone, the importance of positive health to the physical and social well-being of the individual can hardly be doubted.   Occupying a prominent position among the conditions of modern life is the need that a great majority of the people work regularly in order to support themselves, their families, and their dependents and, beyond this, to share in any additional advantages that contemporary society has to offer.   Furthermore, many of the tasks at which people must work, if they work at all, are arduous; they require a great deal of physical strength and endurance. The person who is ill has neither the motivation nor the ability to meet the demands of these occupations.   He is at a disadvantage in competing with his fellow workers, his illness makes him less efficient and productive, and these conditions lead to low pay and sometimes, even, to the loss of employment.   Not only does illness deprive the individual of much needed income during the time that he is unable to work, but also it creates conditions entailing the greater expenditure of money than otherwise would be necessary.   Most illnesses, if they are of any degree of seriousness and for any prolonged duration, are accompanied by heavy expenses for doctors and hospitals, nursing care, and medicines.   The case is not unusual in which the savings of a lifetime are wiped out and staggering debts incurred in paying for the professional care received during a single major illness.   When the illness results in death the economic loss is even greater.   Then it involves not only the time lost and the money spent in providing care for the deceased during his illness but also the loss of his earning power; and this may bring serious difficulties, both economic and social, to his dependents.

The losses to the individual that result from the lack of positive health cannot, however, be expressed solely in economic terms. There are other losses—less subject to objective measurement, to be sure—that are very important.   The relationship between the possession of good physical health and the development of a desirable personality has long been recognized as a positive one.   There can be little doubt that the person who suffers constantly from physical pain has difficulty in developing those personal traits that enable him to maintain pleasant and friendly relations with his associates. In extreme cases the individual suffering from physical illness may become anti-social and withdraw from society, or his illness may so far upset his mental balance that he resorts to crime and other anti-social acts. He may even commit suicide.

THE IMPORTANCE OF HEALTH TO SOCIETY

Society's interests in the physical well-being of its members are of no less importance than the concern of the individual over his own health. There is good evidence supporting the contention that health is a major basis of social progress; it seems just as certain that the widespread existence of uncontrollable disease within a country may be a predisposing cause to national decay. Along this line are the observations of more than one historian that the appearance of an endemic disease within an area has so reduced the vitality of the people as to result in serious depopulation or even their ultimate disappearance. Certainly, the decay of such highly developed civilizations as those of Greece and Rome, each of which was unsurpassed in its time, is difficult to understand without assuming the appearance of some factor that adversely affected the vitality of the population. Some historians believe that this devitalizing factor may have been some disease such as malaria or tuberculosis. This explanation is plausible. If the onslaught of a physical illness can so debilitate the individual as to put him either temporarily or permanently out of the labor force, the widespread existence of an uncontrollable disease among the members of a society can lead ultimately to its decay.

But of even greater significance, because it is more generally applicable to society at large, is the twofold fact (1) that illnesses not only constitute social problems in themselves but (2) that they lead to the development of other social problems. With respect to the former, it is sufficient to note that in modern life the incidence of certain diseases is on the increase in spite of everything that medical science has been able to do to bring them under control and that many others still constitute major hazards because they cannot be controlled readily enough. It is noteworthy, too, that many of the so-called minor illnesses, which in themselves are of no particular consequence, become serious problems when they reach epidemic proportions, or when they so weaken the resistance of their victims that the latter become easy prey to more serious diseases.

The social problems connected directly with illnesses are too numerous to mention. They have a bearing on every segment of society. Any standard text on the family lists illnesses and diseases among the major family problems. Frequently they are discussed as being closely related to other family problems—such as poverty, broken homes, crime, and delinquency (which are social in nature) and sterility and the eventual extinction of the family (which are biological). For the group as a whole, the presence of illness means that a large percentage of its resources must be spent for the training of medical personnel and for the support of health and medical institutions, such as hospitals, infirmaries, and clinics. And since many persons who become ill are themselves unable to pay for medical and hospital care, the expenses of their illnesses are added to the general tax burden in the form of appropriations or other payments made to both public and private agencies for the care of the medically indigent. Further general effects of illness and disease on society may be observed in the depletion of the labor force both in numbers and in productivity. This may become particularly acute during times of crisis, such as wars, when the total man power that can be summoned for military service as well as the operating efficiency of the armed forces is contingent to a considerable degree upon the health status of the population.

THE LEADING CAUSES OF DEATH

In Table 14.1 data are assembled which show the ten leading causes of death in the United States in 1950 and the comparable death rates from these same causes in 1900 and in 1930. An analysis of these causes in terms of their nature as, chiefly, degenerative or infectious, or other, will permit a more vivid presentation of the particular problems they present as the nation's number one killers.

The Degenerative Diseases

The degenerative diseases, strictly defined, are those that cause a deterioration of the circulatory system and its peripheral organs. The most important of these are the diseases of the cardio-vascular system, including, among others, vascular lesions, rheumatic heart condition, hypertension, syphilitic heart ailments, and general arteriosclerosis, nephritis (Bright's disease), and diabetes mellitus. In contrast with the infectious diseases, most of the degenerative diseases are characterized by a long period of onset and development, and although in some instances—as is the case with certain diseases of the heart—death may come quickly following an attack, in most cases it is preceded by a long and gradual period of deterioration.

TABLE 14.1: PRINCIPAL CAUSES OF DEATH IN THE UNITED STATES IN 1950, WITH THE COMPARABLE DEATH RATES FROM THESE SAME CAUSES IN 1900 AND 1930

Cause of Death	1950 Number	1950 Rate Per 100,000	1930 Rate Per 100,000	1900 Rate Per 100,000
ALL CAUSES	1,452,454	963.8	1132.1	1719.1
Diseases of the heart	535,705	355.5	214.2	137.4
Malignant neoplasms	210,733	139.8	97.4	64.0
Vascular lesions	156,751	104.0	89.0	106.9
Accidents	91,249	60.7	77.9	72.3
Certain diseases of early infancy	60,989	40.5	—	—
Pneumonia, except of newborn, and influenza	47,120	31.3	102.5	202.2
General arteriosclerosis	43,297	28.7	—	—
Tuberculosis (all forms)	33,959	22.5	71.1	194.4
Chronic and unspecified nephritis	24,677	16.4	86.7	81.0
Diabetes mellitus	24,419	16.2	19.1	11.0
All other causes	223,555	148.2	374.2	849.9

Source: *Statistical Abstract of the United States* (Government Printing Office, 1952), p. 75.

Five of the ten leading causes of death in the United States, in 1950, were degenerative diseases. Two of these, diseases of the heart and vascular lesions, ranked first and third, respectively, among the nation's killers.   Furthermore, the proportion of the total deaths attributed to diseases of the heart increased constantly throughout the period 1900–1950.   Whereas in 1900 only one out of each 16 or 17 deaths occurring was attributed to these causes, by 1930 heart diseases accounted for one out of every 5 deaths, and by 1950 for slightly more than one out of every 3.   During this same period the death rate from vascular lesions, which in 1950 exacted a toll of 156,751 lives, was constant and high.

The three other degenerative diseases listed among the ten leading causes of death in 1950 are general arteriosclerosis, chronic and unspecified nephritis, and diabetes mellitus.   Of these three diseases, which taken together accounted for nearly 7 per cent of all deaths during the year, the death rate for nephritis only has shown any considerable tendency to decline during the last fifty years.

Certainly the control of the degenerative diseases constitutes one of the nation's most serious health and medical problems.   As a group, these are the diseases that scientific research has been least successful in controlling or eliminating.   The most promising efforts so far made are those directed against degenerative diseases that are produced by, or related to, previous conditions of infection, such as myocarditis, rheumatic heart disease, and syphilitic heart ailments. The death rate from the degenerative and other chronic, non-infectious diseases increased from 415.5 per 100,000 population in 1900 to 643.8 in 1949, and since these diseases appear to be little amenable to control and the deaths resulting from them are concentrated in, although by no means confined to, the ages over 45, they are almost certain to assume a more prominent position among the causes of death as the median age of the population increases.

The Infectious Diseases

It is a well-known demographic fact that the rapid gains in the population of the Western world since 1750 have been due more largely to reductions in the death rates than to increases in the birth rates.   The drastic reductions in the death rates have been made possible largely through the conquest of the infectious or communicable diseases, including such historically important, deadly killers as bubonic plague, cholera, dysentery, smallpox, syphilis, typhoid fever, typhus, and yellow fever, all of which formerly existed in epidemic proportions and threatened the existence of whole populations. The death rates from these and other infectious and epidemic diseases had already been substantially reduced and the high places held by these diseases among the causes of death had been taken over by the degenerative diseases when the United States established its original death-registration area in 1900. But the further progress made in controlling them (during the first half of the current century) constitutes one of the outstanding successes of medicine and sanitation. So great was the success in fact, that only two groups of the infectious diseases, pneumonia (and influenza) and tuberculosis, remained, in 1950, among the ten leading causes of death in the United States. And even in the cases of pneumonia and tuberculosis the death rates have dropped phenomenally. Whereas, in 1900, pneumonia (and influenza) occupied first position among the causes of death and accounted for 202.2 deaths per 100,000 population, by 1930 it had dropped into second position with a death rate of 102.5 and by 1950 into sixth position with a death rate of only 31.3. Tuberculosis, which occupied the second position among the causes of death in 1900 and had a death rate of 194.4, had dropped into seventh place with a death rate of 71.1 by 1930, and into eighth place with a death rate of 22.5 in 1950.

Although the gains made in reducing the death rates from these diseases are outstanding, the same degree of success has not been experienced in reducing their incidence. Of all of the respiratory diseases, pneumonia and influenza continue to be the most prevalent as well as the most damaging. Their control has been difficult for several reasons. An important one, certainly, is the fact that they cannot be traced to a specific germ, but represent both a group of diseases and a group of causes, only some of which have been identified. Also they are spread through human contacts and, frequently, by healthy carriers. Their existence has been known to medical science for centuries, but it is only in recent years that they have been controlled effectively and the death rates from them reduced substantially. The current success in controlling them is the direct result of many years of careful and meticulous research leading to the recent discovery of serum treatments, the sulfa drugs, and the antibiotics, to all of which at least some of the forms of pneumonia and influenza are yielding.

For centuries tuberculosis, like pneumonia and influenza, has been one of the leading causes of death. Though during the current century great progress has been made in controlling this disease it continues to be one of our major health hazards. No specific treatment for it has been discovered and the methods of treatment to which it responds are experimental, expensive, and disruptive to both family organization and individual careers. Furthermore, like pneumonia and influenza, the decline in its incidence, although general, has been much less spectacular than the reduction of the death rates attributed to it. Tuberculosis continues to be a tremendous problem among the industrial population and, except for accidents in all forms, it is the leading cause of death among males in the ages 15 to 44 in the general population.

The success of medical science and sanitation in controlling all of the infectious diseases and in eliminating them as leading causes of death indicates that the often-stated goal of public health—that deaths should ensue only from degenerative causes—may ultimately be approximated, if never quite attained. The decline in the death rate attributed to the infectious diseases—from 676.2 per 100,000 population in 1900 to 78.7 in 1949—is no less than phenomenal. Nevertheless, since most of these diseases are preventable, the mere fact that they continue to kill many persons—they accounted for nearly 100,000 deaths in 1950—and to disable many others is a tragedy in itself. It must be remembered that the causes of the infectious diseases have not been exterminated but only suppressed; their control has been the direct result of an extensive and complicated system of social organization created and maintained specifically for this purpose. Except for the protection afforded by vaccinations and immunizations, the population is probably as susceptible to them today as formerly. Should the machinery through which they have been controlled be disrupted or eliminated, either through wars, depressions, or the lethargy of society, they again might become as deadly as they ever were.

Cancer

Cancer is not classified as a degenerative disease; nevertheless it is like this group in that its causes are poorly understood and it is believed to be the result of a number of factors operating over a long period of time.   It is listed generally in mortality reports as malignant neoplasm, and is described as an "ungovernable, erratic growth and destructive migration of cells that are normally present in the body." It is rapidly becoming one of the most terrifying diseases with which the population is faced.   In the United States the death rate attributed to cancer more than doubled between 1900 and 1950 and, in the latter year, when it accounted for 139.8 deaths per 100,000 population, or about 14 per cent of all deaths occurring, it ranked second only to diseases of the heart among the nation's killers.

Accidents

In 1950, accidents in all forms exacted a toll of 91,249 deaths in the United States and ranked fourth on the list of causes of death. Nearly two fifths, or a total of 34,763, of these deaths were attributed to motor vehicle accidents.

The death rate from accidents places them among the five leading causes of death for all age groups in the population.   They are the leading cause of death for both sexes in all of the age groups up to 25 and for males in all of the age groups up to 45.   The great tragedy of the excessive number of deaths from accidents is that a large part of them could be prevented through the conscientious use of safety devices, educational measures, and other precautionary techniques. Not only would the successful application of these considerably reduce the annual death toll; it would also prevent much partial and permanent disability.

SICKNESS AND DISABILITY

As yet there is no census of sickness in the United States. Consequently, there is no such thing as a compilation of morbidity statistics for the general population. The statistics on morbidity that do exist are fragmentary in nature, are representative only of particular localities, of certain groups of people, and of certain classes of diseases, and, therefore, are limited in their applicability. One of the difficulties that would be encountered in compiling morbidity statistics is inherent in the various shades of meaning that surround the term *morbidity* itself. But a more serious problem is the fact that comprehensive official statistics exist only for certain groups of diseases for which compulsory reporting is required, and even the recording of these is inadequate and incomplete.[1] Until certain positive measures are taken that provide for the compilation and classification of morbidity data for the general population, our knowledge along these lines will remain particularly meager.

There are, however, a number of sources of information concerning the incidence of those diseases and cases of disability that require medical services. Although these are fragmentary and, for the most part, not comparable in their findings, they constitute important soundings into the incidence of sickness and disability. Among the most important of these sources are the National Health Survey of 1935–36, the records of the Selective Service System from the inauguration of the program in 1940 until the end of World War II in 1945, and the inventories of sickness and disability among selected groups conducted by the Metropolitan Life Insurance Company, the Milbank Memorial Fund, the Committee on the Costs of Medical Care, the United States Public Health Service, and various agencies of one type or another at the state and local level. There is not space here to exhaust the findings of all of these sources but some of the results of three of them—the National Health Survey of 1935–36,

[1] For a more complete discussion of the nature of the available morbidity statistics in the United States, see W. Wallace Weaver, *Social Problems* (Sloane, 1951), pp. 72, 91–98.

the records of the Selective Service System, and a recent study of health needs and medical care in Michigan—will be reviewed.

The National Health Survey

One of the most complete sickness surveys conducted to date is the National Health Survey of the United States Public Health Service. Carried out during the winter months of 1935–36, it included a sample of 2,800,000 persons in eighty-three cities and twenty-three rural areas. Its primary purpose was to determine the number of people who were unable to attend to their usual activities, such as work, school attendance, and so forth, each day during the winter months because of sickness, injury or physical impairment resulting from disease and accident.[2]

The data from this study that have been published pertain only to the urban areas, with none of the rural data ever having been made available, except indirectly through other sources. The results for the urban part of the sample show that 4.5 per cent of the 2,300,000 persons surveyed were disabled on the day of the canvass, which could have been any day from November to March. By age, the highest proportion of sickness was found among persons 65 and over, 12.1 per cent, and the lowest proportion among persons 15 to 24, 2.5 per cent. The corresponding proportions for persons under 15 and persons from 25 to 64 were 4.2 per cent and 4.4 per cent, respectively.[3] A breakdown of the diseases and disabilities from which these persons were suffering showed that nearly one fourth were sick with acute respiratory diseases (influenza and pneumonia, colds, grippe, etc.); approximately two fifths were suffering from chronic ailments (asthma, cancer, diseases of the heart, nervous disorders, rheumatism, and tuberculosis) or from permanent disabilities caused by prior diseases and accidents, and about one twelfth were disabled because of injuries received in accidents. The infectious diseases accounted for

[2] The results of this study are reported in U.S. Public Health Service, *Preliminary Reports, The National Health Survey, 1935–36: Significance, Scope and Method of a Nation-wide Family Canvass of Sickness in Relation to Its Social and Economic Setting* (Government Printing Office, 1938). A separate mimeographed "Sickness and Medical Care Series," gives the more detailed summaries.

[3] U.S. Public Health Service, *An Estimate of Disabling Illness in the Country as a Whole*, National Health Survey, Sickness and Medical Care Series Bulletin 1 (mimeographed, Government Printing Office, 1938), p. 1.

the disablement of about one in twenty-five of the persons who were
ill; diseases of the appendix, liver, and stomach disabled a similar
proportion; and other acute diseases caused the disability of the remainder.[4]

The data on the incidence of illnesses that were disabling for a week
or longer show that 172 such illnesses per 1,000 population had occurred during the twelve months preceding the canvass. Here again
the rates were lowest among persons 15–64, 144 per 1,000; highest
among persons 65 and over, 265 per 1,000; and in between for persons under 15, 232 per 1,000. The average days of disability per
person averaged 9.8, and were distributed by age as follows: 32.6 days
for those 65 years old and over; 9.1 days for those 15–64; and 6.0 days
for those under 15.[5] Forty-nine of the 172 disabling illnesses were
diagnosed as respiratory diseases, 46 as chronic ailments, 29 as due to
infections, 15 as diseases of the puerperal state, 16 as due to accidents,
9 as digestive ailments, and 10 as due to other causes.[6]

This study also reveals some of the relationships between the incidence of disabling illness and economic status. As noted above,
disabling illnesses lasting a week or longer occurred at the rate of 172
per 1,000 persons in the general survey population. Of these illnesses,
124 were classified as acute and 48 as chronic. The incidence of such
illnesses among the population on relief, however, was much higher,
234 per 1,000 persons, and of these, 163 were classified as acute and
71 as chronic. Of the non-relief population, each 1,000 of those
with incomes of less than $1,000 had 174 disabling illnesses which
lasted a week or longer, those with incomes of $1,000 to $2,000, 155,
those with incomes of $2,000 to $3,000, 150, and those with incomes
of $3,000 and over, 149. Also, 5.2 per cent of the heads of families on
relief were kept from seeking work because of chronic disability.
This compared with only 2.4 per cent of the heads of non-relief
families in the lowest income group and less than 1 per cent of those
with yearly incomes of over $1,000.[7]

[4] *Ibid.*, p. 2.
[5] *Ibid.*, p. 4.
[6] *Ibid.*, p. 5.
[7] U.S. Public Health Service, *Illness and Medical Care in Relation to Economic
Status*, National Health Survey, Sickness and Medical Care Series Bulletin 2
(mimeographed, Government Printing Office, 1938), pp. 2–3.

Although the National Health Survey has been subjected to a great deal of criticism for one reason and another, it probably continues to be our most important source of information on the prevalence of sickness and disability in the general population. Certainly it has done more than any other study to define the extensiveness of the problem and to show how different groups are affected by it. As such it deserves the attention of anyone who is interested in the prevalence of sickness and disability in the nation.

The Selective Service System

More than 17,000,000 adult males were examined by the Selective Service System between the beginning of its program in 1940 and the end of World War II in 1945. More than ten million of these were accepted for military service, of whom 10 per cent were subsequently screened out and discharged. Also, of the six million who were initially rejected, about 1,500,000 were later re-examined and inducted.[8] The examination records of the men called up for induction naturally do not provide a representative sampling of the nation's population. The majority of these men were confined to the ages from 17 to 37, and even in these ages the system of voluntary enlistments had taken large numbers before Selective Service got to them. Also, the standards for acceptance or rejection must have varied—despite efforts to keep them constant—because of the varying pressure of quotas as the war moved through its different phases. It is likewise true that the purpose of the examination administered to the draftees was not to discover physical defects, as such, but to determine their fitness or unfitness for military service. Many men who had defects were inducted anyway, when these defects were of such nature as not to interfere unduly with the performance of military occupations. It should be observed, furthermore, that many of the defects for which men were rejected do not necessarily constitute serious handicaps in civilian life.

But even with these limitations, the mass of data on the prevalence of defects among the nation's males assembled by the Selective Service System during World War II is one of our most valuable pools of

[8] Weaver, *op. cit.*, pp. 93–94.

information on the incidence of defects and disabilities. Some of these data, showing the number of defects per 1,000 registrants examined are set forth in Table 14.2.

The information included is for whites and Negroes and is broken down with each category further subdivided by occupation into agricultural and nonagricultural. For both races, it will be observed, the prevalence of defects was about the same for the farmers and the nonfarmers, although there were important differences in the prevalence of particular defects. Among the whites, the farmers were considerably less likely to have defects of the eyes, teeth, nose and ears, skin trouble, ailments of the abdominal viscera, varicose veins, hemorrhoids, tuberculosis, syphilis, neoplasms, kidney and urinary troubles, and gonorrhea and venereal diseases. On the other hand, they were much more likely to be illiterate and mentally deficient and to have defects of the mouth and gums, and were slightly more likely to be troubled with defects of the feet, mental disease, disorders of the genitalia, neurological difficulties, and endocrine conditions. Among the Negroes, the primary differences were found in the rates of illiteracy and mental deficiency, which were twice as high among the farmers as among the nonfarmers, and in the rates of syphilis, hemorrhoids, defects of the feet, teeth, genitalia, nose, and abdominal viscera, all of which were higher among the nonfarmers.[9]

The materials presented above are only a minute sounding into the Selective Service data on the prevalence of defects among the men called up for induction into military service. They represent the defects recorded for all registrants between November 1940 and December 1943, irrespective of whether they were accepted or rejected. Thus, they give a more complete picture of the actual prevalence of defects and disabilities than would be the case if they pertained only to rejectees. For one of the healthiest nations in the world, the picture is not a pleasing one and it becomes less so when it is remembered that many of the defects are either preventable or remediable and represent the result of gross neglect in matters pertaining to personal health. It is not particularly heartening to know either that

[9] Marcus S. Goldstein, "Physical Status of Men Examined through Selective Service in World War II," *Public Health Reports*, LXVI (May 11, 1951), 587–609.

TABLE 14.2: DEFECTS PER 1,000 WHITE AND NEGRO REGISTRANTS IN AGRICULTURAL
AND NONAGRICULTURAL EMPLOYMENT EXAMINED THROUGH
SELECTIVE SERVICE, NOVEMBER 1940 TO DECEMBER 1943

Type of Defect	Rate per 1,000 White Registrants Examined		Rate per 1,000 Negro Registrants Examined	
	Agricultural	Nonagricultural	Agricultural	Nonagricultural
Eyes	99.4	132.3	57.5	69.1
Musculoskeletal	99.2	90.1	57.7	67.8
Illiteracy and mental deficiency	96.0	24.3	269.0	121.3
Feet	86.6	85.2	105.2	125.7
Teeth	83.6	131.5	36.4	65.3
Mental disease	67.2	55.8	47.3	47.7
Cardio vascular	57.0	56.9	57.3	64.5
Hernia	53.8	52.2	35.4	41.4
Mouth and gums	50.2	31.7	35.2	37.9
Genitalia	45.8	45.4	34.4	48.8
Nose	40.3	46.8	6.8	15.2
Throat	37.7	25.8	24.4	30.4
Skin	36.9	39.1	12.9	18.5
Ears	35.6	44.1	10.6	15.6
Neurological	29.8	26.2	18.5	19.1
Abdominal viscera	18.1	22.7	3.7	8.2
Varicose veins	17.4	20.9	10.5	14.2
Hemorrhoids	15.2	17.7	8.4	13.7
Lungs	15.2	15.1	11.3	12.4
Tuberculosis	12.8	16.4	9.5	13.3
Endocrine	12.6	12.2	2.9	4.1
Syphilis	11.0	14.1	127.7	167.4
Neoplasms	9.5	11.0	5.6	7.0
Kidney and urinary	7.6	10.1	5.0	8.4
Gonorrhea and other venereal	1.9	2.4	23.6	30.5
Infectious and parasitic	0.8	0.5	0.6	0.6
Blood and blood forming organs	0.7	0.9	0.2	0.3
Other medical	61.7	68.6	32.8	45.6
Nonmedical and not stated	327.3	349.3	259.2	298.3
Total	1430.9	1449.3	1309.6	1412.3

Source: Marcus S. Goldstein, "Physical Status of Men Examined through Selective Service in World War II," *Public Health Reports*, LXVI (May 11, 1951), figs. 6a and 6b, pp. 602–603.

during this period of great international tensions the nation's potential fighting forces are vastly depleted because of physical defects that disqualify men for military service. The same thing is true of the wasted man power in civilian pursuits because of these same defects.

Unmet Medical Needs in Michigan

The Department of Sociology and Anthropology at Michigan State College conducted a state-wide survey of health needs and health care in Michigan in which some attempt was made to inventory sickness and disability among the population.[10] This study used the "Symptoms Approach" developed in the U.S. Department of Agriculture to study a total of 3,786 persons in a sample of 1,113 households.[11] The sample population was distributed by residence as follows: open country, 1,317; village, 421; metropolitan, 548; and urban, 1,500.[12]

Of the persons included in this study, 40.2 per cent reported having one or more of 27 positive symptoms during the six months preceding the survey interview. However, the percentages of persons reporting positive symptoms varied considerably with such factors as residence, income, education of the wife or female head of the family, and the distance to the nearest town having a doctor. The differences in these respects may be summarized as follows: [13]

1. By residential categories, the percentage of persons reporting one or more positive symptoms was 42.9 for the open country, 45.9 for the village, 35.2 for the metropolitan, and 38.3 for the urban.

2. By income groups, the differences in the percentage of persons reporting one or more positive symptoms were somewhat greater and ranged from as high as 61.2 for those in families with gross incomes of less than $1,000 in 1948 to as low as 33.1 for those in families with gross incomes of $5,000 and over. In the other income groups, positive symptoms were reported as follows: persons in families with gross

---

[10] The results of this study are reported in Charles R. Hoffer *et al.*, *Health Needs and Health Care in Michigan*, Michigan AES Special Bulletin 365, East Lansing, 1948.

[11] For the details concerning this method of study, see Edgar A. Schuler, Selz C. Mayo, and Henry B. Makover, M.D., "Measuring Needs for Medical Care: An Experiment in Method," *Rural Sociology*, XI (June, 1946), 152–158.

[12] Hoffer *et al.*, *op. cit.*, p. 11.

[13] *Ibid.*, Table 2, p. 15; Table 6, p. 20; Table 7, p. 21; and Table 8, p. 22.

incomes of $1,000–$1,999, 44.2 per cent; $2,000–$2,999, 41.7 per cent; $3,000–$3,999, 34.9 per cent; and $4,000–$4,999, 36.6 per cent.

3. Positive symptoms were reported for 47.1 per cent of the persons in families in which the wife or female head had completed 0–8 grades in school, for 36.1 per cent of those in families in which she had completed 1–4 years of high school, and 35.8 per cent of those in families in which she had completed 1 or more years of college.

4. For 1,223 persons in the open country sample, positive symptoms were reported for 56.2 per cent, 42.3 per cent, and 41.8 per cent, respectively, of those living 11 miles or more, 6–10 miles, and 0–5 miles from the nearest town having a doctor.

The data from this study, like those from the National Health Survey and those from the examination records of the Selective Service System, point up some of the more significant, if not too well understood, problems concerning the prevalence of sickness and disease and defects and disabilities in the nation.   Not only do they outline the extent of the problem in the general population and reveal the prevalence of many diseases and defects on an unsuspected scale but also they underline the seriousness of the problem in specific groups and classes.   Of particular importance in this respect is the inverse relationship between income and the prevalence of sickness and disability demonstrated by both the National Health Survey and the study of unmet medical needs in Michigan.   It is a well documented sociological truth, of course, that the disadvantaged groups in a society, whatever their nature, enjoy fewer of the good things that the society has to offer than others, and health seems to be no exception.

SOCIAL ORGANIZATION FOR HEALTH

The complexity of our modern social organization for assisting mankind in his struggle with disease is tremendous.   Personnel includes —in addition to physicians, dentists, and registered nurses—a wide range of other specialists and paramedical workers, such as osteopaths, chiropodists, chiropractors, cultists and religious healers, clinical psychologists, dietitians, health educators, hospital and medical administrators, medical technologists, medical record librarians, nurse anesthetists, optometrists and opticians, sanitary engineers and sanitarians, medical and psychiatric social workers, occupational and physical therapists, veterinarians, x-ray technicians, dental technicians, and practical nurses and mid-wives. All together in the United States today these number nearly one million persons. In the way of facilities and services, there are in the country over 6,000 hospitals, containing more than 1,500,000 beds; as many, or more, health centers and clinics, maintained either by hospitals, private health agencies, governmental organizations, commercial and industrial establishments, schools, colleges, trade unions, courts, prisons, and charitable agencies; and a variety of voluntary health agencies, such as the National Anti-Tuberculosis Association, Cancer Society, Society for Crippled Children and Adults, National Foundation for Infantile Paralysis, and the American Heart Association, all of which have organized chapters scattered throughout the country.

There are certain social and economic problems connected with our social organization for health, that need to be pointed out. These may be stated as follows: (1) Even if there is no actual scarcity of certain types of personnel and facilities for meeting the needs of the population for health and medical care, these certainly are disproportionately distributed within the country, so that it becomes difficult for certain groups to secure medical and health care when they are needed. (2) There is an extreme differential in the use of medical services and facilities which correlates highly with such factors as residence, race, income, education, and distance from services, and which indicates that large numbers of the population are not getting the health and medical care they need. (3) Paying for services for health and medical care as the need for them arises is a problem with which many families in the United States are unable to cope. It is generally agreed that this country has as good personnel and equipment for medical care as any other, but perhaps a third or more of the population do not get complete care because they cannot pay for it and do not get it free.

Number and Distribution of Selected Types
of Personnel and Facilities

In 1949, there were 183,997 active civilian physicians and 77,820 active dentists in the United States; and, in 1951, there were 366,134 active graduate nurses. The specialist-person ratios—that is, the number of each type of specialist per 100,000 population—was 125 for physicians, 52 for dentists, and 239 for nurses. In 1951, there also were 640,207 beds in registered general hospitals, providing a bed-person ratio (the number of beds per 1,000 population) of 4.2. These ratios for the country as a whole are quite favorable and conform closely to the specifications that have been set forth for maintaining adequate health and medical care standards.

But, as the data assembled in Table 14.3 indicate, there are some important inequalities in the distribution of health and medical personnel and facilities from one region of the country to another. In general, these differences appear to be associated directly with the degree of urbanization and show that the more urban and metropolitan the region, the more favorable are the physician-person, dentist-person, and other such ratios. For example, of the ratios shown in Table 14.3, those for the Southeast and the Southwest, the two most rural regions in the country, are consistently lower than the national average, while those for New England, the Central Atlantic States and the Far West (except for general hospital beds) are consistently above the average for the nation. Essentially the same thing is true of the distribution of medical services and facilities from one state to another and between the city and the country. Whereas for the United States as a whole there is one active civilian physician for every 1,200 persons, in New York State (highly urban) there is one for every 500, and in Mississippi (predominantly rural) there is one for every 1,500. Between the city and the country the differences are just as exaggerated, or more so. According to a publication of the Public Health Service, which describes the distribution of physicians in the United States by region and degree of urbanization, the greater metropolitan areas have 173 physicians per 100,000 population; the lesser metropolitan areas, 131; areas adjacent to metropolitan areas,

TABLE 14.3: THE NUMBER OF PHYSICIANS, DENTISTS AND NURSES PER 100,000 POPULATION AND THE NUMBER OF GENERAL HOSPITAL BEDS PER 1,000 POPULATION, UNITED STATES, 1949–52

United States and Region	Physicians (1949)	Dentists (1949)	Nurses (1952)	General Hospital Beds (1952)
United States	125	52	239	3.7
New England	155	59	357	4.0
Central Atlantic	161	69	295	4.0
Southeast	86	27	150	3.1
Southwest	98	30	162	3.6
East North Central	120	54	238	3.4
West North Central	116	56	217	4.3
Rocky Mountain	123	49	255	4.8
Far West	137	65	298	3.4

Source: The President's Commission on the Health Needs of the Nation, *Building America's Health*, 3, "America's Health Status, Needs and Resources" (Government Printing Office, 1953), Table 183, p. 140; Table 227, p. 176; Table 252, pp. 186–187; and Table 329, pp. 236–247.

78; isolated semi-rural areas, 80; and isolated rural areas, 50.[14]   Similar or greater inequalities could be shown to exist between rural and urban areas in the distribution of dentists, nurses, and general hospital beds, but the point has been made and there is little need for further elaboration.

The basic causes for the concentration of health and medical services in the cities, or closely adjacent to them, appear to be rather obviously economic in nature: not only are there greater opportunities to practice in the city, but also city practice is more lucrative than rural practice.   There are indications that this concentration is becoming even more pronounced, and although the city and the country, through improvements in transportation and communication, have become more accessible to one another than ever before, it is extremely doubtful that this fact offsets the disadvantages to the rural areas created by the lack of physicians, dentists and hospitals in the community.   The acuteness of this problem has been recognized and a number of positive steps have been taken to alleviate it.   In some states the shortage of physicians in the rural areas is being met by the award of medical scholarships which bind the recipients to maintain their practices in the smaller towns and cities for a specified

[14] *Health Manpower Source Book* (Government Printing Office, 1952), Table 35, p. 42.

number of years, usually five, after their graduation from medical school. Likewise, the quick response of many of the states to accept the provisions of the Hospital Survey and Construction (Hill-Burton) Act is rapidly eliminating the shortage of both hospitals and health centers in the rural areas.

Differentials in the Use of Medical and Health Services

Numerous studies made in recent years have shown the great disparity in the use of the services of physicians and other medical personnel and of the facilities of hospitals and other health agencies by different groups in the population. These studies demonstrate quite clearly that rural people, Negroes, the low-income families, the poorly educated groups, the more isolated groups, and the unskilled workers use these facilities far less than their counterparts, the urban dwellers, the whites, the high-income families, the better educated groups, the less isolated groups, and the professional and skilled workers.

In 1945, the Interbureau Committee on Postwar Problems of the United States Department of Agriculture issued a report in which were summarized some of the more obvious discrepancies between the rural and urban populations in the use of medical services and facilities. Particularly noteworthy are their statements to the effect that (1) each 1,000 people in towns under 5,000 and in the open country receive only 2,240 physicians' calls per year as compared with 2,679 calls per 1,000 persons in cities of 5,000 to 100,000, and 3,003 calls per 1,000 persons in cities of over 100,000, and (2) that each 1,000 persons in the rural areas have only 42 cases of hospitalization per year, as compared with 68 cases per 1,000 persons in cities of over 100,000. The report states also that the rural population gets far less dental care and far less surgical care, especially elective surgery, than the urban population; and about the only health items that rural people use in relatively greater quantities than the urban are patent medicines. These differences are explained largely on the basis of the lower income levels in the rural areas, but also are observed to be partially due to the absence of physicians and other health facilities in the country.[15]

[15] *Better Health for Rural America: Plan of Action for Farm Communities* (Government Printing Office, 1945), p. 6.

The Department of Sociology and Rural Life at Mississippi State College has studied the health practices of 909 rural families, including 3,443 family members. The results show some of the major differentials in the use of health and medical personnel and facilities by different groups in the population. The most important of these differences may be summarized as follows: (1) Each 1,000 persons in the lowest socio-economic group (classified by Sewell's Socio-economic Status Scale) had 1,376 physicians' calls, 116 dental calls, and spent 300 days in general hospitals during the year, as compared with 3,242 physicians' calls, 1,232 dental calls and 636 days in general hospitals for each 1,000 persons in the highest socio-economic group. (2) Females accounted for twice as many physicians' calls and days in general hospitals as males, and nearly one third more dental calls per 1,000 population than males. (3) The farm population had 1,631 physicians' calls, 357 dental calls, and 343 days in general hospitals per 1,000 persons as compared with 2,373 physicians' calls, 554 dental calls, and 447 days in general hospitals per 1,000 persons in the nonfarm population. (4) Each 1,000 persons in families in which the wife or female head had completed less than 5 years of schooling had 1,188 physicians' calls, 110 dental calls, and 304 days in general hospitals as compared with 3,418 physicians' calls, 1,014 dental calls and 507 days in general hospitals for each 1,000 persons in families in which the female head had completed 13 years of formal schooling or more. (5) Each 1,000 whites accounted for 2,497 physicians' calls, 612 dental calls, and 455 days in general hospitals, as compared with 1,048 physicians' calls, 166 dental calls, and 494 days in general hospitals for each 1,000 Negroes. (6) Persons living less than 10 miles from the nearest of each type of facility had 1,930 physicians' calls, 459 dental calls, and 426 days in general hospitals per 1,000 population as compared with 1,729 physicians' calls, 343 dental calls, and 342 days in general hospitals per 1,000 population for persons living 10 miles or more from the nearest of each type of facility.[16]

These differentials in the use of health and medical personnel and facilities do not mean at all that the groups receiving the fewer services

[16] See Marion T. Loftin and Robert E. Galloway, *The Health Practices of Rural People in Four Mississippi Counties,* Mississippi State College Sociology and Rural Life Series No. 5, 1954.

actually need less care than the others. They do mean, however, that many of their needs for health and medical care are not being met. The causes of the differentials appear to be mainly economic, although they are associated with many other factors, such as race, residence, education, occupation, and degree of isolation. But whatever the causes, the problem remains. Not all groups in the population are receiving adequate health and medical care.

Paying for Health and Medical Services

The cost of personal health and medical care. The amount of money spent by families in the United States for personal health and medical care runs into billions of dollars annually. In 1927 Louis I. Dublin, statistician for the Metropolitan Life Insurance Company, placed the total cost of medical care in the United States at $2,000,000,000,[17] and two years later W. S. Rankin placed the figure nearly a half billion dollars higher, at $2,460,000,000.[18] In 1932 the Committee on the Cost of Medical Care published its final report in which the conclusion was reached that medical expenditures in the United States in 1929 had reached a total of $3,656,000,000.[19]

The Health Information Foundation with the assistance of the National Opinion Research Center, University of Chicago, is currently conducting a National Consumer Survey of Medical Costs and Voluntary Health Insurance, which, when completed, will provide, for the first time in twenty years, a comprehensive, nationwide picture of personal medical costs incurred by families. This survey, which covers the period from July 1952 to June 1953, is based on single interviews of 2,809 families, including 8,846 family members. It represents a national sample of the population of the United States subdivided by age, sex, income, size of family, residence, occupation, and region.[20] According to the preliminary reports released to date, this

[17] *Health and Wealth* (Harper, 1928), p. 8.
[18] "Economics of Medical Service," *American Journal of Public Health* (April, 1929), pp. 359–365.
[19] *Medical Care for the American People* (University of Chicago Press, 1932), p. 14.
[20] Odin W. Anderson, *National Consumer Survey of Medical Costs and Voluntary Health Insurance*, Summary Report No. 2, "Voluntary Health Insurance and Consumer Expenditures for Personal Health Services in the United States, July

study shows that the total annual charges for personal health services incurred by families is $10.2 billion. Broken down by types of services for which the charges were made, this total is distributed as follows: physicians, $3.8 billion; hospitals, $2.0 billion; prescriptions and medicines, $1.5 billion; other medical goods and services, $1.3 billion; and dentists, $1.6 billion. These reports show further that, exclusive of insurance premiums and the portions paid by insurance, the average charges for medical care incurred by families in the United States is $178 per year, and that eleven per cent of the families experience charges in excess of $395, seven per cent in excess of $495, and one per cent in excess of $995. This latter figure, projected to include the entire population, means that some 500,000 families in the United States are each experiencing personal charges for medical services that approach $1,000 annually. These reports also indicate that 6,500,000 families, representing 15 per cent of all families in the country, were in debt for personal-health services as of July 1953. The total amount of this indebtedness was $900,000,000. The average amount owed per family in debt was $121, with nine per cent of the families owing under $94, three per cent from $95 to $194, and two per cent $195 and over. In addition to the amount shown above, families in the country also owed financial institutions and individuals another $200,000,000 for charges arising from personal-health services.[21]

The study shows further that of the $10.2 billion dollars charged families for personal-health services annually, approximately 15 per cent, amounting to $1.5 billion, is paid by insurance benefits. These benefits pay about 50 per cent of the $2.0 billion charged for hospital services and about 13 per cent of the $3.8 billion charged for physicians' services. Included in this latter amount, however, are $300 million, or 38 per cent of the $800 million charged for surgical care, and $100 million, or 25 per cent, of the $400 million charged for obstetrical care. Only $100 million, or four per cent, of the other $2.6 billion charged by physicians are paid from insurance benefits.

1952 Through June 1953" (mimeographed, New York: Health Information Foundation, 1954), p. ii-3.

[21] Anderson, *National Consumer Survey of Medical Costs and Voluntary Health Insurance*, Summary Report No. 4. "Debt among Families in the United States Due to Costs of Personal Health Services as of July 1953" (mimeographed, New York: Health Information Foundation, 1954), pp. iv-3–iv-7.

For no other major item in the national health bill is the amount paid by insurance benefits in excess of one per cent of the total charges.[22]

The prepayment of medical costs through voluntary health insurance. The prepayment of the costs of medical care is a relatively new development in the United States. Since 1929, however, health-insurance plans offering various degrees of protection have been publicized extensively and, in spite of heated opposition from certain quarters, the health-insurance movement on a voluntary basis has grown extremely rapidly. To a large extent this movement has followed the principle of group insurance. The most notable examples are the plans developed by the larger companies and industrial concerns to provide blanket coverage for their employees and their families, and those developed by physicians, hospital administrators, or other agencies within local communities. There are other plans available that can be purchased by the individual on the same basis as other types of insurance, but the developments in this direction have been much less extensive than in the area of group insurance.

The most recent estimate of the extent to which the population of the United States is enrolled in voluntary prepayment health-insurance plans of which the writer is aware is the one issuing from the National Consumer Survey of Medical Costs and Voluntary Health Insurance referred to above. The preliminary reports from this study indicate that 87 million people in the United States, or 57 per cent of the population, had some hospital insurance, and 74 million people, or 48 per cent of the population, had some surgical and other medical insurance as of July 1953. However, the extent to which the population is enrolled varies widely from one section of the country to another, for occupational groups, between rural and urban areas, and by family income. A larger percentage of the population is enrolled in the Northeast and North Central parts of the country than in the South and West. By occupation, enrollment varies from as low as 33 per cent for families employed in agriculture, forestry and fisheries to as high as 90 per cent for those employed in mining and manufacturing. Only 41 per cent of the families whose annual income is under $3,000 are enrolled as compared with 71 per cent of those whose annual in-

[22] Anderson, *National Consumer Survey of Medical Cost and Voluntary Health Insurance*, Summary Report No. 2, *op. cit.*, Table 2.

come is from $3,000 to $4,999, and 80 per cent of those whose annual income is $5,000 and over. Seventy per cent of the urban families, 57 per cent of the rural nonfarm families, and 45 per cent of the farm families have voluntary health insurance. The study shows also that 80 per cent of all families with health insurance had policies which had been obtained through their place of work or through an employed group, 9 per cent held policies which had been obtained while members of a group but which they had retained on an individual basis after leaving the group, and 32 per cent had policies which had been obtained as individuals.[23]

Since the rationale behind health insurance is to distribute the cost of personal health and medical care equitably so that no one family incurs heavy costs at any one time, two questions are primary for evaluating the adequacy of any health-insurance program. First, is it of such nature that it can include all major segments of the population? And second, to what extent do its benefits take care of the charges for personal health and medical care incurred by the participants? These are some of the primary problems facing the proponents of voluntary health insurance today and unless satisfactory solutions can be found for them on the voluntary prepayment principle, our future developments in the field of health insurance are almost certain to move in the direction of compulsory health insurance sponsored by the government.

The data from the National Consumer Survey of Medical Costs and Voluntary Health Insurance presented above show some of the difficulties that the voluntary plans are facing in extending their coverage to all major segments of the population. The primary problem appears to be with the self-employed and with people employed in very small groups who do not meet the requirements for group enrollment and who, for one reason or another, are not availing themselves of the health insurance that can be had on an individual basis. Among the deterring factors to widespread enrollment of individuals that do not hamper group enrollment are the unavoidably high cost of acquisition, extended waiting periods, and the limitations on benefits to prevent self-selection. To meet this problem the voluntary health-

[23] Anderson, *National Consumer Survey of Medical Costs and Voluntary Health Insurance*, Summary Report No. 1, "The Extent of Voluntary Health Insurance in the United States as of July 1953" (mimeographed, New York: Health Information Foundation, 1954).

insurance programs must undertake the development of methods for grouping the self-employed and the very small groups of employed for enrollment purposes so that they can be offered as low an acquisition cost, as few limitations on benefits, and as favorable premiums as the larger employed groups are now enjoying.

The preliminary reports of the National Consumer Survey of Medical Costs and Voluntary Health Insurance also offer some information on the extent to which the voluntary health-insurance program is taking care of the charges for personal health and medical care incurred by the families with health insurance. Of the 2,809 families surveyed on a national scale, 602, or 21 per cent, had received some services, from July 1952 through June 1953, for which insurance benefits had been paid in whole or in part. These benefits amounted to less than 20 per cent of the gross charges for 29 per cent of the families, 20–39 per cent of the gross charges for 28 per cent of the families, 40–59 per cent of the gross charges for 20 per cent of the families, 60–79 per cent of the gross charges for 10 per cent of the families, and 80 per cent and more of the gross charges for 7 per cent of the families. However, the extent to which the gross charges were covered varied widely with the type of medical care received. Fifty-nine per cent of the insured families who had hospital charges, 49 per cent of those who had surgical charges, and 35 per cent of those who had obstetrical charges had 80 per cent or more of each of these charges paid by insurance.[24]

A final problem confronting voluntary health insurance today is the question of more comprehensive coverage to take care of physicians' charges for such services as home calls and office calls and outpatient diagnostic services. To date most of the plans in effect have not included benefits to cover these charges. Indeed, much of the prevailing philosophy in the field of health insurance seems to be that these are not important unpredictable items in the family medical bill and that families can afford to pay for such care as the need for it arises. On the other hand, physicians' charges for services other than surgery and obstetrics, although they are usually incurred in small amounts, may constitute a relatively large item over the period of a year. It is also true that there is a high positive correlation be-

[24] Anderson, *National Consumer Survey of Medical Costs and Voluntary Health Insurance,* Summary Report No. 2, *op. cit.,* Tables 16–18.

tween participation in health-insurance plans and the use of those services for which benefits are provided. Thus, if the coverage were more comprehensive more families would get more of the medical care which they actually need. The most recent study underlining this relationship, and perhaps the only one to do so on the basis of a nationwide sample, is the National Consumer Survey of Medical Costs and Voluntary Health Insurance. For all families included in this study the general hospital admission rate was 12 per 100 persons per year. But for families with health insurance the rate was 13 per 100 persons per year while for families without insurance it was only 10 per 100 persons per year. Likewise, the number of hospital days varied from 110 per 100 persons per year for families who had insurance to only 80 per 100 persons per year for families who did not have insurance. Among the insured families the number of surgical procedures was 7 per 100 persons per year as compared with 4 per 100 persons per year among the families without insurance.[25]

Compulsory health insurance. Every important country in the world, except China, India, and the United States, has developed some form of health insurance under the auspices of the government. Germany pioneered in this field as early as 1883, and Great Britain and Russia have developed it to the greatest extent, being the only two countries to provide so-called "universal protection" under their programs. The United States has been reluctant to take any concerted action in this direction. However, the proposal for compulsory health insurance in this country has been made, the need for such a program has been demonstrated by its proponents, and during the last twenty years the whole issue has become one of the most hotly contested ones on the national scene.

The majority report of the Committee on the Cost of Medical Care, an independent organization made up of physicians and laymen, in 1932 recommended, among other things, that the costs of medical care be placed on a group-payment basis through the use of both insurance and taxation for those who desired it. But the principal

[25] Anderson, *National Consumer Survey of Medical Costs and Voluntary Health Insurance*, Summary Report No. 3, "Voluntary Health Insurance and Utilization of Personal Health Services in the United States, July 1952 Through June 1953" (mimeographed, New York: Health Information Foundation, 1954), p. iii-3.

minority report of the Committee, prepared by eight physicians and one layman, disagreed violently with this proposal, as well as with most of the other recommendations. With the advent of the New Deal in 1933, attention became focused more sharply than ever before on compulsory health insurance under government supervision, but the Social Security Act of 1935, as finally enacted, contained no provisions for it. In 1938 the National Health Conference, basing its proposal on the National Health Survey of the Public Health Service, recommended the consideration of a medical-care program for the entire population supported by both insurance and taxation, but again no action was taken beyond the introduction of a bill into Congress which never advanced beyond the committee stage. The National Health Assembly, which met in 1948, made even more explicit proposals to develop a program of compulsory health insurance and President Truman assumed the obligation of initiating and supporting a bill for compulsory health insurance. Because of severe opposition, however, the enactment of the necessary legislation by Congress to get the program under way was impossible.

Study Questions

1. Discuss the importance of good health from the personal and from the social points of view.

2. Outline the changes in the principal causes of death in the United States since 1900.

3. In one or two paragraphs point out the primary differentials in mortality rates in the United States.

4. Describe the relationship between (1) age and mortality, (2) sex and mortality, (3) race and mortality, and (4) residence and mortality. Show the differences in the causes of death in relation to each of these factors.

5. Why have the degenerative diseases posed so great a problem in so far as controlling them is concerned?

6. Why do pneumonia and influenza and tuberculosis continue to be listed among our major health hazards?

7. What are the primary problems connected with the distribution of medical and health personnel and facilities in the United States?

8. Discuss the differentials in the use of medical services and facilities in the United States.

9. Point out the reasons why all attempts to establish a compulsory health-insurance program in the United States have failed.

10. Do you think that voluntary health insurance is the answer to our problems on how to pay the costs of personal health and medical care? Why or why not?

Selected References

Anderson, Odin W., *National Consumer Survey of Medical Costs and Voluntary Health Insurance*, Summary Reports 1–4 (New York: Health Information Foundation, 1954). These reports contain our most recent nationwide data on the extent of voluntary health insurance, consumer expenditures for personal health services, and debt among families due to the costs of personal health services.

Bachman, George W., and Lewis Meriam, *The Issue of Compulsory Health Insurance* (Washington: The Brookings Institution, 1948). One of the few objective evaluations of this controversial issue available.

Bauer, Louis Hopewell, *Private Enterprise or Government in Medicine* (Springfield, Ill.: Charles C. Thomas, 1947). The case against compulsory health insurance.

Dublin, Louis I., and Alfred J. Lotka, *The Money Value of a Man* (rev. ed., Ronald, 1946). Two statisticians for the Metropolitan Life Insurance Company present an unusually interesting and unique analysis of the costs and values of human workers.

Ewing, Oscar R., *The Nation's Health: A Ten Year Program* (Government Printing Office, 1948). A clear presentation of the health program advocated by the federal government under the Truman administration, including the proposal for compulsory health insurance.

Goldman, Franz, and Hugh R. Leavell (eds.), "Medical Care for Americans," *The Annals of the American Academy of Political and Social Science*, vol. 273 (1951). A comprehensive coverage of many aspects of medical care, including public medical-care and health insurance.

Mott, Frederick D., and Milton Roemer, *Rural Health and Medical Care* (McGraw-Hill, 1948). The most comprehensive study available of rural health and medical care and of the special health problems presented by rural areas.

National Health Assembly, *America's Health* (Harper, 1949). The report on the national conference held in 1948 to evaluate the nation's health status and proposals for improving medical care.

President's Commission on the Health Needs of the Nation, *Building America's Health* (Government Printing Office, 1953), 5 volumes.

An extensive documentation of the health needs of the nation and a massive collection of data from many sources on the health status of the American people, health personnel and facilities, utilization of health services, and financing health services.

Weaver, W. Wallace, *Social Problems* (William Sloane Associates, 1951), chs. 4–6, pp. 69–151. In these three chapters the author presents detailed data for the United States on the health status of the population, the causes and consequences of disease, disability, and death, and the social provisions for medical care.

15

Minority and Racial Problems

In Iowa, a veteran's widow had to change the plans for her husband's burial when cemetery officials discovered that he was an American Indian. In the Rio Grande Valley, another veteran, alive and decorated, was ejected from a night club because his complexion was swarthy and his surname was Spanish. In Cicero, Illinois, the attempt of a Negro to move into an apartment in an all-white community led to a riot. In North Carolina, a Negro man was arrested on the charge of having insulted a young white woman by ogling her in a manner disapproved for Negroes.

Such occurrences serve to remind Americans that minority and racial problems continue in our society. The first chapter of this text pointed out that some problems arise, are faced, and are resolved, while other problems remain, in one form or another, for generations. "Race relations" provide a striking example of problems that persist. They developed very early in American life and have continued to plague our heterogeneous society.

Not only have such problems been persistent, but they have ranked, and still rank, among the most important of our social issues. The greatest internal crisis of our history, resulting in our most deadly and devastating war, was intimately tied to the issue of Negro slavery. Political events have repeatedly demonstrated that questions concerning the Negro are capable of producing sectional dissension. Our relationships with the rest of the world are also affected in no small degree by our treatment of minorities; racial discrimination has provided the communists with one of their most effective themes in anti-American propaganda. Quite apart from communist propaganda, news stories damage our prestige and effectiveness in world leadership, both by alienating colored peoples and by causing all peoples who aspire to democracy to question our sincerity.

Concern with the conflict between American racial practices and our democratic ideals is far from confined to other nations; throughout our history many Americans have felt this discrepancy to be a major shortcoming in our democratic structure. In his monumental study of the American Negro, Gunnar Myrdal dubbed the clash between our national ideology and our traditional racial practices "an American dilemma." He noted that all the world recognizes it as an American problem because of our own concern with it.[1]

Because our racial and minority problems are of long standing, because we are keenly aware of them, and because we recognize the inconsistency between our ideals and practices, Americans of all points of view are likely to have strongly-felt opinions concerning these problems. For many Americans, the emotional impact of these problems exceeds that of most other social problems and makes careful and objective analysis difficult but all the more necessary. These questions deserve careful attention for still another reason: they represent a study in cultural change. More changes have occurred in American race relations since 1940 than in any similar period since Reconstruction. The rate of change may seem painfully slow to a Negro who continues to meet barriers at almost every turn; it may seem painfully rapid to the Southerner schooled in the traditional customs of his region. Neither, however, will question that basic revisions are under way.

TYPES OF MINORITY GROUPS

Terms in Current Use

The term "race," familiar as it is, offers a number of difficulties to the serious student. Despite its apparent simplicity, the concept is actually exceedingly difficult to define with scientific precision.[2]

[1] Gunnar Myrdal, An American Dilemma (Harper, 1944), I, 21.

[2] The student may refer to any college text on racial or minority relations for a discussion of the concept of race. One of the better presentations is found in Brewton Berry, Race Relations (Houghton-Mifflin, 1951), ch. 3.

Furthermore, the term has been applied, popularly and scientifically, both to the major subdivisions of mankind and to subgroups within these categories. For example, we speak of the Caucasian "race" and of its subgroups, the Nordic, Alpine, and Mediterranean "races." Popularly, the term has often been extended even further, as in references to the "French race" or the "Jewish race." Thus the concept has come to lack the precision requisite for objective study. Beliefs and actions based on ideologies of racial supremacy have surrounded the term "race" with emotional implications that make its scientific application even more difficult.

An oddity of American usage derives from our tendency to group together all people with some Negro ancestry, even though their physical variation may be about as great as that of the total population. Thus, a small fraction of Negro blood, if known, makes a person a member of the Negro "race" in ordinary American usage.

Despite all objections, the term "race" remains thoroughly established in both popular and sociological usage. In this chapter, "race" will designate those groups composed of persons physically distinguishable from other Americans, plus any persons who, despite appearance but on the basis of ancestry, are considered to belong to such groups. The term will not be used to refer to nationality, linguistic, or religious groups as such.

There is a need, however, for a term broad enough to include groups singled out on the basis of national, linguistic, and religious, as well as racial, differences. A widely used term is "minority group" or simply "minority," which, for our purposes, designates a grouping of people who are distinguishable by certain easily ascertained characteristics and who, thus identified, become the objects of discriminatory, unequal treatment. The "easily ascertained characteristics" include not only racial but cultural, religious, and nationality differences. Literally, "minority" carries a numerical implication lacking in the above definition and in ordinary sociological usage. Thus, it seems inappropriate to speak of the native "minority" in South Africa or of the Negro "minority" in the Mississippi Delta when in each instance the subordinated group is much the larger part of the population. Indeed, in much of the United States, no one group is

in the "majority," although it may be agreed that one particular segment of the population is in many respects dominant.   To a specific
minority, however, all the rest of society often functions as the
dominant group.   Thus, to the Negro the dominant group consists
of all whites; to the Jew, of all Gentiles.   The term "minority" also
becomes awkward when one speaks of the relationships between the
group and the rest of society.   "Minority relations" implies relationships between different minority groups; "minority-majority relations"
or "minority-dominant relations" are clumsy expressions.   Nonetheless, the usage, "minority group," divested of its strict numerical
connotation, has gained wide acceptance.

Bases of Classifying Minority Groups

Probably the most common basis for classifying minority groups
emphasizes their distinguishing characteristics.   Thus we may speak
of minorities as racial groups (Negroes, Indians), as cultural groups
(Louisiana French, Pennsylvania Dutch), as nationality groups
(Italians, Swedes), as religious groups (Jehovah's Witnesses, Jews),
or as any combination of these.   Nineteenth-century Chinese immigration to the United States, for example, introduced a new racial,
nationality, and cultural type, all in one.   Nationality and cultural
groups typically, but by no means always, coincide.   To give one
example of divergence, there are Middlewestern communities founded
by the "Volga German" immigrants who were German in culture but
Russian in nationality.

The classification of Americans of Jewish background on the basis
of the above categories is not easy, bringing up the old, difficult question, "Who is Jewish?"   Many, probably most, Jews are members
of a distinctive religious faith.   However, whereas the Methodist,
Catholic, Seventh-Day Adventist, or other religious participant loses
his group identity if he abandons his church ties, this often is not true
of the Jew.   Even the Jew converted to Christianity may be considered Jewish by others and may face discrimination.   Certainly,
mere lack of participation in the Hebrew religion does not divest a
person of identity as a Jew either in the eyes of the general population or of Jews themselves.   Even so, designating them as a religious

group is customary and probably involves less inaccuracy than classification on the basis of any other single factor.[3]

One of the most significant classifications of minority groups is based on the degree of acceptance extended by the rest of society. Dominant groups may so nearly accept the minority that discrimination against it is not institutionalized and, except for activities implying close personal intimacy, may seldom appear. In other instances the rejection by the dominant group may be so emphatic that the minority is seriously handicapped. One might plausibly expect the degree of acceptance to vary directly with the degree of similarity between the dominant group and the particular minority. America has tended to extend greater acceptance to Europeans than to non-Europeans and to immigrants from western than from eastern and southern Europe. Religious similarity has also affected the degree of acceptance of European groups—that is, physical and cultural traits being similar, Protestants have met the quickest, smoothest acceptance in America.

Our marked rejection of non-European groups results much less from cultural or religious differences than from our rejection of certain physical types. Roughly, the degree of social acceptance of nonwhite groups in the United States varies inversely with their darkness of pigmentation. Thus the American Negro, culturally the most typically "American" of all minorities, nonetheless meets the most elaborately institutionalized patterns of social rejection.

Minority groups may be categorized on the basis of the presumed duration of their status as a minority. The European nationality groups are temporary minorities and are, indeed, in the process of disappearing as minorities. Others of our minorities may be labeled "lasting" minorities. No prediction is implied that these groups will continue as minorities "forever," but, on the basis of present trends, we cannot foresee their disappearance as such. Nonwhite groups and Jews are in this sense lasting minorities.

Still another basis of classification concerns the volition of the minority status of the particular group: Is the separate existence of

---

[3] For a more detailed discussion, see Melville J. Herskovits, "Who Are the Jews," in Louis Finkelstein (ed.), *The Jews: Their History, Culture, and Religion,* II (Harper, 1949), 1151–1171.

the group imposed or is it self-chosen? To be sure, a clear-cut answer can seldom be given. A circular reaction is often established. Members of a group faced by discrimination rely on themselves for associations, develop bases of group solidarity, and create strong emotional bonds, all of which function henceforth as restraints discouraging those members who can leave the group from doing so. It is more important, perhaps, that the same factors function as conspicuous evidence to society at large of the group's separateness and "clannishness." The continued separate existence of a group, then, sometimes reflects elements both of society's unwillingness and the group's unwillingness to blend. It is important, however, to note that some minorities would continue to be treated as such, even if their members all sought to lose their group identity. No example is more convincing than that of American Negroes. Other groups could disappear rather quickly as distinct groups if they so chose. Various small religious groups, which, in their localities, meet discrimination and possibly even abuse because they do not conform to general community standards clearly exemplify the latter.

THE PROBLEM OF PREJUDICE

The Analysis of Prejudice

To claim that all problems of minorities arise from prejudice would be to exaggerate. Actual American experience, however, has demonstrated that prejudice underlies many such problems and can lead to their perpetuation. Otherwise, for example, there should be no barrier to mutual understanding between Negroes and Southern whites, since they have lived side by side, sharing language, religion, and cultural tradition, from earliest colonial days. Prejudice, then, preserves group separateness by erecting a psychological barrier that hinders mutual understanding. In this sense, it is not the existence or perception of differences in such matters as skin color, but the meaning we attach to them, that creates "race" problems.

In the present context, prejudice refers to those negative attitudes that create a predisposition toward unfavorable response to a racial or minority group. Such a predisposition may characterize both minority and dominant groups—that is, prejudice may exist among Jews toward Gentiles, among Negroes toward Caucasians, as well as the reverse. Moreover, the negative attitudes of prejudice not only predispose groups toward unfavorable response, but provide also a basis for interpreting present or past interaction, and thereby color both expectations and reactions. These negative attitudes may vary from mild aversion to intense hatred. The more intense prejudice becomes, the more elaborate its defenses and the more complex its emotional support. As a general rule, "lasting" minorities suffer the more intense forms of prejudice.

Some writers treat prejudice as if it were a single attitude, explicable in simple terms. Others, recognizing its complexity, try to understand, in general terms, the bases of antipathy in human relationships. Still others attempt to explain the particular sources of only one kind of prejudice, such as anti-Semitism. It will be possible here to mention only a few of the many theories of prejudice.

Certainly, one basis of antipathy and suspicion lies in the foundation of group solidarity itself. The process of identification with a group involves the development of preference for one's own group, of in-group solidarity, implying a certain devaluation of comparable out-groups. In this sense, prejudice is the obverse of ethnocentrism. This principle applies, of course, to prejudice against any out-group and as adequately explains animosity between Minneapolis and St. Paul as between whites and Negroes. To be sure, "social visibility" derived from physical or cultural traits facilitates the application of such prejudice. Even so, antipathy based on recognition of out-group membership hardly explains the complexity and intensity of prejudice against minorities. No doubt such antipathy will continue to be a factor as long as minorities are designated as out-groups, but it is by no means the entire source of such prejudice.

Prejudice often functions to rationalize and justify existing practices; examples abound in almost any situation in which a distinguishable group is exploited. From the first, slave traders and planters needed to justify the enslavement of their fellow men. Beliefs that Negroes were inferior, incapable of self-direction, irresponsible and barbaric, obviously helped serve this purpose. If one observes the conditions in which migratory Mexican laborers often live and work today he sees why many Southwesterners find prejudice against Mexicans convenient. Prejudice, then, often justifies existing exploitation, giving rise to a typical vicious circle: exploitation creates a need for prejudice against a group; the prejudice, once developed, justifies continued exploitation.

At the same time, subconsciously, emotional processes may similarly produce prejudice. The very image of those whom we have wronged may be disquieting, for it threatens us with the awareness of guilt. We prefer to avoid such persons. Failing avoidance, we react with dislike—a dislike which we fortify, consciously, with explanatory rationalizations. Through the interlocking of these processes we may develop negative stereotypes strongly supported by emotion. At this stage, the hated (that is, the wronged) persons often become objects of aggression. If these persons are easily identifiable and their position is subordinate, the dominant group may actually institutionalize means of venting hostility on them. This pattern then serves the additional function of providing insecure, frustrated members of the dominant group with a scapegoat on whom they may safely wreak hostility of whatever source, while bolstering their own egos by demonstration of power. Numerous examples occur; in none has the deliberate manipulation of scapegoating been more ruthless than in Hitler's Germany. Lynching, as a means by which lower-class Southern whites reassured themselves that, whatever else they lacked, they at least had authority over the Negro, is an equally pertinent example.

The stereotype, a mental picture of an out-group, personifies group characteristics in our thoughts. Stereotyping is by no means limited to racial and minority situations; we have our stereotypes of the college athlete and the proper Bostonian. The stereotype of an out-group which is the object of considerable prejudice, however, is likely to be heavily weighted with undesirable traits. Even more, such a stereotype may give a negative interpretation to traits that in other circumstances are considered desirable. An oft-cited example is the different emotional response to a trait common to the stereotypes of Scotchman and Jew. Those who admire the Scot for his "thrift" may deplore the "stinginess" of the Jew.

Prejudice in general, and stereotypes in particular, are learned by the child as are other attitudes and values. Thus one's mental conception of a Jew is gained, not through original, empirical observation, but through contact with one of the most persistent minority stereotypes in our traditions. Having learned elements of the stereotype, one then expects to find the characteristics. One observes a Jew who seems to fit the traditional stereotype and thinks, "How like a Jew"; one meets a Jew who fails to fit the stereotype and makes an exception, "He's Jewish, but he doesn't act like it." In this manner, the classic preface to the anti-Semitic statement, "Some of my best friends are Jews, but . . . ," may be literally true. The person speaking may have high regard for Jewish friends but maintain prejudice against Jews—not against his friends, but against those "other Jews." The tendency to confirm the stereotype when confirmation seems indicated, and to ignore its contradictions as exceptions, should discourage those who blandly assume that if members of groups only knew each other, prejudice would automatically disappear. After all, millions of white Southerners "know" a number of individual Negroes, and esteem some of them, but the prejudice against Negroes and its embodiment in stereotypes persist. One reason, no doubt, for persistence of stereotypes is our tendency to perceive what we expect to perceive. Possibly a greater cause is the constant reinforcement of the stereotype through its own repetition. Just as we initially learned it through cultural transmission rather than by observation, so do we continually relearn it.

When the traditions of a culture embody a particular form of prejudice, finding such prejudice in individuals is to be expected. The white child on the cotton plantation acquires race prejudice in the same way that he acquires religious beliefs, patriotism, and enthusiasm for football. Lack of prejudice in this child would indicate a failure of the socialization process.

Our discussion thus far offers little basis for understanding why, in any social milieu, individuals vary widely in their degree and intensity of prejudice. Some individuals become skeptical of their biases, while other persons from the same background not only accept the usual quantum of prejudice but intensify it until it becomes obsessional. We often label rabid haters as mere cranks or crackpots and refuse to take them very seriously. Under usual circumstances they may exert little influence; but when other elements of social disorganization lead to increasing tensions, the "professional hater" may provide that intensity of feeling which can lead desperate men into violence, persecution, and slaughter, as events of the twentieth century illustrate only too strikingly.

The attempt to understand the intense incorporation of prejudice into some individual personalities has led to investigation of the psycho-dynamics of prejudice. Despite variations in emphasis and interpretation, the studies of "prejudice-prone" or "authoritarian" personalities have tended to agree that certain types of individuals find in prejudice a prop to their own personalities. Just as a frustrated, bewildered group may seek release by scapegoating, so do certain types of insecure, inhibited but conformity-minded individuals find in intense prejudice a reassurance of their own worth.[4]

Means of Combating Prejudice

If one grants the complexity of the negative attitudes of prejudice, then it becomes evident that no single, simple formula can eliminate prejudice. If one grants the existence of the prejudice-prone or authoritarian personality, it follows that our goal must be to minimize the potential influence of such persons.

Efforts to reduce prejudice assume such various forms and involve so many diverse organizations that only the most general summary can be given. Many organizations in our society, as a major part of their activity, maintain programs to reduce intergroup tensions and to combat prejudice. Among these are many associations of the minority groups themselves, such as the National Association for the Advancement of Colored People, the National Urban League, the American Jewish Committee, the American Jewish Congress, the Anti-Defamation League of B'nai B'rith, the League of United Latin American Citizens, the Japanese American Citizens' League, and the National Congress of American Indians. Each of these is naturally most concerned with prejudice against its own group, although some

[4] For a detailed presentation, see T. W. Adorno, Else Frenkel-Brunswik, Daniel J. Levinson, and R. Nevitt Sanford, *The Authoritarian Personality* (Harper, 1950).

of them (especially the Jewish groups) recognize that no group can be safeguarded against manifestations of prejudice unless all groups are so protected. Countless other American organizations, such as the National Conference of Christians and Jews, include among their goals that of combating prejudice. Many religious associations emphasize this goal. The Y.W.C.A. maintains one of the most active of such programs, as do some labor organizations. Governmental commissions, educational associations, business groups, service clubs, women's clubs, and a wide variety of other organizations have likewise, to one degree or another, interested themselves in fighting prejudice. From this welter of activity no systematic, overall approach could emerge. Some of these organizations attempt little more than making their own members aware of prejudice as a problem. Many attack it by emphasizing its harmful effects, its irrationality, and its inconsistency with Christian morality and democratic principles. Many confine themselves to an "educational" approach; others seek to bring representatives of diverse groups together in congenial association; some try to alter those practices in their communities which reinforce prejudice and discrimination. It is impossible, of course, to evaluate this multiplicity of programs in any overall sense. Although the actual accomplishments of most individual programs are probably quite limited, nonetheless their aggregate effect may be very important. They may, for example, have helped make blunt expressions of prejudice unfashionable in many circles today. To the extent that this feeling spreads, the transmission and reinforcement of prejudice in society is correspondingly weakened.

There is growing opposition to the perpetuation of unfriendly stereotypes in the schools and by the mass media of communication. In particular, action groups representing the various minorities seek to prevent depiction of unfriendly stereotypes, and in 1952 the United States Supreme Court upheld an Illinois "group libel" law which forbids the exhibition of certain types of entertainment and artistic productions held to be unfair to minorities. Doubtless such efforts are well meant and may, in time, reduce the prevalence of the undesirable stereotypes. As long as the protests rely on persuasion, no valid objection can be raised, but such activities, when relying on

legislation or other techniques of forced compliance, are often criticized as infringements of our civil liberties that establish dangerous
precedents of censorship. Also, minority protests against unfavorable
materials in literary and other classics may defeat their purpose by
creating resentment against the protesting minority. Less controversial are the efforts to encourage the presentation, in schools and
through the mass media, of favorable characterizations of minority
groups. Newspaper coverage concerning members of minority groups
has become markedly fairer. Stereotypes are persistent and continue
to be expressed through the mass media, but the trend is definitely
toward fairer, more realistic presentation of minorities.

Many persons believe that the termination of educational, economic, residential, political, and other discrimination is necessary to
end the prejudice justifying these practices. Proponents of this point
of view insist that the most effective attacks on prejudice are the efforts (discussed below) to end segregation and discrimination.

MINORITIES IN THE AMERICAN POPULATION

Our total minority population cannot be accurately stated. Although the census provides an enumeration of racial groups, religious
and nationality minorities must be estimated, and estimates vary with
differing interpretations of membership in minorities. Many authors,
for example, include all Catholics in the American minority population. For our purpose, Catholics are not considered "a" minority.
This is an arbitrary matter; it seems doubtful, however, that individual Catholics, otherwise indistinguishable from their neighbors,
meet general and serious discrimination.

The number of foreign-born residents of America is reported by
the census, and in 1950 the number of native-born whites of foreign
or mixed parentage is also given. One may, therefore, as of 1950,
ascertain the size of the Italian minority in that he may quote the
sum of American residents born in Italy and born to Italian-born
parents. This definition, however, has no functional significance.
Operationally, it is absurd to call all second-generation Americans of

Italian background members of a minority; it is equally meaningless
to exempt all the third generation from that status.

Nonwhite Minorities

In 1950, there were 15,755,333 Americans classified as nonwhites;
over 15,000,000 were Negroes. The nation's Negro population has,
for some decades, been approximately one tenth of our total population. Table 15.1 shows the Negro population of each state containing
100,000 or more Negroes (in 1950). About two thirds reside in
those states which the census classifies as "the South." If we add to
these the Negro population of Missouri, we find that ten and one-
half million of our Negro citizens reside in areas where slavery existed
and segregation prevails. The proportion of the population which is
Negro varies widely, ranging downward from a top of 45 per cent in
Mississippi; many counties of the Deep South have more Negro than
white residents.

The Southern Negro population grew only slightly from 1940 to
1950; in several states it declined. Rapid gains were general in the
North and West, reflecting the continuation of migration from the
South. The preference of Northern employers for immigrant labor
and the Negroes' lack of industrial skills prevented a large-scale northward migration until World War I, when the combination of a
virtual cessation of immigration, expansion of war industry in the
North, and a crisis in cotton farming resulting from the boll weevil,
started a major northward migration of Negroes. This flow, once
under way, never ceased, although it slowed considerably during the
depression. With the industrial expansion of World War II the
migration speeded up and also became directed toward the West
Coast.

Few groups in America are so highly concentrated in great cities as
non-Southern Negroes, ninety per cent of whom, in 1950, resided in
metropolitan areas. The great bulk of these lived in very large
metropolitan centers. The New York–Northeastern New Jersey
metropolitan area alone contained over a million Negroes, more than
Mississippi or Alabama. In 1950 seventeen American metropolitan
centers contained 100,000 or more Negroes each. Of these, nine

TABLE 15.1: NEGROES IN SELECTED STATES

	Negro Population, 1950	Per Cent of Total Population	Negro Population, 1940	Change 1940–1950
Georgia	1,062,762	30.9	1,084,927	−22,165
North Carolina	1,047,353	25.8	981,298	66,055
Mississippi	986,494	45.3	1,074,578	−88,084
Alabama	979,617	32.0	983,290	−3,673
Texas	977,458	12.7	924,391	53,067
New York	918,191	6.2	571,221	346,970
Louisiana	882,428	32.9	849,303	33,125
South Carolina	822,077	38.8	814,164	7,913
Virginia	734,211	22.1	661,449	72,762
Illinois	645,980	7.4	387,446	258,534
Pennsylvania	638,485	6.1	470,172	168,313
Florida	603,101	21.7	514,198	88,903
Tennessee	530,603	16.1	508,736	21,867
Ohio	513,072	6.5	339,461	173,611
California	462,172	4.4	124,306	337,866
Michigan	442,296	6.9	208,345	233,951
Arkansas	426,639	22.3	482,578	−55,939
Maryland	385,972	16.5	301,931	84,041
New Jersey	318,565	6.6	226,973	91,592
Missouri	297,088	7.5	244,386	52,702
Dist. of Columbia	280,803	35.0	187,266	93,537
Kentucky	201,921	6.9	214,031	−12,110
Indiana	174,168	4.4	121,916	52,252
Oklahoma	145,503	6.5	168,849	−23,346
West Virginia	114,867	5.7	117,754	−2,887
North	4,246,058	5.1	2,790,193	1,455,865
South	10,225,407	21.7	9,904,619	320,788
West	570,821	2.9	170,706	400,115
Total, U.S.	15,042,286	10.0	12,865,518	2,176,768

Source: Bureau of the Census, *United States Census of Population*, 1950, vol. II, *Characteristics of the Population*, Part 1 (Government Printing Office, 1952).

(New York, Chicago, Philadelphia, Detroit, Los Angeles, St. Louis, Cleveland, San Francisco, and Pittsburgh) were in the North and West; eight (Baltimore, Washington, Birmingham, New Orleans, Memphis, Atlanta, Houston, and Norfolk) were Southern. The proportion of Negroes who live in cities is about the same as that of the general population, but Negroes are more concentrated in very large cities. Paradoxically, proportionately more Negroes than other Americans live on farms; they are underrepresented in villages, suburban areas, and small cities.

All other nonwhite persons in the United States number less than three quarters of a million. Over 100,000 of these, labeled by the census "All Other," include Filipinos, Koreans, Polynesians, and Hindus, plus a sizeable number of residents of mixed or dubious ancestry who are found in isolated racial "pockets" in the older states. They often are a tri-racial white, Indian, Negro mixture.

In 1950, there were 343,410 American Indians in the United States. The largest numbers were in New Mexico, Oklahoma, and Arizona. Only Delaware had no Indians, while twenty-one states had 2,500 or more.

Americans of Japanese and Chinese ancestry are far less numerous than is popularly believed (141,768 and 117,629, respectively, in 1950). The formerly intense prejudice in the West led us to exclude them as immigrants, an act contributing to Japanese resentment against the United States before World War II. The hotly-disputed Alien Land Act in California and our treatment of the Japanese-Americans during World War II also focused attention on these small populations. Almost half of the Chinese, and more than half of the Japanese, reside in California. If Hawaii becomes a state our population of Oriental descent will be about doubled. There is every indication that the forbearance of Japanese-Americans during World War II, and the bravery of their sons in combat, have earned them a more assured status in American life.

Other Minorities

Census materials provide no basis of estimating the number of Jews. Table 15.2 contains an estimate of the Jewish population of the nation and of certain states made in 1937. In the main the concentration of Jews indicated in Table 15.2 probably still applies, but the Jewish population of the South and West is now larger than shown due to its rapid increase in Florida and California. An estimate in 1950 indicated 5,000,000 American Jews, but provided no basis for state and regional estimates.[5] About two fifths of the nation's Jews reside in New York City.

The foreign-born white population has declined proportionately since 1910, when it was 14.5 per cent of the total, and absolutely since 1930. In that year it numbered 13,983,000, but by 1950 it numbered only 10,161,000 or 7 per cent of the population. This decrease results from the low rate of present immigration and the dying of older immigrants. Table 15.2 shows the numbers of American residents in 1950 born in Italy, Germany, Russia, and Poland, the largest European contributors of our present foreign-born population. Table 15.2 also indicates the size, in 1950, of the "foreign-white stock" (foreign-born whites and native-born of foreign and mixed parentage), when 33,750,000 Americans were so classified. Their

TABLE 15.2: FOREIGN-BORN WHITE POPULATION OF CERTAIN NATIONALITIES, 1950; TOTAL FOREIGN-WHITE STOCK, 1950; AND ESTIMATED JEWISH POPULATION, 1937; FOR SELECTED STATES

	Population, 1950, Born in				Total Foreign White Stock, 1950 *	Jewish Population, 1937
	Italy	Germany	Russia	Poland		
New York	503,175	270,661	353,835	254,065	6,803,774	2,206,328
California	104,215	70,791	66,552	23,776	2,982,388	157,471
Illinois	83,556	96,517	59,753	111,376	2,684,567	387,330
Pennsylvania	163,359	59,532	80,541	87,947	2,830,289	434,616
Massachusetts	101,548	15,439	52,353	46,597	2,272,919	262,945
New Jersey	150,680	75,823	50,620	69,404	2,013,656	267,970
Michigan	38,937	45,323	30,804	81,595	1,967,465	105,201
Ohio	56,593	48,528	23,114	41,820	1,578,548	183,570
Connecticut	74,270	17,036	21,180	34,530	964,354	93,080
Texas	5,059	15,380	4,592	3,914	932,280	49,196
North	1,239,092	804,370	745,462	794,472	26,338,396	4,221,215
South	56,835	69,893	51,889	34,231	2,545,434	330,110
West	131,218	110,068	97,493	32,481	4,866,823	219,322
Total U.S.	1,427,145	984,331	894,844	861,184	33,750,653	4,770,647

Source: U.S. Census of Population, 1950; Bureau of the Census, 1950 Census of Population, Series PC-14, No. 20, March 29, 1954; World Almanac, 1949, p. 249, quoting the Jewish Statistical Bureau of the Synagogue of America.
 * The "total foreign white stock" is the sum of foreign-born whites plus the native-born whites of foreign or mixed parentage.

[5] American Jewish Yearbook, 1953, p. 197.

concentration in the populous industrial states is indicated by the table.

The Spanish-speaking minority is one of America's largest. In portions of the Southwest it sometimes suffers discrimination approaching that experienced by Negroes. There are probably more than 3,000,000 Spanish-speaking residents of America. The 1950 Census, in a report on the population with Spanish surnames in five states, indicated 2,289,000 such persons in these states, as follows: Texas, 1,034,000; California, 760,000; New Mexico, 249,000; Arizona, 128,000; and Colorado, 118,000. In popular speech these Spanish-speaking Southwesterners are often lumped together as "Mexicans." Actually, many are descendants of the early settlers of the Southwest; Santa Fe, after all, was founded before Plymouth.

Large numbers of Mexicans, however, do cross back and forth over the international border. Many (called "wetbacks") enter illegally, so that no one knows the exact volume of movement. Although living and working conditions for migratory agricultural labor in the West are often extremely poor, the volume of illegal entrants has increased greatly in recent years. In 1952, some 618,000 were caught and returned to Mexico, but for every one caught, one or more probably went undetected, making a total illegal entry of perhaps 1,500,000 persons. The influx in 1953 apparently was even greater.[6] In addition, about 200,000 Mexican laborers enter legally for seasonal work in the United States, under provisions arranged by the two governments. It is impossible to estimate how many illegal entrants will remain in the United States. Doubtless many intend to return to Mexico and will do so, whether detected or not.

Another Spanish-speaking group in the United States is the rapidly-increasing Puerto Rican minority. Since their homeland is American territory, they are not technically immigrants, but sociologically they are, for the transition from Puerto Rico to New York City is quite as great as that usually experienced by immigrants. In 1950 there were 300,000 persons of Puerto Rican birth or parentage living on the mainland; 245,000 of them were in New York City. About 90 per

[6] These estimates and remarks are based on articles by Gladwyn Hill in *The New York Times*, January 18 and June 14, 1953.

cent of the Puerto Ricans and virtually all the Southwestern Spanish population are classified as "white" by the Census.

NEGROES IN AMERICAN SOCIETY

The Importance of Our Negro Minority

From almost any approach, it is evident that Negroes compose our most important single minority. They are the largest numerically; they face the greatest intensity of prejudice, strongly buttressed by emotional reaction; discrimination against them is both widespread and formally institutionalized. Certainly, public interest today in civil rights and, indeed, in race relations in general, is overwhelmingly the expression of concern over Negro-white relations. Finally it is worth repeating that Negroes are the most "American" of all of our minorities. When their behavior patterns differ from those of white Americans, the differences appear largely to represent adaptations that Negroes perforce have made to their status in American society.

Negroes in the South

For demographic, emotional, and historical reasons, the study of the American Negro is, to a large extent, the study of the South and its plantation heritage. Since emancipation provided the ex-slaves with no new skills, no land, and no capital, it left them little choice but to resume their traditional role of plantation laborers. The much publicized sharecropping system, which reached its peak about 1930 and by that time actually involved more white than Negro croppers, was but one of several systems developed to enable plantation operations to continue. Significant features, common to all these systems, included the retention by landowners of managerial responsibilities and prerogatives, direct supervision of Negro workers, and paternalistic obligations of landowners to laborers. Under these conditions, interactional patterns characteristic of slavery continued: whites made decisions; Negroes followed them. Independence and self-reliance by Negroes were systematically discouraged.

The basic premise of the traditional Southern pattern was that the white race was innately superior in intellect, character, and qualities of leadership. The ideology of white supremacy insisted that the white man was ordained to fulfill the role of superior race and that any violation of this role led only to individual and societal degeneracy. To preserve this superiority, the supreme taboo was placed on intermarriage and on sexual contact outside marriage between Negro men and white women. Biologically, this was popularly interpreted as maintaining racial purity; culturally, it implied the ability of the males of the dominant race to retain exclusive possession of the women of their own group. The cultural interpretation was more meaningful than the biological, since sexual relationships between white males and Negro females were not similarly taboo. During slavery, offspring had derived status as freemen or slaves from the mother, so such intermixture had "lightened" the slave population rather than "darkened" the white group. In addition to this antebellum precedent, the greater emotional emphasis placed on sexual propriety of females than of males led to an emphasis on "protecting" the women of the dominant race from Negro males. To nineteenth-century America, sexual relationships often implied male "dominance" and female "submission." Since the white race had to maintain supremacy—that is, dominance—under all circumstances, sexual relationships between Negro men and white women were intolerable.

Many of the elements present during the formulation of this taboo have altered. There is virtually unanimous agreement that cross-racial sexual contacts have declined greatly in frequency, but the strongly fortified emotional insistence that white women must avoid sexual contact with Negro men persists as the fundamental element in Southern racial traditions.

Indeed, many other characteristics of the traditional pattern function to prevent situations which might conceivably jeopardize this taboo. Of course, the details of Southern race relations were not deliberately planned with this end in mind. Most practices, in their origin, developed in response to the needs of specific situations. However, practices that helped avoid situations that might endanger the sexual taboo had, by virtue of that characteristic, survival value;

even today, proposals to change such practices typically arouse the bugaboo of racial intermarriage.

To emphasize the social distance between the races, there has developed an "etiquette of race relations" which governs white-Negro interaction in personal or potentially personal relationships. The etiquette controls any relationship approaching the "primary group": that is, employer and employee, mistress and servant, white and Negro neighbors. The Negro addresses the white person by titles such as "sir," "ma'am," "Mister," "Miss," or "Mrs.," whereas the white person addresses the Negro by first name, by last name without status designations, or as "boy," "girl," "uncle," or "auntie." A white person may address a Negro with the peremptory voice of command; a Negro observing the etiquette answers in the ingratiating voice of humility. The Negro makes indirect requests, avoiding contradiction of a white person. The white man, entering a Negro's home, may stride to the front door, perhaps calling to announce his arrival; the Negro, entering the home of a white man, traditionally goes to the back door. The pattern thus governs a wide variety of such interactional situations. It is intricate, varies somewhat from place to place, and is often confusing to strangers. Yet there is a thread of consistency. The Southern etiquette of race relations constantly stresses white superiority, constantly underlines Negro inferiority. It is an ingenious pattern facilitating continuous, even friendly, interaction between members of the two races while constantly emphasizing the racial barrier. Quite logically, this traditional etiquette is most rigid in relationships between Negro males and white females.

Not all racial contacts, however, involve patterned interaction. In public facilities where large numbers meet anonymously, the Southern states, by custom and law, have segregated the races as if to prevent, under such relatively fluid, unpatterned conditions, the development of interaction between individuals of the two groups. Separate schools seem to serve the similar purpose of preventing the development of close ties in a setting where relationships otherwise might not imply any particular inequality. To summarize and admittedly to oversimplify very complex patterns, it appears that in the South segregation functions to reduce the frequency of interaction between the races in those situations where the etiquette does not function automatically to emphasize status differences.

Compliance with the etiquette earned for Negroes some measure of assistance from white people. The plantation tradition produced not only inequality, but a certain white paternalism, which, like the development of friendships between the races, softened somewhat the arbitrary nature of the system. On the other hand, paternalistic traditions had little hold on those large numbers of whites to whom Negroes were more likely to be economic competitors than servants. Also, although it was good form, upperclass whites were not compelled to treat Negroes in a kindly, paternalistic manner. For Negroes, however, strict conformity to the traditional pattern was required.

Discrimination under the Southern pattern of race relations. In order to comply with constitutional requirements, Southern laws state that separate facilities should be equal. In actuality, however, facilities and institutions for Negroes have been far inferior to those provided whites, and Negroes have faced discrimination in almost every line of activity. It will be impossible, in this single chapter, to trace the inequalities in detail, but some of the major areas of discrimination must be briefly discussed.

Negroes have traditionally performed the less skilled and more menial tasks in the South. In addition, their training has often been limited. Thus they have consistently received lower incomes than have Southern whites. That this income differential is due only in part to deficiencies in training is indicated by the reluctance of the South to permit trained and gifted Negro individuals to advance to positions of power, and by a marked tendency to pay Negroes lower wages than white workers performing identical tasks. During periods of full employment, Negroes have met relatively little white competition for traditional "Negro jobs"; occasionally Negroes have secured positions ordinarily reserved for whites. Periods of depression have had precisely the opposite effect; whites have sought, successfully, to enter occupations formerly reserved for Negroes. The overall trend from Reconstruction days until recent years indicated increased vulnerability of the Southern Negro worker, as one by one, occupations traditionally his were entered by white workers, without a corresponding entrance of Negroes into "white" jobs. Rather generally, Negroes have been discouraged from positions that involved authority over white workers, that implied white-collar status, or that placed Negro males and white females in frequent contact.

Unionization in the South has been hampered by the existence of a labor force divided by race, each race suspicious of the other; many unions, especially the older craft unions, have specifically restricted membership to whites, thus in effect barring Negroes from certain lines of employment. Even in the industrial unions and those craft unions admitting Negro workers, the Negroes have often assumed a more or less passive role, and leadership has been disproportionately white. Even so, unionization offers great potential gains to Southern Negro workers, vulnerable as they are to low pay and unemployment. Such gains have already been realized in many instances, and the recent progress of integrated unions in the South has been heartening.

Since the beginning of World War II Negroes have made important economic gains in the United States. While their most spectacular advances in entering new occupations and in promotion to new levels of responsibility have occurred in the North, gains in both employment and income have likewise been achieved in the South. Indeed, their relative gains have been greater, both North and South, than those of the whites. Even so, Negroes everywhere, and especially in the South, continue to receive far lower incomes than the general population.[7] The relative increase in the income of the Negro masses reflects in part the greater proportional improvement in the wages of manual laborers than of white-collar workers and in part the declining number of Negroes in Southern agriculture, where their earnings have always been extremely low. Whether the relative gains in income would survive a sharp break in the general prosperity, and whether Southern Negroes have actually achieved a significant advance in occupational security and employment opportunities, cannot be stated with certainty. At best, the Southern Negro remains one of the least privileged segments, economically, of the American population.

In no aspect of Southern life have legal assurances of equal facil-

[7] In this connection, *Time*, in its feature on the United States Negro, 1953, stated: "The Negro's average yearly income is still only a little more than half of the white average, but ten years ago it was about 35 per cent." *Time* (May 11, 1953), p. 55.

ities been more consistent, and actual inequalities greater, than in education. It is quite true that in recent years the South has narrowed the gap between white and Negro educational facilities. Even so, as recently as the school year 1948–49, Mississippi spent an annual average of $123 per white pupil in average daily attendance in grade and high schools, and only $27 per Negro pupil.[8] Similar, if less marked, differentials have been characteristic of most Southern states. Within each state inequalities have generally been more extreme in rural than in urban communities and in plantation areas of large Negro population than in upland farming areas where few Negroes reside. Indeed, segregation has been an expensive luxury for the many Southern counties with few Negro children. In contrast, the utilization of the bulk of the educational funds for white schools has often enabled plantation counties to provide excellent educational facilities for their white children while providing Negro children with extremely limited opportunities. Consolidation of rural Negro schools has lagged years behind that of white schools; even today, transportation for Negro school children is often lacking. The curriculum, even in urban Negro schools, has typically been more limited, the buildings more crowded, equipment and teaching aids less adequate, playground facilities skimpier, and sports and other extracurricular activities more restricted, than in white schools. Much of the South long paid white and Negro teachers at differential rates, but equalization of salaries has been under way the last few years. Comparable contrasts have existed between the tax-supported colleges provided for white and Negro students.

Discrimination against the Negroes has also been marked in respect to legal rights. About 1890, the Southern states began to explore means of preventing political participation by the Negro masses. Several techniques were developed. One, the poll tax, discriminated against the very poor of both races and thus has been an instrument maintaining, not merely white supremacy, but the supremacy of the more prosperous whites. Only Virginia, Alabama, Mississippi, Arkansas, and Texas continue this tax as a voting requirement today. Another such measure—-the requirement of an educational or literacy

[8] Milton R. Konvitz, "The Extent and Character of Legally-Enforced Segregation," *The Journal of Negro Education*, XX (Summer, 1951), 428.

test—likewise does not, in principle, discriminate against Negroes as such, but in actuality, registrars of voters long tended to ignore literacy requirements for whites but applied them very strictly to Negro applicants. Two other techniques were bluntly discriminatory and have been declared unconstitutional. They were (1) the so-called "grandfather clause," which exempted from certain require-ments those whose forebears possessed the ballot, and (2) the white Democratic primary, which, in the one-party system of the South, denied Negroes any effective role in state and local affairs. The total effect of these regulations, buttressed by white hostility toward the individual Negro who challenged them, was the disfranchisement, until very recently, of nearly all Negroes in the Deep South and of large numbers in the Upper South.

A voteless people in our society is a people with no real power over local officials. It is not surprising, therefore, that after the loss of the vote, Negroes had little influence on other aspects of Southern legal structure. Although marked improvements have been made recently, for decades the Negro suspected of wrongdoing was arrested by a white sheriff, deputy, or policeman and tried before a white judge by a white jury. Throughout this entire procedure there was too often the feeling that Negroes were likely to be guilty of crime, and ap-parently there was sometimes little inclination to worry about the guilt or innocence of an individual Negro. Southern law enforce-ment often seemed to consider offenses of Negroes against Negroes unimportant and sometimes appeared to assume, in altercations be-tween whites and Negroes, that upholding white supremacy required the presumption of Negro fault. The Negro convicted of an offense against a white man was likely to receive a disproportionately severe sentence. Thus, law-abiding Negroes received inadequate legal pro-tection against criminal elements of their own race or against abuse by white individuals or groups.

The political impotence of Southern Negroes permitted many other instances of discriminatory treatment. The educational inequalities described above could hardly have developed had Negroes possessed equal rights in selecting school boards. Similarly, the neglect of streets, lighting, water and sewage systems, and parks and playgrounds in the Negro sections of Southern towns and cities was facilitated by their inability to protest through the vote. In housing, hospital facilities, provisions for orphans and defective children, and many other respects, similar inequalities developed. Southern society is a biracial society, approaching the caste principle, with the inferior status of the Negro exemplified in most areas of activity.

Enforcement of Southern pattern of race relations. The traditional pattern of white supremacy has been maintained in the South by the full weight of custom and law. Such customs as the racial etiquette have often, in effect, had the weight of law, since local law enforcement officials, on one pretext or another, punished the Negro who challenged any aspect of the regional code. Moreover, Southern legislative actions cast interesting light on the oft-stated assumption that customs cannot be legislated. To be sure, segregation was compatible with traditional Southern attitudes, and in some respects (the Negro church, for example) Negroes themselves, during Reconstruction, sought establishment of their own institutions rather than integration into those of the whites. Yet, for more than a decade after the end of Reconstruction, many public facilities in the South were not segregated; many Negroes did vote, and a few, here and there, were even elected to office. Legislation during the 1890's provided for rigid public segregation and for disfranchisement, and these changes soon became reinforced by custom. Recent experience has likewise shown that innovations in the other direction—such as the admission of Negroes into graduate schools—can quickly be accepted by the public as routine. Governmental policies may not change attitudes directly, but, if not so sweeping that enforcement bogs down, new policies can alter the manner in which attitudes are translated into action. Action which becomes customary sometimes operates to alter the attitudes themselves.

There was occasional mob violence in the South when custom and law seemed insufficient to enforce racial traditions. Violence in race relations has not been restricted to the South, but the acceptance of violence as an extra-legal, semi-institutionalized aid to white dominance has been more general there than elsewhere. Until recent years, many white Southerners insisted that the prerogative of violent action was essential to protect their way of life, maintain the purity of white womanhood, and so forth. Such arguments are not fashionable today, and indeed, even in the Deep South, lynching is virtually extinct.

Southern mob violence was never the routine, casual sport of the masses which exaggerated accounts indicate. Although in one year during the 1880's the number of lynchings exceeded 200, these were scattered in many states, not all in the South, in a base population of many millions. A Southern Negro, indeed, was always in far greater danger, statistically, of death in some altercation with an individual white or another Negro than of becoming a mob victim. The greatest significance of lynching, sociologically, arose from the realization that such action *could* occur at any time on almost any pretext. The Negro felt defenseless. The deliberate injection into some mob scenes of torture and mutilation further enhanced the symbolic terror of lynching. The pattern functioned, as its white defenders maintained, to "keep the Negro in his place" through terrorization. No statisticians expounded to Negroes the slight probability of death by lynching; on the contrary, stories of such deaths, often growing with repetition, circulated among Negroes to serve as the ultimate threat to the violator of tradition.

The effects of lynching on the whites were hardly less serious, though quite different in character. The very fact that regional traditions approached the condoning of lynching and that participants were seldom prosecuted weakened the entire law-enforcement structure of the region, provided the rest of the world with spectacles of America at its worst, and contributed to the one-sided administration of law and justice described above. Lynching is virtually extinct, to be sure, but many of the attitudes it exemplified and reinforced survive.

Whatever reservations Negroes may have felt, they accepted the system rather than risk the consequences of racial conflict—a realistic approach, under the circumstances. Within the framework of the Southern pattern, Negroes sought to obtain as many schools, public facilities, and services as the dominant whites could be persuaded to yield. This pattern, however, could only produce a psychological as well as a physical withdrawal of the Negro from general community activities. As much as possible, Negroes reproduced in their community the institutional structure and associational patterns of the greater community. In both South and North, a dual community organization came to be the expected situation.

Within the Negro community, segregated both spatially and psychologically, there developed vested interests in maintaining the *status quo*. Negro teachers who perhaps would find employment difficult in competition with white teachers; Negro businessmen who benefited from a concentrated Negro population; Negro professional men who, constrained to practice only among their own people, were thus freed from general competition; Negro leaders whose very position arose from their access to the dominant white community—these and many others found secure roles behind the walls of segregation. Myrdal designated such vested interests by the neat phrase, "the advantages of the disadvantages." [9] Doubtless even today many Negroes have ambivalent attitudes toward ending segregation.

Two qualifications must be made to the above description of the Southern scene. First, the description is historical; it most nearly fitted the South in the first three decades of the present century, perhaps. It is significant today as the background against which present changes must be considered and as the cultural environment which millions of Negroes experienced.

The second qualification is that the pattern was never entirely consistent throughout the region. There always were variations, sometimes even from one community to the next. This generalized description has of necessity been an oversimplification, most nearly approached in rural areas of the Deep South. In the tier of "border" states from Delaware to Oklahoma, certain forms of legalized segregation exist, but many aspects of the Southern pattern have never taken root.

Negroes in the North

The small Northern Negro population was reinforced, before the Civil War, by escaped slaves and by a steady drift of free Negroes from the South. A few rural communities were established by Negroes,

---

[9] Myrdal, *op. cit.*, p. 795. Myrdal here attributes the phrase to H. B. Frissell, former principal of Hampton Institute.

and in some areas, Negroes became agricultural laborers; in general, however, their role in Northern agriculture was negligible. Even before the Civil War, most Northern Negroes lived in cities and towns. After emancipation, the drift of Negroes northward was somewhat accelerated, but even so, in most parts of the North, Negroes were far less numerous than European immigrants. Not until World War I did movement to the North become a major migratory stream.

The North developed patterns of Negro-white relations that in some respects resembled the Southern forms. Like the South, the North tended to assume that the Negro was a separate and inferior type of mankind, incapable of assimilation. The melting-pot tradition seldom embraced the Negro. Racial intermarriage, banned in most states admitted to the Union after 1850, was frowned on even in those states permitting it. In its own way, then, the North also implicitly accepted the dogma of white supremacy.

Yet, there developed striking regional contrasts in race relations. Perhaps the greatest difference lay in intensity of concern. To the Northerner, the Negro was, after all, only one of a wide variety of minorities, and many Northerners, having little contact with Negroes, gave them little thought. This indifference, of course, directly contrasted with the constant fixation of Southern concern. The area of civil rights provided another contrast between the regions. Provisions in the constitutions and laws of most Northern states guaranteed civil rights to all citizens. To be sure, there was often neglect of law enforcement and of municipal services in Negro areas of Northern cities, but this neglect more often arose, perhaps, from heavy Negro concentration in neglected slum areas than from racial discrimination as such. Although the North, in its police and judicial administration, has not been free from the tendency to stereotype Negroes as prone to certain types of crime, there has not been the semi-institutionalization of a double standard of legal penalties so characteristic of the South. Here and there in Northern states, segregation in schools and other public facilities has occurred, but again, such practices could usually be fought, and often altered, through legal challenges. In short, although blunt discrimination against Negroes has existed, such behavior has run counter to the laws and best traditions of most of the North and as a result has frequently been vigorously fought and defeated.

Yet, in some other respects, Northern segregation has been quite as, or even more, complete than Southern. Ecological processes, buttressed by restrictive covenants, have produced a high degree of residential segregation of various minorities in Northern cities. More, perhaps, than any other large group, the Negro has been confined to "Negro" districts. Since the Negro population in Northern cities has increased rapidly, there has been constant pressure of population within the segregated districts, leading to higher rents than the facilities warranted, to a constant pressure on Negroes to establish housing "footholds" elsewhere in the city, and thus, to a major source of racial friction. Segregation in housing often leads, in effect, to segregation in parks, clinics, schools, and other public facilities. It is often alleged that Negroes (or other groups) prefer to live with their own kind. Indeed, new arrivals do seek the security of neighbors from a similar background. Their initial adjustment to the new environment is facilitated by such neighbors. This, however, is a very different matter from expecting the newcomers, their children and their children's children, to remain forever in a separate community. The latter situation requires of all a pattern meeting the needs of some and perpetuates a separateness that otherwise would be merely a phase of acculturation.

During periods of prosperity, Negroes have benefited from the variety and abundance of jobs available in Northern cities. During the depression, however, unemployment among Negroes rose to proportionately greater heights than among whites, indicating the existence of a "last-hired, first-fired" pattern for Negroes in Northern industry. Many lines of work, as the result of either managerial or labor policies, or both, were traditionally restricted to white workers, but the North did not develop the Southern intensity of resistance to the entrance of Negroes into new jobs, nor did it as consistently deny Negroes promotion or authority over other workers. In recent years Northern Negroes have entered many occupations, including a variety of white-collar jobs, formerly seldom offered them. For this and other reasons, Northern Negroes may be in a stronger position than those in the South to retain recent economic gains.

Unlike the South, the North never extended general approval to violence against Negroes as a means of maintaining their inferior status. Violence between the races there has been, and frequently; the riot has been its typical form. Race riots have usually been preceded by a period of mounting racial tension over competition for housing, jobs, or recreational facilities. Given a background of tension, an incident, perhaps insignificant in itself, sometimes produces violent conflict between many Negroes and many whites. Even under such conditions, however, there has not been that white solidarity usually characteristic of Southern communities during periods of racial conflict.

RECENT TRENDS IN RACE RELATIONS

Some Factors Encouraging Change

The institutionalized pattern of Southern race relations has, these past few years, been seriously challenged for the first time since Reconstruction, and Northern states and communities have shown increasing concern with minority problems. Factors leading Americans to re-examine their traditional racial patterns are so numerous and complex that no real discussion of them can be undertaken here. The following list of such factors, neither conclusive nor arranged in any presumed order of importance, is suggestive:

(1) An increasing number of Negroes have become eligible through training and professional accomplishment for consideration for non-traditional positions.

(2) Increased scientific knowledge has led to a questioning of the belief in the innate superiority of the white race, thus removing the fundamental premise of the traditional Southern pattern.

(3) The "accident of history" that during World War II one of our major enemies based its national ideology on racism led us to oppose such concepts, abroad and at home. White Americans be-

came increasingly aware of the inconsistency of our position, and Negro Americans vigorously protested it.

(4) Our continued concern, now that the United States is the leader of the free world, with our influence abroad, focuses our attention on race relations. Our ability to gain the confidence of the darker peoples of the world is reduced by domestic discrimination. Other nations may well be skeptical of our sincerity as long as we practice discrimination, and enemies overlook no opportunity to publicize our flaws.

(5) Wartime demands for the fullest utilization of our labor potentials made it apparent that segregation and discrimination are wasteful luxuries in times of emergency. Prosperity and full employment have further encouraged us to question why the best equipped men available, regardless of race, may not be chosen for unfilled jobs. Equally important is the other side of this same point; the existence of full employment has minimized the opposition of white workers to a wider utilization of Negro manpower.

(6) Recent political trends have increased the ability of all minorities to exert political and other pressures. Concentration of Northern minority groups in certain key states has led both political parties to show increasing interest in minority problems. Also, in nonpolitical matters, the organized action groups of minorities have become increasingly influential.

(7) The spirit of liberalism and social experimentation, which characterized much of the 1930's and 1940's, was doubtless a major impetus toward re-evaluating traditional American racial practices.

(8) The recent strength of organized labor in America has opened new opportunities to Negroes. As stated previously, organized labor has not been consistent in its approach to Negro-white relations. Certain unions have excluded Negroes. Nonetheless, the concentration of the masses of urban Negroes in the labor ranks, the liberal racial policies of the national leadership of both the C.I.O. and the A.F. of L. and many of their member unions, and the increased ability of the unions to influence public policy have all been major factors leading to change.

(9) The entire complex of recent changes in the South itself is transforming that region. Such changes include the transfer of

political power within the rural South from the plantation areas to the upland white areas, mechanization of agriculture, migration from rural areas. These changes also include the rapid urbanization of the South, its expanding industrial development, and the accompanying spread of unionization. By reducing the power within the region of the plantation tradition, these changes produce a social climate more receptive to change in race relations.

Some Factors Resisting Change

Counteracting factors resisting change likewise are complex. One of the most important in American minds is the residue of prejudice, with all its emotion. Also, to the many influential whites with vested interests in the maintenance of current racial practices, the traditional rationalizations have obvious appeal. Negroes too, as we have noted, often have vested interests in segregation. Quite aside from direct vested interests, millions of Americans of both races are simply accustomed to the existing patterns and manifest the usual reluctance to abandon known and familiar ways. In the South many people who acknowledge that changes in race relations are inevitable hope the changes will come gradually by local action rather than in response to outside pressures. Such people often state, in apparent sincerity, "Such changes will come, but now is not the time." Memories of past violence, of the Ku Klux Klan during Reconstruction and of lynching more recently, cause many sincere Southerners to dread the prospect of rapid readjustments in race relations.

These and other factors of resistance are real and should not be underestimated; nor should they be overstated. In recent years, forces producing change have been more powerful than those resisting it, so that today race relations are in a state of flux. Each recent innovation—the admission of Negroes to Southern universities, the ending of white primaries, the integration of military units, and so forth—was presaged by fears of violence and threats of "blood in the streets." Actually, recent changes have proceeded with surprisingly little overt resistance, even in the Deep South, and violence in race relations has declined during the period of these innovations. There seems every reason to believe that additional changes will likewise be accepted by the South, if not without opposition, at least without the widespread violence and mass terrorism so often feared.

Means of Effecting Changes in Race Relations

Emphasis on broad social trends conducive to change should not cause one to forget that changes seldom occur automatically or spontaneously. Most of the recent alterations in traditional patterns have resulted from specific efforts to bring about change.

Many of the organizations, whose various roles in fighting prejudice were discussed above, have also worked to combat discrimination or to eliminate segregation in areas related to their own principal interest. This is, of course, especially true of the action groups representing specific minorities, but it has also been true of a wide variety of other organizations. To cite one example, the United Packinghouse Workers of America (C.I.O.) is engaged in an aggressive program of eliminating segregation and discrimination from its locals even in the Deep South. While many recent economic gains have come automatically to Negroes as members of the national labor force, other gains have resulted from deliberate programs sponsored by community groups, business associations, or organized labor. In other fields, similar gains have been made. The rapid emergence of Negro "stars" makes the shift from the former all-white policy of organized baseball an especially dramatic example. A number of professional associations formerly barring or discouraging Negro membership have altered their policies. Some universities have added Negroes to their staffs for the first time; "quota systems," often directed especially toward limiting the number of Jewish students, have been under increasing attack; some college fraternities have revised their rules forbidding Negro or Jewish members. Such changes have usually resulted from organizational activity urging new policies.

The fight against discrimination, however, has been waged with particular success through governmental action. Greatest emphasis has, of course, been on national policies; the most successful avenue has been the judiciary. The most striking gains, perhaps, have been in education. In a series of decisions, from 1938 to the present, the Supreme Court and, on occasion, lower courts have ruled that each state must make available for Negroes the same advanced training extended to whites. When these facilities do not exist the state must admit qualified Negroes to any of its public-supported universities. This obligation may be evaded neither by sending the Negro student outside the state nor by hastily erecting a substitute professional school which cannot offer the facilities, prestige, or professional contacts of the "white" school. Nor may the state impose undue hardships on the student through denial of campus facilities, segregation in classrooms, etc. These decisions have opened graduate and professional schools to Negroes in most of the segregated states. Undergraduate admissions for programs of study provided only at "white" colleges are also covered.

On May 17, 1954, in a momentous decision, the Supreme Court declared segregation in public schools unconstitutional. Reactions by the seventeen affected states and the District of Columbia fall into three patterns: (1) Preparation for immediate desegregation. Washington and scattered border state communities started the desegregation process in September, 1954. A flurry of protests followed, but in most instances the protests died down without seriously impeding the process. Significantly, actual violence developed in none of these protest movements. (2) A search for legal means to circumvent the decision. Two possible techniques are under consideration by some states of the Deep South: (a) Abolishing "public" schools by assigning the operation of schools to a technically private agency, (b) Enforcing segregation under the constitutional police authority granted the states, thus matching one constitutional provision against another. The legality of these techniques, if they are actually undertaken, will doubtless be challenged. (3) A "wait-and-see" policy pending clarification and implementation of the initial decision. This reaction appears to characterize most Southern states. Spokesmen for these states usually avoid challenging the Court's decision, but emphasize a desire to effect gradual compliance over a period of time.

Judicial decisions in other fields have also been very significant. A series of decisions has ruled that segregation on buses and trains imposes undue restraint on interstate commerce. As long ago as 1914, the Supreme Court invalidated the "grandfather clause" as a voting requirement. A principal support of "white supremacy" in political matters was removed by a 1944 decision invalidating the all-white Democratic primary; subsequent judicial rulings have invalidated some of the techniques by which various localities and states sought to evade the implications of this decision. Southern intimidation of Negro voters has not ended, but Negroes now vote in cities all over the region and do so increasingly in the rural areas. Restrictive convenants (real estate agreements forbidding sale or rental to Negroes or other designated groups) were declared, in 1948, not enforceable by state courts, thus weakening a principal technique effecting urban residential segregation. In a number of instances, decisions in criminal cases involving Negro defendants have been overruled because Negroes were barred from jury service. A state decision of international implications was the 1952 invalidation, by the California Supreme Court, of the Alien Land Act. This law forbidding ownership of land by aliens ineligible for citizenship had applied, when passed, to most Oriental peoples, but in recent years had principally affected the Japanese.

Federal executive action has accounted for other recent gains for minority groups. The Fair Employment Practices Commission (F.E.P.C.), created by executive order of President Franklin D. Roosevelt under his wartime powers, forbade discrimination in any defense program and provided some sanctions against employers refusing to comply. Actually, serious sanctions were usually avoided, rather than risk interference with wartime production; thus the order was enforced rather loosely, especially in the South. It was, however, effective enough to open, for Negroes and other minorities, new lines of employment in many Northern plants, and it played no small part in the wartime economic gains made by minorities.

President Truman created, and President Eisenhower has continued, a Committee on Government Contract Compliance to seek conformity with the provision in federal contracts barring discrimination against minority groups. This committee has more limited scope than the earlier F.E.P.C. Its enforcement powers lie in the potential ability of the federal agency concerned to cancel any contract whose provisions are not being fulfilled.

One of the most important changes resulted from President Truman's order ending segregation in the armed forces. As recently as the beginning of World War II the Navy utilized Negroes only as mess boys, and the tradition of Army segregation was thoroughly ingrained. Despite many predictions to the contrary, desegregation in the armed services was achieved very smoothly, and, with the exception of the regionally-based National Guard units, has been virtually completed. The importance of this move in opening new opportunities to Negro youth and in improving their morale in the armed forces is obvious, but perhaps even more significant is the experience for all American youth of living, working, and fighting together. A variety of other executive acts of more restricted scope have been taken by Presidents Roosevelt, Truman, and Eisenhower. Among the more significant results have been fuller opportunities for government employment and the ending of segregation in government facilities in the District of Columbia.

The fight against discrimination and segregation has been much less successful in the legislative branch of the government than in the judicial and executive branches, and immediate prospects for legislative action appear limited. Congressional opposition to F.E.P.C. legislation in particular has been resolute.

State and local governmental action has likewise assumed a variety of forms. Among the most significant forms has been the passage, by the end of 1952, of reasonably efficient F.E.P.C. legislation in nine states. A number of American cities also have established municipal fair employment practices commissions.

OUTLOOK

The principal goal of our minorities is a thoroughly American one. They simply want the full privileges of American citizenship. Stated another way, the goal of our minority groups is to eliminate disabilities resulting from minority status. In 1944 Myrdal pointed out that the "rank order of discrimination" of the white Southerner placed the greatest insistence on maintaining the sexual taboo, followed by the retention of the barriers against "social equality"— that is, drinking, eating, dancing, and the like. The white Southerner seemed most amenable to changes in political, judicial, and economic relationships. To Negroes, a roughly inverse "rank order" prevailed; they were most interested in jobs, credit, police protection, fair court procedures, and the vote, and least concerned with the barriers against close social intercourse.[10]

Some minority leaders wish to remove the barriers preventing full participation in American life but at the same time reserve for their group the right to maintain its distinctiveness. This goal of equality and unity combined with diversity is often called "cultural pluralism." Concerning American Indians, the assimilationist-versus-pluralist debate has been underway for years and shows no signs of diminishing. A comparable difference of opinion exists among Jews and among many nationality minorities. Agreed upon in all of these groups, however, is the desire of the minority to participate fully in American life. Disagreement exists only over the degree to which the group should retain its unique traditions in the American environment.

All indications today point to a continued trend toward fuller incorporation of minorities into American life. Many signs, indeed, indicate an acceleration of this trend. If we assume the implementation of democratic principles to be a continuing goal of American society, we have every reason to anticipate further progress toward democracy in race relations. How nearly complete this process may become within the lifetime of any reader is beyond estimation.

Study Questions

1. It is often stated today that American race relations, far from being of only regional concern, have come to possess international significance. In what respects is this an accurate statement?

2. Describe the advantages and disadvantages implicit in the use of the terms "race" and "minority group." What other terms might be substituted to express the same concepts?

3. Discuss the question, "Who Is a Jew?" Point out the difficulties of classifying this particular group on the basis of any single principle of distinctive characteristics.

4. Discuss possible means by which society might neutralize the potential danger from the prejudice-prone personality.

[10] Myrdal, op. cit., pp. 60–61.

5. Enumerate elements of the prevalent stereotype which your community carries of its most numerous minority. What fallacies can you discern in this process of stereotyping?

6. "If one grants the basic premise of the innate superiority of the white race, then the traditional Southern form of race relations becomes a consistent and systematic culture pattern." Present your reasons for agreeing or disagreeing with this statement.

7. Compare and contrast Northern and Southern practices concerning the Negro.

8. Debate the question, "Resolved, that the most appropriate means of attacking racial discrimination in America today lies through federal action."

9. In your opinion, which have been the most significant of the factors which have led, in recent years, to a reevaluation of American racial practices?

10. Assume that you were asked to formulate the policies for an action group organized to fight discrimination and prejudice. What policies would you sponsor?

Selected References

Berry, Brewton, *Race Relations* (Houghton Mifflin, 1951). Emphasizes the various forms which race relations may assume, with examples from over the world. Chapter 5 on prejudice is especially recommended. Excellent bibliography.

Dollard, John, *Caste and Class in a Southern Town* (Harper, 1949). A study of a plantation community in the Mississippi Delta, with descriptive and theoretical materials on social stratification.

Drake, St. Clair, and Horace Cayton, *Black Metropolis* (Harcourt, Brace, 1945). A description of Chicago's Negro community, with excellent presentation of the problems of Negroes in large Northern cities.

Finklestein, Louis (ed.), *The Jews: Their History, Culture, and Religion* (Harper, 1949), vol. II. Part III of this volume contains materials on the characteristics of the Jewish group, their migrations, role in the national economy, and community life.

Frazier, E. Franklin, *The Negro in the United States* (Macmillan, 1949). A sociological account of America's largest minority, which emphasizes historical factors and community and institutional organization.

Marden, Charles F., *Minorities in American Society* (American Book, 1952). A comprehensive text covering all minorities mentioned in this chapter, with additional materials on Catholic-Protestant relations, the minor sects, and Hawaii and Puerto Rico.

McDonagh, Edward C., and Eugene S. Richards, *Ethnic Relations in the*

United States (Appleton-Century-Crofts, 1953). Especially useful in this combination text-reader is Part 3, "Improving Ethnic Relations," which discusses needed research, action programs, and recent gains of minorities.

Myrdal, Gunnar, *An American Dilemma* (Harper, 1944). A comprehensive analysis of the Negro in American life, emphasizing the conflict between democratic values and American racial practices.

Rose, Arnold M. (ed.), *Race Prejudice and Discrimination* (Knopf, 1951). The selections on prejudice (Part IV, section B) are particularly recommended. This collection of readings also contains interesting accounts of various specific minorities.

Tuck, Ruth, *Not with the Fist* (Harcourt, Brace, 1946). A readable and sympathetic description of Spanish-speaking Americans in an inland city of Southern California.

16

Problems Arising from Cultural Contacts

Until recently, problems arising from cultural contacts have been treated under a variety of specialized headings, such as minority group relations, assimilation, personality disorganization, social disorganization, culture change, and acculturation. The approach utilized in this chapter attempts to focus attention upon the common aspects of cultural adjustment problems previously discussed as separate topics. This change of emphasis reflects both the increased numbers of cultural-contact problems produced by industrial technology and the recognition of their shared properties.

Technological improvements in communication and transportation have multiplied the contacts between peoples of different backgrounds. A hundred years ago it required at least three weeks to send a message from Europe to America and to receive a reply. Today, the average American can hear over his radio on-the-spot descriptions of events taking place half way around the world. Fifty years ago, almost a week was required to travel from the Atlantic Coast of the United States to the Pacific, and this feat itself represented a remarkable advance in long-distance transportation. Now, jet airliners make it possible to travel completely around the earth in less than half the time.

Improvements in transportation and communication, while facilitating intercultural contacts, have not been solely responsible for bringing more people of different backgrounds together. Momentous social and economic changes have served toward the same end through forcing peoples to move, socially as well as physically, in unprecedented numbers. To cite a single example, more than twenty million people moved to the United States alone during the first half of the twentieth century. Social cataclysms, including two gigantic wars within a period of 25 years, forced countless millions of others into motion. During and immediately after World War II at least thirty million Europeans were displaced from their homes, many going to other lands. The wars also moved military personnel into the most remote sections of the world. At the close of hostilities in 1945, some five million Americans were on foreign soil. It is not possible here to list even the major influences of world trade developments upon intercultural relations. Suffice it to say that it is a remote spot of the world, indeed, where one cannot find a discarded gasoline tin or bottles of carbonated beverages originating in the United States.

The important point is that today peoples of different cultures can scarcely avoid coming into contact. When they do, relational difficulties of varying degrees of seriousness frequently—perhaps, usually—develop. If these difficulties are to be resolved, *some* adjustments must be made. The socio-cultural processes of encounter and adaptation provide the common focus for the problems of cultural contact with which we are here concerned.

THE NATURE OF CULTURE REVIEWED

The varieties and complexity of cultural contact problems being what they are, a logical starting point for their analysis is a review of the general nature of culture and its influence upon individual personality and group relations.

The noted English anthropologist E. B. Tylor defined culture as "that complex whole which includes knowledge, belief, art, morals, law, custom, and any other capabilities and habits acquired by man as a member of society." Approached from a slightly different direction, culture consists of the socially accepted and implemented products, both material and non-material, of human thought. Man possesses a culture, which other animals do not, because his brain structure makes it possible for him to make and retain mental abstractions of his experiences and to transmit these abstractions to others of his species through the use of symbols, chiefly language. Further, he is able to relate his own experiences with those communicated to him by others and develop new composite abstractions. These mental abilities of abstracting, communicating, and relating make it possible for humans to "know" more about the world in which they live than they can personally experience. Nor are they limited to the vicarious experiences of the living. Knowledge can be transmitted from one generation to another, and, although some of it is lost in the process, the stockpile of ideas, lore, and techniques of a society can be steadily enlarged.

Man is seldom content with merely reciting his experiences, however. He also seeks to explain them, to arrange them into more comprehensive patterns. By so doing he feels better able to take appropriate actions in new situations as well as in those for which he has some guide based on experience. Such explanations, natural and supernatural, and a code of prescribed actions are also communicated to other members of the group. If accepted, they become part of the group culture. The processes of retention and communication within a restricted group lead the members to develop behavioral similarities that distinguish them from members of other groups with different culture patterns.

The development of behavioral uniformities within a group is more than a matter of subjection to the same cultural environment. Each member of a social group may by his actions threaten the security of the other members of the group, just as the actions of others may threaten his security. Hence, the action of each member becomes to some extent the concern of the others. If a given behavioral form is accepted as the appropriate one under given conditions, care must be taken that this procedure is followed by all. Deviations present a potential threat to the group, so social pressures are brought to bear against the deviant. Of course behavioral changes do occur, but seldom without resistance, even when old forms have proved ineffective under altered circumstances. Traditional behavior may be stamped with the authority of supernatural will, and dire consequences predicted as the penalty for nonconformance. The fearful members of the society constantly seek to avert any action by the more daring that may unleash the wrath of the gods. It is only fair to note, however, that the cautious and conservative members of various societies, while most frequently criticized for retarding progress, have undoubtedly been responsible on many occasions for preventing action which would have proved socially disastrous.

Each society in addition to exerting pressures to force its members to conform to accepted modes of action is also faced with the problem of indoctrinating the offspring with the ways of the group. This process of indoctrination is called *socialization*. It is accomplished, in the main, through the differential bestowal of rewards and punishments (sanctions) to the child in accordance with his actions. This channeling of behavior into socially approved forms may be extremely subtle. In fact, even those who are doing the channeling may not be conscious of their own influence. The gradualness and thoroughness of socialization formerly led to the erroneous belief that some culture traits are inherited and that they develop with physical maturation. This same belief is held, to a considerable extent, even today.

After the child has learned the language of his group, those who have assumed responsibility for his behavior may communicate their approval or disapproval more directly. They may go even further, explaining or justifying to the child why he should act in a prescribed manner. This, however, is not necessary to force his conformance; the application of sanctions remains the fundamental means of implementation. For many behavioral prescriptions, the original reasons or justifications have been lost, if they were ever clearly defined. The American child who has been taught to prefix his requests with the magic word "please" because "it's polite, that's why" probably did not respond to this vague justification. He learned—if his parents were strict on the subject—because his request was more quickly granted if he said "please" than if he didn't.

As a consequence of the socialization process, it soon becomes unnecessary for the individual to have actual social pressures brought to bear in order that he may behave in the acceptable manner. He retains, and unconsciously applies, memories of earlier experiences of his own or accounts of the experiences of others. He is able to conceptualize a situation, possible actions of his own, probable reactions of others. He may direct his own behavior in order to receive desired reactions. But a large part of his behavior requires no conscious consideration of reactions of others. "Accepted" behavior implies approval, so that as long as the individual operates within the limits of group habits, customs, and routines, his actions receive an automatic endorsement. It is only when he is placed in an unfamiliar situation or strays from charted behavioral paths that he faces the necessity of thinking about alternative actions and their possible reception.

The tendency of each society to justify its own way of life leads to a corollary tendency to consider the differing ways of other groups not only as peculiar but also as wrong. This belief in the superiority of one's own groups and culture is termed *ethnocentrism*. So much is it an accepted outlook of many individuals that they are frankly amazed, and not a little resentful, to find that members of other culture groups do not concede or even recognize this superiority. Even more shocking is it to many to find that their way of life is actually considered inferior.

The characteristics of culture groups that are especially relevant in a consideration of cultural contact problems may be summarized briefly as follows:

(1) Members of human social groups, by virtue of their mental equipment, tend to develop uniform behavioral characteristics based, in large measure, upon the communicated experiences (and their rationalizations) of past and present members of the particular society. These similarities of individual behavior appear as group culture patterns, or configurations, which distinguish the society from other societies possessing different behavioral patterns.

(2) The same factors that make culture possible tend also to perpetuate accepted patterns over varying periods of time. Dependent upon the size of the group and the efficiency of the communication process, the members of a society are exposed to many of the same "secondary" experiences, explanations, rationalizations, that influence their behavior. Efforts are made to restrict the behavior of

group members to forms that have proved, or are thought to have proved, effective in the past, lest some deviant action prove harmful to the group.

(3) The behavior of new members of the society is channeled into patterns acceptable to the group by the selective application of sanctions. The "socialized" individual responds to mental images of group reactions in "choosing" his behavior. This process of response is sufficiently automatic in many cases to require no conscious thought. Actually, the choice of action—even that which is disapproved—is limited by the content of the culture and the creative ability of the individual.

(4) Each society tends to justify its patterns of culture, partly as a measure for inducing the conformance of the members. As a consequence, the well-indoctrinated member feels the assurance that the beliefs and values of his group are fundamentally and eminently "right," while any conflicting values and beliefs of others are, by the same token, fundamentally "wrong."

CULTURE CONTACT AND ADJUSTMENT

It should be apparent from what has been noted about the nature of culture that relations between persons of different culture groups may present a number of problems. First, people of each group recognize that people of other groups engage in behavior that differs from their own. In some cases the behavior may be so completely "strange" that it elicits only a reaction of wonder. In other cases, the behavior may be of a type that is disapproved in another society. Then, the reaction is not mere amazement, but also condemnation. But these are only surface difficulties. If relations become more involved, other complications arise. These will be discussed shortly, but all involve difficulties of adjusting to new traits, beliefs, and values. The adjustments necessary to surmount such difficulties depend upon the particular cultures involved and the nature of the contacts. It is the latter variable with which we shall be concerned for the most part since the great variety of identifiable culture groups precludes the possibility of any comprehensive analysis of specific group contacts.

Diffusion, Acculturation, Assimilation

Before proceeding to the discussion of types of cultural contacts, it would be well to review some of the terms and concepts associated with culture group relations that will be used.

The term *diffusion* as applied to culture refers to the transmission of one or more traits from one culture group to another. This transmission may occur directly through observation and imitation or it may be brought about by communication between representatives of the groups involved. It is, in either event, a learning process, but there must be both the desire and ability of one group to take over some trait before diffusion occurs. The content of the culture determines what traits can be taken over. As Lowie has pointed out, primitive peoples could borrow the use of friction matches from the West, but they could not borrow the match industry, for that requires a more complex level of technological development.[1] Most culture traits possessed by any group probably consist of those which they have borrowed from others.

The term *acculturation* denotes a fusion of culture traits of two or more groups, producing a synthesis derived but distinct from any predecessor. It is probably rare that any trait or group of traits is taken over without some modification being made by the receiving group either in the form or function of the trait.

Assimilation refers to the change in individual or group behavior as the prescriptions and values of one culture are discarded and those of another adopted. The process of assimilation may be said to be completed when the individual or group is able to operate comfortably within the adopted system, and both feels a part of the assimilating group and is accepted as such. The term *assimilation* is frequently confused with the process of biological fusion through interbreeding —a process more accurately called *amalgamation*.

Socialization, discussed above, differs from *assimilation* in that in

[1] Robert H. Lowie, *An Introduction to Cultural Anthropology*, enlarged edition (Rinehart, 1940).

the former the subjects involved are immature and have not been previously indoctrinated in some other culture. The net result of the socialization process, however, is the same as that of assimilation: the channeling of the individual's behavior into the accepted patterns of the group.

Types of Cultural Contact Situations

Three categories of cultural contact situations have been selected for analysis here, although it should be made clear that the classification is an arbitrary one. The bases for this particular selection are situational in terms of those involved and the nature of the involvement. The categories are:

1. Cases of relatively isolated individuals seeking to operate in an alien culture.

2. Cases of minority culture groups seeking to operate in an alien culture.

3. Cases of distinct culture groups in a tangential rather than an incorporative relationship.

The first two types of contact involve the possibility of assimilation; the third, as conceived here, does not—at least not as an immediate prospect—although diffusion and acculturation may take place.

It should be remembered, too, that considerable differences in group behavior may be found within a larger society that is nominally culturally homogeneous. In some cases, differences between groups in the same society are so marked that contacts offer difficulties as great as if entirely different societies were involved. Beyond doubt the adjustment of a youth reared in the mountains of eastern Tennessee to the culture of Brooklyn would be a difficult matter even though the people of both areas are citizens of the United States and share many aspects of the national culture. Social classes as well as regional groups display distinctive behavioral patterns that require intrasocial relational adjustments. The person seeking to rise into a group of higher social status must alter his behavior in accord with the views of that group before he is accepted as a bona fide member. In short, true social mobility is a special type of assimilation.

The intent of the foregoing is simply to emphasize that boundaries of nationality and race are only incidental to cultural differences. It is quite possible that an upper-class American reared in metropolitan New York would have less difficulty adapting to the culture of upper-class Europeans than to the life of lower-class rural Americans. It should be obvious that an American Negro would find the life of an African tribesman quite as strange as would a white American. Aside from personal idiosyncracies, it is the culture that determines the individual's adaptability to unfamiliar modes of life. It is neither his nationality nor his race, but what he believes in, what he does.

THE INDIVIDUAL IN AN ALIEN CULTURE

The account that follows is a remarkable one in the clarity with which it depicts the process of moving from one socio-cultural sphere to another as experienced by the isolated individual. It is apparent that the "cultural distance" traversed in this particular case is relatively short. However, this fact does not invalidate the basic principles of adjustment involved. Rather, it emphasizes the truly great emotional problems that attend any basic shift of behavior from conformance with one set of norms to conformance with another.

While I lived in —— I was perfectly happy and essentially religious. I had been taught that it was well to be moral—in the way the preacher defined morality—because then I could be sure that God would always be on my side, so to speak. Church attendance and church work were taken for granted. About the only people who didn't participate in church were the social outcasts, or at least they were so defined by the rest of us. What could be more convincing evidence of the preacher's rationalizations? . . .

But then I moved to —— [a metropolitan city]. Many of my companions are seemingly as innocent of the church as if they were cave men. Their daily sins of commission and omission at first shocked me, then puzzled me, and now almost intrigue me. I observe that no dire consequences befall them. . . . As time went on I thought less and less of the church. This was made possible partly because when I came to —— I did not know where to go to church and nobody asked me to go. I waited and no one has asked me yet. My recreation now consists of things and thoughts which I regarded six or seven years ago to be "sinful." I think now that they are not, but I still do not feel right about it, but I don't know why. . . .

When I go home I always feel my worst about this. My folks (parents, fiancee, friends) don't know what I do think or that I do not go to church when I am away. I feel like a hypocrite when I am home. I see that the church and the preacher are very narrow, provincial, superstitious, and not really religious in many matters. I am unmoved by discussions about "sin," "repentance," "backsliding" and by most of the doctrinal lingo about "eternal salvation," baptism, and other eternal principles. I am sure they are not, but I do not know why . . . I have an awful sense of guilt when ——— (my fiancee) brings up religious matters. She is so innocent and yet so sure, that she gets on my nerves. Someday I am going to blow up, but that will bring me nothing good. But it's going to happen sure. . . .

I have tried going to church alone, but I feel even worse then. I am truly wasting my time, and I feel even more like a hypocrite. . . .

Deep down I am sure that it is me who is wrong. Everybody else can't be wrong . . . I may pay for my irreligion. . . . How do I know but that the preacher is right? But he can't *prove* to me that he is. Or do you have to *feel* it only or have what they call "faith"? . . . Sometimes I worry a great deal and then again I forget the whole thing for a day or so. . . . But when I go home and when I think of marriage I get a cold sweat. I can't always go on making believe to others. There's going to be a showdown.[2]

Five phases of adjustment may be identified in this case history. The final phase—restored equilibrium—had not yet been completed. The phases do not represent the only adjustment process, but they are relatively "normal," if we may equate normalcy with frequency of occurrence.

The first stage is prior to the alien culture contact. The socialized individual is able to operate freely and easily with his group. (The case subject uses the words "perfectly happy" and "sure.") There is more or less uncritical acceptance of the "rightness" of the group norms. Deviants have been effectively ostracized and serve as examples of the unhappy consequences that attend violation of accepted behavior.

The initial encounter with the "alien" culture marks the second stage. The individual observes behavioral differences. He may be

[2] John F. Cuber, "Marginal Church Participants," *Sociology and Social Research* (September–October, 1940), pp. 57–62.

simply interested in them as curiosities; he may try to understand
them; he may try to evaluate them. The subject of our case history
reported "shock" as he measured the behavior of his new companions
against the norms of his home community. Their transgressions, he
had been led to expect, would be attended by quick and sure punishment—but the expected sanctions failed to materialize.

The third phase may be any one of several possibilities. In our
case history the subject himself began to indulge in behavior which
the people in his home community adjudged "sinful." Again, the
material sanctions failed to develop—but he could not completely
discard the values inculated over a long period of years. As a consequence he developed a vague sense of guilt (". . . I still do not feel
right about it, but I don't know why . . .").

The fourth phase is a condition that has been termed "marginalism." It is a realization of the relativity of cultural values, accompanied by indecision of action. Our case subject was unsure of his
own behavior because its rightness or wrongness depended upon the
particular standards against which he measured it—and he was no
longer sure of his standards. He resented the security of his fiancee
who still accepted the absoluteness of values, a view which he had
come to feel was naïve.

The fifth phase is a search for a new equilibrium—a new equation
of behavior and standards. Failure to regain this equilibrium results
in a condition of *anomie*—a lack of behavioral guides—which Durkheim considered to be the grounds for many cases of suicide.

Since our case subject had not yet achieved a new balance, we may
examine his alternatives and their associated problems. First, he
could return to the norms of the group into which he was socialized.
(It might be mentioned that he could have held fast to them all along
as an alternative to phase three.) This type of reaction would reduce internal conflict, but it might also weaken or destroy the possibilities of harmonious social relations in the new social environment.
In fact, it is almost sure to do so if the individual strongly indicates by
word and deed that he considers the behavioral traits of the host
society vastly inferior to those of the group he has left.

At the other extreme, the individual could completely discard the
beliefs, customs, and artifacts of the earlier group and adopt the

culture of the host society. This procedure, assuming his acceptance by the recipient group, would undoubtedly improve his social relations, although it might also rob him of some of the individualistic distinction which he would otherwise enjoy. The major disadvantages would lie with whatever relationships he sought to maintain with the original group. (Recall the words of the case subject: "But when I go home and when I think of marriage I get a cold sweat.") By that group he is likely to be viewed as an apostate whose very defection is an implied insult. The convert, who is considered by one group to have "seen the light," is the deserter, who has "forfeited his birthright," to another.

Between these two alternatives of rigidity, or steadfastness, on the one extreme and complete assimilation on the other, come the bulk of individual adjustments. It may be argued that the range of adjustments is not a true continuum inasmuch as discrete differences may be identified in the types of adjustment. One type we call cultural synthesis; another we may call cultural compartmentalization. Both represent attempts on the part of the individual to adjust to the demands of different systems.

Cultural synthesis is simply the process of acculturation on the individual level. The individual adopts certain traits which he feels will enable him to operate more successfully in the newly-encountered system while retaining traits of his earlier culture group. The success of this procedure is dependent upon the extent of cultural diversity and, of course, upon the content of the cultures. In some instances it may be possible to fuse traits from each into a compatible whole. In other cases the fundamental outlooks may be so completely variant that mixture of compatible traits is practically impossible. It has been widely observed that the traits most readily adopted and rejected are those least associated with fundamental culture values. One frequently finds "culture immigrants" who have adopted the superficial trappings of dress and language but who remain firmly committed to the philosophy and values of their native heritage.

The disadvantages attending adjustment through synthesis are several. One is that the individual, particularly if he has selected and rejected the "wrong" traits, may find that he has placed himself in a position of permanent marginalism rather than transitional marginalism. Instead of being able to maintain successful relationships with the two or more cultures involved, he may be rejected by all parties. Even should he achieve a successful fusion so far as his relationships are concerned, he may be plagued by guilt feelings as was the subject of our case history. Particularly will this be true if consistency of action with belief is one of the cultural values to which he subscribes, and he recognizes that the behavioral traits derived from one culture are at variance with the beliefs derived from another.

Another mode of operating successfully in two or more cultures is what has been termed cultural compartmentalization. This type of adaption is advocated in the adage, "when in Rome, do as the Romans do." It assumes that the individual can make automatic adjustment to the cultural environment in which he is placed. Indeed, there do appear to be some persons who, through the maintenance of so-called "logic-tight mental compartments," are able to switch from one system to an almost completely contradictory one and back again with no apparent disturbances. This is not to be confused with the adaptation of the truly flexible individual whose broad philosophy enables him to participate in a variety of cultures without necessarily committing himself to any. In the case of cultural compartmentalization, the individual *does* commit himself but to different systems at different times. Some social psychologists hold that the apparent separation of internalized value systems is not so complete as it might appear on the surface and that the attempt to consolidate conflicting systems may lead to mental disorders of varying severity.

MINORITY-MAJORITY CULTURE GROUP CONTACTS

The second type of culture contact situation with which we are concerned is one which involves two groups rather than an individual and a group. Various aspects of this particular class of relationship have already been discussed in some detail in the preceding chapter, which is concerned with the social problems of minority and racial groups. Hence, the discussion here will be limited to the ways in

which the existence of the group may influence the process of individual adjustment.

It should first be made clear that not all problems of minority-
group relations are the products of cultural differences. In fact, quite
the opposite is frequently the case: cultural differences may appear as
the result of social exclusion, for whatever grounds, that prevents
the free communication of ideas. In other cases, the processes of
assimilation are impeded—even though the minority group members
may actually desire to become assimilated—because of exclusion from
social participation. The most ironic situation is one in which the
social exclusion is allegedly based on cultural differences, since in this
case the differences serve as the basis for their own perpetuation.
These facts about ethnic groups are related simply to point out that
while some aspects of cultural contract problems and minority group
problems may overlap, the two sets of problems are by no means
identical.

For analytical purposes, four major types of minority-majority culture group relations may be set forth:

(1) A relational situation in which both groups desire assimilation.

(2) A relational situation in which neither group desires assimilation.

(3) A relational situation in which the majority rejects the assimilatory attempts of the minority.

(4) A relational situation in which the minority group resists assimilatory pressures from the majority.

For our purposes, the fourth type is of greatest interest. In the
situation where both groups desire assimilation of the minority, the
major problems focus around the most effective methods for securing
this end with the least disturbance to both groups. It should be
recognized that some disturbances are normal even in this case because assimilation inevitably involves changes in the organizational
systems of both groups. Some members face the threat of losses in
prestige and power, and they resist in various ways. In general, however, the social problems associated with this type are less serious than
those associated with the other types.

Where neither group desires assimilation, the problems are basically
the same as those of culture groups in tangential contact discussed

below. Hence, they need not be taken up at this point. Europe, more than the United States, offers examples of cultural enclaves that have preserved their distinctiveness despite centuries of living in close proximity to other culture groups.

So far as the rejected minority group is concerned, the problems that arise are only incidentally those of cultural contact. They belong more to the class of racial and minority problems discussed in another chapter in which social and psychological factors are of greater importance.

The situation of particular concern here is the competitive one in which a relatively small group seeks to retain its cultural characteristics despite variant cultural surroundings. The history of the United States is rich in examples of such relations ending, in most instances, with the loss of the minority culture identity. What may be rightfully termed a national culture of the United States has been developed through the fusion of characteristics drawn from many minority groups. Despite the recent trend to deprecate the so-called "melting pot" theory as applied to the United States, the fact still remains that history records no more numerous instances and rapid rates of acculturation and assimilation than have prevailed in this nation.

The significant effort of the culture group in resisting assimilatory pressures is that of the direct exercise of social controls upon the individual member. It is true that the individual, even separated from the group, is subject to social restraints. But these are "internal," the mental products of socialization. Highly effective as these may be, without reenforcement they are subject to the dissipations of time.

The group serves, through the application of social sanctions, to reenforce the culture pattern. The forces are external as well as internal—teasing, ridicule, social isolation, even physical punishment accorded to those who violate the group norms. A typical example is offered in the following statement by a Norwegian-Lutheran student in a midwestern town who broke from the minority group pattern:

Those kids [the other Norwegian-Lutheran students in the high school] gang together except for me. They stick together just like glue. I was ostracized from them because I danced and went to shows and we play bridge. We dance and go to shows and play cards, but over there they're against everything. In fact, every time we had a dance at the high school they threw some kind of a party at the church and tried to make the kids come. Those who didn't were ostracized. The Lutherans just wouldn't let us run around with their crowd.

I quit going to church. The kids over there are all right, but I'm kind of left out of things, and since I've been going out they have left me alone. They are very strict, and they don't want you to go out to dance and out on parties and dates, and they watch what you do.[3]

It should not be assumed that the majority group always emerges the victor in the struggle for cultural dominance. Indeed, many cases may be offered in which a militant minority superimposed its way of life upon a quiescent majority. Even more frequently, minority groups continue to maintain their own cultural characteristics through the exercise of efficient social controls. Newspapers, special schools, fervent observation of holidays and other symbolic events peculiar to the group, all may be utilized in the interests of culture preservation. Not infrequently expatriate minority groups celebrate commemorative events with greater intensity than is the case in the "homeland."[4]

The pressures upon the individual member of the cultural minority come from more than one direction. He is subject to the sanctions of both the majority group and the minority, each of which seeks to win his allegiance. The choice is not a simple one, and is generally made in an atmosphere charged with emotional issues. There is no "right" decision in the sense that favorable consequences attend the one exclusively and unfavorable consequences the other. Family ties may have to be weighed against personal ambitions attainable only through cultural mobility. Certainly the child in such an ethnic minority group is an ideal recipient for the facetiously suggested educational toy for the modern age: a puzzle that doesn't work out no matter how the pieces are put together.

The crucial issue upon which the survival of a minority culture

[3] W. Lloyd Warner and Associates, *Democracy in Jonesville* (Harper, 1949), p. 187.

[4] Many world travelers have noted, for instance, that United States citizens living in American communities abroad celebrate Independence Day with greater fervor than they do in the United States. This reflects the felt need to intensify "American beliefs" and solidify group bonds.

hinges is whether it provides for the social, emotional, mental and physical needs of the group members in the competitive cultural environment. If it can do so, and the members firmly believe that it is doing so, there is no reason short of physical elimination why the minority culture should not persist indefinitely. What frequently occurs, however, is that the group leaders fail to recognize the demands engendered by changed social surroundings. Continued devotion to past ways in the mistaken belief that they are independent of environmental circumstances (or that they exercise complete control over them) may lead to cultural malfunctioning. New needs are unrecognized and unmet. Members seeking to meet them as individuals rather than as a group desert the older pattern in increasing numbers. Cohesive pressures are increased by the "loyalist" members; strains and dissension develop; and the disorganization process accelerates. Soon there are too few remaining members to fill the social positions required for autonomous existence, and the ethnic minority as a functional group is dissipated. The losses to the assimilating group are the cultural traits of the minority which failed to survive the assimilatory process, some of which are of primary functional value, others of which served secondary emotional and aesthetic needs.[5]

CULTURE GROUPS IN TANGENTIAL RELATIONSHIP

The third class of contact situations mentioned above (see page 464) comprises those cases in which distinct culture groups are in some type of association (direct or indirect, formal or informal) but with no immediate likelihood of assimilation. It is doubtful that there are any major culture groups in the present age of rapid communication and transportation without multiple contacts of this nature. The relations between the English-speaking peoples of North America and the Spanish- and Portuguese-speaking peoples of Central and South America offer a typical example. Group similar-

[5] In our own society may be cited the changing structure of the family to a form that is suited to the requirements of our economic system but that fails to provide for the social integration of aged persons, a function which was filled by the so-called institutional family.

ities and differences are recognized, and there is a two-way diffusion of culture traits ranging from music to baseball; but no general fusion of the distinct language groups appears likely—at least in the near future.

Two basic types of social problems may develop from such a tangential contact situation. One results from the use by the members of a culture group of their own culture references to interpret the actions and beliefs of another group. The other type is disorganizational, the effect of the diffusion of alien culture traits into a society that is not prepared to deal with the resulting changes.

Relational Problems

The analysis of cultural relational problems is not a difficult matter when we understand that any social action derives its meaning for a group from the culture of the group. This is true not only of the actions of the group itself but also of the actions of other groups which it considers, interprets, or evaluates. Stated simply, an action can have as many meanings as there are those to give it meaning. Understanding develops only when common meanings can be attached to the same actions, and this is not an easy task. Furthermore, the development of understanding is impeded by the common belief held by many groups that the particular meaning which they attach to an action is absolute and universal. Misinterpretation of their own actions by others is viewed as conscious distortion to serve malevolent ends, while any denial of their own interpretations by those whose actions they seek to explain is often viewed as sheer duplicity.

One need only review a current newspaper or magazine to find numerous examples of the types of misunderstanding which lead to hostility and possible conflict. The government of the United States offers economic aid to a financially-depressed nation whose "ungrateful" leaders reject the "wedge of economic imperialism." The Western allies establish military bases in Europe and Asia as "the first line of defense" amidst communist cries of "capitalist aggression." The Soviet Union concentrates troops along the border of a neighboring country as a "protective measure" and the action is interpreted by non-communist nations as a "prelude to attack." A Negro man is sentenced to death for rape in Alabama, and the item is headlined in

European communist newspapers as "another American lynching."
A deposed political leader is summarily tried and executed for "trea-
son" in a communist nation as accusations of "Star Chamber methods" and "inquisition" are hurled from the West. These are only a
few of the more dramatic examples of relational difficulty in a widely
publicized area of cultural contact. Thousands of less noted but
equally confounding cases of socio-cultural conflict occur daily in all
parts of the world.

Despite their frequent association, misunderstanding does not always lead to disapproval and denunciation, nor does condemnation
necessarily imply misinterpretation. We may not understand, for
example, why the males in certain preliterate tribes practice mother-
in-law avoidance, but at the same time we may feel no strong antipathy to the practice and some of us may even heartily endorse it.
Or, to choose a simple case of understanding without agreement, we
may appreciate the fact that a dish of properly prepared snails is
pleasing to the palate of a French gourmet, but that does not necessarily mean that we think snails are fit for human consumption.
Relational problems are seldom the immediate products of misunderstanding or even disagreement, although these may be the roots of
discord. The problems result when action is taken, whether it be a
measure based on misconception or one to eliminate or alter some
considerable cultural element. As Sumner pointed out nearly half a
century ago in his classic *Folkways*, the determination of undesir-
ability is dependent upon the behavioral norms of the evaluating
group. The average American may feel an aversion to eating snails
because they are not part of his food habits or folkways but he is not
likely to take any strong action to prevent their being eaten by others.
There are, however, more fundamental beliefs which serve as guides to
action, the violation of which is intolerable because such transgression,
ultimately, is considered a threat to group life. In such cases, it is
felt, measures must be taken to block the anticipated effects. This
may be done through severance of relations or through the direct
application of sanctions against the offending group.

Rarely are relational problems the result of single issues over which
there is misunderstanding or disagreement. They are the cumulative
effect of numerous events together with their interpretations or mis-

interpretations. Where suspicion already exists, interaction is likely to be somewhat curtailed. Each group then, in an attempt to fathom the actions of the others, organizes into a plausible pattern the fragmentary information gathered through contacts and hearsay, binding the pieces together with a tissue of deductions. Since the deductions are commonly formed within the cultural framework of the deducing group, the images thus constructed may be far from realistic, and even farther from the self-images held by the groups whose understanding is sought. No matter how distorted the image is, however, it serves as the basis for further interaction. Moreover, the action based upon it is then interpreted and utilized by the other group or groups in an effort to fathom the acting group, thus compounding the initial miscomprehension. Obviously, the less factual information there is available, the greater the fictitious contribution to the group images developed. It would be difficult to estimate how many major and minor culture groups interact with others in this tension- and hostility-producing atmosphere of "reciprocal delusion." [6]

Disorganizational Problems

Problems arising from cultural misunderstandings and conflicting values receive wide attention in contemporary literature, but it is doubtful that they are more serious in terms of human lives affected than disorganizational problems resulting from culture diffusion. To understand these latter, we must again look at the fundamental relationships between culture and society.

Each society maintains its existence through the development and application of behavioral modes by which individual and group needs are met under existing environmental conditions, both natural and cultural. There may be any number of equally effective methods of dealing with the same conditions, but the society adopts, and thus limits itself to, a relatively few which are taught to each new generation. Behavioral uniformities do alter, of course, since conditions change, perfect transmission is never completely achieved, and new techniques are introduced through diffusion and invention. The

---

[6] The author is indebted to A. T. Hansen for this descriptive conceptual designation.

rapidity of change depends upon a variety of factors: the extent of environmental change, the size of the culture base, the efficiency of communication techniques, the effectiveness of socialization and social control, and the values of the culture with respect to change itself as being either desirable or undesirable. However, if there were not a certain amount of stability and uniformity, there would be no recognizable culture configurations.

To a considerable extent the forms of social organization and technology of any culture group are interdependent variables. The tools and skills of the group shape the cooperative patterns through which they are applied, and the social structure developed imposes certain limitations on the types of tasks which the group can perform. No hoe culture ever developed a social equivalent of the business corporations of industrial society, nor could a council of ten or twelve tribal elders govern by oral dicta a nation of 160 million people. Regardless of its simplicity or complexity, the prime function of a socio-cultural system remains that of filling the basic biological and derived cultural needs of the society. When this function is efficiently performed a relative equilibrium of the system is achieved.

The equilibrium of a socio-cultural system may be upset in several ways. Basic biological needs are not likely to alter appreciably, but cultural, or "learned," needs may undergo radical transformation. It is commonplace but nonetheless true that the luxuries of one generation can become necessities for the next, that is, they become an integral part of the functioning system. An agrarian society may operate very effectively without timepieces, mechanical power, and even reading and writing; but an industrial society cannot. Industrialists seeking to develop their operations in culture areas lacking a business tradition almost invariably find it necessary to create new needs before potential workers will respond to such incentives of the industrial society as money, medical care, and housing. Once these needs become a part of the culture pattern, however, then the equilibrium of the system is upset and is not restored until the necessary alterations have been made to fill them.

It is not necessary to change the kinds of needs to upset the equilibrium of a system. The sheer increase of existing needs through population growth may prove more than the system can meet. This, however, is not primarily a problem stemming from cultural contacts, except when the introduction of medical and hygienic techniques reduces "normal" population losses. It may be noted, though, that proponents of Western culture patterns with the high value they place upon the preservation of human life frequently fail to anticipate the disorganizing effects of a diffusion of life-saving techniques into societies that are not prepared to care for the resulting population increase.

A third way in which socio-cultural equilibrium is vulnerable is through the "supply" system. This segment is not limited to the supplying of basic economic needs; it is concerned also with the more abstract social and psychic needs. The alteration of the supply system through the introduction of new tools, skills, ideologies, or related culture traits requires corresponding adjustments throughout the entire socio-cultural system.

Consider the hypothetical case of an agricultural society dependent upon human and animal energy for the operation of its technological system. The basic tillage instrument is the wooden plow drawn by oxen; planting and harvesting are done by hand. The basic economic structure is the family. Some families work their own land; others, as tenants, cultivating land which they do not own. In each case, however, the size of the plot worked by the family is small—geared to the amount of land that can be effectively cultivated with available tools, skills, and power. Most of the produce is utilized to feed family members and animals; whatever is left is traded at small local markets or used to pay the land rent. Upon this base, the social and cultural superstructure is developed, both guided and limited by the socio-economic foundation.

What would be the effects of introducing mechanical energy and equipment into such a society? Actual experiences in similar cases attest to a probable radical reorganization. Primarily, more land can be cultivated with greater productive efficiency by fewer persons. With the disappearance of the need for great concentrations of human energy per land unit, the family economic structure and the family work plot lose their former significance. Tenant families are displaced from the soil and, if the supply of land is limited, must migrate to other areas in search of work. The relationships between family members themselves change as their cooperative work functions are altered or lost.   New economic structures develop in response to larger-scale operational needs.   With fewer producers, smaller proportions of the agricultural product are consumed locally, and a more elaborate market economy must be developed to dispose of the surplus.   Perhaps the products must be transported and processed before they can be utilized, so facilities to serve these functions must be developed.   One can trace endlessly the consequences of introducing such a trait, since the whole interrelated socio-cultural system is eventually affected.

Major disturbances in the equilibrium of a system are seldom produced by the introduction of one or two isolated traits.   This is not because their introduction couldn't produce the disturbances. Rather, it is because the culture that is willing to accept one new trait is usually willing to accept others at the same time.   The total effect is a complex pattern of changing functions and structures like the wave pattern produced by scattering a handful of stones into a small pond.   The social problems attending the diffusion of alien traits into a relatively stable system are associated with the adjustments that must be made to gain a new equilibrium.   The very nature of the social system developed through the establishment of patterned functions and relationships is such that new demands placed upon it cannot be instantaneously met.   There is a period of lag in which the differences between desired conditions and existing conditions are recognized by the group as social problems.   These problems may become exceedingly critical if the group becomes so disorganized that traditional methods of meeting crises cooperatively cannot be utilized. Similarly, the development of problem conditions for which there is no traditional guide in the cultural history of the group may retard the process of adjustment, especially if the group culture heavily stresses dependence upon traditionalism.

Adjustment is a necessary consequence of culture diffusion, but problems of a catastrophic nature are not.   The adoption of new traits by a culture group may well solve more problems than are created by the introduction and, in fact, may spell the difference between group survival and extinction.   It must be remembered that only through cultural adaptation have human societies been able to meet the demands of varying environmental circumstances. Adjustments frequently are painful, but the failure to make them in the face of altered conditions may prove fatal.

TOWARD SOLVING CULTURAL CONTACT PROBLEMS

To admit the inevitability of adjustment problems as a consequence of cultural contacts is not to say that nothing can be done to lessen their severity. In fact, those who subscribe to such a pessimistic view should, by the same reasoning, reject hygienic and medical techniques because pathology and death are inevitable consequences of human existence.

There are several conceivable approaches to the prevention and solution of cultural contact problems. One of the more obvious possibilities, of course, is to restrict the contacts themselves. At first glance, this proposal may seem to be of the same order as King Canute's legendary command for the ocean to cease its motions. Yet it is one of the more common proposals and has frequently been implemented in varying degrees. Contact restrictions may range from a censorship of "undesirable" alien ideas, either in oral or written form, to attempts at complete prevention of social and cultural contacts with outside groups.[7] The erection of barriers to contact may be relatively effective in the securing of immediate objectives. The greatest potential danger in a restrictive policy is that ideas, skills, and techniques that might aid the society in meeting changing conditions are likely to be excluded no matter how careful the selection of the culture traits that are allowed to pass. It is extremely doubtful that any society of limited numbers can create within itself the necessary techniques for dealing with a rapidly changing and threatening environment.

A second approach to the prevention of cultural contact problems is to control the cultural environment. Man has been relatively suc-

[7] Contemporaneously the so-called "Iron Curtain" of communist Europe marks the boundary of a culture area where deliberate contact restrictions have been imposed, presumably in the attempt to protect the developing system from disruptive influences until it has achieved a relative stability.

cessful, to judge by his survival and numerical increase, in dealing with the physical environment, although it is quite conceivable that even those conditions could change with sufficient rapidity to extinguish human life. The major current threats to survival are cultural in nature. Human history is replete with examples of culture groups that have considered the possibility of establishing a relative cultural uniformity in order to remove such threats. Some have attempted to impose their own system through conquest. Others, more peaceable but no less determined, have resorted to persuasive proselytizing. Their successes have varied widely in extent, but none has come even close to achieving the elimination of major cultural differences throughout the world. Incomplete success in the past, however, offers no positive warrant of continued failure in the future. Improvements in communication and transportation—not to mention war material—have been so great during the industrial era that these means of alleviating problems attributable to major culture differences must still be considered as a possibility. But even among those who agree on the approach, there are wide disagreements as to what patterns the cultural uniformity should take—a problem itself based upon cultural differences.

However effective they may prove in the future, neither isolation nor complete domination by one culture appears to offer a feasible approach to preventing problems arising from cultural contact at the present time. The spread of industrialism has increased intercultural contacts not only because it has provided more efficient means of communication but more especially because of the interdependent nature of industrial society. Yet the formation of a tighter web of relationships does not seem to have made more generally acceptable the imposition of any single culture pattern by a dominant group. Quite possibly a considerable cultural uniformity may evolve as a natural consequence of the widespread adoption of industrial technology, but this is yet to be demonstrated since a large part of the world has not made the transition.

The expectation of continued cultural differences and contacts means that social problems stemming from them can also be anticipated for some time in the future. It would be misleading to suggest that clear-cut solutions to these problems exist, but the preceding analyses do pose the possibility of an approach that is neither isolationist nor imperialistic in nature. It is an approach geared to change rather than, as in the case of the other approaches, being dependent upon restricting change. The following are prerequisite steps to the implementation of this approach:

First, and basic, those concerned with the prevention or solution of relational problems must understand the nature of culture and how it is related to the behavior of individuals and societies.

Second, not only must the general principles of culture be known but also the content of specific cultures whose contacts produce serious problems. The fallacy of approaching the problems from any single direction should be apparent. No one culture provides in itself all that is necessary to the understanding of another. The necessary understanding for effective analysis and action requires a knowledge of all culture groups that figure in the problem situation. Until there exists a sympathy (in the projective rather than the compassionate sense) for the members of a culture group, no claim can be laid to the type of comprehension that must be had if solutions are to be achieved through this approach.

Third, the processes of socio-cultural change resulting from the introduction of new culture traits must be observed and interpreted as a constant guide to action. There must be the realization that major changes in social structure and function are never the products of pure whimsy but the adjustment of a system to new demands placed upon it. The taking of appropriate action implies some anticipation of future developments, a venturesome task considering the complexities of any socio-cultural system. But it must also be considered that all planning involves some prediction. Thus, the question reduces itself to what shall serve as the basis for predictions and planning. Here it is proposed that the socio-cultural sciences, even in their present stage of development, provide a better source of knowledge for effective understanding than any previously available.[8]

It is realized that the provision of a foundation for an approach to the solution of problems of cultural contact, is by no means equivalent

---

[8] For evidence in support of this position, see Edward H. Spicer (ed.), *Human Problems in Technological Change: A Casebook* (New York: Russell Sage Foundation, 1952) and Alexander H. Leighton, *Human Relations in a Changing World* (Dutton, 1949).

to the presentation of solutions themselves. Nor should the bald fact be ignored that there are types of cultural contact problems which this approach is not likely to solve. There are incompatible cultures whose differences are not to be bridged simply by mutual understanding, however strongly some may feel that understanding automatically leads to harmonious relations. Countering those cultures that value individual freedom are those that would completely subjugate the individual to the social structure; in opposition to those that value government by popular consent are those that favor rule by the oligarchic elite; some glorify technological achievement while others disdain it; some honor peace, while others reverence war. Finally, whereas some groups seek harmony through compromise, there are others that admit of no compromise, that wholeheartedly subscribe to the view that those who do not act as they act, believe as they believe, live as they live cannot and should not be tolerated. Such aggressive ethnocentrism is not uncommon, and it excludes the possibilities of peaceful relations short of submission.

Current limitations of information and skills do not invalidate the claim that many problems arising from cultural contacts can be successfully dealt with by utilizing available scientifically-derived knowledge. The very foundation stone of social science is the premise that human behavior can be rationally explained and, within limits, predicted and controlled. At the risk of repetition, it should be emphasized that the question of whether action should or should not be taken is largely academic. If social problems are serious enough, ameliorative action *will* be taken. The major decisions, and this is especially true of cultural contact problems, are those of taking appropriate action at the favorable time to secure the desired ends.

Study Questions

1. What evidence supports the author's belief that problems of cultural contact have increased numerically in the twentieth century?

2. What techniques of socialization are used in our culture? How might they affect an individual's adaptation to a different culture?

3. What cultural and social factors in our society contribute to easy adaptation to a different culture? What factors make adaptation difficult?

4. In what respects are social classes and culture sub-groups similar? In what respects are they different?

5. How are the following concepts distinguished from one another? Acculturation, assimilation, amalgamation, socialization.

6. What conditions might make assimilation of a culture group easier than the assimilation of an individual separated from the group?

7. Is it possible for a numerical minority to assimilate a majority?   If so, give the necessary conditions and cite examples.

8. Under what conditions is social conflict likely to arise from cultural misunderstandings?

9. What types of cultural innovations are most likely to be resisted by a group? Why?

10. What are the advantages and disadvantages of the various approaches to the prevention and solution of cultural contact problems discussed in the chapter?

Selected References

Bowers, David F. (ed.), *Foreign Influences in American Life* (Princeton University Press, 1944).   Essays and critical bibliographies.   Various authors discuss foreign elements affecting American social life, politics, art, literature, and other aspects of the culture.

Buaken, Michael, *I Have Lived with the American People* (Caldwell, Idaho: The Caxton Printers, Ltd., 1948).   Account of a Filipino's adjustment to American life, assessing both discriminatory treatment and generosity.

Herskovits, M. J., *Acculturation: The Study of Culture Contact* (New York: J. J. Augustin, 1938).   A book concerned more with problems of studying acculturation than with problems of culture contact.

Kardiner, Abram, and Lionel Ovesey, *The Mark of Oppression. A Psychosocial Study of the American Negro* (Norton, 1951).   Study is concerned with racial minority but has direct implications for cultural minority groups.

Leighton, Alexander H., *Human Relations in a Changing World* (Dutton, 1949).   Thoughtful discussion of the implications of applied social science to intercultural relations problems.

Park, R. E., "Human Migration and Marginal Man," *American Journal of Sociology*, xxxiii (May, 1928), 881–893.   An early but discerning treatment of cultural marginalism, its conditions and consequences.

Sone, Monica, *Nisei Daughter* (Little, Brown, 1953).   An entertaining description of Japanese-American life in the United States.   Includes experiences on visit to Japan.

Spicer, Edward H. (ed.), *Human Problems in Technological Change.* A
    Casebook (Russell Sage Foundation, 1952). A unique collection of
    analyzed cases illustrating problems produced in various societies by
    cultural innovations.
Stonequist, Everett V., *The Marginal Man* (Scribner, 1937). A more
    extensive treatment of cultural and social marginalism and its effects
    upon personality.
Tuck, Ruth D., *Not with the Fist* (Harcourt, Brace, 1946). Mexican-
    Americans in a Southwest city. Treats of problems of acculturation
    and assimilation.

17

Problems of International Relations

In the second half of the twentieth century, citizens in all parts of the world are appalled by the number, the magnitude, and the complexity of the international problems with which they and their fellows are confronted. Each day the morning paper features the difficulties that arise in the dealings of one nation with another, and the weekly news magazines scarcely have space in which to summarize the more important of the happenings. Radio and television do their share to bring international problems into the living rooms, the kitchens, and the bedrooms of people in the United States, and various media of communication serve a comparable purpose in the other countries of the world. In these days of rapid means of communication and transportation, rare is the person who can ignore the problems of war and the rumors of war, the difficulties confronting statesmen in their conduct of international affairs, the obstacles in the way of successful international organization.

WAR

War is a social institution. It is not an end in itself (as the family, industry, the state or religion) but is basically predatory. It thrives on the destruction and maiming of the outsider, as well as, to a limited extent, on those inside the institution. It employs violence, fraud, intimidation, destruction—in fact, all the available means to accomplish its purpose. War is a form of intergroup conflict highly organized, which stems from the very character of the groups that engage in it. It is usually the culmination of prolonged tension between two or more nations.

Within a year after the end of World War II in Europe and Asia, portentous, war-like events already overshadowed the talk of peace. Renewed rioting in India, mobilization for full-scale civil war in China and Palestine, and a drastic deterioration of relations between Soviet Russia and the Western powers focused attention on underlying tensions in the unstable postwar world. The killing of the American airmen flying over Yugoslavia's territory aroused grave concern in the United States and Britain.

These were but a few of the symptoms of the war mentality of the war-weary world. The subsequent years have only accelerated the tempo of "small wars" and of the various ramifications of the "cold war." A terrible climax came with the Korean "police action" and the documented atrocities, not to speak of the blood-letting communist-sponsored wars carried on in Southeast Asia. Why is it that, in spite of all the earnest prayers of millions of people for peace—and the persistent insistence of Soviet Russia and her satellites that all their governments want is "peace, peace, peace"—we are involved in a series of declared and undeclared wars?

The Causes of War

The search for some reasonable answer to the above question is and will continue to be one of the chief preoccupations of mankind. Books and articles, libraries of them, try to pin down the causes of the outbreaks of war between nations and within nations. Probably the most popular and traditional approach is that which views war from the standpoint of the historian, or as an ethical problem. For instance, Roman Catholicism maintains the concept of the "just war," and conservative Protestantism retains the emphasis on sinful nature of man. The legalist, on the other hand, tries to define the circumstances under which resort to war is legitimate and the activities that are legitimate during war. Following World War I, especially, efforts were made to outlaw war and to define it by establishing the fact of aggression (the Draft Treaty of Mutual Assistance of 1923, the Geneva Protocol of 1924, and the Kellogg-Briand Pact of 1928).

Many philosophical concepts of war are in existence. According to Machiavelli and Hobbes war is implicit in the nature of man and society. Hegel believed that war is an instrument of a universal historical plan. Henry von Treitschke's theories expounding the power of the state have been of tremendous importance due to their acceptance of the aggressive German elements. To him, the state is an end in itself and its value lies in its value of national unity and might. "Might is at once the supreme right; the dispute as to what is right is decided by the arbitrament of war."

During the nineteenth century new "scientific" arguments were introduced emphasizing and justifying war. Doctrines were propounded preaching that social progress in general, over and above that of any particular nation or race, is promoted by war. The principle of natural selection was applied to the struggle of nations on the analogy of the struggle of individual and of species. This overextended analogy is often referred to as the Neo-Darwinian theory of social conflict and struggle. It became associated with the doctrine of race differences and with the assumption that war is a necessary factor in the origin and preservation of the state and society.

Following World War I, international conflicts were generally attributed to economic causes; much was heard about the "have" and "have-not" nations, especially the *Lebensraum* cries of Hitler and Mussolini. Others discovered that war does not pay and hence should not be carried on.

Although there is lack of a clear-cut socialist doctrine of war, much has been said about the connection between war and class struggle, and in condemnation of modern wars as imperialistic. It is true that particular groups or organizations can get economic advantages from war through selling war supplies, by securing promotions in the military profession, or from charging for various services essential to the conduct of war; but it is not known how far these economic motives are intermingled with the other elements promoting war. The Marxian theory, as reinterpretated by Lenin, claims that the "imperialist" war is the result of the steady pressure exerted by capitalists for colonial, commercial, and financial expansion because of a declining internal market and an increase of productive capacity of the capitalist system; but the historical evidence shows that the "capitalists" have often been willing instruments of a politically motivated imperialism rather than the hidden promoters of diplomatic or militarist expansion. Yet the dominant Soviet theory still emphasizes the horrors of "imperialism" and maintains that the only solution to the ever-widening cycle of wars is the "dictatorship of the proletariat . . . over the bourgeoise; a rule enjoying the sympathy of the laboring and exploited masses." [1] It is only fair to admit, however, that a considerable group of socialist thinkers are definitely anti-militaristic; they, too, try to promote the idea that the general strike should be used to prevent war and that national defense is unjustified.

Bernard claims that the most frequent "ideologically sanctioned wars are now the political ones, waged in defense of a class, a political philosophy, a social program, or a popular economic philosophy. . . ." [2] In this respect, the movement that brought Fascism to power in Italy and Nazism in Germany shows what a powerful social force a warlike ideology can become. In fact, politics during the two decades between the two world wars were characterized by the conflict between the democratic and the Nazi-fascist-communist ideologies (a conflict resembling the bloody struggle between the Catholics and Protestants in the sixteenth century). All of these ideologies stood for rearmament, violence, no compromise, unrestricted sovereignty, and a carefully organized party as the supreme organ of government and the instrument of internal dictatorship and international dominance. The activities of these totalitarian states, in turn, caused the democracies by instituting many controls over economic and social life and by putting their economies on a defense basis to become military or semi-military states.

Political and geographical theories of war put the emphasis on the state and its tendency to expand and grow. Although it is not always apparent on the surface, all these "geopolitical" plans are built on a political theory of war as a major premise. They assume that a sys-

---

[1] Joseph Stalin, *Foundations of Leninism* (New York: International Publishers, 1939), p. 53.
[2] L. L. Bernard, *War and Its Causes* (Holt, 1944), p. 55.

tem of autarchy, *Lebensraum*, pan-regions, "Heartland," can lead to world domination and the solution of the particularistic national problems.

Along with the other thinkers bothered with the ever-recurrent problem of war, the psychologist also has made his addition to the numerous theories, by stressing the importance of aggressive dispositions in the individual. The psychologist's emphasis upon the fundamental drives of aggression, frustration, psycho-pathological conditions, national neurosis, animism, displacement, or the projection of conscience, is merely a claim that fighting is a fundamental tendency in human beings: that human nature forever will make mankind fight.

These numerous theories on war may be summarized into three categories: (1) the philosophies accenting the moral problems of war; (2) the legal approaches; and (3) the theories of social scientists who deal with war, as empirically as possible, by seeking to learn its causes. Most social scientists overemphasize the factors with which their particular science or approach is concerned, whether it is psychology, sociology, economics, politics, geography, or anthropology.

Sociological Aspects of War

Since we are basically concerned with the sociological aspects of this problem, we must emphasize that wars are likely to be due to a multiplicity of causes, more properly to a variety of conditions rather than to any specific cause. Furthermore, wars can be analyzed most profitably by thinking of them in terms of the special maladjustments which threaten the breakdown of a given society. One should particularly avoid discussing the problem of war in terms of legalistic judgments and pronouncements. For example, according to American terminology, we could not have decided whether we were at war with Hitler between 1939 and Pearl Harbor because, according to our constitution and legalistic reasoning, wars must be declared. However, Japan and Germany had been carrying on an "undeclared" war. We were confused by the fiction of the American Neutrality Act, although President Roosevelt ordered the shooting of the Nazi submarines "on sight"; we were even more puzzled about the "non-legal" aspects of the war—the psychological, moral, and economic warfare. This confusion greatly perplexed America's public mind. Later, in 1946, Tito's Yugoslavian airmen deliberately shot down American planes although we were at peace with this member of the United Nations. The U.S.S.R. has been carrying on an "undeclared war" against the United States, sometimes even downing planes and shooting American soldiers—and yet we have been legally at peace with each other.[3]

War as a transitional phenomenon. When analyzing war, sociologically, we must remember that (as pointed out by Comte) the transition from one social order to another has always been accompanied by periods of definite unrest, each a sort of interregnum of anarchy, which may last for several generations. No one alive today can escape the realization that we are living through one of the greatest crises of history. The long-heralded world revolution has broken upon us. This revolution is a reconstruction of the political order of Europe and consequently of Asia and Africa. As usual, in cases where revolutions are the methods of change, the old political and social systems of the world have proved grossly inadequate for the further development of economic and social life.

Sovereignty and the changing world order. Sovereignty is the supreme power of the state over its territory, and it is claimed by some seventy political organizations in the contemporary world. They are the authorities that negotiate treaties, submit or refuse to submit to negotiations in international disputes, initiate or conclude wars, and enforce laws. Although we are told that the age of absolute national sovereignty is passing, due to the modern means of communication, actually states are now more reluctant than ever to renounce their sovereignty. On the one hand, the mass of the people in most nations regard war with abhorrence; and on the other hand, they oppose, or it is claimed that they oppose, any surrender of national sovereignty. Those who favor a strong international government with police power abhor war and are willing to modify national sovereignty. The con-

---

[3] We have been passing through a series of "undeclared wars" utilizing Trojan horses, spies, traitors, "fifth columns," treachery, espionage, and economic and psychological warfare, although these methods are not classified, in international law, as acts of war. For their descriptions, see William J. Donovan and Joseph S. Roucek, "Secret Movements, Espionage, and Treachery," in T. V. Kalijarvi and Associates, *Modern World Politics* (Crowell, 1953), pp. 308–330.

temporary period is one of anarchy wherein all values are in a state of flux, contradicting and conflicting with one another. This anarchy is particularly obvious in international relations.

The War of Ideologies

The anarchy mentioned above is particularly evident when two or more societies with different systems of values come into direct and continued contact. Note, for example, the case of the relationship of the U.S.S.R. and the United States. In it appears to be the very depth of irreconcilable social conflict, producing a universal, all-pervading "war of ideas."

In earlier years, the propaganda battles of Goebbels were not merely far-fetched, airy dialectics. From the hour of the Berlin-directed assassination of Chancellor Dollfuss to the concluding days of World War II, Berlin was occupied with war; its conclusion was the disappearance of the Nazi Germany from the map of Europe. The battle was inaugurated by an international propaganda assault. The "mental armament" first used to defend a Germany without military defense, later launched its gangster offensive down the Danube and eventually against the rest of the world. The Third Reich, and today Russia, are the clearest example of the connection between the ideological battle and international violence. They produced in the end the most devastating results. This battle of ideological differences may also be viewed from another angle. Consider the basic difference between American politics and politics as propounded and practiced in the U.S.S.R. The main function of politics, in a democracy such as ours, is to equalize and adjust, in useful compromises, all forms of social activity. But if all creative forces of human life are in crisis, politics cannot produce anything acceptable and stable; hence, they too, are in a critical stage. The resulting social uncertainties produce regimes that are anything but peaceful—regimes that are actually war, additional symptoms of our critical times.

If, in the old sense, politics means civic life, in modern dictatorships, it signifies a war mentality. The case goes far beyond the externals of military organizations, drill, banners, uniforms, parades, salutes, leaders, war-orders and crises, challenges, and defiances.

Theirs is the system of permanent mobilization. It is the life of a war-footing.

When war breaks out a democratic people announces that politics are adjourned and the party system is suspended for the duration of the crisis. The modern dictatorships have discarded the party systems altogether. In the stress of war the democracies abdicate their basic liberties. Dictatorships have as their basic principle the destruction of the historic liberties of the individual. In wartime the democracies acquiesce in what is virtually a suspension of sovereign law, and the national interest becomes the sole criterion of official conduct, as long as the enemy is at the gate. In the autocratic states the national interest as interpreted by the leader is at *all* times the sole criterion. He rules by decree. In peace the democracy spends as much as it can afford; in war it spends whatever is called for. In the autocratic state, popular sacrifice is continuously on a war footing. Privation under this system becomes *ipso facto* heroic, as it does in wartime with free people.

It is no accident that the dictatorships use a militaristic vocabulary to describe actions which in free countries are regarded as peaceful activities. Democracies stimulate wheat-growing by bounties and tariffs, but dictatorships fight the "Battle of Wheat." Democracies build tractor factories but dictatorships hurl their "shock brigades" into the trenches against the enemy within and outside the gates. A state under dictatorship is always fighting a civil war.

Modern autocracy, therefore, is a permanent war system. It is basically an armed camp. It has the singleness of purpose, the swift efficiency, the crisp discipline of the military method, geared to the aims of the dictatorship. The participants who are fighting for the mastery are drawn from the same armory, their doctrines are variations of the same theme, and they go forth to battle singing the same tune with slightly different words. Their weapons are the coercive, warlike doctrines of the life and labor of mankind. Their doctrines presuppose that disorder and misery can be overcome by more and more warlike measures. Their promise is that through the war power of the State men can be made happy.

In the name of progress, men who call themselves communists, socialists, fascists, nationalists, progressives, and even liberals, have been holding that government with its instruments of war must, by telling the people how they shall live, direct the course of civilization and fix the shape of things to come. This is the dogma which all the prevailing dogmas presuppose. Although despotism is no novelty in human affairs, probably at no time in twenty-five hundred years has any Western government claimed for itself a jurisdiction over men's lives comparable with that which has been officially attempted in the totalitarian states. This governmental coercion has created the very chaos it purported to conquer. The consequence of collectivism is regimentation, censorship, despotism, and impoverishment, all tending to militarism and finally to war.

Militarism of social processes is itself a cause as well as a result of social disorganization. It is inherent in the striving of contemporary authoritarian systems to achieve internal stability, resembling a state of siege, by the determined policies that unsettle the established order surrounding them. These contradictions are paradoxes indicating that war is not merely an outgrowth of the ever-accelerating changes in our social institutions. It results not only from social causes, but also is produced by man's irrationality. Modern man is frequently a genius in dealing with the physical and external world, but often a driveling idiot in dealing with himself and in his relations with his fellow men.

Disruption of social equilibrium. Our war crises can also be traced to the disruption of the social equilibrium. Man, confused by numberless conflicting ideologies appealing to him, is not merely unable to determine the sense of striving and the sense of direction of his definite social goals; he has also lost the cultural orientation that rests on a certain balance of material and spiritual values and he has lost the sense of an obligation to something not himself.

In the nineteenth century, theorists of violence, such as Nietzsche and George Sorel, created among many ideologists a state of mind hostile to everything that for two thousand years had been the human ideal. In the doctrines of violence, common to the extremists of the right and left, war has a fertile ground fostered by the common assumption that man is sovereign in his spiritual values and can refuse to accept any supernatural (or shall we call it "divine") ideology of life. Hence, no rules are imposed on him in his warfare on others, and war may, in fact, become an end in itself.

The ideology of capitalistic nationalism. Related to this trend is an ideological over-emphasis on the acquisition of material goods as the source of happiness—of the kind so well described in Lynd's *Middletown in Transition.* In our economic system, based on competition and the insistence that any reasonable person must strive for the ever-growing consumption of the ever-increasing type of goods, we have another kind of warfare. It permeates all spheres of international and national life and is inseparably connected with our modern culture.

This type of "business ideology" shades into the war mentality of those who believe in the creation of a perfect world by proletarian action; who believe that a new golden age will dawn for mankind after a period of necessary violence, be it revolution or war. Because of their particular class or race ideologies, men cut one another's throats, asphyxiate one another, and willingly undergo the most horrible torments.

We can only reach the tragic conclusion that war is a cause as well as a result of the transitory state of all cultural patterns.

Related to this is our ideological insistence that the ever-accelerated tempo of daily life, speeded up by the ever-growing number of inventions (the fastness with which we can shoot, jump, travel, hear, and see, *farther* and particularly *faster*) is real "progress." This, in turn, disrupts the most stable elements of our culture—the concepts of human personality, the institutions, the doctrines, and social hierarchies.

The Battle of Business

Another kind of conflict is carried on in the economic world, for continuous conflict characterizes the commercial front. Although war interrupts free communication and trade among the nations, we are also familiar with the slogan that "trade follows the flag." All too often commercial interests have welcomed an alliance with the military in order to push the sales of home industries, collect debts from recalcitrant, backward people, and drive out rival tradesmen belonging to other nations.

Even though the Marxians (excluding Marx) have overstressed the economic factors, insisting that all modern wars have been due to the existence of capitalism, it must be admitted some economic advantages are derived from war. The most obvious is the looting of the vanquished. Wars have also been waged to expel the occupants of a given area so that it could be permanently occupied by the victors. There are also economic advantages derived from the possession of such populated regions as Hong Kong or the Philippine Islands. Of primary importance in this respect is the ability of the ideologists to indoctrinate their followers with certain forms of reasoning. For instance, in addition to the Nazis, who claimed to represent a "have-not" nation, the Italian fascists and Japanese imperialists used similar claims. What these leaders really wanted was empires that they could entirely exploit for their exclusive benefit, and they supported their demands with the argument that abundant natural resources were necessary for their prosperity and happiness.

PROBLEMS OF INTERNATIONAL ORGANIZATION

Each state claims a monopoly of the use of force for the resolution of fractional-tensional situations within its boundaries; but for the control of force among states, no one state is entirely adequate. The world is now struggling with the problem of how to develop a social organization capable of exercising such control. The pace of modern technology, and such weapons as the long-distance rocket, guided missiles, and the hydrogen bomb have made the problem of the utmost urgency.

The dream world of universal peace imposed by force has had a long and largely honorable history. Although the prototype existed in such early alliances as the Greek Achaean League, international policing prior to the nineteenth century flourished chiefly in the realm of ideas. It was part of the Great Design of Henry IV of France and his Minister Sully. Rousseau included it in his *Project for Perpetual*

Peace. Mild William Penn was its advocate, as was Abbé de Saint Pierre. But not until 1815, when the reactionary genius of Prince Metternich produced what has accurately been called the "Unholy Alliance" was international policing given the test of action. The victorious powers of Russia, Prussia, and Austria got together and kept the peace by force. They kept the "peace" of east-central Europe for a few decades—and with it the *status quo.* Inasmuch as keeping the imperial *status quo* meant squelching every liberal chick in the egg, the Alliance eventually could not stand against the rise of liberal fervor in Europe. In 1848 both Italy and France kicked over the traces; revolt spread to Austria and Germany, and Prince Metternich, for 33 years the master mind of the Alliance, had to flee from his country. The Unholy Alliance was dead, but its influence on the minds of men lived on. This despotic use of international force by the club of contented war-winners gave the whole idea of international police an unsavory aura which lasted well into the twentieth century.

Meanwhile, the British Navy, with the help of France, the United States, and other countries, began to maintain a world patrol on its own. In Mexico, Chile, and Argentina, at Navarino in Greece, at Dulcigno on the Adriatic, and at Peking during the Boxer Rebellion, against the Barbary pirates and the pirates of the Far East, the British and others used force or the threat of force to keep peace. The peace thus kept involved in each case the national interests of the intervening powers, and the actions were against groups too weak to fight back. But such an impromptu and largely naval police force could not prevent a major conflict. The big explosion was World War I.

Out of the caterpillar of war, through the cocoon of Versailles was hatched that beautiful butterfly, the League of Nations. Ardent apologists for the League—which still existed in form up to 1946—insisted that its prime purpose was not to stop wars once they were at the boiling point, but rather to promote international cooperation. "A place for talk" is the way League-loving Sir John Fischer Williams described it.

The Weakness of the League of Nations

There is no doubt that the League was sold to the people of the world—and turned down by the United States Senate—largely on the basis of Article 16 of the Covenant, which clearly contemplated the prevention of war by the use of military force. The sorry failure of the League to employ force made it a laughing stock long before World War II. The use of military power was not mandatory, under Article 16, and in any case no written words in the document could have forced the member nations to call out their armies and navies to stop aggression. The League of Nations refused to use its teeth simply because the two member nations that dominated it had no will to use them. Those nations were Great Britain and France. European politicians came to believe that the League was no more than an alternate tool of the French and British balance of power—a belief that was confirmed when the ignoble Hoare-Laval pact, by giving Mussolini a free hand in Ethiopia, put an effective end to the League's lone effort to apply not military but merely economic force against the aggressor.

International Police Schemes

Roughly speaking, international police schemes are of three types. First there is the proposal for a police force made up extensively of national military units which would take orders directly from an international boss, or indirectly from their own national governments acting as agents for the international boss. This is the type incorporated in the United Nations organization, and particularly in the provisions regarding the Security Council. The Council has the power to investigate disputes by amicable means. In case the Council fails to bring about a peaceful solution, it may rule that a threat to peace exists, call out an armed force, and take forcible means to preserve peace. This is to be done through the Military Staff Committee on which only the "Big Five" powers are represented. But difficulty is found in the stipulation that provides that forcible measures can be taken only by unanimous vote of the Council. Thus by a negative vote any of the Big Five can prevent the Security Council from taking any action against itself or against any other state.

A second net of proposals would provide for a truly international police force, recruited or drafted from different nations and owing allegiance, in theory, to none. Obviously, it would have to be Samson-strong or its establishment would have to be linked with a program of general national disarmament.

The third group of proposals represents a combination of the two preceding ideas. There would be an international force, supplemented by national armies and navies, as reserves. This type was to have been used by the United Nations.

The Weakness of the United Nations

Without going into the details of the United Nations charter, which is accessible to everyone, let us consider its basic nature. The union is one of states. Each of them retains its absolute national sovereignty and total political independence. All past history shows that war is the ultimate outcome of relations among states of equal sovereignty that exercise unrestricted sovereign power—regardless of pacts for international order and collective security, non-aggression, mediation, or arbitration, or any organizations formed to facilitate pacific settlement of disputes and conflicts.

One fundamental weakness of the Charter lies in the right of any one of the Great Powers to veto any formal investigations or action by the Council. Obviously, no state is likely to vote against its own interests; hence, the unanimous vote of these permanent members required on any issue before action can be taken will not be forthcoming if the decision will adversely affect one of them. Thus the Charter continues the conflict between national self-determination and the total economic interdependence of the world.

The International Control of Atomic Energy

The fate of Hiroshima and Nagasaki has brought into startling relief the monstrous dangers humanity is facing unless it speedily finds a road to permanent peace. Since the explosion of the atomic bomb and the announcement of hydrogen power, a countless number of people have risen to warn of the annihilation with which mankind is threatened unless man's outlook on international relations catches up with potentially all-destructive scientific progress. Not only is a warning sounded by educational leaders, such as former President Hutchins of Chicago; the scientists themselves are gravely alarmed. The latter resemble Frankensteins viewing their own creations. Like the rest of their fellowmen, very few of them have hitherto taken an active interest in world affairs. Now they suddenly perceive that human moral progress has not kept up with the mechanical aspects of scientific progress, with the result that the scientific discoveries are surely threatening the undoing of the human race.

Many proposals have been made for the international control of atomic power. In discussing these proposals, we accept the premise that atomic and hydrogen power are weapons of unprecedented potentialities, that for the time being no effective technological defense against them will be found, and that, sooner or later, all major countries will be in possession of them. These facts have convinced many that some sort of international regulation of atomic energy is absolutely necessary. These proposals can be grouped under two headings: first, "outlawing" the bomb, a thoroughly unrealistic solution until war itself is successfully outlawed; and second, renouncing the development of atomic energy altogether, another unrealistic proposal as no nation can be sure that "others" have done their "renouncing." In this respect, possibly the strongest element influencing the decisions of the aggressor nations will always be the fear of reprisals by those attacked or their allies.

These two courses having been dismissed, what alternatives remain? Some believe that there should be no production, manufacture, or stockpiling of potentially explosive fissionable materials—except under effective international supervision and control. Doubtless all agree that there should be full realization of the scientific and industrial potentialities of atomic fission for peaceful purposes. But inasmuch as no nation will give up its private and secret activities, the only remaining solution would seem to be international control by an international organization. A world state, according to most proposals, would be superimposed upon the existing states. The individual states would be deprived of their foreign policy and their armed force.

But it should be noted that differences in economic interests, government structures, and domestic ideologies are precisely among the most potent weapons and causes of war. In short, world federation, international government, and an international police force could be a solution to these basic problems. But a world federation will not be established overnight; and international atomic control cannot be called into being by the touch of a wand. It must be built up little by little and gather momentum as it proceeds.

Although there is no immediate political solution to the atomic problem, it does not necessarily follow that a third world war is inevitable. A panic may be produced by the steady repetition of the slogan: "time is running out." We are told constantly that we have only a few days or a few months or a few years to reorganize the world.

What Can Be Done to Avoid a New Cataclysm?

As 1954 dawned, new hope filled the hearts of men. A mighty vision was set before a war-weary world—the vision of beating atomic swords into atomic ploughshares. A man of peace—though a soldier by profession—saw the silver lining behind the dark, mushroom-shaped cloud that had hung ominously over the world for seven years. President Eisenhower told the people of the world that there was an alternative to atomic war. The alternative was atomic peace, nuclear construction, instead of nuclear destruction, world peace instead of a world in pieces.

The historic atoms-for-peace proposal was made by President Eisenhower in a dramatic appearance before the General Assembly in New York on December 8, 1953. The President's plan was—and that's part of its greatness—essentially simple. It called for the creation of an atomic energy agency under the supervision of the United Nations. Nations possessing atomic fuel would contribute part of their supply to this agency "to serve the peaceful pursuits of mankind."

Before an audience tense with expectations the President discussed what he called "the awful arithmetic of the atom bomb." He disclosed to the world that "atomic bombs today are more than 25 times as powerful as the weapons with which the atomic age dawned." (The first A-bomb, exploded in 1945, carried the equivalent of 20,000 tons of TNT.) Moreover, the President said, there are now hydrogen weapons "in the ranges of millions of tons of TNT equivalent." The stockpile of the United States at present, he went on, "exceeds by many times the explosive equivalent of the total of all bombs and all shells that came from every plane and every gun in every theater of war through all the years of World War II." This stockpile, he said, is increasing daily, but, he added, "the dread secret and the fearful engines of atomic might are not ours alone." He pointed out that in addition to "our friends and allies," Britain and Canada, "the secret is also known to the Soviet Union." The President of the United States served notice that "should an atomic attack be launched against the United States, our reactions would be swift and resolute." He warned that "such an aggressor's land would be laid waste," but added "all this, while fact, is not the true expression of the purpose and the hope of the United States." He continued—and this was one of the most moving passages in his eloquent and memorable speech: "To pause there would be to confirm the hopeless finality of a belief that two atomic colossi are doomed malevolently to eye each other indefinitely across a trembling world." What are America's goals? The President proposed an international atomic energy agency, to be created under the United Nations. Nations possessing stockpiles of atomic fuel would contribute part of their supply to this agency, as previously stated.

The new plan did not mean the abandonment of the United States' plan for international control of atomic energy—a plan for foolproof guarantees against cheating. What the President did was to sidestep the plan for the time being. It was hoped that if agreement with Soviet Russia could be reached on constructive uses of atomic energy, the way would be paved for an agreement on outlawing its destructive uses. Throughout the free world, including even the so-called "neutral" countries, Eisenhower's address was enthusiastically acclaimed as a practical means toward easing world tensions. After some hedging the Kremlin said that it would join in considering the proposal, but asked that the nations involved also take up the question of outlawing the atomic and hydrogen bombs, as well as "other weapons of mass annihilation," under "strict international control." Americans greeted the Soviet's reply hopefully, but cautiously.

Even the hopes produced by President Eisenhower's proposal indicate that, in the final analysis, in the immediate future, in our system of national states and the supremacy of three major powers, peace will have to be preserved by varying means of day-to-day foreign policy. These are hard facts which all men who like the safe and solid sound of the phrase "international government" will have to face for the time being.

As a nation, we are woefully ignorant of world affairs and realities. Our press is the freest and best informed in the world, but our ignorance of the history, geography, economics, institutions, languages, and customs of the rest of the world remains. For example, generation after generation of our youth have been brought up in ignorance of the Slavic world, although both world wars started directly there. Only our direct participation in World War II gave us our present international interest. Previously, the stress in American education had been toward nationalistic isolationism. Subjects with an international content, such as geography, modern history, world economics, foreign languages, have languished in favor of bread-and-butter subjects, the "social sciences," and "good citizenship," the content of which usually was narrowed and restricted to domestic affairs. In the midst of education becoming more isolationist in form, came the attack on Pearl Harbor. After our entrance into the war, desperate measures were taken to remedy the gaps in our education in international subjects. Army-sponsored language courses and area studies introduced by numerous institutions of higher learning were but a few steps taken in the right direction. That the situation worries representative educators had been evident in recent years.

The diversity of opinions that exist on the possible solution of the problems of war and international organizations makes it obvious that sociology (or the social sciences) has no ready-made answer. We may never be able to find the final answer since the values that men hold subjectively on this problem are themselves social facts that the sociologist must take into account, and they vary. The utilization of all available knowledge is essential, while emotion, in the process of reasoning, must be reduced to its lowest point. The substitute for war must give the same satisfaction to a state that war promises to give.

Study Questions

1. Outline the historical and ethical approaches to war.
2. What are the main philosophical and scientific concepts of war?
3. What are the allegedly "scientific" concepts of war?
4. Restate the main socialist arguments, pro and con, concerning war.
5. Outline the main arguments of the totalitarian state in favor of war.
6. What is the sociological approach to the study of war?
7. Why is war characteristic of the transitional periods in history?
8. How are economic factors related to international organization?
9. What are the main hopes for international government?
10. What can education do to solve the problem of international organization?

Selected References

American Journal of Sociology, LI (March, 1946), 359–487. The entire issue is devoted to the sociology of war.

Dahl, Robert A., "The Impact of Atomic Energy," *The Annals of the American Academy of Political and Social Science*, vol. 290 (November, 1953). A collection of articles on nuclear weapons, nuclear power, atomic energy and political power, and the impact of atomic energy on individuals in society.

Friedrich, Carl, *War, the Causes, Effects, and Control of International Violence* (Washington: National Education Association, 1943). A brief but useful summary of various theories of war.

Heard, Gerald, *Man and Master* (Harper, 1941). Viewing conflict as a social revolution brought on by man's loss of faith in some authority outside himself.

Kirk, Grayson, *The Study of International Relations in American Colleges and Universities* (New York: Council of Foreign Relations, 1947). How instruction in international relations can promote international understanding.

McMurray, Ruth, and Muna Lee, *The Cultural Approaches: Another Way in International Relations* (University of North Carolina Press, 1947). How the governmental agencies operate in cultural relations.

Read, Herbert, *Education for Peace* (Scribner, 1949). How modern education can help in the maintenance of peace.

Sheen, Fulton J., *Philosophies at War* (Scribner, 1943). Mgr. Sheen explains the underlying causes of war and the best ways in which war may be most truly won.

Index